KOREA'S GLOBALIZATION

South Korea has cast its lot with globalization arguably to a greater extent than any other Asian country in the post–Cold War era. This book, edited by Samuel S. Kim, presents the first sustained analysis of Korea's globalization and its ramifications for all aspects of the Korean state and society. The authors critically probe the promise and performance and the myths and realities of Korea's globalization drive. Each chapter is a case study designed to explain how globalization works and what its positive or negative consequences are for the Korean state and society. They examine the effects of globalization on business conglomerates, workers and labor unions, women, foreign migrant workers, the military, politicians, and government officials. More broadly, they examine how Korea, as a newly industrialized and newly democratizing country, is coping with the twin challenges of democratic consolidation from below and within and globalization from above and without.

Samuel S. Kim is Adjunct Professor of Political Science, Senior Research Associate, and Associate Director of the Center for Korean Research, East Asian Institute, Columbia University. He is the author or editor of fifteen books on East Asian international relations and world order studies including *China and the World: Chinese Foreign Policy Faces the New Millennium* (1998), *North Korean Foreign Relations in the Post–Cold War Era* (1998), and *China, the United Nations, and World Order* (1979). His articles have appeared in *American Journal of International Law*, *World Politics*, *World Policy Journal*, and other publications.

CAMBRIDGE ASIA–PACIFIC STUDIES

The Cambridge Asia–Pacific Studies series aims to provide a focus and forum for scholarly work on the Asia–Pacific region as a whole and its component subregions, namely, Northeast Asia, Southeast Asia, and the Pacific Islands. The series is produced in association with the Research School of Pacific and Asian Studies at the Australian National University and the Australian Institute of International Affairs.

EDITOR: John Ravenhill

EDITORIAL BOARD: James Cotton, Donald Denoon, Mark Elvin, Hal Hill, Anthony Low, Ron May, Anthony Milner, Tessa Morris-Suzuki

KOREA'S GLOBALIZATION

EDITED BY

SAMUEL S. KIM

Columbia University

CAMBRIDGE
UNIVERSITY PRESS

PUBLISHED BY THE PRESS SYNDICATE OF THE UNIVERSITY OF CAMBRIDGE
The Pitt Building, Trumpington Street, Cambridge, United Kingdom

CAMBRIDGE UNIVERSITY PRESS
The Edinburgh Building, Cambridge CB2 2RU, UK   http://www.cup.cam.ac.uk
40 West 20th Street, New York, NY 10011-4211, USA   http://www.cup.org
10 Stamford Road, Oakleigh, Melbourne 3166, Australia
Ruiz de Alarcón 13, 28014 Madrid, Spain

© Samuel S. Kim 2000

First published 2000

Printed in the United States of America

Typeface New Baskerville 10/12 pt.   *System* QuarkXPress   [TW]

A catalog record for this book is available from the British Library.

Library of Congress Cataloging in Publication data

Korea's globalization / edited by Samuel S. Kim
p. cm – (Cambridge Asia-Pacific studies)
Includes bibliographic references and index.
ISBN 0-521-77272-9 (hbk.) – ISBN 0-521-77559-0 (pbk.)
1. Korea – Economic policy. 2. Korea – Social policy.
I. Series. II. Kim, Samuel S., 1935–

HC467.K6265 2000   99-040255
338.9519 21 – dc21

ISBN 0 77272 9 hardback
ISBN 0 77559 0 paperback

Contents

Tables and Figures

Figure

Contributors

SAMUEL S. KIM (Ph.D., Columbia) is Adjunct Professor of Political Science, Senior Research Associate, and Associate Director of the Center for Korean Research, East Asian Institute, Columbia University. He is the author or editor of fifteen books on East Asian international relations and world order studies including *China, the United Nations, and World Order* (1979), *The Quest for a Just World Order* (1984), *North Korean Foreign Relations in the Post–Cold War Era* (ed., 1998), and *China and the World: Chinese Foreign Policy Faces the New Millennium* (ed., 1998). He has published more than 150 articles in edited volumes and leading international relations journals, including *American Journal of International Law, International Interactions, International Journal, International Organization, Journal of Peace Research, World Politics,* and *World Policy Journal.*

BARRY K. GILLS (Ph.D., London School of Economics and Political Science) teaches in and directs the postgraduate programs in international political economy and transnational development at the Department of Politics, University of Newcastle upon Tyne, U.K. He is a founding editor of the *Review of International Political Economy* and a frequent guest editor for *Third World Quarterly* (three special issues to date). His latest works include *Korea versus Korea: A Case of Contested Legitimacy* (1996) and *The World System* (coedited with A. F. Frank), reprinted in paperback in 1996.

DONG SOOK GILLS (Ph.D., University of Sheffield, U.K.) teaches sociology and international development at the School of International Studies, University of Sunderland, U.K. Dr. Gills is a specialist on women and development. Her latest work is *The Forgotten Workers: Rural Women and Triple Exploitation in Korean Industrialization* (forthcoming, Macmillan IPE series).

YONG CHEOL KIM (Ph.D., Ohio State University) is Assistant Professor of Political Science at the Chonnam National University. He has written extensively on labor politics in South Korea. He is currently completing a book on the state, labor, and coalitional dynamics.

CHUNG-IN MOON (Ph.D., University of Maryland) is Professor of Political Science at Yonsei University. He has published twelve books and more than 110 scholarly articles in edited volumes and such scholarly journals as *World Politics, Journal of Asian Studies,* and *World Development.* His most recent publication is *Democracy and the Korean Economy* (1998), coedited with Jongryun Mo.

C. S. ELIOT KANG (Ph.D., Yale) is an assistant professor in the Department of Political Science, Northern Illinois University. His recent publications have appeared in *International Organization* and *Asian Perspective.* He has held numerous fellowships, including the International Affairs Fellowship of the Council on Foreign Relations, the Brookings Research Fellowship, and the Mellon Fellowship in Social Sciences. He was a visiting research fellow at the Japan Institute for International Affairs in Tokyo, Japan, from July 1997 to June 1998.

EUN MEE KIM is a sociologist trained at Ewha Women's University (B.A.) and Brown University (M.A. and Ph.D.). She is Associate Professor in the Graduate School of International Studies at Ewha Womans University. She is the director of the International Cooperation Division of the Institute for International Trade and Cooperation at Ewha and Associate Editor of the journal *International Studies Review.* Before joining Ewha in 1997, she was an associate professor and the director of graduate studies in the Department of Sociology at the University of Southern California (1987–97), a visiting scholar at Harvard University (1994), and an assistant professor of sociology at Temple University (1990–1). Her numerous publications include *Big Business, Strong State: Collusion and Conflict in South Korean Development, 1960–1990* (1997) and an edited volume, *The Four Asian Tigers: Economic Development and the Global Political Economy* (1998). Her research focuses on political and economic development in East Asia and South Korea, and, in particular, the state, the *chaebol,* and the relations between capitalist development and democratization.

SEUNGSOOK MOON (Ph.D., Brandeis University) is an assistant professor of sociology at Vassar College. She has taught on gender and social change in East Asia and Asian American communities. She is a corecipient of the 1997 SSRC International Migration Research

Planning Grant. Her most recent work includes "Gender, Militarization and Universal Male Conscription in South Korea" in *The Women and War Reader*, Lois Lorentzen and Jennifer Turpin (eds.) (1998) and "Begetting the Nation: The Androcentric Discourse of National History and Tradition in South Korea" in *Dangerous Women: Gender and Korean Nationalism*, Elaine H. Kim and Chungmoo Choi (eds.) (1998). She is currently working on a book examining the relationship between the institution of military service and gender hierarchy in the labor market in South Korea.

KATHARINE H. S. MOON (Ph.D., Princeton) is an assistant professor of political science at Wellesley College. She teaches and researches on international relations and Asian politics, with a focus on topics concerning women and gender issues. She is the author of *Sex among Allies: Military Prostitution in U.S–Korea Relations* (1997) and articles related to women and gender in militarism and human rights. With grant support from the American Association of University Women, she is currently working on a book that analyzes the roles of gender and culture in foreign policy.

CHAE-JIN LEE (Ph.D., University of California–Los Angeles) is Bank America Professor of Pacific Basin Studies, Professor of Government, and Director of the Keck Center for International Strategic Studies at Claremont McKenna College. He also taught at the University of Washington, University of Kansas, and University of California–San Diego, and served as dean of the School of Social and Behavioral Sciences at California State University (Long Beach). His publications include *China and Korea: Dynamic Relations* (1996); *U.S. Policy toward Japan and Korea* (coauthored with Hideo Sato) (1983); *Zhou Enlai: The Early Years* (1996); *China and Japan: New Economic Policy* (1984); *China's Korean Minority* (1986); and *Japan Faces China: Political and Economic Relations in the Postwar Era* (1976). He edited or coedited *North Korea After Kim Il Sung* (1998); *The Korean Peninsula and the Major Powers* (1998); *Political Leadership in Korea* (1976); *The Prospects for Korean Unification* (1993); *U.S.-Japan Partnership in Conflict Management: The Case of Korea* (1993); and *The United States and Japan: Changing Relations* (1992).

B. C. KOH (Ph.D., Cornell) is Professor of Political Science at the University of Illinois at Chicago. He is the author of four books, including *The Foreign Policy Systems of North and South Korea* (1984) and *Japan's Administrative Elite* (2nd edition, 1991). His articles have appeared in such journals as *Asian Survey*, *Comparative Political Studies*, *Comparative Politics*, and *Journal of Politics*.

VICTOR CHA holds an A.B. in economics from Columbia University (1983), B.A./M.A. in philosophy, politics, and economics from Oxford University, England (1986), and Ph.D. in political science from Columbia (1994). He is currently Assistant Professor in the Department of Government and the School of Foreign Service at Georgetown University. He is a recipient of numerous academic awards including the Fulbright (Korea) and MacArthur Foundation Fellowships, and the John M. Olin National Security Fellowship at Harvard University's Center for International Affairs, and is a postdoctoral fellow at the Center for International Security and Arms Control, Stanford University. He has published on Korea and East Asian security-related topics in various scholarly journals. He is the author of *Alignment Despite Antagonism: The United States–Japan–Korea Security Triangle* (1999). He also published numerous articles in edited volumes and various journals including *Asian Survey, Asian Perspective,* and *Korean Studies.*

Preface

The first words of Charles Dickens's *A Tale of Two Cities,* written more than a century ago – "It was the best of times, it was the worst of times" – might be used to describe Korea's globalization in the midst of what President Kim Dae Jung characterized as "the greatest crisis since the Korean War." For good or otherwise, this project was conceived in early 1997, several months before the Asian crisis first erupted in Thailand, but was carried out against the backdrop of the global financial crisis and what many Koreans quickly dubbed "the IMF era."

The project was based on the premise that the Korean concept of *segye-hwa* (globalization), first formally introduced by President Kim Young Sam in 1994, has obvious theoretical and real-world significance for democratization, development, foreign relations, and a host of other related social and cultural issues. Perhaps no state in the post–Cold War world has cast its lot with globalization as decisively or as publicly as Korea did under the Kim Young Sam government. No government launched its globalization drive with such a bang or ended with such a whimper, as Seoul's continuing decline in global competitiveness and the economic crisis of 1997–8 have made it clear. And yet, President Kim Dae Jung has continued Korea's globalization drive with greater determination and vigor, as if there were no other way of overcoming the greatest crisis since the Korean War. Apparently, then, for Korea there is no escape from the payoffs and penalties of globalization.

Indeed, Korea's globalization drive, riddled with contradictions, poses a challenge for scholars and policymakers alike. This collaborative volume presents the first focused analysis of the various and multiplying ramifications of globalization dynamics upon all aspects of the Korean state and society. In doing so, we seek to avoid the pitfalls of the neoliberal "hyperglobalization" chant, with its heroic assumptions, and neorealist "globaloney" castigation, which does not adequately take into account the patterns and dynamics of contemporary globalization. Combining a broader conceptual framework with case studies, this book critically probes the promise and performance, the myths and realities, of Korea's globalization drive and the complex and evolving interaction of globalization challenges and Korean responses, especially how Korea as a newly industrialized and newly democratizing country is coping with the twin challenges of democratic consolidation from below and within and globalization from above and without.

In pursuit of this line of inquiry, the contributors address several major challenges, dangers, opportunities, and consequences of Korea's globalization. They compare *segyehwa*'s actual performance with its promise in the economic, sociocultural, diplomatic, and security domains. They also shed light on the "winners" and "losers" in Korea's *segyehwa* drive – at who in the Korean state and society gets what, why, and at whose expense in the IMF era. Each chapter is a case study designed to explain how globalization works and what its positive or negative consequences are for the Korean state and society in general and for the state-capital-labor relationship, business conglomerates (*chaebol*), workers and labor unions, women, foreign migrant workers, foreign relations, security, and U.N. diplomacy in particular.

The McCune–Reischauer romanization system is used throughout this book, with some familiar exceptions for well-known place names (e.g., Pyongyang, Seoul, and Pusan) and personal names (e.g., Syngman Rhee, Park Chung Hee, Kim Dae Jung, Lee Hong-koo) that would otherwise be difficult to recognize.

Like my most recent work on North Korea, *North Korean Foreign Relations in the Post–Cold War Era* (1998), this book emerged from a major research conference under the auspices of the Center for Korean Research of Columbia University's East Asian Institute, held at Columbia on 22–23 May 1998. The project would not have been possible without the generous financial support of the Korea Foundation, which provided the Center with a major grant, for which we are grateful. I would also like to express my profound gratitude to my colleagues at the East Asian Institute, especially Professors Charles Armstrong, Thomas Bernstein, Gerald Curtis, Gari Ledyard, Andrew Nathan, and Madeleine Zelin, for their abiding support and encouragement for this and other ongoing projects.

In addition to thanking the contributors whose revised and updated chapters appear in this volume, I wish to acknowledge our individual and collective debts to the lively audience at the Columbia conference and all others who took part. In the course of the peer-review and vetting process at Cambridge University Press, three anonymous readers provided excellent suggestions for improving and updating the chapters to take into account the changes and continuities in the globalization drive not only during the entire tenure of the Kim Young Sam government but also during the first fourteen months of the new Kim Dae Jung government (February 1998–April 1999). For indispensable logistical and managerial support, we express our thanks to two helpful and hard-working graduate students in Korean studies at Columbia, Katelyn Choe and George Kallander.

Finally, Mary Child, our editor at Cambridge University Press, has been an invaluable navigator for the project. Special thanks also are due to Jennifer Chang, Cathy Felgar, and Andy Saff at Cambridge University Press for their efficient steering of the manuscript through the various stages of the administration and production process. The usual disclaimer still applies: The editor alone is responsible for any errors that remain in the book.

SAMUEL S. KIM
New York, New York
December 1999

CHAPTER 1

Korea and Globalization (Segyehwa): A Framework for Analysis

Samuel S. Kim

Fellow citizens: Globalization is the shortcut which will lead us to building a first-class country in the 21st century. This is why I revealed my plan for globalization and the government has concentrated all of its energy in forging ahead with it. It is aimed at realizing globalization in all sectors – politics, foreign affairs, economy, society, education, culture and sports. To this end, it is necessary to enhance our viewpoints, way of thinking, system and practices to the world class level.... We have no choice other than this.
President Kim Young Sam, 6 January 1995[1]

"Globalization" advertised by the Kim Young Sam group is, in every respect, a motto of treachery which is aimed at fully reducing South Korea to a colony of outside forces and a market of international capital, ridding the people of the consciousness of national independence and making them cripples depending on outside forces.
Korean Central News Agency (Pyongyang), 10 January 1995[2]

The world is now advancing from industrial societies where tangible natural resources were the primary factors of economic development into knowledge and information societies where intangible knowledge and information will be the driving power for economic development. The information revolution is transforming the age of many national economies into an age of one world economy, turning the world into a global village.... Diplomacy in the 21st century will center around the economy and culture. We must keep expanding trade, investment, tourism and cultural exchanges in order to make our way in the age of boundless competition which will take place against a backdrop of cooperation.
President Kim Dae Jung's inaugural speech, 25 February 1998[3]

[1] Seoul KBS-I Television in FBIS-EAS-95-004, 6 January 1995 (Internet version).
[2] FBIS-EAS-95-006, 10 January 1995 (Internet version).
[3] For a full text of the inaugural address, see *Korea Herald*, 26 February 1998 (Internet version).

1

In this increasingly interconnected world, the forces for good and evil travel with equal speed and ease. Globalization has an immense potential to improve people's lives, but it can disrupt – and destroy – them as well. Those who do not accept its pervasive, all-encompassing ways are often left behind. It is our task to prevent this; to ensure that globalization leads to progress, prosperity and security for all. I intend that the United Nations shall lead this effort.

U.N. Secretary General Kofi Anan, 3 September 1998[4]

The *Segyehwa* Paradox

To examine Korea's drive toward globalization or *segyehwa* in the 1990s is to be confronted with several riddles.[5] For good or otherwise, *segyehwa* has become the self-styled hallmark, indeed the self-designated litmus test, of President Kim Young Sam's administration (February 1993– February 1998), the first civilian government in thirty years. Indeed, no state in the post–Cold War world cast its lot with globalization as decisively or as publicly as Korea did under the Kim Young Sam administration, which viewed it as the most expedient way for Korea to become a world-class, advanced country. *Segyehwa* has been touted as no longer a matter of choice but one of necessity – globalize or perish! At the end of his single five-year presidency, however, Korea was forced to apply to the International Monetary Fund (IMF) for help in order to avert the imminent financial meltdown; the IMF responded with a $58 billion rescue package, the largest bailout program in IMF history, with disbursements disproportionately front-loaded.

Like the North Koreans in their insistence on projecting *juche* (self-reliance) as the primary element of their national identity and "the cornerstone of the internal and external policies and approaches of our Republic,"[6] the Kim Young Sam government announced on 6 March 1995 that it had decided to keep, not translate, the Korean word *segyehwa* in its romanized form, as the official name for its globalization drive. Too many foreigners interpreted *globalization* as simply "economic liberalization," according to the Ministry of Information and Communications, when in actuality *segyehwa* was far more comprehensive, embracing political,

[4] Annual Report of the Secretary-General on the Work of the Organization, U.N. Doc. A/53/1 (3 September 1998), par. 168.
[5] Unless otherwise indicated, Korea refers to the Republic of Korea (ROK), or South Korea, to be consistent with globalization debates and literature, where North Korea is rarely noted and South Korea, as the world's eleventh largest economy, figures prominently.
[6] U.N. Doc. GAOR, forty eighth session, seventeenth plenary meeting (5 October 1993), 11. North Korea has long since stopped translating *Juche* in its English-language publications, and it is almost impossible to find North Korean foreign policy pronouncements that do not contain this kind of compulsive lip service to *Juche*.

cultural, and social openmindedness.[7] Indeed, *segyehwa* was meant to describe Korea's unique concept, encompassing political, economic, social, and cultural enhancement to reach the level of advanced nations in the world.

And yet the interplay between Korea and globalization was complex, and somewhat surprising, with several paradoxical consequences. First, Korea's globalization drive was initiated by the state. In striking contrast to the extreme version of globalization being put forward by its proponents in the West, who foresee an inexorable demise and irrelevance of the territorial nation-state, *segyehwa* was initiated by the government as a state-enhancing, top-down strategic plan. The concept of *segyehwa* as articulated by President Kim Young Sam – and embraced by President Kim Dae Jung – is broader than the Western version would lead one to believe.

Second, tellingly, North Korea lost no time in launching a war of calumnies against South Korea's *segyehwa* drive, as if it still remained a model island of autocentric and self-reliant development in the sea of the capitalist world economic system. That the country so mired in a theocratic trinity of Father, Son, and *Juche* but eking out a bare existence by relying on a sort of tenuous external "life-support" system could be so vehemently opposed probably helped more than hurt Seoul's globalization drive.

Third, Seoul's globalization drive, especially President Kim Dae Jung's conceptualization of participatory democracy and the market economy as mutually complementary – as "two wheels of a cart" – is espoused at just that moment when globalization has contributed at one and the same time to an expansion of the liberal democratic state's functional responsibilities and to an erosion of its capacity to deal effectively on its own with many of the demands placed upon it.[8]

Fourth, President Kim Young Sam's *segyehwa* drive started with a bang but ended with a whimper, as Seoul's continuing decline in global competitiveness and the economic crisis of 1997–8 have made clear. And yet, President Kim Dae Jung has continued a globalization drive with greater vigor, even as the new administration has been disassembling the Presidential *Segyehwa* Promotion Commission (PSPC) set up by the previous administration. Apparently, then, there is no escape from the payoffs and penalties of globalization, as the new leadership has been espousing the "five great reforms" as the only assured way to survive in the brave new

---

[7] See *Far Eastern Economic Review*, 22 June 1995, 48.

[8] David Held, *Democracy and the Global Order* (Stanford, CA.: Stanford University Press, 1995), and Richard W. Mansbach and Dong Won Suh, "A Tumultuous Season: Globalization and the Korean Case," *Asian Perspective* 22, no.2 (1998), 245.

world of infinite global competition. Put another way, the Kim Dae Jung administration seems to realize that the genie of globalization cannot be stuffed back into the bottle, even if it were desirable to do so.

Finally, the greatest irony of all is that President Kim Young Sam's success lies not in *segyehwa* but in his localization (deglobalization) campaign of sorts – the restoration of local autonomy in South Korean politics. To the extent that globalization means or requires greater deregulation, decentralization, and democratization via local autonomy, Kim Young Sam's globalization drive cannot be dismissed as a complete failure.

The purpose of this introductory chapter is to provide a conceptual framework for a comprehensive assessment of the promise and performance of Korea's globalization drive, of the various and multiplying ramifications of globalization dynamics upon all aspects of the Korean state and society, a framework that shies away from the thinking of both the "hyperglobalization" school, with its heroic assumptions, on the one hand, and the neorealist "globaloney" school, which does not adequately take into account new patterns and dynamics of contemporary globalization, on the other. The chapter seeks to examine critically the nature of the globalization debates in the West and to propose a broader framework to appraise the successes and failures of Korea's *segyehwa* drive in the economic, sociocultural, diplomatic, and security domains from the early 1990s to early 1999.

Segyehwa in the Globalization Debates

There is no doubt that globalization is a much-contested concept. There is no coherent or dominant theory of globalization that commands or enjoys a paradigmatic status in social science. The debates about globalization have remained largely jejune, dominated by two extreme views: On the one hand, the neoliberal and even some neoconservative proponents claim that globalization heralds the rise of a new post-Westphalian global order and the demise of the state system; on the other hand, the neorealist and neomercantile opponents argue that it amounts to nothing new.

Most neoliberal proponents take a Panglossian view, claiming that globalization heralds the emergence of truly open and free global markets in capital and goods, the rise of a new post-Westphalian global order, and the functional demise of the state system. According to this "hyperglobalization" school, social and economic processes now function at a predominantly global level and nation-states are no longer decision *makers* but have become decision *takers*. As Kenichi Ohmae argues, "We are finally living in a world where money, securities, services, options, futures, information and patents, software and hardware, companies and know-how, assets and memberships, paintings and brands are all traded without national sentiments across traditional borders."[9] In a similar vein, Robert Reich argues that "there will be no national products or technologies, no national corporations, no national industries" and that "all that will remain rooted within national borders are the people who comprise a nation."[10] For the British political economist Susan Strange, the nature of international competition in the post–Cold War world has fundamentally changed such that states no longer compete for control over territory and the wealth-creating resources, with the inevitable diffusion of authority from states based on territorial control to transnational enterprises and associations based on other sources of power. With the inner core of their authority in social and economic affairs so impaired by relentless globalization dynamics, the states become hollow or defective institutions.[11] Paradoxically enough, the Marxist "withering away of the state" thesis that was revised to extinction in the former Soviet Union and all other communist states has been brought back in the neoliberal hyperglobalization school.

Indeed, the hyperglobalization school rests on the assumption that economics increasingly takes command over politics. It is a case of economic globalization transforming political and social affairs of interconnected human communities throughout the world. National economies are said to be immersed in and perforated by a sea of transnational forces and actors eroding differences between and among nation-states. Multinational corporations (MNCs) have already become truly global companies, transnational corporations (TNCs), able and willing to shift production sites around the world in response to differences in local conditions – thinking globally, producing locally! The claim is thus made that as a consequence of an integrated global economy, the castle of state sovereignty has been rendered an empty fortress. In short, the demise or at least the functional irrelevance of the nation-state is central to the neoliberal hyperglobalization argument – to wit, there has occurred a fundamental paradigmatic change in the principles and organizations of human social and economic affairs.

On the other hand, the critics of globalization, in spite of diverse political, methodological, and normative orientations, argue that all the fuss about globalization amounts to no more than "globaloney." As the conservative economist Milton Friedman put it, "The world is less internationalized in any immediate, relevant, pertinent sense today than it

[9] Kenichi Ohmae, *The Borderless World* (London: Collins, 1990), 171.

[10] Robert Reich, *The Work of Nations* (New York: Vintage Books, 1992), 3.

[11] Susan Strange, "The Defective State," *Daedalus* 124, no. 2 (1995), 55–74; idem, *The Retreat of the State: The Diffusion of Power in the World Economy* (New York: Cambridge University Press, 1996).

was in 1913 or in 1929."[12] The "globaloney" school proceeds from two diametrically opposed starting points: On the one hand, the neorealist skeptics argue that there is nothing new in today's world economy and the state is as powerful as ever; on the other hand, the populist resistance skeptics argue that globalization has gone too far at the risk of state sovereignty or social democracy. Sleeping in the same antiglobalization bed but having different dreams, countries such as Iran, Malaysia, Saudi Arabia, and North Korea have vehemently stated that globalization is the extension of American hegemony and that the IMF is just doing America's bidding, even as many Americans see globalization as beyond their country's control.[13]

The argument that globalization is a threat to social stability, state sovereignty, national and cultural identity, and environmental protection has come from a wide range of competing interests, from cultural fundamentalists to neomercantile protectionists to environmentalists, including the unlikely globaloney partnership of labor unions decrying unfair competition from underage workers in developing countries, environmental groups, and hypernationalists such as Patrick Buchanan, billionaire business people such as Ross Perot, and Sir James Goldsmith in railing against North American Free Trade Area (NAFTA) and World Trade Organization (WTO).[14]

From the left of social democracy, neo-Marxist *dependencia* theory, and non-Marxist world order populism, it is often argued that the claims of diminished state capacity have less to do with the pressures of globalization and more to do with hierarchy and unevenness in state structure and policy. For example, Walden Bello, a leading *dependencia* theorist in the Philippines, argues as if to parrot North Korea's *juche* model that the answer to the unrelenting pressure of globalization controlled by the North is clear and simple enough – deglobalize or perish! The way out of chronic and continuing crisis afflicting the global South (the periphery) is prescribed to be the deglobalization (delinkage) of the domestic economy from the global system controlled and exploited by the North (the Center) – that is, its reorientation toward greater reliance on the internal market.[15] From a populist post-Westphalian world order perspective,

[12] Milton Friedman, "Internationalization of the U.S. Economy," *Fraser Forum*, February 1989, 10.

[13] Helen Milner, "International Political Economy: Beyond Hegemonic Stability," *Foreign Policy* 110 (1998), 121.

[14] Dani Rodrik, "Sense and Nonsense in the Globalization Debate," *Foreign Policy* 107 (Summer 1997), 19; idem, *Has Globalization Gone Too Far?* (Washington, DC: Institute for International Economics, 1997), 2.

[15] Walden Bello, "The Answer: De-Globalize," *Far Eastern Economic Review* (29 April 1999), 61.

Richard Falk argues that globalization has not so much gone too far as it has gone the wrong way by making a distinction between "globalization-from-above" and "globalization-from-below." The former had to be resisted through the latter, as globalization-from-above involves the expansion of an international division of labor, the growing power of multinational corporations, and the influence of Western-dominated global economic institutions (e.g., the World Bank, the IMF, and the WTO), whereas globalization-from-below is energized by new democratic social movements.[16]

Viewed in this way, globalization is nothing less than an ideological fig leaf for a process in which governments have willingly abandoned many of the tools of governance and passed power from the democratically legitimated sphere of politics to the unaccountable realm of the market. A similar argument can be heard from conservative nationalists of various kinds, such as the Gaullists in France, and Buchanan and Perot in the United States, advancing a more protectionist economic policy. Such a neomercantile defense of the state is often allied to and conflated with a cultural politics of defensive and exclusionary nationalism.[17]

Speaking for the Islamic world, Abdallah Bin-Abd-al Muhsin al-Turki, Saudi Arabia's minister of pilgrimage affairs and religious trusts, defines contemporary globalization in hegemonic terms, as "an effort on the part of the North – using its edge in the field of science and technology – to establish dominance over the South from an educational, cultural, social, economic, and political perspective, under the pretext of helping the South as it pursues across-the-board development and to achieve fairness in investment and prosperity for all sides."[18]

For post-Soviet Russia, globalization, not unlike the mighty Yangtze River in China for which Beijing is constructing the world's biggest dam (the Three Gorges Dam), may be impeded, but not stopped. The biggest danger is that the globalization process, dominated by the IMF and the Paris Club (the Organization for Economic Cooperation and Development [OECD]), is "punching big holes in the holy of holies of the Russian state – its sovereignty." However, defense of Russian national interests in an era of globalization calls for navigating between the Scylla of total isolationism and the Charybdis of total openness. What is required instead is "the development of cooperation with states of the CIS

---

[16] Richard Falk, "Resisting 'Globalisation-from-above' through 'Globalisation-from-below,'" *New Political Economy* 2, no. 1 (1997), 17–24.

[17] David Goldblatt et al., "Economic Globalization and the Nation-State: Shifting Balances of Power," *Alternatives* 22, no. 3 (1997), 269–85; Samuel Huntington, *The Clash of Civilizations and the Remaking of World Order* (New York: Simon & Schuster, 1996).

[18] See FBIS-TOT-98-200, 19 July 1998 (Internet version).

[Commonwealth of Independent States] and Russia's strategic partners in the far abroad, primarily with China, Iran, Iraq, and Yugoslavia."[19]
The most serious challenge comes from the neorealists, who are skeptical about the extent of globalization and the extent to which state power and autonomy have declined. Recent developments are said to be far short of globalization, and it is claimed that the state is as robust as it ever was, with an impressive array of political options, and that the contemporary state of international economic affairs is not without historical precedent. The postwar growth of international economic transactions represents "internationalization" or "regionalization" rather than the emergence of a truly global economy, and current levels of global flows are said to be comparable to, or even lower than, those during the classical gold-standard period (c. 1870–1914) and so that the postwar growth is little more than a return to the status quo ante after the disruptions of the 1930s and World War II.[20] That the global corporation acts autonomously in international economic affairs is a myth, it is also argued – the world's leading MNCs continue to be shaped decisively by the policies and values of their home states; they are not converging to create a seamless global market. Only a fraction (about 2 percent) of the corporate directors of America's MNCs are not Americans. In short, globalization is not homogenizing corporate structures nor causing the demise of the state nor diluting the national identities of corporate leadership.[21]

Both the hyperglobalization and globaloney schools are misconceived, proceeding from the dubious premise of globalization as an ideal end – a fully globalized economy – rather than as a process situated or moving somewhere on a continuum from the local at one end, as in North Korea and Somalia, and the global at the other, as in many developed and developing countries that are heavily dependent on trade and foreign investment. Such either/or conceptions of globalization underlying the current debates – that either a paradigmatic change has already occurred heralding a new post-Westphalian global order or there is nothing new in contemporary international life – stand on shaky historical and empirical grounds.

The problem with the neoliberal hyperglobalization school has a lot

---

[19] Anatolly Gromyko, "The Present Is Not a Shrine for Contemplation," *Pravda* 14 April 1998, 4–5 in FBIS-SOV-98-119 (Internet version).

[20] Peter Beinart, "An Illusion for Our Time: The False Promise of Globalization," *New Republic*, 20 October 1997, 20–4; Paul Hirst and Grahame Thompson, *Globalization in Question?* (Cambridge, UK: Polity Press, 1996); Stephen Krasner, "Compromising Westphalia," *International Security* 20, no. 3 (1995), 115–51.

[21] Paul N. Doremus et al., *The Myth of the Global Corporation* (Princeton, NJ: Princeton University Press, 1998).

to do with the heroic assumption of costless adjustment in a hypothetically perfect global economy. Contrary to the neoliberal argument, globalization remains incomplete and global markets are not yet perfectly integrated. Nearly half of the people in the developing world have yet to be fully integrated by contemporary globalization dynamics, especially by the much-touted rise in the volume of international trade and capital flows, and roughly three-quarters of the world's population, not owning a telephone, let alone a modem and computer, are effectively outside an increasingly interconnected cyberworld.[22] The majority of the sales and assets of even the largest MNCs tend to remain in the home country, and their core operations remain essentially national companies with international operations but subject to national controls. The world's financial regulatory agencies and central banks still remain national in scope and location. The neoliberal argument stereotypes and overgeneralizes MNC strategies, skating over the possible diversity of their responses.[23] Intrafirm trade engenders significant deviations from the ideal type of global competitive markets, and non-tradables remain a large proportion of national economies because intra-industry trade countries typically face less than perfectly elastic demand for their exports.[24]

This is not to deny that MNCs have become the main agent and catalyst in the increasing globalization of capital, goods, services, and manufacturing sites or that many people in "emerging markets" have been brutalized by the globalization process, especially in the wake of the Asian financial crisis of 1997–8.[25]

Competent states are not nearly as constrained by globalization as many of its proponents would have us believe. States still hold substantial

---

[22] World Bank, *World Development Report 1997: The State in a Changing World* (New York, 1997), 12; Robert O. Keohane and Joseph S. Nye, Jr., "Power and Interdependence in the Information Age," *Foreign Affairs* 77, no. 5 (September–October 1998), 82.

[23] Beinart, "An Illusion for Our Time"; Doremus, *The Myth of the Global Corporation*; Jonathan Perraton et al., "The Globalization of Economic Activity," *New Political Economy* 2, no. 2 (1997), 257–77; Louis Uchitelle, "Globalization Has Not Severed Corporations' National Links," *New York Times*, 30 April 1998, D1, D6.

[24] Perraton et al., "The Globalization of Economic Activity"; Goldblatt et al., "Economic Globalization."

[25] See Nicholas D. Kristof and Edward Wyatt, "Who Sank, or Swam, in Choppy Currents of a World Cash Ocean," *New York Times*, 15 February 1999; Nicholas D. Kristof and David E. Sanger, "How U.S. Wooed Asia to Let Cash Flow In," *New York Times*, 16 February 1999; Nicholas D. Kristof and Sheryl WuDunn, "World Markets, None of Them an Island," *New York Times*, 17 February 1999; and Nicholas D. Kristof and Sheryl WuDunn, "The World's Ills May Be Obvious, But Their Cure Is Not," *New York Times*, 18 February 1999.

autonomy in regulating their economies, social policies, and institutions that differ from those of their trading partners.[26] Even the revolution in communications has weakened but not completely compromised state control, because "information does not flow in a vacuum but in political space that is already occupied."[27] The significance of contemporary globalization therefore needs to be assessed in a situation- and actor-specific way; it varies according to actors' respective resources, skills, and strategic choices or policies. The impact of globalization upon a state's power or role depends not only on the type of state involved – whether the state in question is the United States, China, Myanmar (Burma), or North or South Korea – but also on the state's globalization strategy. Far from making states functionally obsolete or irrelevant, globalization has in effect redefined what it takes to be a competent and effective state in an increasingly interdependent and interactive world. Globalization is a double-edged sword in this respect: It threatens both minimalist and maximalist states and provides an opportunity for competent and adaptable states.

Consider how three quintessentially globalist institutions – the World Bank, the International Institute for Management Development (IMD) in Lausanne, Switzerland, and the World Economic Forum (WEF) in Geneva – perceive the role of the state in globalization dynamics. Thanks to the "East Asian Miracle," the World Bank has come a long way from the neoclassical laissez-faire view, reassessing by the early 1990s the respective roles of the state and the market. Pride of place was finally given to "effective but carefully limited government activism" for rapid economic growth in the developing world, with states (governments) doing less and less in those areas where markets work, and more and more in those areas where markets cannot be relied upon (e.g., education, health, nutrition, family planning, poverty reduction, administrative, regulatory, and legal infrastructure).[28] By 1997, the World Bank had embraced the concept of "an effective state" as vital for development while acknowledging that state effectiveness varies across countries at different stages of development. Reflecting upon the benefits and the limitations of state action in the last fifty years, the World Bank has finally embraced the notion that "the state is central to economic and social development, not as a direct provider of growth but as a partner, catalyst, and facilitator."[29] Most recently, the state capacity to absorb, generate, disseminate, and

[26] Rodrik, "Sense and Nonsense in the Globalization Debate," 21.
[27] Keohane and Nye, "Power and Interdependence in the Information Age," 84.
[28] World Bank, *World Development Report 1991* (New York: Oxford University Press, 1991), 9–10; idem, *The East Asian Miracle: Economic Growth and Public Policy* (New York: Oxford University Press 1993), 8–11.
[29] World Bank, *World Development Report 1997*, 1–15, quote on 1.

apply knowledge has come to be viewed as critical for economic and social well-being because everything one does in life depends on knowledge.[30]

In a similar vein, the IMD analyzes and ranks the world competitiveness of forty-six (forty-seven since 1999) industrialized and emerging economies – including Korea – based on the ability of a state (government) to provide an environment that sustains and enhances the competitiveness of its business enterprises, particularly how the countries involved manage their economic environment according to what it calls the "four forces of competitiveness" – proximity versus globality, attractiveness versus aggressiveness, assets versus processes, and individual risk versus social cohesiveness.[31] The WEF, which parted company with the IMD in 1995 and issues its own annual *Global Competitiveness Report*, evaluates and ranks the global competitiveness of fifty-three industrialized and emerging economies based on the definition of competitiveness as the ability of a state to provide economic conditions and institutions for economic growth over the next five to ten years. One of the criteria it uses in assessing a state's ability to achieve sustained high rates of economic growth is "corruption and official malfeasance, not only because good governance aids political stability, but also because it has become a crucial factor in international competitiveness. A growing body of empirical evidence suggests that widespread corruption hurts the ability of a country to attract foreign direct investment and generally raises the costs of doing business in the country."[32]

States still command the loyalty of their citizens, have control over material resources (a third to half of gross domestic product [GDP]) and define the policies and rules for those within its jurisdiction, even as world politics and the United Nations remain largely state-centric. Globalization has not rendered any state policy impossible, nor has it substantially compromised state sovereignty. Instead, globalization processes reflecting and effecting global events, the global transparency revolution, trade, capital, investment, and a global web of multilateral agreements have changed the payoff structure of certain state policies or strategic choices, especially those of states widely interconnected with and deeply enmeshed in the global economic system.

Consider the responses of the capitalist United States and "socialist" China. Faced with the challenge of doing more and more with less and

---

[30] World Bank, *World Development Report 1998/99: Knowledge for Development* (New York: Oxford University Press, 1998).

[31] See IMD, *World Competitiveness Report 1998*, in http//www.imd.ch/wcy/approach/competitiveness.html.

[32] See Jeffrey D. Sachs, "Ten Trends in Global Competitiveness in 1998," in *Global Competitiveness Report 1998*, http://www.weforum.org/publications/GCR/sachs.asp.

less – the globalization-localization antinomy – many governments, including the United States, according to Deputy Secretary of State Strobe Talbott, have sought to leverage scarce resources by forming coalitions with nonstate actors – MNCs, NGOs, and such global inter- governmental organizations as the United Nations, the World Bank, and the IMF – since such coalitions help the United States "to work not only multilaterally, but multi-multilaterally, through several organizations and institutions at the same time."[33] Indeed, what really halted America's hegemonic decline – the received conventional wisdom in the late 1980s when "Japan as Number One" was a popular global chorus – and sus- tained its status as the only superpower, according to Thomas Friedman, was "that under the pressure of globalization America would slash its defense budget, shrink its government, and shift more and more powers to the free market."[34]

For all the habit-driven trumpery about the Deng Xiaoping theory of building socialism with Chinese characteristics, Beijing has been subject to all the external pressures and dynamics of globalization. In a revealing manner, President Jiang Zemin in his political report to the Fifteenth Chinese Communist Party (CCP) Congress on 12 September 1997 admit- ted just as much when he stated that there is no longer an escape from "the globalization (*quanqiuhua*) of economy, science, and technology" and that there is no choice but to reform, restructure, and open up state- owned enterprises (SOEs) to the "survival-of-the-fittest" competition if China is not to forfeit its "global citizenship."[35] Indeed, some Chinese scholars see globalization as the functional equivalent to unprecedented wars – economic wars, commodity wars, technology wars, and wars over talented people – between developed and developing countries and among developing countries. To win the global economic warfare, China

[33] Strobe Talbott, "Globalization and Diplomacy: A Practitioner's Perspective," *Foreign Policy*, 108 (Fall 1997), 79.

[34] Thomas L. Friedman, *The Lexus and the Olive Tree* (New York: Farrar, Straus & Giroux, 1999), xvii.

[35] For Jiang Zemin's political report to the Fifteenth CCP Congress, see FBIS- CHI-97-255 (12 September 1997) (Internet version). Without specifically using the term "global citizenship" (*qiuji*), Jiang's political report brings back the central point of the intense but short-lived 1988 debate on "global citizen- ship": that in an era of globalization, China can choose not to emancipate its political-economy thinking and fall behind in the technological race, forfeit- ing its "global citizenship" in the process, or it can more fully integrate itself into, and make more creative use of, the world market, whereby it will leap into the front ranks of world power. That is, reform of state enterprises is justified as a way of responding to the pressures of globalization from above and without (see Lu Yi et al., eds., *Qiuji: Yige shijiexing de xuanze* [Global citizenship: a world- wide choice] [Shanghai: Baijia chubanshe, 1989]).

should raise as many foreign trade or economic marshals and generals as possible.[36]

With the rise of China as the world's second largest foreign direct investment (FDI) host for four successive years – the first being the United States – some Chinese scholars argue that the prime motive force of globalization is MNCs with the state playing a spurring and regulative role. As a consequence, Beijing must adapt to the irresistible tide of globalization by establishing a strategic partnership of long-term cooperation with MNCs.[37] Wang Yizhou, a leading Chinese international relations theorist, breaks new ground in defining globalization as more than an economic globalization. Globalization is an economic process, to be sure, but it is also a complicated political and historical process. "To each country, it is a 'double-edged sword,' which can help break through brambles and horns, but may also harm the user. Under this situation, a new security concept should be established which pays equal attention to economic, social and political aspects." Security in the era of globalization "refers not only to 'safety' in the military and diplomatic sciences, but also to economic and technological security, including financial, trade and investment security, the avoidance of big rises and falls, the ability to have stronger competitive methods and a grasp of information factors."[38]

Thus, it seems more useful to explore the changes brought about by globalization pressures in terms of the shifting balance of costs and benefits of any given state policy. With the rapidly growing exit options of mobile (footless) global capital, as shown in the recent Asian-cum-global financial crisis, states, especially such indebted export-dependent developmental states as South Korea, have few viable options for defying the logic of globalization. One thing remains clear: Globalization has exerted pressure on all states to change their policies and institutions in certain ways, but states' willingness and ability to change or adapt their policies and institutions to the logic of globalization vary. Practically all states, including "socialist" China, face a number of crucial strategic choices, each of which is in a larger sense a decision on how best to cope with the challenges and opportunities of globalization.

Moreover, what constitutes a competent and effective state not only differs across countries, as earlier noted, but at different stages of political

---

[36] *Ta Kung Pao*, 25 January 1999, A2 in FBIS-CHI-99-025 (Internet version).

[37] Long Yongtu, "On Economic Globalization," *Guangming Ribao*, 30 October 1998, 6 in FBIS-CHI-98-313 (Internet version).

[38] Wang Yizhou, "New Security Concept in Globalization," *Beijing Review* 42, no. 7 (15–21 February 1999): 7. See also Wang Yizhou, *Dangdai guoji zhengzhi xilun* [Analysis of contemporary international politics] (Shanghai: Renmin chubanshe, 1995), especially chapter 1, 19–46.

and economic development in the same state. In the Korean case, for example, the much-vaunted developmental state that brought about the "Miracle on the Han River" has been out of sync at least since the mid-1980s with the twin pressures of democratization from within and below and globalization from without and above. As the following chapters show, the Korean state is no longer a competent, effective, or adaptable state in an era of globalization. In short, the neoliberal hyperglobalization school commits the fallacy of premature optimism about the benefits of globalization as well as about the demise of the putatively defective or obsolescent state. That post-Mao China joined the global economy without giving up much of its state sovereignty and still managed to establish an all-time global record in doubling per capita output in the shortest time period (1977–87) speaks volumes about the relationship between state sovereignty and globalization.[39]

The neorealist argument that states are more important than ever before because they have the means to resist and reshape the pressures generated by globalization dynamics is problematic for all but the few great powers that enjoy relatively low sensitivity, vulnerability, and security interdependence due to massive resource and skill differentials and relative economic self-sufficiency. As already noted, even such relatively self-sufficient great powers as the United States and China have been forced to change or adapt their state actions in order to swim with, rather than against, globalization trends. The neorealist argument that the more something changes, the more it stays the same ignores the unprecedented scale, intensity, and rapidity of contemporary globalization processes in five separate but mutually interconnected realms – trade, finance, investment, production, and multilateral treaties and institutions – fueled by rapidly falling communication and computing costs.

There are several major differences between the pre-1914 first-wave globalization and the contemporary second-wave globalization. If the first-wave globalization was catalyzed by falling transport costs, the second-wave globalization has been fueled by a convergence of several momentous changes.[40] First is the end of the Cold War and the demise of socialist challenge accompanied by reprioritization of the dominant issues in global politics. What used to be called "global high politics" (global peace and security) has become "global low politics," and what used to be called "global low politics" (global developmental issues) has become "global high politics." An event crucial to this transformation

[39] World Bank, *World Development Report 1991*, fig. 1.1, p. 12.
[40] Jeffrey Sachs, "International Economics: Unlocking the Mysteries of Globalization," *Foreign Policy* 110 (Spring 1998), 97–111. See also Friedman, *The Lexus and the Olive Tree* and UNDP, *Human Development Report 1999* (New York: Oxford University Press, 1999).

was the Uruguay Round, which resulted in the formation of the WTO. Second, the extraordinary advances in the communications revolution, interacting with financial and trade liberalization, have brought about rapidly declining transport, telecommunication, and computing costs, causing the natural barriers of time and space that separate national markets and borders to fall as well. The third major difference is the extent to which developing countries, especially East Asian countries, are linked with developed countries and integrated in the global system of trade, finance, investment, production, and multilateral treaties and institutions as never before and this time as partners rather than colonial dependencies. As Jeffrey Sachs points out, the rapidly growing linkage of rich and poor countries in the world economy is not only the great novelty but also the cornerstone of political challenges to contemporary globalization.[41] The recent Asian crisis has highlighted with particular clarity the ineluctable fact that the Asian emerging markets are now too important to the global economy to be relegated to the periphery. The combined synergistic effects of these momentous changes are most evident in all aspects of contemporary life, especially in the economic area, as the world moves beyond global interdependence – the buzzword of the 1970s – to confront new opportunities and dangers of globalization.

International trade has continued to expand as a proportion of world GDP. Trade-GDP ratios increased to 15–20 percent – or even higher for some developed countries – compared to around 12–13 percent for advanced industrial countries during the gold-standard era. If current trends continue, world exports of goods and services will reach $11.4 trillion, or 28 percent of world GDP, by 2005, or nearly double 1998's projected $6.5 trillion, or 24.3 percent of world GDP, up from a mere 9.3 percent twenty years ago. The volume of international merchandise trade is now about sixteen times what it was in 1950, whereas the world's total output is only five and a half times as great. When government expenditure is removed from a comparative calculation, the proportion of trade in relation to national economic activity has grown by as much as a third. The intensity of trade has also increased as trade has risen faster than income. Services trade has more than doubled in the past decade to more than $1 trillion annually, more than 20 percent of total trade. Contemporary international trade is more extensive, more entrenched, more technologically driven, and relatively cheaper to conduct than it was during the gold-standard era.[42]

Global financial flows have expanded more rapidly than world trade or income, with daily turnover in the foreign-exchange markets rising from

---

[41] Sachs, "International Economics," 97–8.
[42] *Business Week*, 31 August 1998, 116; Goldblatt et al., "Economic Globalization."

$15 billion in 1973 to $820 billion in 1992 and to $1.5 trillion by 1998 and still rising, more than ten times the level of trade in 1979 and fifty times the level of world trade today. The volume of international banking transactions increased from $265 billion in 1975 to $4.2 trillion in 1994. The current globalization of finance capital is more extensive and more intensive than in the gold-standard era, with more currencies and more types of assets traded more frequently at greater speed and in greater volumes than in earlier eras. Because of new tools of communication (e.g., Internet, cellular phones, fax machines), the infrastructure of exchange is more institutionalized and technologically more advanced.[43] The trend in financial globalization has been toward ever higher levels of global interdependence, putting governments distinctly on the defensive, eroding much of the authority of the contemporary sovereign state.[44] The Internet revolution continues to fuel the transition to informationization – a global information-based economy. Global FDI flows and FDI outflows (OFDI) respectively at $400 billion and $424 billion in 1997 are nearly twice what they had been in 1990, and some sevenfold their volume in 1980. Even the Asian financial crisis of 1997 has not substantially dampened as 1998 figures are projected to reach a level of around $430–$440 billion for both FDI inflows and FDI outflows.[45]

Without sacrificing their national identity, the MNCs with 53,000 parent companies – large and small – and 448,000 foreign affiliates throughout the world have to come to play the dominant role in global finance, trade, investment, and production. Thanks to rapidly falling costs of transport and communications, MNCs account for about one-third of world output, 70 percent of world trade, 70 percent of patents and technological transfers, and 80 percent of FDI. In the late 1970s, the industrial nations invested $34 billion a year overseas. By 1990, that figure had reached $214 billion. The value chain of production can now be globalized, with different stages of the production process of a single output carried out in different parts of the world. With the exit options for MNCs making direct investments grow by the day, the balance of power has shifted in favor of mobile global capital vis-à-vis both national governments and national trade unions. Indeed, one of the defining features of the contemporary global economy is the multi-tasking role of MNCs in trade, finance, and direct foreign investment; they play a much more central role today than they have done in the

[43] Perraton et al., "The Globalization of Economic Activity"; Goldblatt et al., "Economic Globalization" and *Human Development Report 1999*, 30.

[44] Benjamin Cohen, "Phoenix Risen: The Resurrection of Global Finance," *World Politics* 48, no. 2 (1996), 268–96.

[45] United Nations Conference on Trade and Development (UNCTAD), *World Investment Report 1998* (New York and Geneva, United Nations, 1998), 2, 8.

past.[46] MNCs' ability to outsource abroad in response to fierce global competition has not so much brought about an end of the nation-state as it has significantly changed the costs and benefits of particular national economic institutions and policies.

In sum, there is considerable evidence to rebut the neorealist claim that the contemporary international economy is not so very different from that of the gold-standard era. New tools of communication, new markets, new actors – states and nonstate – and new rules and institutions have all combined to fuel globalization dynamics, radically increasing the *scope, intensity, speed, sheer numbers* and *modalities*, and *impact* of human relations and transactions, both regional and global, and eroding the boundaries between hitherto separate markets (e.g., Sino-ROK trade, which, starting from a zero base of about $40,000 in 1978, ballooned to $23.6 billion in 1997). As a consequence, more state, nonstate, and transnational actors are involved in more extensive and intensive transactions in more ideas, goods, and services than ever before.[47] Falling telecommunications costs and protectionist barriers, the shift from virtually autarchic trade-GDP ratios to extensive participation by the United States and China (thanks to post-Mao China's reform and opening), the collapse of the COMECON system, and the subsequent liberalization of Eastern European centrally planned economies (CPEs) have all contributed to the emergence of a global trading system.

A Broader Conceptualization

As shown above, much of the globalization debate dominated by the hyperglobalization and globaloney schools has been marred by tenuous on-the-fly conceptualization, by ideological polemics, by inattention to the full range of available empirical evidence, and above all by overgeneralization based on the experiences and politics of Western industrial democracies. It is time to move beyond chant or castigation to a more specific analysis of the complex and evolving interplay between globalization dynamics and Korean performance. Before formulating an alternative notion of globalization for this country-specific case study, however, it seems useful to clear away some of the major misconceptions underlying the recent globalization debates in the West, particularly in the United States. Globalization is not a singular condition, let alone an ideal end. It is not a linear or irreversible or necessarily homogenizing process. Globalization can foster more globalization, to be sure, but it

---

[46] Beinart, "An Illusion for Our Time," and UNCTAD, *World Investment Report 1997* and *World Investment Report 1998* (New York and Geneva: United Nations, 1997 and 1998).

[47] *Human Development Report 1999*, 30.

can also foster deglobalization (localization) in various backlash forms. As Sachs aptly put it, "Globalization, in short, is pulling decision making in two directions, to the local (and sometimes dangerously parochial) and the global (and sometimes dangerously distant from the citizenry)."[48]

Globalization does not inevitably signal the end of the nation-state or the arrival of a borderless global society. It is one thing to claim the emergence of global markets but quite another to equate global markets with a perfectly integrated global economy, let alone a global civil society. Globalization is not the same as "globalism" or "universalism" as it does not refer to values or structures.[49] This is not to say or argue that contemporary globalization is all benign or without any polarizing and marginalizing normative and structural effects, but rather to spotlight the conceptual and methodological dangers of eliding and conflating globalization with such normative concepts as globalism, universalism, and transnationalism.[50] Above all, globalization is more than a unidimensional phenomenon (i.e., economic globalization).

For the purpose of this analysis, I define globalization as a set of processes of stretching and intensifying worldwide interconnectedness in all aspects of human relations and transactions – economic, social, cultural, environmental, political, diplomatic, and security – such that events, decisions, and activities in one part of the world have immediate consequences for individuals, groups, and states in other parts of the world. Whether globalization is the new international *system*, which replaced the Cold War system, as Friedman argues, is debatable. But Friedman does capture the two faces of globalization by defining it as a kind of a dynamic but double-edged ongoing process that is empowering more individuals, groups, nation-states, and corporations "to reach around the world farther, faster, deeper and cheaper than ever before," while at the same time "producing a powerful backlash from those brutalized or left behind by this new system." If the symbol of the Cold War system was "a wall, which divided everyone," according to Friedman, "the symbol of the globalization system is a World Wide Web, which unites [connects?] everyone."[51] Put succinctly, globalization is a worldwide revolution with far-reaching but differentiated consequences for people's security, well being, and identities.

---

[48] Sachs, "Ten Trends in Global Competitiveness in 1998," 12.

[49] James N. Rosenau, "The Dynamics of Globalization: Toward an Operational Formulation," *Security Dialogue* 27, no. 3 (1996), 247–62.

[50] For a cogent normative analysis of the polarizing and marginalizing effects of globalization, see Richard A. Falk, *Law in an Emerging Global Village: A Post-Westphalian Perspective* (Ardsley, NY: Transnational Publishers, 1998). See also *Human Development Report 1999* for a balanced description and analysis.

[51] Friedman, *The Lexus and the Olive Tree*, 7–8.

Consider the multiple and multiplying effects of the Asian-cum-global financial crisis, which has forced 20 million Asians back into poverty, made 40 percent of the Russian people poorer than ever, forced 6.1 million Indonesian children to leave school, and produced growing unemployment in Korea and Brazil.[52] It is a boundary-expanding or boundary-penetrating process of intensifying the levels of interaction and interconnectedness within and among states and societies. The boundary-expanding dynamics of globalization have been developing in tandem with a mushrooming of the communications facilities, economic and social interests, and overseas markets through which globalization can foster more globalization worldwide. The end of the Cold War may not have given birth to the globalization system, as Friedman argues, but it certainly has accelerated the globalization process. Thanks to the end of the Cold War, for many states, including the United States, economic globalization is increasingly in the driver's seat, both reflecting and effecting sociocultural, diplomatic, and security globalization.

As a consequence, the separation between the local and the global, between "domestic" and "foreign" affairs, has become increasingly blurred if it has not been completely erased.[53] Far from being a singular condition in a single domain of human activity, globalization is a multi-dimensional process. As such, globalization takes place in all the key domains of contemporary international life, not only in the economic but also in the social, cultural, diplomatic, and security domains, albeit at a varying pace and intensity. Globalization is not a preprogrammed or determinative process. Its nature and direction are shaped and reshaped by the dynamic interplay of objective and subjective factors, or what Chung-in Moon calls "spontaneous" and "managed" globalization.[54] The concept of globalization suggested here refers to an interactive and interpenetrable process that interrelates multiple levels and domains of modern life – economics, politics, society, culture, and security.

To understand the multiple cascading ramifications of globalization for the Korean state and society requires careful examination of the differential patterns and intensity of global interconnectedness in each of these domains (as the chapter essays in the volume demonstrate). Globalization and regionalization need not be seen in mutually conflictive terms; regionalization can take place at the same time as globalization,

---

[52] Roger Cohen, "Redrawing the Free Market: Amid a Global Financial Crisis, Calls for Regulation Spread," *New York Times*, 14 November 1998, B9.

[53] Held, *Democracy and the Global Order*; Rosenau, "The Dynamics of Globalization"; Anthony McGrew, ed., *The Transformation of Democracy? Globalization and Territorial Democracy* (Cambridge, UK: Polity Press, 1997).

[54] Chung-in Moon, "Globalization: Challenges and Strategies," *Korea Focus* 3, no. 3 (May–June 1995), 64–7.

given the lower communications and transport costs associated with geographic proximity. Rather than being viewed as contradictory to globalization, regionalization is perhaps better seen as part and parcel of globalization dynamics, especially in the case of such trade-sensitive countries as Korea. Even in Europe, where regionalization has gone further and deeper than in other regions of the world, the European Union has been a spur, not a barrier, to more globalization. In the 1990s, more than ever before, globalization and regionalization are mutually reinforcing with globalization fostering both *de facto* and *de jure* regionalization, on the one hand, and regionalization fostering globalization only insofar as it stimulates the forces of competition, not the forces of protectionism, within a region, on the other.[55]

Still, the processes of globalization are only capable of global reach. This does not mean that any group, government, or MNC has actually accomplished complete globalization.[56] Globalization dynamics stemming from the density and intensity of patterns of global interconnectedness generate a host of subnational (local), national, and transnational problems and stimulate the growth of multilateral regulatory regimes to manage these transnational problems while at the same fueling antiglobalization resistance movements. Because of such global interconnectedness in economics, politics, society, culture, ecology, and security, "no one area of human activity is isolated; and within each area, no one is untouched by the conditions and activities of others."[57]

Although no aspect of Korea's globalization is so "soft" as to be beyond specification, measurement of Korea's global interconnectedness is likely to depend on the issue area in question. Hard data on international trade, investment, MNCs, and flows of capital provide an empirical base for assessing the extent and intensity of Korea's economic globalization, as well as its actual performance (see table 1.1).

Social and cultural globalization refers to the spreading of information, ideas, and social and cultural practices, products, and institutions throughout the world. The globalization impact of the modern communications media can be seen virtually everywhere. In 1892 it was observed that an inhabitant of a village who reads a newspaper "interests himself simultaneously in the issue of a revolution in Chile, a bush-war in East Africa, a massacre in North China, a famine in Russia," and is,

---

[55] This is the major finding of an OECD-sponsored study. See Charles Oman, *Globalisation and Regionalisation: The Challenge for Developing Countries* (Paris: OECD, 1994); see also Goldblatt et al., "Economic Globalization," and Perraton et al., "The Globalization of Economic Activity."

[56] Rosenau, "The Dynamics of Globalization."

[57] Robert Cox, "Democracy in Hard Times: Economic Globalization and the Limits to Liberal Democracy," in McGrew, *The Transformation of Democracy?*, 49.

therefore, likely to be better informed about the world "than the Prime Minister of a hundred years before."[58] It is equally remarkable that in 1946 the world had just one computer, built at the University of Pennsylvania, weighing thirty tons and covering fifteen-hundred square feet and that as late as the late 1940s nobody predicted wide use of computers. The most extensive market research conducted in the late 1940s concluded that the world computer market would absorb no more than one thousand computers by the year 2000.[59] The spread of social and cultural activity across the globe has been made possible by, and depended heavily on, the revolution in microelectronics, information technology, and computers, with their virtually instantaneous worldwide connections. In 1996 dollars, for example, the cost of a three-minute international phone call between New York and London has dropped over the past couple of decades from $300 to $1 – to virtually zero-marginal cost through the Internet – and the cost of computer processing power has been falling by an average of 30 percent a year in real terms.[60]

Today, the practices and products of social and cultural globalization, from the global human-rights norms, especially women's rights in the Korean context, to the transnationally popular cultural products – movies, TV programs, music, books, and computer software – can be produced and disseminated across a variety of separate but "sovereign" state boundaries. Overseas sales of American-made software and entertainment products totaled $60.2 billion in 1996, more than any other U.S. agricultural or industrial product. In 1997 Hollywood films alone earned more than $30 billion worldwide. Even such fundamentalist antiglobalization states as Iran and Malaysia are not immune to the global spread and penetration of American cultural products.[61]

The relevance of social and cultural globalization goes far beyond the spread of such products, for it may serve as a catalyst for other, related processes of change. However, the impact on national identities of social

---

[58] Quoted in Held, *Democracy and the Global Order*, 122.

[59] W. Michael Blumenthal, "The World Economy and Technological Change," *Foreign Affairs* 66, no. 3 (1987/88), and Thomas W. Millburn, "Successful and Unsuccessful Forecasting in International Relations," in eds. Nazli Choucri and Thomas W. Robinson, *Forecasting in International Relations: Theory, Methods, Problems, Prospects* (San Francisco: W. H. Freeman and Co., 1978), 80.

[60] See "Thinking about Globalisation: Popular Myths and Economic Facts," *The Economist* (London), http://www.economist.com/editorial/freeforall/18-1-98/sb0225.html.

[61] On the global spread and penetration of American pop culture, see Paul Farhi and Megan Rosenfeld, "American Pop Penetrates Worldwide," Sharon Waxman, "Holly Attuned to World Markets," and John Lancaster, "Barbie, 'Titanic' Show Good Side of U.S.," in *Washington Post*, 25, 26, and 27 October 1998, respectively, all on A1. See also *Human Development Report 1999*, 4.

Table 1.1 Matrix for the Study of *Segyehwa*

	Globalization Processes	Segyehwa's Challenges	Segyehwa's Strategies (1994–9)	Assessment and Coverage
Economic Globalization	Trade Capital Investment MNCs	Competitiveness FDI R&D Knowledge-industry E-commerce	Financial reform Corporate reform Labor reform Public sector reform Shift from loans to FDI	Chapter 1 Chapter 2 Chapter 3 Chapter 4 Chapter 5 Chapter 11
Social and Cultural Globalization	Mass media Pop culture Tourists Students Professionals Workers Social practices and institutions	Informationization Nationalism v. globalism Workers' rights Women's rights; Welfare state; Cultural exclusivism v. cultural pluralism	Education reform Mass media reform Knowledge-intensive industrial policy "Universal Globalism" Social concertation Welfare state and social safety nets	Chapter 1 Chapter 3 Chapter 6 Chapter 7 Chapter 11
Diplomatic Globalization	Democratization Diplomatic exchange IGO connection NGO connection Global conferences	"Intermestic" challenge Bilaterlism v. multilateralism; Global democratization Diffuse reciprocity	Status drive Economic diplomacy "Independent collective security" ODA Financial contribution OECD membership	Chapter 1 Chapter 8 Chapter 9 Chapter 10 Chapter 11

↕ ↕ ↕ ↕ ↕ ↕ ↕ ↕	Proliferation of WMDs	Redefining security;	"Independent collective security"	Chapter 1
	Arms trade	UNPKOs	Bilateralism v. multilateralism	Chapter 8
	Defense production	NPT regime; ACD treaties;	UNPKO participation	Chapter 9
Security	UNPKOs	Information warfare	US-ROK alliance	Chapter 10
Globalization		Diversification of overseas arms acquisitions	Burdensharing for USFK NEASED	Chapter 11
		Arms trade	"Sunshine Policy"	

Note: The direction of the arrows in column one indicates interactive or influence flow.

and cultural globalization processes dominated by the United States is uncertain and controversial. One of the defining features of the post–Cold War world is the extent to which virtually all states are subject to the twin pressures of globalization from above and ethnonational localization from below. With the clarity, simplicity, and apparent stability of East-West conflict gone, practically all states face wrenching national-identity difficulties as they try to adjust to a world in which conflict no longer takes place along an East-West divide. The question of national identity is of theoretical and real-world significance, for the state defines itself not only essentially – by what it is – but also behaviorally – by what it does.[62] Does globalization foster a clash of civilizations on a grand scale, as Samuel Huntington argues?[63] Or can social and cultural globalization serve "to detach, or disembed, identities from particular times, places and traditions," and "have a 'pluralizing impact' on identity formation, producing a variety of options which are 'less fixed or unified' "?[64]

   In the diplomatic domain, globalization dynamics underlie any developments that facilitate the expansion of authority, policies, and interests beyond the existing socially constructed, territorial boundaries, as well as shared cooperative security based on coalition politics of state and non-state actors.[65] Indicators of a country's diplomatic globalization include its increasing or decreasing membership in myriad international organizations, both international intergovernmental organizations (IGOs) and international nongovernmental organizations (INGOs), but more importantly changing policies and practices in or with respect to these organizations. The extent to which globalization influences the making and execution of a state's foreign policy is closely keyed if not determined by the extent of its involvement in the global system – the more involved, the more impact, the greater imperative for change.

   Globalization is also blurring the traditional separation between "foreign" and "domestic" affairs, creating the "At Home Abroad, Abroad at Home" antinomy.[66] As a consequence, foreign policy challenges and responses must be rethought. The Clinton administration's response to

---

[62] Lowell Dittmer and Samuel S. Kim, "In Search of a Theory of National Identity," in eds. Lowell Dittmer and Samuel S. Kim, *China's Quest for National Identity* (Ithaca, NY: Cornell University Press, 1993), 1–31.

[63] Huntington, *The Clash of Civilizations.*

[64] Held, *Democracy and the Global Order,* 124.

[65] Rosenau, "The Dynamics of Globalization"; Talbott, "Globalization and Diplomacy."

[66] John Gerard Ruggie, "At Home Abroad, Abroad at Home: International Liberalisation and Domestic Stability in the New World Economy," *Millennium: Journal of International Studies* 24, no. 3 (1994), 507–26, and James N. Rosenau, *Along the Domestic-Foreign Frontier: Exploring Governance in a Turbulent World* (New York: Cambridge University Press, 1997).

globalization challenges is revealing. Like the Kim Young Sam administration, the Clinton administration considers its globalization policy to be its hallmark. As one neorealist critic put it, "Globalization – powered by the inexorable march of technology and trade – will do democratization's work more effectively than State Department pressure ever could," providing the lone superpower with the false promise and comfort of a post–Cold War world. Indeed, globalization is said to have become "the narcissism of a superpower in a one superpower world. It allows America to look at the world and see its own contentment and its own fatigue."[67]

In response to globalization dynamics, the United States, at the beginning of the Clinton administration, created the National Economic Council as a counterpart to the National Security Council, as well as the position of undersecretary of state for global affairs, charged with responsibility for actions in several crosscutting functional issues, such as environmental protection, promotion of democracy and human rights, population and migration issues, and law enforcement. Globalization has increased interdepartmental cooperation on matters of economics, defense, and law enforcement in a more aggressive pursuit of American economic interests abroad. U.S. diplomatic officials at home and abroad are more actively engaged than ever before in meeting with local representatives of U.S. corporations to work out commercial negotiating strategy, and in pressing foreign officials in more than sixty countries to accept U.S. positions, thus advocating and promoting the interests of U.S. businesses around the world. As a result, the number of nondiplomatic U.S. government personnel stationed overseas has significantly increased in recent years. Roughly 63 percent of Americans abroad who are under the authority of U.S. ambassadors and other chiefs of mission are not State Department employees. "As globalization moves forward," according to Strobe Talbott, "that number is likely to grow, as will the challenge of coordinating the American government's presence abroad."[68]

The impact of globalization on military and security matters is varied and even confusing. In a fundamental sense, the nature of "national security" has changed. The traditional boundaries delimiting national (internal) and international security or internal and external threats are substantially blurred. Yet even in the United States, according to Deputy Secretary of Defense John Hamre, "we have a 19th century view of national security. If a problem develops outside of the borders of the United States, it is a national security problem. If it is inside of U.S. borders, it is law enforcement." America's defense infrastructure, which is

[67] Beinart, "An Illusion for Our Time," 20–1.
[68] Talbott, "Globalization and Diplomacy," 78.

increasingly connected to the Internet (a technology for which there is no assured embedded security), is now wide open to sabotage and disruption by faceless and borderless hackers. And yet the U.S. government screens "kids for drugs" but "has no idea where the operating codes for most of our computer systems [are] written. . . . we continue to operate a security system that largely worries about the nationality of the board of directors or the geographical location of the corporate headquarters, which is very naive."[69] All the same, the United States, as the lone superpower in the post–Cold War world, has emerged at one and the same time as the world's largest arms dealer and the world's most vociferous defender of arms-control regimes, especially the Non-Proliferation Treaty (NPT) regime.

On the positive side but still at the margins, the United Nations, as the most legitimate institutional expression of the idea of global community, is working hard to facilitate, however imperfectly, global consciousness-raising, consensus-building, standard-setting, and law-making processes to deal with problems that threaten international – and increasingly "intermestic" – peace, human security, and social, economic, and ecological well-being. Despite, or perhaps even because of, the initial euphoria and hyperactivism in the early post–Cold War years, the United Nations soon began to experience what former Secretary-General Boutros Boutros-Ghali called "a crisis of over-credibility" stemming from its overextension. Local and regional armed conflicts, mostly "internal state-making conflicts" that had previously been overshadowed and repressed by global superpower contention, have broken out in many parts of the world. In responding to such post–Cold War security and humanitarian challenges, U.N. "peacekeepers" soon found themselves involved in a wide range of more demanding but less clearly mandated state-building activities, such as supervising ceasefires, demobilizing forces, destroying weapons, overseeing the return of refugees, providing humanitarian assistance, supervising administrative structures, training new police forces, and supervising and organizing elections. The General Assembly has also shifted its primary attention to the development of a more synergistic conception of human security by sponsoring a series of global conferences on the environment (Rio de Janiero, 1992), human rights (Vienna, 1993), population and development (Cairo, 1994), social development (Copenhagen, 1995), women (Beijing, 1995), and human resettlement (Istanbul, 1996).

Still, globalization as such was not on the United Nations' agenda until

---

[69] John Hamre, "How Do Free Trade and Globalization Impinge on U.S. Security and How Does Defense Policy Affect U.S. Economic Welfare?" The Council on Foreign Relations, 5 June 1998, in hppt://www.foreignrelations.org/studies/transcripts/hamre.html.

the Asian financial crisis of 1997–8. In 1998 alone, three major discussions were held respectively in April, July, and September under the U.N. auspices on the impact of the globalization process on the world economy. For the first time, the U.N. secretary-general's annual report on the work of the organization released on 3 September 1998 – an annual state of the world message – declared that the United Nations shall take up the challenge of ensuring that "globalization leads to progress, prosperity and security for all." For the first time UNDP's *Human Development Report 1999* has devoted its primary attention to globalization, providing a most comprehensive and balanced assessment of its new benefits as well as new threats to human security broadly defined.

The ugly and subversive side of military and security globalization is an accelerating marketization of arms production and distribution. The impact of globalization on conventional arms sales is more and more market-driven competition and less and less cooperative security. The end of the Cold War means that political leaders everywhere are more subject than ever before to the dictates of global market forces with little countervailing socialist challenge or normative constraint. Although the North Korean nuclear case was quickly billed the first nuclear proliferation crisis of post–Cold War global politics, it has remained the tip of the iceberg. With the weakening of ideological and national identities associated with the Cold War, the development, production, and distribution of advanced weapons systems began to follow the logic of economic globalization. The globalization of arms production and dual-use technology is a new kind of proliferation that threatens the extant and emerging norms concerning weapons of mass destruction. Even before the end of the Cold War, many new arms exporters – Brazil, Bulgaria, China, Egypt, Israel, both Koreas, Spain, and Yugoslavia, among others – joined the fray as second-, third-, and fourth-tier merchants of death, weakening whatever normative constraints or central mechanisms were present in the global system. Today, the United States is the world's largest arms dealer, supplying nearly 43 percent of the world's arms. The U.S. approach to arms exports has already given way to the frenzy of global arms trade, even as U.S. ambassadors and representatives of the military-industrial complex are actively lobbying foreign procurement officials, Saudi princes, and heads of state everywhere for an ever larger share of the global arms market.[70]

The following chapters reveal many dimensions of Korea's understanding or misunderstanding of globalization as a double-edged sword posing at one and the same time dangers and opportunities. Not unlike

---

[70] For a trenchant analysis, see William W. Keller and Janne E. Nolan, "The Arms Trade: Business as Usual?" *Foreign Policy*, 109 (Winter 1997–8), 113–25.

Putnam's "two-level-games" approach,[71] a successful execution of the *segyehwa* drive requires far more than policy or rhetorical pronouncements. Indeed, it requires an effective ongoing negotiating process of choosing among various competing strategic options and in right sequencing (as argued in Chapters 2–3), not a finalized decision for self-execution, even as the Korean state, situated strategically between domestic and international politics, is constrained simultaneously by what globalization agents (IMF, OECD, EU, the MNCs, the United States, and global markets) will accept and what domestic constituencies (*chaebol* and labor unions) will ratify. In pursuit of this line of inquiry, the contributors pose and address several – and enduring – questions about the major challenges, dangers, opportunities, and consequences of Korea's *segyehwa* drive. They describe and explain what is in, of, and by *segyehwa's* promise as measured against its actual performance – in the economic, sociocultural, diplomatic, and security domains. They also shed light on the "winners" and "losers" in the course of Korea's *segyehwa* drive – who gets what, why, and at whose expense in the Korean state and society in the era of globalization (the 1990s). As shown in table 1.1, each chapter is an interaction-specific or issue-specific case study designed to explain how the pressure of globalization works, and with positive or negative consequences for the Korean state and society in general and the state-capital-labor relationship, business conglomerates (*chaebol*), workers and labor unions, women, foreign migrant workers, foreign relations, security, and U.N. diplomacy in particular.

In the concluding chapter, the major arguments and findings of the volume will be drawn together in a systematic fashion so as to deliver an overall assessment of the causes, patterns, and consequences of Korea's globalization drive. The final chapter will also sketch out a series of challenges confronting the Kim Dae Jung government, each of which will involve a strategic decision and sequencing regarding how to cope with globalization challenges and how to redefine the role of the state as a competent, efficient, knowledge-intensive, and adaptable state needed in surviving and even prospering in the era of globalization. As well, three plausible future scenarios – breakdown, breakthrough, and muddling through – will be delineated and assessed as a way of speculating about the shape of Korea's *segyehwa* life to come.

---

[71] Robert Putnam, "Diplomacy and Domestic Politics: The Logic of Two-Level Games," *International Organization* 42 (Summer 1988), 427–60, reprinted as Appendix in Peter B. Evans, Harold K. Jacobson, and Robert Putnam, eds., *Double-Edged Diplomacy: International Bargaining and Domestic Politics* (Berkeley, CA: University of California Press, 1993) 431–68. This is the best single volume applying and testing Putnam's two-level-games model in various security and economic issues as well as in several North-South case studies.

CHAPTER 2

Globalization and Strategic Choice in South Korea: Economic Reform and Labor

Barry K. Gills and Dongsook S. Gills

Introduction

This chapter investigates the impact of economic globalization on South Korea's transition to a mature economy and democratic society, with special emphasis on the role of organized labor. South Korea is an important case study of national responses to globalization. For the past decade, South Korea has undergone a transition characterized by increasing pressure on the developmental state model and a changing power configuration among government, business, and labor. The authoritarianism of the past has been replaced by democracy, and the character and composition of the ruling coalition has undergone important alterations.

At the center of the old model was a government-*chaebol* alliance, whereby organized labor was strictly controlled and excluded by law from direct political activity or the funding of political parties. The model was sustained by a "growth first" orientation, neomercantilist trade practices, and a robust industrial policy, all of which tended to promote *chaebol* expansion.

In the changing context of the international economy in the 1980s and 1990s, the old model began to unravel. South Korean companies sought greater independence from government tutelage. Domestic labor demanded greater autonomy from both government and management. Foreign trade partners pressed for greater openness of the Korean economy. These combined pressures brought about a crisis of the old model, culminating in the International Monetary Fund (IMF) agreement of 1997.

Each element in the triad – government, business, and labor – has attempted to redefine the situation. The rough balance of forces, however, produced a sociopolitical impasse for much of the 1990s. President Kim Young Sam's policy of globalization (*segyehwa*) failed to bring about necessary structural reform. The "IMF crisis" challenges the new government of President Kim Dae Jung to redefine South Korea's strategic direction.

Globalization and Strategic Choices in South Korea

Globalization remains a highly contested concept, not a single, received, or self-evident theory.[1] In any definition, globalization demands fundamental choices. A "strategic choice" suggests a political decision taken about the basic structure and goals of the economy and the society, which will determine the nature of its development. A strategic choice is a matter of prioritization of one set of goals over another involving the speed and sequence of key reforms. In South Korea's case, the key problem has been how to reconcile globalization with the need for fundamental reform in the domestic economic and political structures.

We construct the following schema of strategic choices based on the needs of the South Korean situation in the early 1990s in order to analyze the globalization policy of President Kim Young Sam:

A. *Deconcentration first*
B. *External opening first*
C. *Democratization first*

South Korea needed all three elements: deconcentration of *chaebol*; external opening and liberalization; and a deepening of democratization. However, the outcome of reform depended upon the prioritization of these needs. We will now examine each option in turn.

A. Deconcentration First

While the *chaebol* had once been considered an asset for the disciplining of industrial investment and pursuit of international export advantages, by the mid-1990s they increasingly became a liability. The litany of *chaebol* sins included ambitious but reckless investment strategies; antiquated management structures; confrontational industrial relations; private

---

[1] See B. K. Gills, ed., Special Issue of *New Political Economy*, 2, no. 1 (1997); B. K. Gills, ed., *Globalisation and the Politics of Resistance*, Macmillan, forthcoming; L. Amoore, R. Dodgson, B. K. Gills, P. Langley, D. Marshall, and I. Watson, "Overturning 'Globalisation': Resisting the Teleogical, Reclaiming the 'Political'", *New Political Economy*, 2, no. 1 (1997): 179–95.

family financial control (albeit reduced to 15 percent of total equities in the top thirty companies); dangerous financial practices (e.g. the mutual guarantee system); hidden debt structure; and rent-seeking behavior.[2]

Long-term national industrial health and economic growth were in question as capital fled from productive industrial investment into "Jai tech" or financialization and speculation. National employment levels were threatened as companies increasingly sought to relocate the production process abroad. The traditional strategy of growth first pursued by the government-*chaebol* alliance, which had involved government financial support for business, was plagued by increasing corruption and concomitant corporate debt, creating fundamental weaknesses in the national financial system.

Some economists have long argued that both constraints on the *chaebol* and promotion of small- and medium-size enterprises (SMEs) were indispensable to establishing a pluralistic and competitive national economic structure. The precondition to achieve vigorous domestic competition and fair trade was the implementation of effective regulation to control monopolistic business behavior. However, despite the existence of rules governing the establishment of cartels, many loopholes in the regulatory system allowed the *chaebol* to circumvent restrictions, especially in the finance and insurance sectors.[3] Furthermore, despite the regulatory focus on prevention of concentration, Korea lacked a direct and enforceable antimonopoly or antitrust law.

A strategic choice for "deconcentration first" would have emphasized domestic reform *prior* to acceleration of external opening. The primary goal would have been to create a competitive, nonmonopolistic domestic market structure. This would have required gradual and selectively deferred external market opening. The strategic goal here was to cushion the national economy against destabilizing external shocks while preparing a new domestic regulatory structure. The sequence emphasizes adequate domestic preparations before accelerating external opening. In relation to democratization, deconcentration is a necessary condition but not a sufficient one.

B. External Opening First

External opening first should be understood in the context of increasing external pressure to liberalize the Korean economy. When questioned about the degree of external pressure for liberalization, South Korean

---

[2] Kim Jun Il, senior counsellor to the deputy prime minister, minister of finance and economy, interview with author, Kwachon, Korea, 26 August 1997.

[3] You Jong Keun, economic adviser to the president, interview with author, Seoul, 14 August 1998.

economic officials routinely cited U.S. demands as a key impetus for the acceleration of economic liberalization.[4] This pressure extended to industrial, service, and agricultural sectors, including financial liberalization and eventual full capital market opening.

In an environment characterized by demands for market opening, technological innovation, and increased capital mobility, this option prioritizes international competitiveness. In the case of South Korea, this implies moving toward a market-regulated economy rather than a state-regulated one. The emphasis on international competitiveness included a preference for flexibilization of labor. With aspirations to join the WTO and the Organization for Economic Cooperation and Development (OECD) high on the agenda, the need to conform to prevailing international norms became more urgent. *External opening first* was preferred by the *chaebol* to deconcentration, while being deemed by many to be an effective means of bringing about reform in the economic structure. However, placing emphasis on external opening before deconcentration ran the risk of further entrenching the *chaebol* and thus reducing the scope for democratization. Moreover, it entailed increased risks of macroeconomic destabilization from external shocks.

C. Democratization First

The option of *democratization first* is related to social, economic, and political problems that persisted from the legacy of military rule. It implied that the traditional "growth first" model would be abandoned, accepting lower rates of growth in order to achieve other social goals. The priority would be on increased welfare spending, a redistribution of income from capital to labor, and social inclusion. This option is not incompatible with the goal of business deconcentration. However, its goals are much broader than achievement of a competitive capitalism and may imply a social democratic model and expansion of the welfare state.

In South Korea's case, *democratization first* required a new democratic industrial relations system, based on a social contract with labor protecting its rights in law and allowing it to play a constructive role in national politics. Labor-management relations under the *chaebol* system were characterized by hostility and confrontation. Government-business relations were marked by increasing pressure from business to decide economic policy, posing problems of corruption and political paralysis. The weakening or breaking of the government-*chaebol* alliance would have provided a possibility for a new social alliance between government and labor in pursuit of broad reform and a new economic model.

---

[4] Various ministries of the government of the Republic of Korea, interview with author, summer 1994.

Breaking the Mold?

As the first civilian democratic regime in decades, the government of President Kim Young Sam recognized the need to engage in a politics of economic reform, expanded welfare, and social inclusion. His first policy initiatives focused on deconcentration – for example, the real name financial disclosure system, a reform which Roh Tae Woo had abandoned. His deconcentration policy included a battery of measures such as the "core company system" or specialization policy; credit control restrictions on borrowing and *chaebol* financial holdings in private commercial banks; limitations on the expansion of *chaebol* subsidiaries; limitations on equity holdings by *chaebol* family members; efforts to separate ownership and management of large firms; and restrictions on cross-payment guarantees.[5]

The Kim Young Sam government attempted to stipulate streamlined strategies of technological investment by the *chaebol* and curtail their ambitious horizontal expansion into multiple business lines. The government decided to phase out the traditional financial practices of preferential (subsidized) policy loans for *chaebol* and encourage them to raise funds independently on capital markets, including abroad.

The government was also wary of *chaebol* exodus, fearing the consequences for national industrial capacity and employment levels. In October 1995 the government imposed more stringent financial requirements for Korean firms investing overseas, though apparently with little real impact. The problem of capital flight was partly addressed by the decision to accelerate liberalization of foreign investment into Korea, in hopes of attracting new technologies and sustaining international competitiveness. The *chaebol* were pressured to produce greater efficiency gains and to commit increased resources to research and development.

At the same time, however, another set of policy proposals arose around the goal of accelerated external opening. As early as the spring of

---

[5] Interestingly, President Park Chung Hee initiated reform measures in 1972 such as indictment of "anti-social" businessmen alleged to have misused borrowed funds while their firms became incapacitated. The Public Corporations Inducement Law gave the ministry of finance (MOF) the power to designate groups with healthy financial structures to go public – but few *chaebol* did so in the 1970s. The Real Name System was also proposed, but dropped in 1972. These measures came in response to the "kerb market" financial crisis of 1971, in which the government bailed out indebted corporations. In 1974 Park decreed a special directive to reform the *chaebol*, requiring all *chaebol* to submit a three-year plan to reduce debt/equity ratios, increase paid-up capital, sell subsidiaries, undergo merger and rationalization, and modernize the family management system. In 1976 the Park regime attempted to use the banking system to police *chaebol* borrowing and investment, but this system failed as the Office of Bank Supervision could not enforce the banks' recommendations.

1994, the Economic Planning Board (EPB) began preparing a comprehensive plan in anticipation of the inauguration of the WTO scheduled
for January 1995.[6] The guidelines included the further liberalization of
finance, foreign direct investment, and agriculture and fisheries. A new
Economic Globalization Planning Agency was recommended to oversee
ministerial task forces.

In the EPB's view, globalization would "allow Korean firms to make
use of the optimal combination of production factors around the world"
and make Korea "the world's best location for foreign investment." The
goal was an "open and fair competition system," which required "ceasing
[the government's] practice of market intervention and removing regulations which had become entrenched in the past when concerns regarding market failure were much greater."[7]

The EPB wanted to remove both the support system for SMEs, which it
called "inherently anti-competitive," and the various support systems for
chaebol as well. Moreover, the EPB advocated removal of government
restrictions which "specifically penalizes conglomerates" in favor of "fair
competition." Foreign firms would be treated "in the same manner as
domestic firms" and "all possible sectors of the Korean economy should
be opened to foreign competition." Moreover, the EPB assumed that,
"Globalization necessarily entails rapid and sweeping financial deregulation," which would mean reduction of government financial privileges to
both *chaebol* and SMEs alike.

In contrast, the Ministry of Finance (MOF) was skeptical of rapid
external liberalization, particularly in the financial sector, an area in
which U.S. pressure was playing a particularly important role. The Bank
of Korea (BOK) shared the same concern that opening Korea's financial
sector too fast could be potentially damaging to the economy, threatening future macroeconomic stability. Traditional fiscal and monetary policy techniques might lose their efficacy in the new liberalized and dereg-
ulated environment.[8] The EPB concluded that this was an inevitable risk
of globalization. MOF and BOK caution on accelerated liberalization was
eventually overwhelmed by a combination of the presidency, the EPB,
the Ministry of Foreign Affairs, and the Ministry of Trade, Industry, and
Energy (MOTIE).[9]

[6] Kwon Ok Guy, director, Regional Cooperation Division 1, International Economic Policy Bureau, Economic Planning Board, "The Economic Globalization
   Plan for Remaking the Korean Economy," *Republic of Korea Economic Bulletin*,
   July 1994, EPB/KDI.
[7] Ibid.
[8] Ministry of Finance, and the Monetary Research Division, Bank of Korea,
   interviews by author, summer 1994.
[9] Various ministries of the government of the Republic of Korea, interviews by
   author, summer 1994; and Kwon Ok Gyu, "The Economic Globalization Plan ..."

The shift in emphasis from deconcentration to external opening may be explicable in political terms. The cabinet system was weakened by frequent turnover, a result of the long queue of politicians expecting high office. President Kim received constantly changing and conflicting advice on the economy and was prone to make a sudden change of direction. Kim Young Sam represented a middle class political constituency interested in stability. His initial anti-*chaebol* measures and attempts to dismantle vested interests and root out corrupt practices made part of the middle classes uneasy, reviving a conservative backlash against reform.[10] The first instance of this backlash was the defeat of the administration's attempt to reform the legal system and the judiciary at the expense of entrenched vested interests.[11] More fundamentally, Kim Young Sam concluded he could not conduct his economic policy without the cooperation of the *chaebol*, and thus turned away from the idea of a decisive break in the government-*chaebol* alliance. However, he successfully tackled the problem of smashing the power of the old military ruling clique, such as the secret society known as *Hanahoe*, and carried out significant reforms of the military and security apparatus, making these institutions more subject to the rule of law.

The Reverse Course

The initial anti-*chaebol* or deconcentration program was met by a "strike by capital." In the first quarter of 1993, investment in machine facility dropped by 12.4 percent, following a drop in the previous quarter of 10.2 percent, the lowest levels in three decades. This situation continued into the second quarter of 1993 and overall economic growth fell to 3.4 percent, the lowest since the severe recession of 1980–1. This created a fear in the government of increased unemployment. The economic bureaucracy and the incoming presidential chief economic secretary argued for restoration of "growth first" rather than a priority on welfare goals. It was clear that the business community sided with this argument.[12] Kim Young Sam chose to restore business confidence and revive the investment climate. Therefore, he called an extraordinary meeting with leading *chaebol* business magnates at the Blue House, imploring them to resume investment in manufacturing and industry and soliciting their involvement in large-scale new infrastructural projects.

---

[10] Park Jin, political advisor to the president, Blue House, interview by author, Seoul, 22 August 1997.

[11] Cho Won Dong, policy planning staff, Blue House, interview by author, 28 August 1997; and Park Jin, Blue House, interview by author, 22 August 1997.

[12] Park Jin, political adviser to the president, Blue House, interview by author, Seoul, 22 August 1997.

Thus, during 1994 the Kim Young Sam administration embarked on a "reverse course" on deconcentration policy, and shifted back to a traditional emphasis on the needs of big business, export promotion, and rapid economic growth. President Kim's fundamental commitment to economic growth and his political weakness (despite the supposed strength of the presidential office) worked to defeat his early attempts at deconcentration.

The reverse course clearly demonstrated the increased power of big business. This was illustrated in business's impact on government policy regarding industrial relations reform. The price demanded by the *chaebol* for their cooperation with government included the removal of the labor minister, who was regarded as too liberal. Revision of the old authoritarian labor law, promised by the new government and demanded by labor, was deferred to the future. In October 1994 the new minister of labor announced that a draft of the revised labor law would not be ready until late 1995.

The "growth first" camp favored accession to the OECD in anticipation of enhancing competitiveness and absorbing foreign technologies (while also expecting to bargain for exceptions during the accession negotiations – to reduce the "cost" to Korea). The idea of joining the OECD, which required accession to additional International Labor Organization (ILO) conventions, promised an element of reform, both in terms of changing *chaebol* behavior and promoting better conditions for workers. However, while some understood this primarily as a matter of improving workers' welfare, others, especially *chaebol* elements, believed the key goal was to enhance Korea's international competitiveness by giving management increased power to discipline and flexibilize labor.

Segyehwa: A Critique

Long before the formal announcement of the *segyehwa* (globalization) policy in the Sydney Declaration of 17 November 1994, the "New Diplomacy" initiated under Foreign Minister Han Sung Joo had enunciated a new willingness to work cooperatively with other nations in "strengthening the liberal trade system." Han viewed internationalization (*kukjehwa*) as "an inevitable process which every nation-state must undergo to ensure sustained stability and prosperity."[13] In May 1994, he stressed the necessity for Korea's "striving for globalization, trying to induce foreign investment, liberalizing its financial market and preparing to join the

[13] Foreign Ministry of the Republic of Korea, "Fundamentals of Korea's new diplomacy" (an address delivered by Foreign Minister Han Sung Joo to the Korean Council on Foreign Relations, May 1993).

OECD."[14] The best means of meeting the challenge of globalization was to "enhance competitiveness."[15]

In December 1994, the government announced an important cabinet reshuffle and administrative reorganization specifically intended to be "suited for the pursuit of globalization strategies."[16] The EPB and the Ministry of Finance were merged into a new super-agency called the Ministry of Finance and Economy (MOFE), while MOTIE was superseded by the new Ministry of International Trade and Industry (MITI). A new policy planning staff position was created at the Blue House specifically to assist in the formulation of globalization policy.

It was at the same time that the Globalization Commission (*Segyehwa Ch'ujin Wiwonhoe*) was formally established on 27 December 1994 by presidential order (no. 14504), and the commission was formed by 21 January 1995. In structure, it was headed by the prime minister (Lee Hong-koo), and consisted of a set of committees on policy planning, administrative reform, educational reform, and science and technology. Its membership was composed of representatives from government ministries, research institutes, academia, and "socially eminent persons" and consultation with a special grouping called the Association for Economic Justice (*Kyongshil Ryun*).[17]

President Kim Young Sam delivered the first major domestic pronouncement on *segyehwa* on 25 January 1995 before members of the new commission. This speech, along with a subsequent one delivered on 23 March 1995, outlined the meaning of globalization. He described globalization as a "global trend" and an era characterized by "a borderless global economy" in which "room for asserting national sovereignty in economic affairs is sharply diminishing."[18] Rapid liberalization of capital, technology, goods, and service flows across nations, and ushers in a period of "boundless global competition."[19] A critical reading of the government's initial statements on the globalization policy reveals a clear tendency to combine elements of all three strategic options, though there is an emphasis on external opening. In "Principles for National

---

[14] Foreign Ministry of the Republic of Korea, "Post-UR international order and Korea's foreign policy," (an address delivered by Foreign Minister Han Sung Joo to the Korean Council on Foreign Relations, 12 May 1994).

[15] Ibid.

[16] *Korea Times*, 22 December 1994.

[17] Cho Won Dong, Blue House, Policy Planning Staff, interview by author, Seoul, 28 August, 1997.

[18] "Explanatory Notes on President Kim Young Sam's Blueprint for the *Segyehwa* Policy," in *The Segyehwa Policy of Korea under President Kim Young Sam*, Korean Overseas Information Service, Seoul, Korea, July 1995, 7–16, p. 7. See also the Globalization Commission Report, 1995, 3–19.

[19] Ibid., 8.

Development in the Globalization Era," the government stressed that it must ensure "fair competition in all sectors and take greater interest in issues related to social development such as the environment, labor, income distribution and social welfare." Each citizen was entitled to an "adequate social safety net against unemployment and disease." However, there was a continuous emphasis on increasing competition in all sectors, public and private.

The government claimed "*segyehwa* entails rationalizing all aspects of life" and "reforms in every area." It meant "a sweeping transformation of society"[20] requiring "productivity and flexibility" in all areas of national life.[21] Segyehwa included economic reform to meet global standards of practice (including transparency of all transactions, fair competition, deregulation of the financial sector, and a fairer tax system); industrial relations reform; expansion of the social security system; political reform toward a more open competitive system; and administrative reform.

The government called for a mission to "abolish all outmoded or unreasonable elements in society and in attitudes and behaviour which resulted from the past single-minded pursuit of economic development." The Kim Young Sam government criticized previous regimes for having been "so obsessed with growth that they ignored the serious implications of the increasing concentration of economic power in the hands of a few business tycoons, the worsening income distribution and the intensifying strife among different regions and classes."[22] Economic growth alone was insufficient and must be "accompanied by an equally substantial endeavor for balanced and equitable social development."[23]

The 1996 Globalization Commission report included measures for deconcentration, and acknowledged the need to prepare a legal foundation to prevent monopoly behavior. It cited evidence that, "Until 1994, 117 cases which breached the controls on economic concentration, and 76 cases of improper internal trade, contrasted to only 3 cases of industrial combination."[24] Furthermore, "insufficient controls on monopoly

[20] Kwon Ok Gyu, Director, Regional Cooperation Division 1, International Economic Policy Bureau, Economic Planning Board, "The Economic Globalization Plan for Remaking the Korean Economy," *Republic of Korea Economic Bulletin,* July 1994, EPB/KDI, Seoul, Korea.
[21] "Explanatory Notes on President Kim Young Sam's Blueprint for the Segyehwa Policy," in *The Segyehwa Policy of Korea Under President Kim Young Sam* (Seoul: Korean Overseas Information Service, July 1995), 7–16, p. 12.
[22] Ibid., 10.
[23] "President Kim Envisions Enhanced Well-being and Quality of Life through the *Segyehwa* Policy," in *The Segyehwa Policy of Korea under President Kim Young Sam,* 17–23.
[24] *Kyongjaeng chokjin ul wihan Kongjong korae jedo kaeson bang-an* [Improvement plan for the fair trade system for promotion of competition], 1996, *Segyehwa*

not only prevents successful anti-concentration policy, but limits the competitiveness of Korean enterprise against giant MNCs."[25]

In pursuit of this aim, the Fair Trade Commission was elevated to ministerial level.[26] The government recognized the task of making Korea's competition policy conform to that of other advanced countries. Old principles of state regulation of the economy, such as price stabilization, prevention of "excessive competition," and "reinforcement of competitiveness" had worked to protect the monopolistic status of enterprises and legitimize business combinations, all of which facilitated concentration and thereby hampered "market competition," technological innovation, and productivity gains.[27]

However, the substance of *segyehwa* was quite limited, and primarily oriented to achieving greater productivity in the private sector. For example, the promised extension of the social insurance and welfare system consisted of a modest expansion of coverage for the indigent.[28] Reform of the social security system took the form of computerization and appeals to business to become more involved in employee welfare, primarily on a workfare basis. Finally, the promise to increase public support for the socially marginalized relied largely on appeals for private sector involvement or self-help programs. Such programs are "in tune with the neo-liberal governments' calls for greater self-help, active citizenship and a reduced dependency on the state."[29]

The reforms in welfare and attempts to achieve social justice were insufficient in scope, depth, and speed. No consequential measures followed to support the announcement of the welfare state. ROK social welfare spending remained the lowest in the OECD except on education.[30] The failure to expand the social safety net sufficiently during the Kim Young Sam period left Korean workers badly exposed when the subsequent economic crisis in 1997–8 brought high unemployment. The general failure of Kim Young Sam's social and welfare policy was related to the government's return to the policy of growth first.[31]

chujin chonghap bogoso [Globalization Commission Comprehensive Report] (Seoul: Globalization Commission, 1997), 345.

[25] Ibid., 346.

[26] Ibid., 344.

[27] Ibid., 345.

[28] *The Globalization Commission Report 1996*, 536, provides figures on extension of coverage for minimum income support to the indigent from 70 percent to 80 percent by 1996, and 90 percent by 1997 and 100 percent by 1998.

[29] Ankie Hoogvelt, *Globalisation and the Postcolonial World* (New York: Macmillan, 1997) 149. This is mentioned in the section entitled "The Politics of Exclusion."

[30] Soon Won Kwon, "Economic Justice and Social Welfare: New Principles of Economic Policy" (paper presented at the International Conference on Democratization and Globalization in Korea, 18–19 August 1997, Seoul, Korea).

[31] Ibid.

Kim Young Sam's *segyehwa* policy failed to make a clear strategic choice and therefore lost the opportunity for sequential reforms. This exacerbated the fundamental structural weaknesses of the Korean economy. On the whole, *segyehwa* policy was more rhetorical than substantive, more of a slogan than a coherent policy. In hindsight, it resulted in missing the window of opportunity for timely reform at less cost to the Korean economy and society.

Segyehwa and Labor Reform

From 1987 until the present, the issue of labor reform has been central, involving longstanding union grievances against restrictive elements of the law, including the prohibition on plural unionism, third-party intervention, public sector unions, and union participation in party politics. While labor has tried to gain social and political acceptance as a legitimate partner of government and business, the *chaebol* have demanded new powers to discipline labor.

When President Kim Young Sam was inaugurated in February 1993, he initiated a policy of nonintervention in labor-management disputes and appointed a former human rights lawyer as minister of labor. However, the *segyehwa* policy, with its emphasis on growth first and flexibilization of labor, brought about a reactivation of the government-*chaebol* alliance and a strong defensive response from organized labor.

On the other hand, the preparations for South Korea's entry into the OECD increased the urgency of making headway in labor reform. The ILO was dissatisfied with South Korea's low compliance with international labor standards and the OECD required revision as a precondition of Korean membership. On 9 May 1996, President Kim Young Sam established a Presidential Commission on Industrial Relations Reform (PCIR), including representatives from both the FKTU[32] and KCTU.[33]

From the government's point of view, there were two goals of labor reform: 1) to reduce the rigidity of the labor market, and 2) to bring Korea's labor practices up to international norms and ILO standards in preparation for OECD membership.[34] The FKTU and KCTU submitted similar proposals to the PCIR calling for the abolition of the prohibitions on plural unionism, union political activity, third-party intervention, and public sector unions. Business submitted proposals to the PCIR via

---

[32] The Federation of Korean Trade Unions is the officially recognized peak organization. It has a reputation for moderation and "bread and butter" unionism.

[33] The Korean Confederation of Trade Unions was formed in November 1995, as an illegal rival national confederation, composed of "democratic" trade unions espousing a broad social agenda.

[34] Cho Won Dong, policy planning staff, Blue House, Seoul, interview by author, 28 August 1997.

the Korean Confederation of Employers (KCE), insisting on maintaining prohibition of plural unions and union political activity. In addition, KCE called for the right to replace striking workers and abolish severance payments on redundancy.[35]

In spite of the withdrawal of KCTU from the PCIR,[36] draft proposals were forwarded to the government by the committee on 12 November 1996. A new government committee was established to finalize the draft legislation, headed by Prime Minister Lee Hong-koo. The committee arrived at a final draft on 3 December 1996. The draft legislation provided the basis for flexibilization of labor, including relaxed rules for dismissal of workers and substitution for striking workers. Third-party intervention was to be allowed for registered organizations and the teachers' union was to be recognized from 1999, but banned from striking.

The draft permitted multiple unions at industry level effective from 1997 but delayed their introduction at enterprise level. However, at the crucial National Assembly stage of the process, the ruling party introduced a controversial change: a decision to delay implementation of multiple unions by three years. Apparently, this decision was taken by key members of the committee and the ruling party, reportedly without the full knowledge of the Blue House.[37] In the absence of opposition MPs,[38] in the early hours of the morning of 26 December 1996, the bill was passed along with ten others in seven minutes flat.

The passage of this bill delayed the implementation of multiple unions until 2000 and maintained the prohibition of political activity by unions and the prohibition of the national teachers' union. As a result, the government's original agreement to recognize the KCTU from March 1997 was rescinded. Workers would not be allowed to form multiple unions at enterprise level until 2002. A clause in the new law threatened the legal status of unions if their main purpose was regarded as being aimed at solidarity for political or social purposes. This particularly affected KCTU, since many of its member unions explicitly espouse political and social goals. The KCTU's reputation for militancy and politicization made it unpopular with both business and government. The new legislation would slow the progress of KCTU and undermine the legal protection of its members.

The National Strike

The labor reform policy of the Kim Young Sam government led directly to a major national confrontation with organized labor, led by the KCTU.

---

[35] Ibid.
[36] The KCTU claimed that the PCIR was biased towards the interests of business.
[37] Cho Won Dong, Blue House, interview by author, August 1997.
[38] Ibid.

The ruling party's blatant reversion to improper methods in the National Assembly raised public fears over potential reauthoritarianization. The attempt to legislate flexibilization of labor threatened the job security of a wide section of the working population. There had already been layoffs and downsizing in Korea, and a trend to impose early retirement or involuntary dismissal, which had reached even into the white collar and professional sectors of the economy. This trend had set a tone of fear, insecurity, and anger among the Korean workforce.

The KCTU responded by immediately declaring a national strike, mobilizing both unions and wide sections of civil society in an historic protest movement. A central goal of the KCTU was recognition of the right of full freedom of association for unions. The two-month period of the national strike was remarkable not only for the extent to which it sustained coordinated nationwide strike activity, but also for the amount of public sympathy it gathered, despite decades of anti-union sentiment in South Korean society.[39]

The national strike was led from temporary headquarters at Myong-dong Cathedral in Seoul, the traditional symbol and citadel of the democracy movement. Unions, and especially strikes, generally had lacked social and political legitimacy in the past. The key to KCTU strategy was, therefore, "bringing the public to support, sympathize and understand the general strike."[40] KCTU was successful in communicating to the public that the strikers acted in the general interest in opposing the new trends of job insecurity and flexibilization.[41] Public support for the general strike was polled at a mere 26 percent before the strike, but steadily increased, finally reaching 80 percent in the third stage of the action. The union leadership was also able to calm fears that it represented a radical left-wing threat to society, an image that had often been used against labor in the past. This was possible through growing public awareness of the issues on which the strike was being fought. The national strike was therefore related to society's attitude to democratization as well as to "globalization."

When FKTU joined the strike action, this produced a massive protest movement. The government, facing such a scale of public mobilization, agreed on 21 January to reopen debate on the revision of the labor law. An extraordinary session of the National Assembly convened on 17 February and the new labor law was approved by the National Assembly on 10 March 1997.

The new labor law was a compromise which gave something to each of

[39] Kwon Young Gil, president of KCTU, interview by author, Seoul, 22 August 1997.
[40] Ibid.
[41] Ibid.

the major actors. For business, it increased the flexibility of the labor market – for example, allowing redundancy dismissals and replacement of striking workers. However, labor won a two-year moratorium on the use of redundancy dismissals, approval for union financial support to full-time union officers, and the removal of the prohibition on political activities by unions (except in cases in which the main purpose is to promote political movement). Government gained by establishing the basis for a participatory and cooperative industrial relations system through reform of the collective bargaining system and adjustment of the labor disputes system.[42]

The experience of the rank and file during the national strike in 1997 laid a foundation for a national political role by organized labor. The absence of direct representation of trade unions in the National Assembly has limited the gains that labor could make by action in the streets. Therefore, the next step was to recognize the need for empowerment and the building of a political organization representing labor and increasing labor's political capacity. The three goals of this new strategy would be: 1) transforming enterprise unions into industrial unions; 2) campaigning for social reform; and 3) politically empowering labor. Labor's goal was to reconfigure the political terrain so that the role of labor as a partner in social reform is recognized.[43]

In conclusion, the national strike in 1997, as well as being the first successful national strike in Korea's history, brought about a change in the status of unions in Korean society. The successful organization of such a prolonged and large-scale action itself was more significant than the outcome of reform of the labor law *per se*.[44] The stage was set for a new role by organized labor and a new era of government-business-labor relations.

From "Globalization" to "the Age of IMF"

In the autumn of 1997 there was an abrupt change in the national economic situation, turning sharply from growth to crisis. After a series of major corporate bankruptcies in South Korea (Kia Automobiles, Hanbo Steel) and currency crises in Southeast Asia (Thailand and Indonesia), South Korea entered a full-scale financial crisis, revealing deep structural problems in the banking and corporate sectors. The crisis was suddenly exacerbated by an acute short-term credit crunch, as mobile capital fled from Korea, and by attacks on the value of the *won*.

[42] Korea International Labor Foundation, *Labor Reform in Korea Toward the 21st Century* (February 1998), 41–67, contains complete details of the procedures of industrial relations reform under Kim Young Sam.
[43] Ibid.
[44] Ibid.

In response, the government of South Korea struck a historic agreement with the IMF on 3 December 1997, on a $55 billion rescue package. The agreement stipulated far-reaching reforms in the financial sector, accelerated liberalization of trade and investment, and radical corporate restructuring measures.[45] The IMF rescue package initially entailed sharp budget cuts, higher interest rates and taxation, and reduced growth. Such deflationary measures threatened to set off a national unemployment crisis.

Quick and decisive legislative action was taken to remedy the financial crisis. At President-Elect Kim Dae Jung's urging, the National Assembly passed a package of financial reform bills on 29 December 1997 establishing the independent Financial Supervisory Commission (FSC), liberalizing foreign ownership in the Korean stock market, and enforcing the independence of the central bank. The aim was "the end of government-controlled financial resource allocation,"[46] and the restoration of foreign investor confidence in the Korean economy.

The dawning of the "IMF *shidae*" or "the Age of IMF" coincided with a historic political transition. Kim Dae Jung was the first opposition party candidate to be elected president of the Republic since its founding in 1948. He identified the source of the crisis in the corrupt relationship between the government-*chaebol*-banking triad and the failure of the old state-led development model.[47] President Kim Dae Jung was forced to begin his administration by responding to the immediate financial crisis and the onset of a major recession and national unemployment crisis. High unemployment threatened both economic prosperity and political stability. The government made relieving distress from unemployment a high priority, alongside restoring financial stability.

The New Agenda of Reform

Kim Dae Jung's basic strategy, going under the slogan of "Parallel Development of Democracy and Market Economy," is to combine accelerating market liberalization, deepening structural reforms, and extending the democratization process. However, it has not been entirely clear what model the new government is attempting to follow, since it combines elements of radical free market ideology, liberal democracy, and corporatism.

[45] "Seoul, IMF Agree on $55-bil. in Bailout Loans," *Newsreview* 26, no. 49 (6 December 1997), 12–5.

[46] Ministry of Finance and Economy, Overall Economic Policy Division, Republic of Korea, "Challenge and Chance: Korea's Response to the New Economic Reality," June 1998, 3.

[47] Ibid., 1–2.

The Kim Dae Jung administration took the view that the IMF prescriptions for Korea were basically sound, but that there was a need to negotiate on certain parameters, such as the interest rate and the fiscal deficit.[48] The government embraced a radical free-market philosophy in the area of finance and foreign investment. President Kim Dae Jung's administration viewed foreign investment as being necessary for long-term financial stabilization. By shifting from heavy reliance on foreign debt to more foreign direct investment, South Korea would reduce its vulnerability to external shocks, ease the pressures of debt servicing, lower the domestic interest rate and exchange rate, stimulate new corporate governance norms, and attract new technology.[49]

In early 1998, Korea opened its capital market and real-estate markets to foreign investment, and allowed mergers and even hostile takeovers by foreign firms, including in the financial sector. The successful renegotiation of short-term domestic banking debts of U.S. $21.8 billion into long-term government-guaranteed loans in April 1998, alongside significant improvement in the current account balance and substantial increase in foreign reserves, all contributed to a stabilization of the financial crisis by the end of May 1998. The exchange rate, which also stabilized, was now fully determined by the market.[50]

Thus, the new government used the acute short-term financial crisis to bring about a radical deepening of economic liberalization, arguing that, "In the age of globalization, mercantilist notions based on the idea of an independent national economy have no place."[51] The previous decade of "transition" since 1987 had failed to exploit the "window of opportunity" for structural reform. It is widely believed that the root cause of the IMF crisis was the failure of previous administrations, especially those of Roh Tae Woo and Kim Young Sam, to dismantle the old government-business alliance. Market forces, including foreign capital, were not sufficiently in operation to ensure competitiveness and reduce structural distortions in the economy.[52] In this context, the simultaneous combination of internal corporate reforms and external intervention via market forces constitutes the nub of the new government's approach to economic restructuring.

[48] You Jong Keun, interview by author, Seoul, Korea, 14 August 1998; Kim Tae Dong, chief secretary to the president for policy planning, interview by author, Chongwadae, Seoul, Korea, 12 August 1998.
[49] Kim Tae Dong, interview by author.
[50] Ibid.
[51] "Challenge and Chance," 5.
[52] John Burton, *Financial Times* correspondent, interview by author, Seoul, Korea, 30 July 1998. In Burton's analysis, Kim Young Sam's decision to reflate the economy in 1994–5 exacerbated the problem of corporate and banking sector debt, leading to disastrous consequences later.

The key points of reform under Kim Dae Jung will be "to terminate government-business collusion, restructure the *chaebol*, recognize labor as a key factor in production, and bring labor into the policy making process."[53] Nevertheless, some of the president's key economic advisors take a somewhat antagonistic view towards organized labor.[54]Also, as in the past, the resistance of the *chaebol* to pressure for change remains considerable. They have a tendency to invoke economic nationalism to resist the forces of structural reform, especially when that pressure is perceived to come from abroad. Likewise, both the relationship between big business and organized labor and that between government and the unions remains fraught with deeply embedded distrust and sometimes open antagonism.

The IMF crisis presented the nation with both a challenge and an opportunity. The national economic crisis made it explicit that cooperation among business, labor, and government is an objective necessity. The public exposure of colossal corporate debts and mismanagement and the attitude of the IMF towards Korea's major corporations and banks contributed to a weakening of the *chaebol*'s sociopolitical position. In the new situation, big business had no realistic alternative other than to accept a new framework of government-business-labor consultation.

The Tripartite Commission and the New Korean Corporatism

A central aspect of President Kim Dae Jung's reforms is the creation of a new national system of mediation and policymaking involving government, business, and labor. The combination of the IMF crisis, President Kim Dae Jung's policy, and the increase in union power (albeit primarily "negative" via the capacity to strike) created a situation in which the government could not realistically hope to overcome the national crisis nor carry out necessary restructuring without the participation of labor.[55]

Although there have been recent precedents such as the PCIR and the Labor Relations Commission (LRC), the newly established Tripartite Commission (*No-Sa-Jong Wiwonhoe*) represents a new attempt to bring labor into formal consultations. It therefore represents a further movement in the direction of abandoning the exclusion and subordination of labor characteristic of the past. Based on the idea of an equal trilateral representation among government, business, and organized labor, the Tripartite Commission embodies ideas of corporatism.

---

[53] Choi Jang Jip, "Korea's Political Economy: Search for a Solution," *Korea Focus*, 6, no. 2, (March–April 1998), Korea Foundation, 1–20.

[54] Choi Jang Jip, director of the Presidential Commission on Policy Planning, interview by author, Seoul, Korea, 7 August 1998.

[55] Ibid.; and Lee Byong Hoon, *Nodong Yonguwon*, interview by author, Seoul, Korea, 7 August 1998.

The tripartite system initiated by the new government on 15 January 1998 was contingent on certain expectations by each major party to the agreement. Unions aim to ensure that the adjustment to the national crisis occurs on the principle of "fair burden sharing," requiring the corporate sector to make radical changes and accept responsibility for past mismanagement. Organized labor also seeks to establish its influence at national policymaking levels and win acceptance as a legitimate social partner.[56] The *chaebol* seek to avoid social isolation and punitive government action, while pressing the case for business autonomy in the restructuring process and further flexibilization of the labor market. Government wants to construct a nonconfrontational industrial relations system to protect the national interest and to use this system as a vehicle to implement structural reforms throughout the economic system.

The Tripartite Commission's importance was increased by the malfunctioning of the National Assembly during the first half of 1998. Under an opposition party majority (GNP, *Han Nara Dang*), the National Assembly was deadlocked and unable even to elect the speaker, let alone pass significant reform legislation. The long-term role of the Tripartite Commission remains in question, given that it has not yet stabilized and lacks consistent will for genuine cooperation by either business or labor.[57]

The fundamental reasons for this instability are historical. Labor suffered exclusion and repression for decades during rapid industrialization. With political democratization since 1987, organized labor has sought compensation for these sacrifices. In the process, confrontations with employers became intensified. The gains of labor in the first few years of democratization were significant enough to raise fears about maintaining national competitiveness. As a result, many Korean firms channeled their new investment abroad. The IMF crisis and its consequent high unemployment may restore the bargaining power of business over the unions.

Redundancy dismissals remain at the heart of the confrontation. At the outset of the tripartite system, government and business, partly responding to IMF conditionality requiring liberalization of the labor market, demanded that labor accept the abandonment of the two-year moratorium on redundancy dismissals. Both government and business view redundancy dismissal as an inevitable and necessary aspect of economic restructuring. Both FKTU and KCTU reluctantly accepted legalization of redundancy dismissal for reasons of economic restructuring, but did so in exchange for an agreement that the *chaebol* would abide by the "fair burden sharing" principle.

[56] Ahn Pong Sul, International Relations Bureau, FKTU, interview by author, Seoul, 3 August 1998.
[57] Kim Tae Dong, interview by author; Huh Young Gu, vice president of KCTU, interview by author, Seoul, 14 August 1998.

Changes in the law concerning redundancy and worker protection were the key issues of the national strike in early 1997. Therefore, relinquishing the moratorium was a step backward for labor, made acceptable only by the promise of substantial economic and social reform, the so-called "Social Compromise."[58] The first round of tripartite talks resulted in an agreement on a trade-off between the interests of labor and business, bringing about revision of the labor laws in an extraordinary session of the National Assembly in February 1998.

Throughout 1998 and the first quarter of 1999, both labor and *chaebol* moved in and out of the Tripartite Commission. They have been dissatisfied with the progress of negotiations and look to government to take their side. Unions claim that business abuses the situation by excessive resort to redundancies, thus weakening and resubordinating labor. Unions have accused government of maintaining the traditional government-*chaebol* alliance against organized labor.[59] Business claims that fair burden sharing is taking place, via loss of assets, managerial dismissals, and multiple reform measures aimed at *chaebol* restructuring.[60]

Subsequent to the first round of talks in the Tripartite Commission, government has been placed in an awkward position of having to placate first one and then the other party in order to sustain the process of consultation. The success of the first round depended greatly upon the urgency of the national financial crisis and the expectation by labor of substantial change via economic and social reform.[61] By the time of the second round of tripartite talks in June 1998, however, the situation had already changed. The sense of common feeling generated by the shock of the financial crisis had dissipated as the immediacy of the foreign exchange problem subsided. Secondly, there was a growing frustration on the part of labor that the earlier agreement on fair burden sharing was not being carried out by either government or business. Unions, especially KCTU, became more militant in opposing growing unemployment, while the companies demanded autonomy in dealing with internal industrial disputes.

Labor demanded that government punish business for "unfair labor practices," as promised in the first round. Unions felt that the government had failed to carry out its promise and the Ministry of Labor was

---

[58] Korea International Labour Foundation, *Handbook of the Social Agreement and New Labor Laws of Korea*, (KOILAF: Seoul, 1998), i–iii.

[59] *"Wigi ui No-Sa-Jong"* (*No-Sa-Jong* in Crisis), KBS report, 31 July 1998, statement by Cho Hui Yon, policy director of *Chamyo Yondae*.

[60] KBS Report, 31 July 1998, statement by Kong Byong Ho, director of the Free Enterprise Center.

[61] Huh Young Gu, vice president of KCTU, interview by author, Seoul, 14 August 1998.

perceived to be indifferent.[62] Business, on the other hand, demanded punishment of labor for illegal strikes. The government maintained that its role is limited to mediation and suggesting alternatives but not an enforcement of a solution.[63]

The unemployment problem had initially hit unorganized workers in small and medium-sized industries. Later, however, large job cuts spread to previously well-protected organized workers in the large companies, and then into the financial sector. The government announced intentions to make substantial cuts in the public sector. As unemployment rapidly spread, labor-business conflict intensified.

The prolonged strike at Hyundai Motors in the summer of 1998 illustrates the continuing fundamental problems in the tripartite relationship. Militancy at Hyundai was part of a larger national trend in which the rank and file responded to the deepening economic crisis and mounting unemployment by electing new and more militant leadership. The companies' plans for massive redundancies for reasons of restructuring were perceived by labor and business in diametrically opposed ways. Labor viewed these measures as a one-sided shifting of the costs of adjustment onto workers and their families, without the restraint that both business and government had promised. Business regarded these measures as both absolutely necessary and a matter for autonomous management decision-making. Government accepted that reduced demand dictated redundancies, but emphasized the need for both restructuring and unemployment relief.

Hyundai Motors scheduled over two thousand production worker redundancies for the end of July 1998, but claimed that this was only half the level that had been made necessary due to reduced demand in the car market. The union claimed that Hyundai had already implemented some eight thousand dismissals, if not under the name of redundancy dismissal. Therefore it rejected any further redundancies for restructuring. The dispute erupted into illegal industrial action and occupation of the production facilities. The two sides each accused the other of being in the wrong – the unions for illegal strike action, business for illegitimate shifting of the costs of mismanagement onto workers. After a long stalemate, the local union voted to reject a compromise package negotiated by a special committee, including the leaders of KCTU and FKTU, which had been formed to mediate in the dispute.

The Tripartite Commission confronted serious obstacles in implementation of the agreed principles. The result has been a slow deterioration

---

[62] KBS Report, statement by Lee Yong Bom, spokesperson for the Tripartite Commission, 31 July 1998.

[63] KBS Report, statement by You Jong Keun, economic adviser to President Kim Dae Jung, 31 July 1998.

of confidence in the tripartite process and the prospects for a new corporatism. The center of action had moved from the conference table back to the streets by the summer of 1998. KCTU organized a symbolic protest action on May Day, followed by a brief general strike in July. FKTU joined forces with KCTU to stage large protest rallies in Seoul, presenting labor's joint demands for a halt to mass dismissals and for fulfilment of government promises.

Throughout the autumn and winter of 1998, the government continued to pursue a combination of neoliberal and corporatist policies. Although the government belatedly began to use some stimulus measures by September 1998 in order to boost demand and address the recessionary trend, it nevertheless continued to emphasize restructuring as the cornerstone of economic policy. Restructuring entails short-term costs of adjustment which frequently take the form of redundancies. The government's line is that although restructuring brings short-term unemployment, it will create employment in the long term by strengthening competitiveness. The unemployment rate for the first quarter of 1999 (January–March) was approximately 8.5 percent, up from a mere 2 percent prior to the crisis. Real wages had dropped by as much as 10 percent by the end of 1998 compared to the previous year. Labor costs were reduced during the restructuring process, while in some cases, profits were up. This process extended even to the public sector, where, as in the case of Korea Telecom (71 percent government-owned) the workforce was cut by 11 percent in 1998 while operating profits jumped by 43 percent.[64]

In contrast, labor has been persistently demanding the end to spiraling redundancies. This issue has been at the center of the repeated turbulence in the Tripartite Commission. A new crisis emerged in February 1999 as organized labor once again withdrew from the Tripartite Commission. The KCTU, under the leadership of Lee Kap Yong, withdrew on 24 February, and presented the government with a list of demands including stopping the industrial restructuring and redundancies, shortening working hours, and establishing the social safety net. While indicating that KCTU did not intend to undermine the tripartite framework of negotiations, Lee Kap Yong announced that KCTU would engage in direct negotiation with either government or business on any of the issues. FKTU, under the leadership of Park In Sang, on 26 February threatened to withdraw from the Tripartite Commission by the end of March if its conditions were not met. These included prior consultation with unions on industrial restructuring decisions and stronger measures

---

[64] "Korea Telecom's Profit Soars After Cost-Cutting Moves," *International Herald Tribune*, 5 March 1999, 17.

to eliminate illegal labor practices. Both KCTU and FKTU were prepared to initiate a national strike by April 1999 if labor's demands went unmet. In mid March 1999, the Ministry of Labor responded by agreeing to meet directly with FKTU and representatives from the Tripartite Commission, excluding business, in order to discuss normalization of the Tripartite Commission. KCTU took the view that the Tripartite Commission had lost its function as a tool of social negotiation. Some commentators believed that establishing a direct negotiation channel with labor would undermine the Tripartite Commission as the sole negotiation forum, while others concluded that President Kim Dae Jung is manipulating labor into sustaining the status quo. Certainly, the pursuit of industrial restructuring by the government, in both the private and the public sector, has increased the level of antagonism between government and labor and therefore weakened the social base for the success of the new corporatism.

Given the fact that high industrial unemployment is a new experience for Korea and given the prospects for its further increase in the short term, it is inevitable that strains within the new tripartite system can only continue. Its long-term success is therefore very uncertain. The lack of implementation of corporate reform plans on the one hand and the perception of labor's rigidity on the other are issues that will become increasingly important for President Kim Dae Jung's administration.

Conclusion

Globalization is an uncharted sea that requires great skill to navigate successfully. *Segyehwa* policy was originally intended to bring about a new economic structure, conforming to liberal international norms and capable of sustaining international competitiveness and growth. This implied a liberalization of the economy not only in terms of trade, but also of finance and foreign investment. The developmental state was to give way to a liberal regulatory state. The *chaebol* were to be down-sized and prepared for competition on a level playing field, both domestic and international. Society was to be reformed and democratized, allowing for more citizen participation and inclusion. Welfare and social spending were to expand, broadening the social safety net and enhancing human development. However, achieving these aims required clear understanding of the sequentialization and prioritization of reforms and the consequences of such choices.

Kim Young Sam's government failed to make a strategic choice and missed a narrow window of opportunity for timely reform. A clear strategic choice in favor of *deconcentration first* would have broken the traditional government-*chaebol* alliance, enabling government to regulate business in such a way as to reduce structural distortions. The failure to tackle these structural problems in good time revealed the vulnerability of the economy, therefore exposing it to increased risk. The chance to use gradual liberalization, which could have reinforced the intended effects of market reforms without inflicting excessive damage on the domestic economy, was therefore also missed. The failure to prepare sufficiently the social safety net left workers and society in a very exposed position when the economic system entered full-scale crisis in 1997–8.

The failure of the *segyehwa* policy to tame the power of the *chaebol*, and in particular to reform their financial practices, led directly to the onset of the IMF crisis and was perhaps its central cause. The intervention of outside actors set a new agenda which has resulted in rapid rather than gradual adjustment, in a context of serious economic contraction and spiraling unemployment. Domestic reform and external opening have now been compressed into a single and time-shortened framework, which demands drastic adjustments. The key issue here is therefore how this new situation affects democratization, in particular the inclusion of labor.

The crisis brought about a situation in which the state and society could no longer ignore the need for a social safety net and social inclusion. IMF conditionality initially dictated deflationary policies, which exacerbated economic contraction and higher unemployment. The recessionary tendency was intensified by the fall in domestic demand and the general economic downturn throughout Asia. Even the IMF soon realized that the South Korean problem could not be solved by deflationary policies and that the continued alienation of labor threatened the success of reform. The government belatedly shifted to an expansionary fiscal policy by September 1998, in an effort to stimulate domestic recovery.[65]

The government's response to the crisis involves increased welfare expenditure, cautious expansionary deficit spending, and efforts to incorporate labor into the political process via the Tripartite Commission. The Kim Dae Jung government has committed very substantial resources not only to unemployment relief and job retraining, but to ambitious job creation projects.[66] Nevertheless, the government continues to pursue rapid industrial restructuring which in the short-term exacerbates unemployment and recessionary tendencies.

The response of South Korea to globalization challenges some prevalent ideas about globalization based on European experience. In the

---

[65] "Seoul Tries to Tackle 'Spiral of Recession,'" *International Herald Tribune*, 3 September 1998.
[66] Federation of Korean Trade Unions, "The Economic Crisis and Trade Union Responses: A Survey on Living and Working Conditions of the Korean Workers," FKTU, Seoul, 1998, 137.

case of the West European economies, there has been a tendency to question the welfare state and turn to neoliberal market ideology. In Korea, while globalization has exposed the corruption and inefficiency of the past model, it has created conditions that demand not only an increased reliance on the market but at the same time an expansion of the welfare state and the social safety net.

Recent trends in the politics of Western Europe indicate that the response to globalization involves a conflict between the attempt to preserve social democracy and the welfare state and the drive to allow market forces to sustain competitiveness. In the case of Korea, globalization and the crisis it has produced opens the prospect for increasing the social inclusion of labor rather than determining its marginalization. Sustaining a competitive and stable economy may not be possible without further democratization via the social and political inclusion of labor and expansion of welfare institutions.

Globalization combines two contradictory tendencies. On the one hand it fosters competition, fragmentation, and destabilization. On the other hand, these very forces may stimulate a sociopolitical response that emphasizes social stability and cohesion. The paradox of globalization is that it tends to weaken organized labor while at the same time strengthening labor's resistance and activism. The outcome of the process of social reform and democratization will depend on how these two forces are balanced in the spheres of both economics and politics.

CHAPTER 3

Globalization and Workers in South Korea

Yong Cheol Kim and Chung-in Moon

In the last four decades, South Korea has undergone a dramatic economic transformation: From one of the world's poorest countries, it has become the eleventh largest economy in the world. The transformation can be attributed to several factors: the interventionist but market-conforming state, an assertive export-promotion strategy, human capital formation, the Confucian culture, and geopolitics.[1] Beneath the Korean miracle, however, lies an additional contributing factor that is often neglected, namely, the rather unique social and political arrangement between the state, capital, and labor. Strategic intervention by the state was predicated on enforcing the corporatist co-optation of big business while marginalizing labor. The South Korean state virtually reorganized, controlled, and mobilized the labor sector in order to satisfy its developmental objectives.[2] South Korea's catch-up would have never been possible without a strict enforcement of state corporatism in which big business was included, while the popular sector, including labor, was pacified through control and coercion.

[1] Leroy P. Jones and Il Sakong, *Government, Business, and Entrepreneurship in Economic Development: The Korean Case* (Cambridge, MA: Harvard University Press, 1980); Bruce Cumings, "The Northeast Political Economy," *International Organization* 38 (1984), 1–40; Alice H. Amsden, *Asia's Next Giant: South Korea and Late Industrialization* (New York: Oxford University Press, 1989); Robert Wade, *Governing the Market: Economic Theory and the Role of Government in East Asian Industrialization* (Princeton, NJ: Princeton University Press, 1990); World Bank, *The East Asian Miracle: Economic Growth and Public Policy* (New York: Oxford University Press, 1993).
[2] Jang-Jip Choi, *Hankookui Nodong Undongkwa Kookga* [Labor movements and the state in South Korea] (Seoul: Yeolumsa, 1988); Yong Cheol Kim, "The State and Labor in South Korea: A Coalition Analysis," Ph.D. dissertation (Columbus, OH: Ohio State University, 1994).

The myth of the developmental state and pacified labor has recently been shattered, however, by two grand irreversible trends: democratization and globalization. Democratic opening and transition since 1987 have facilitated the expansion of civil society, in which workers have been able to occupy a strategic position. Open political space made Korean workers a major beneficiary of democratic changes by enhancing their organizational and functional strength. The proliferation of labor unions, increased political and industrial bargaining power, and rising real wages testify to the improved status of the working class in South Korea.

Nevertheless, gains from democratization were soon offset by the process of globalization, which involved opening, liberalizing, and rationalizing the national economy. Lifting the mercantilist overlay from the South Korean economic landscape and fostering free flows of goods and services and factors of production in the name of globalization have profoundly challenged business, labor, and other social forces. But the hardest hit was labor. Globalization has imposed a double burden on workers. While intensified pressures for international competition have subjugated workers to the mandate of flexible labor-market conditions, the economic crisis resulting from the failure of the globalization strategy has led to mass unemployment and a sharp reduction in workers' income, wealth, and welfare. Neither improved political and industrial bargaining power through democratization nor the formation of a transnational coalition with international labor movements, a by-product of globalization, has prevented South Korean workers from being trapped in the current predicament.

This chapter explores the crisis of Korean workers in the process of globalization. The first section presents a brief historical overview of labor politics in South Korea and changing industrial relations under the Kim Young Sam government, during which the globalization strategy was actively pursued. The second section examines correlates of globalization and economic crisis as well as the dynamics of labor politics within the framework of structural adjustment imposed by the International Monetary Fund (IMF). The third section elucidates impacts of the economic crisis and IMF conditionalities on labor politics and the quality of workers' lives. The fourth section looks into the Kim Dae Jung government's policy responses to the workers' crisis. Finally, some theoretical and policy implications will be discussed.

Globalization Strategy, Labor Politics, and Precarious Compromise

Prior to the democratic transition in 1987, industrial relations in South Korea were governed by authoritarian, antilabor institutions. Authoritarian regimes, which were obsessed with economic development and national security, regarded the advent of strong labor as a threat to the security of the nation and the regime as well as to capital accumulation. Thus, the developmental coalition between the state and business systematically excluded the labor sector through ideological maneuver and the politics of coercion and intimidation. The ban on labor unions' political activities and prohibition of union organization by government officials in 1963, enforcement of a special law to restrict labor disputes in free trade zones in 1970, a series of notorious labor laws during the *Yushin* period, the prohibition of multiple labor unionism, the ban on third-party intervention in labor disputes, and the implementation of a company union system under the Chun Doo Hwan regime all illustrate legal and institutional measures to exclude and marginalize labor in the process of economic development.[3]

The repression of labor did not last long, however. The democratic opening in 1987 dismantled the template of developmental dictatorship and significantly altered the political landscape in South Korea. By taking advantage of the new political opening, workers began to challenge the existing authoritarian industrial relations order through the expansion of new unions and massive public protests. Since the democratic opening in 1987, the number of labor unions has increased from 2,534 in 1985 to 6,142 in 1988 and 7,527 in 1992. The number of workers' strikes has also risen, from 276 in 1986 to 3,749 in 1987, 1,873 in 1988, and 1,616 in 1989.[4] Workers staged attacks on two fronts. On the one hand, they targeted the government by calling for the abolition of three notorious labor laws (i.e., the ban on political activities, multiple labor unions, and third-party intervention). On the other hand, corporate owners, who were accustomed to state protection and the despotic managerial culture, became a target. Wages were still the primary point of contention, but workplace democracy, workers' welfare, and occupational safety emerged as new items on labor's agenda. The democratic transition coincided with increasing tension and confrontation among the state, capital, and labor. A vicious cycle of strikes and plant closures was set in motion immediately following the transition. The workers can be seen as the victor in this debacle. They enjoyed a better bargaining

---

[3] Jang-Jip Choi, *Hankookui Nodong Undongkwa Kookga*; Yong Cheol Kim, "The State and Labor in South Korea" op. cit.; Martin Hart-Landsberg, *The Rush to Development: Economic Change and Political Struggle in South Korea* (New York: Monthly Review Press, 1993); George E. Ogle, *South Korea: Dissent within the Economic Miracle* (Atlantic Highlands, NJ: Zed Books, 1990).

[4] Chung-in Moon and Yong Cheol Kim, "A Circle of Paradox: Development, Politics, and Democracy in South Korea," Adrian Leftwich, ed. in *Democracy and Development: Theory and Practice* (London: Polity Press, 1996), 139–67.

position than the state and capital, and as a result their real wages rose by almost 50 percent between 1987 and 1990.[5]

Firms could absorb increased labor costs during good times. In 1989, however, the Korean economy entered a protracted recession. Firms could not bear high wage costs any longer, so they began to devise new corporate strategies. Leading firms shied away from labor-intensive industries and introduced labor-saving factory automation. They also attempted to introduce new labor-management principles, such as "no work, no pay," and to replace the seniority system with a merit system. Other alternative measures, such as an hourly wage system, flexible working hours, and hiring of substitute workers during labor disputes, all of which were designed to ease the structural rigidity of the labor markets, were also considered.[6]

Neither capital nor labor was satisfied. While workers called for higher wages, greater bargaining power, and workplace democracy, management was actively seeking wage stability through the creation of more flexible labor-market conditions. The Kim Young Sam government was inaugurated in early 1993, when business and labor were deeply entangled in precarious bargaining. The Kim government was burdened with two contradictory labor-reform objectives: the democratic mandate to compensate workers through an equal burden sharing and distributive justice and the neoconservative globalization campaign to enhance international competitiveness.[7] While the democratic mandate favored workers by pushing for labor reforms that included the lifting of the bans on multiple labor unionism, third-party intervention during labor disputes, and unions' political activities, the globalization campaign to enhance international competitiveness drove the government to side with management by advocating reforms for flexible labor-market conditions. The two conflicting objectives continued to dominate the discourse on labor reforms during the Kim Young Sam regime and led to a messy stalemate in improving relations between industry and labor.

---

[5] The real-wage index was equal to 100 in 1980, 147.2 in 1987, 198.8 in 1990, and 280.0 in 1995 (see Won-Duck Lee, "Hankook Nodong Undongui Miraenun Mooeok Inga?" [What is the future of the Korean Labor Movement?], *Quarterly Labor Review* 9, no. 1 [1996], 95).

[6] June Kim, "Nodong Beop Gaejung Nonuiui Baekyungkwa Pilryoseong" [Background and necessity of the revision of labor laws], *Journal of Legislative Research* 238 (April 1996), 1–32.

[7] Byungtae Lee, "Kunro Gijoon Beop Gaejungaeseoui Nodongja Sangkwa Jaengjum" [The image of workers and issues in revising labor standard laws], ibid., 33–74; Young-Il Im, "Nodong Undongui Jaedowhawa Siminkwon" [Institutionalization of labor movements and citizenship], *Economy and Society* 34 (Summer 1997), 51-66.

Facing the stalemate, president Kim Young Sam announced his "New Thought on Industrial Labor Relations for Leaping into the First Class Nation in the 21st Century" on 24 April 1996. The new initiative constituted an integral part of his globalization strategy. It outlined the following as the guiding principles for new labor-management relations: maximization of public goods, participation and cooperation, balance between autonomy and social obligations, emphasis on education and humanity, and globalization of institutions and consciousness.[8] Along with the initiative, the government launched a new presidential Commission on Labor-Management Relations Reforms, composed of thirty members drawn equally from the academic community, labor, management, and nongovernmental organizations (NGOs). The commission was instrumental in reactivating the long-delayed public debate on labor reforms.

The launching of the commission and the reactivation of the public discourse on labor reforms were initially triggered by domestic political considerations. Despite the Kim Young Sam government's alleged reform drive, no visible progress was made in the area of labor-management relations, and public criticism was on the rise. Thus, the measure was intended to cope with domestic criticism of reform failures. But equally critical were international pressures resulting from the regime's globalization strategy. South Korea joined the United Nations and the International Labor Organization (ILO) in 1991. South Korea's membership in these bodies enhanced the nation's international status, but also imposed new international obligations on the country. The U.N. Human Rights Commission urged South Korea to amend labor laws that violated U.N. human-rights standards; and the ILO called for abolition of the ban on third-party intervention in labor disputes and on multiple labor unionism, restoration of the basic labor rights of public officials and schoolteachers, and termination of government interference in labor-union activities.[9] Pressures from the Organization for Economic Cooperation and Development (OECD) also intensified. As part of its globalization strategy, South Korea applied for membership in the OECD in 1995, but the OECD's Trade Union Advisory Committee made South Korea's admission conditional on its compliance with ILO requirements.[10] Meanwhile, the World Trade Organization (WTO), which began to deliberate on the Blue Round linking global labor standards

---

[8] Won-Duck Lee, *Nosa Gaehyeok: Miraelul weehan Seontaek* [Reform of labor-business relations: the choice for the future] (Seoul: Korea Labor Institute, 1997), 33.

[9] *Naeil Shinmun*, 29 May 1996.

[10] *Hankyoreh*, 27 April 1996; *Hankuk Gyungjae Shinmun*, 25 April 1996.

to sanctions on trade, put additional pressures on the South Korean government.[11]

These international changes and pressures served as new catalysts for labor reforms in South Korea. Nonetheless, forging a new consensus through the commission was not easy. Labor and management were deeply divided, and representatives from the academic community and NGOs were not effective in mediating between the two. Management was critical of labor, attributing the decline in international competitiveness to high wages and rigid labor-market conditions, and called for an immediate implementation of the "no work, no pay" policy, no wages to full-time union officers, hiring of substitute workers during labor disputes, and a flexible system of layoffs. Yet, it sided with labor on other issues, such as lifting the ban on multiple labor unionism and unions' political activities. Labor was diametrically opposed to neoconservative elements of management's proposals. Union representatives regarded flexible layoffs, hiring of substitute workers, and arbitrary adjustment of working hours as serious threats to employment stability, union cohesiveness, and even occupational safety.

The labor-management confrontation virtually crippled the commission. Following its formation on 9 May 1996, the commission held ten public hearings, thirty committee meetings, twenty-three subcommittee meetings to formulate amendments to the labor law, and fourteen general conferences. But no compromise was reached, and the commission adopted an alternative proposal by representatives from NGOs, which it submitted to the president on 8 November 1996.[12] The government was also divided. The Ministry of Finance and Economy and the Ministry of Commerce, Trade and Energy favored the proposal by the management side that could contribute to international competitiveness by easing structural rigidity in labor markets. But Park Se-il, then presidential secretary in charge of social-welfare policy, and Jin Nyom, then labor minister, urged incorporation of the commission's proposal (i.e., the proposal of the NGO representatives) into the labor reform bills, since it was much closer to the labor position.[13]

---

[11] Yoon-Jong Wang, *Mooyeokkwa Nodong Gijoonui Yeongae* [Links between international trade and labor standards] (Seoul: Research Institute for International Economic Policy, 1996); Yong Ho Bae, "Nodong Gijoonkwa Mooyeok Goyong Ganui Kwangae" [The relationship between the labor standard, international trade, and employment], *Journal of Legislative Research* 242 (December 1996), 219–46; OECD, *Trade, Employment, and Labour Standard: A Study of Core Workers Rights and International Trade* (Paris, 1996).

[12] *Hankyoreh*, 12 November 1996.

[13] Ibid., 12 December 1996; Won-Duck Lee, *Nosa Gaehyeok*, 47–8.

On 3 December the government announced new labor-reform bills that comprised many elements of the proposal made by the management representatives in the commission. The new labor reforms bills included (1) the right to substitute workers during labor disputes; (2) an end to payment of wages to full-time union officers starting in the year 2002; (3) endorsement of the "no work, no pay" provision; and (4) adoption of flexible layoffs and adjustments of working hours. Some of labor's demands were also accommodated in the bills. For example, multiple unionism was allowed at the industry and national levels but banned at the enterprise level; and schoolteachers would have collective-bargaining rights starting in 1999.[14] Labor did not endorse the bills. Two top labor organizations, the Federation of Korea Trade Unions (FKTU) and the Korean Confederation of Trade Unions (KCTU), threatened to stage general strikes should the government bills pass the National Assembly.

Despite the labor opposition, the ruling New Korea Party secretly convened the National Assembly in the early morning of 26 December and passed the bills without the participation of opposition party members. The bills passed were more pro-business than the ones proposed by the government; they banned collective bargaining by schoolteachers indefinitely and delayed the implementation of the multiple labor organizations at the industry and national levels from 1997 to 2000. The passage outraged labor. The KCTU immediately called for a general strike, and the FKTU followed suit. December 1996 and January 1997 were months of sound and fury. Public opinion supported the workers not so much because of the content of the amended bills as the ruling New Korea Party's autocratic maneuver in passing the bills. In one public opinion poll conducted by the newspaper *Hankyoreh*, 87.4 percent of respondents said that the bills should be withdrawn.[15] Opposition political parties, as well as NGOs representing a wide range of the civil society, joined workers in opposing the passage of the bills. International pressures were also mounting.[16] The OECD, the ILO, and the International Confederation of Free Trade Unions (ICFTU) sent delegations to the South Korean government to officially protest the new bills. They argued that the bans on collective bargaining by schoolteachers and multiple labor unionism were outright violations of the right to free association. The ICFTU even engaged in a global campaign to boycott Korean products.

Domestic and external pressures forced President Kim Young Sam to reexamine the bills in the National Assembly on 21 January 1997.[17] After lengthy and painful negotiations, both the ruling party and the

---

[14] *Hankyoreh*, 2 December 1996.
[15] Ibid., 10 January 1997.
[16] Ibid.
[17] Ibid., 22 January 1997.

opposition parties agreed to amend the passed bills. New compromises included immediate legalization of multiple labor unionism at the industry and national levels and delayed implementation of flexible layoffs for two years. However, the compromise did not appease labor; both the FKTU and the KCTU defied the bills and continued to work for their removal.

Globalization produced paradoxical outcomes for South Korean workers. Globalization significantly improved the domestic and international status of Korean workers by facilitating the formation of transnational coalitions with international labor organizations. But the costs outweighed the benefits. In the age of waning international competitiveness, the logic of globalization provided the government and business with powerful ideological and institutional weapons to restrain labor. And fear of layoffs, erosion of labor's internal cohesion, and threats to wage and job security emerged as inevitable consequences of globalization.

The Economic Crisis, IMF Conditionalities, and Changes in Labor Markets

Kim Young Sam's promise to make South Korea a first-class nation through the globalization strategy was not realized. His globalization strategy was a dismal failure, resulting in an acute economic crisis even before his tenure had ended. The sudden collapse of the Korean economy in November 1997 alarmed the entire world. During his term in office, foreign debts rose from $43.9 billion in 1994 to $160.7 billion in 1996 and $158 billion in 1997, while foreign-reserve assets dwindled from $20.2 billion in 1993 to $12.4 billion in 1997. At the height of the currency crisis, disposable foreign reserves held by the Bank of Korea amounted to less than $8 billion, spreading the fear of sovereign default. The exchange rate between the won and the dollar plunged from 808.1 won to the dollar in 1993 to 1,415 won to the dollar by the end of December 1997. The average annual stock price index declined from 1,027.4 in 1993 to 375 in December 1997.

Several factors explain the genesis of the crisis. While domestic factors such as corporate failures and mounting nonperforming loans, the dismal banking and financial sector inflicted with moral hazard, connections between politics and business (*Jungkyung Yuchak*), and pervasive rent-seeking behaviors were its structural causes, external factors such as contagion effects of foreign exchange crisis, the panic behavior of international lenders, and the stupidity of credit-rating agencies proved to be the triggering variables. But more critical was the premature and incoherent globalization strategy of the Kim Young Sam government. The rhetoric of globalization overshadowed its substance, fostering an array of policy and institutional mistakes. Economic liberalization in financial and capital markets, which was undertaken without corresponding institutional and policy reforms, is an outstanding example of policy and institutional failures.[18]

After a series of financial and foreign-exchange crises, the Kim Young Sam government filed for national economic bankruptcy, asking the IMF for $57 billion in bailout funds on 2 December 1997. But the IMF bailout was predicated on a set of conditionalities for structural adjustment. They included: "(i) the strong macroeconomic framework designed to continue the orderly adjustment in the external current account and contain inflationary pressures, involving a tighter monetary stance and substantial fiscal adjustment; (ii) a comprehensive strategy to restructure and recapitalize the financial sector, and make it more transparent, market-oriented, better supervised and free from political interference in business decisions; (iii) measures to improve corporate governance; (iv) accelerated liberalization of capital account transactions; (v) further trade liberalization; and (vi) improve the transparency and timely reporting of economic data."[19] Within this broad policy framework, the IMF stipulated that "the capacity of the new Employment Insurance system will be strengthened to facilitate the redeployment of labor, in parallel with further steps to improve labor market flexibility."[20]

Of these conditionalities, the provision on labor-market flexibility became a critical issue for the Korean government on two accounts. First, foreign equity investment was essential in coping with the financial and foreign-exchange crisis. But a lifetime employment system, strong labor unions, and rigid labor-market conditions posed a major barrier to foreign equity investment. In order to induce much needed foreign capital, labor-market flexibility had to be improved. Second, the IMF-led structural adjustment program was predicated on extensive corporate restructuring involving bankruptcies, mergers and acquisitions, and downsizing. Apart from the mandate to enhance international competitiveness, the government realized the importance of flexible labor-market conditions for corporate restructuring.

However, the government's accommodation of the condition of labor-market flexibility in its memorandum to the IMF triggered conflicts

---

[18] Chung-in Moon, "In the Shadow of Broken Cheers: The Dynamics of Globalization in South Korea," in ed. Jeffrey Hart and Aseem Prakash, *Globalization and Governance* (forthcoming, 1998); Jongryn Mo and Chung-in Moon, "Democracy and the Origins of the 1997 Korean Economic Crisis," in ed. Jongryn Mo and Chung-in Moon *Democracy and the Korean Economy* (Stanford, CA: Hoover Press, 1998).

[19] International Monetary Fund, "Korea: Memorandum on the Economic Program" (mimeographed) (Seoul, 1997).

[20] Ibid.

between business and labor. The Federation of Korean Industries (FKI) and the Korean Employers' Association (KEA), two top-level business organizations, welcomed the move and urged the government to implement wage cuts, hiring substitute workers during labor disputes, and flexible layoffs immediately.[21] But the FKTU and the KCTU strongly opposed the move and threatened to engage in general strikes if these new provisions were legalized and implemented. They opposed the move on two counts. First, the IMF conditionality would incur more pain and burden on labor than on business, which was unfair since big business was to blame for starting the crisis. Second, by then the Kim Young Sam government did not have a clear picture of how to deal with mass unemployment and subsequent social instability. Being a lame-duck government, Kim's government could not take any measures.

President-elect Kim Dae Jung intervened at this point. He proposed forming a tripartite national council comprising representatives of the government, business, and labor. In order to persuade labor to join the talks, Kim Dae Jung urged big business to share the burden and pain through corporate restructuring and downsizing. Public pressure made it impossible for labor to refuse to join the council. On 14 January the Labor-Employer-Government Consultative Council was formally launched to "ensure a fair burden sharing in coping with the economic crisis."[22] The council was composed of eleven members (two from labor, two from business, two from government, four from political parties, and the chairman). After lengthy deliberations, on 20 January the council produced its first joint communiqué, in which business promised to ensure transparency in its management, to expedite structural adjustment, and to take prudent measures in laying off its employees, while labor pledged to make every effort to enhance productivity and cooperate with business on wages and working hours in the case of corporate emergencies.

After lengthy and traumatic negotiations, the council reached the Tripartite Accord on 6 February. First, labor and business agreed on an earlier implementation of flexible layoffs and legalization of hiring substitute workers. In addition, the accord relaxed restrictive legal provisions relating to private job placement and manpower leasing. However, the implementation of flexible layoffs was required to clarify the circumstances and procedures for layoffs. Second, labor unions were allowed to engage in political activities. Along with this, government officials and schoolteachers were permitted to engage in collective bargaining, and the unemployed were allowed to join labor unions. Third, the government agreed to strengthen the social safety net and adopt various

---

[21] *Hankyoreh*, 13 December 1997.
[22] *Dong-A Ilbo*, 14 January 1998.

measures to cope with employment stability. In this regard, the budget allocation for the employment insurance fund, including funds for more training and employment stabilization, was to be tripled from 0.7 trillion won to 2 trillion won. Additional social expenditures were to be provided, and the scope of the unemployment benefits was substantially expanded. And finally, a business's greater share of the burden was assured through improvements to corporate financing, transparency, and restructuring. Politicians also pledged to assume a greater share of the burden through political reforms.[23]

The Tripartite Accord was not welcomed by workers, however, who urged the FKTU and the KCTU to renegotiate the provisions on flexible layoffs and hiring substitute workers. The FKTU's opposition to the accord was mild since its president was given full power of attorney in the negotiation, but the KCTU encountered tougher challenges from its constituents because there was no clear delegation of power to its head. On 9 February the KCTU convened an extraordinary meeting of delegates and adopted a resolution denouncing the pact. Delegates argued that the compromise did not reflect a true and fair burden sharing, and they pledged to go ahead with general strikes if flexible layoffs were implemented as scheduled. The Auto Workers Union, the Metal Workers Union, the Medical Insurance Workers Union, and seventy other unions under the KCTU decided to stage a general strike on 13 February. However, the KCTU aborted the general strike because of negative public opinion and instead decided to conduct a long-term struggle against the pact's implementation.[24]

As table 3.1 illustrates, the National Assembly amended the existing labor laws in three major areas on 13 February in accordance with the Tripartite Accord. First, all restrictions on labor unions' political activities were lifted. Second, flexible layoffs were allowed not only in cases of corporate emergency but also in cases of corporate mergers and acquisitions as well as handovers and restructurings. Finally, hiring substitute workers during labor disputes was allowed. Compared to the old labor laws, the new laws represented fundamental changes.

After the passage of the new labor laws, there was a leadership change in the KCTU. Lee Kap Young, the hard-line chairman of the Hyundai Heavy Industry labor union, was elected as the KCTU's second president on 31 March 1998. He defied the amendments and vowed to abolish the provisions on flexible layoffs and hiring substitute workers during labor disputes. He also pledged to ensure employment stability, institutional reforms for a social safety net, dissolution of political-business connections and the *chaebol*, and labor participation in management. He

---

[23] *Hankyoreh*, 7 February 1998.
[24] *Dong-A Ilbo*, 13 February 1998.

Table 3.1 Changes in the Labor-Relations Law, by Major Issues

Clause	Old Labor Laws	Revised Laws (10 March 1997)	New Labor Laws
Multiple unions	Prohibition	Allows multiple unions immediately at the industry and national levels and from the year 2002 at the workplace level	No change
Third-party intervention	Prohibition	Ban lifted, but third-party intervention confined to federations, and organizations registered with the Labor Ministry jointly by labor and management	No change
Unions' political activity	Prohibition	Ban lifted, but restrictions by election laws existed	Practically no restrictions (election laws revised on 20 April 1998)
Flexible layoffs	No clause; handled by court cases	Permitted only under corporate emergency; enforcement delayed for two years	Allowed not only under corporate emergency but also in the cases of merger and acquisition, handover, and restructuring
Hiring substitute workers during disputes	Prohibition	Allows employers to fill job slots vacated by striking workers with other nonstriking workers in the same company but prohibits new subcontractors	Allows hiring substitute workers for professional positions for up to two years, for manual positions for up to six months
"No work, no pay"	No clause	Employers have no obligation to compensate the wage losses incurred by strikes	No change
Payment for full-time union officers	No clause	Bans companies from paying wages to full-time union leaders starting in 2002	No change

Source: Adapted from Jae Hoon Kim, "Shin Nodong Beop: Dallajinun Nosakwangae" [New labor laws: changing labor-management relationships], *Quarterly Labor Review* 10:2 (1997): 63–103; *Dong-A Ilbo*, 16 February and 25 April 1998.

even called for renegotiation with the IMF on its conditionalities.[25] He threatened to boycott the second tripartite talk and to stage a general strike if these terms were not accommodated. Indeed, the KCTU did not participate in the second tripartite talk, so that the FKTU alone represented the labor sector. However, when the government decided to include on the agenda of the tripartite talk prevention of abuses of flexible layoffs, establishment of a special committee to oversee unfair labor practices by employers, and establishment of a special committee on the public sector, KCTU dropped its old demands and joined the second round of the talks. Despite ups and downs, the tripartite council survived a series of crises. Of course, its survival does not mean that there will be smooth sailing. The tripartite agreements are likely to be challenged by industry-level and company-level labor unions, especially over the issue of flexible layoffs.

The dynamics of labor politics in the context of globalization and economic crisis reveal that labor is structurally disadvantaged. Economic imperatives to survive in the age of borderless global competition offer a privileged position to business while weakening labor's position, all the more so because of intervention by the IMF through its conditionalities. However, the economic crisis has brought business and labor together through mediation by the state, and has pressed them to produce the Tripartite Accord among the state, business, and labor. As experiences under the Kim Young Sam government illustrate, such an accord is rarely possible during good times. Hard times, coupled with international pressures, contributed to the forging of a corporatist arrangement as a viable alternative.

Impacts on Labor:
Rising Unemployment and the Workers' Crisis

The economic crisis penalized every sector of Korean society, but the hardest hit were workers. While the amendment of labor laws fundamentally restructured the internal dynamics of organized labor, corporate bankruptcies and flexible layoffs led to mass unemployment and the workers' crisis. The marginalization of workers is more pronounced than ever before.

Organized labor underwent a fundamental realignment. The legalization of multiple top-level labor organizations elevated the KCTU, once an illegal organization, to the position of a major player, intensifying its hegemonic rivalry with the FKTU. The FKTU, which has long served as the dominant labor organization, is now facing new challenges from the

---

[25] *Hankyoreh*, 21 May 1998.

KCTU. The KCTU, which has about five hundred thousand members, is no match for the FKTU, which has 1.2 million members, but the KCTU's aggressive recruitment strategy is seriously undercutting the FKTU's dominance. Despite growing corporate bankruptcies and unemployment, the competition between the two could contribute to increasing the rate of unionization and union memberships in the short term. In the long run, however, the labor sector could be weakened as a result of ideological polarization and organizational competition. The conservative FKTU and the progressive KCTU could easily jeopardize the unified position of labor and ultimately weaken its bargaining position. Japan and France offer convincing testimonials to this trend.[26]

Another related change is the expansion of the industry-level labor unions. Since the amendment of the labor laws in March 1997, seventeen new industry-level labor unions have been established, most of them belonging to the KCTU. Proliferation of industry-level unions, which serve as vital intermediate organizations, could strengthen the labor sector. But the growth of industry-level unions is likely to accompany some structural weaknesses, such as overcentralized bargaining power and increasingly frequent labor disputes, both of which can deepen the structural rigidity of labor markets.

With the new labor laws legalizing the political activities of labor unions, workers have now become significant players in local and national politics. For example, in the 4 June 1998 local elections, three local administrators, nineteen provincial assemblymen, and forty local

---

[26] In the 1960s and 1970s, Japanese unions were divided into two dominant organizations and ideologies, the unions affiliated to Sohyo (the General Council of Japanese Trade Unions) and Domei (the Japan Confederation of Labor) (see Rob Steven, *Classes in Contemporary Japan* [Cambridge: Cambridge University Press, 1983]; T. J. Pempel and Keiichi Tsunekawa, "Corporatism without Labor? The Japanese Anomaly," in eds. Philippe C. Schmitter and Gerhard Lehmbruch, *Trends toward Corporatist Intermediation* [London: SAGE Publications, 1979], 231–70; and Yasuo Kuwahara, "Japanese Industrial Relations," in eds. Greg J. Bumber and Russell D. Lansbury, *International and Comparative Industrial Relations: A Study of Developed Market Economics* [London: Allen & Unwin, 1987], 211–27). In France, fragmentation among labor unions has been much deeper, being divided by ideological lines: the CGT, Marxist-Leninist communism; the FO, social democracy; the CFTC, catholic; the CFTD, nonpolitical; and the FEN, socialist (see Janine Goetschy and Jacques Rojot, "French Industrial Relations," in eds. Bamber and Lansbury, *International and Comparative Industrial Relations*, 142–60; and Martin A. Schain, "Corporatism and Industrial Relations in France," in eds. Philip G. Cerny and Martin A. Schain, *French Politics and Public Policy* [London: Frances Printer, 1980], 191–217). The ideological fragmentation and organizational competition contributed to weakening labor's political and industrial-relations power in both countries.

assemblymen elected were labor-union leaders.[27] This can be seen as a positive sign of workers' improving political status.

Although the legal amendments have boosted the organizational strength and political status of workers, their collective bargaining power at the union shop level is weaker than before. While the flexible-layoff provision gave an upper hand to employers, hiring of substitute workers during labor disputes critically undermined the strategic position of company-level unions.[28] As company-level unions have begun to lose their bargaining power, they have relied increasingly on intervention by industry- and/or national-level labor unions. But third-party intervention by upper-level labor unions has not produced positive outcomes. Economic recession and employers' new bargaining chips, such as flexible layoffs and hiring of substitute workers, have fundamentally delimited the effectiveness of industry- and national-level labor unions' intervention. As of May 1998, 1,780 firms had settled their wage negotiations with unions. Unlike in previous years, wages were cut by 6.8 percent, from 3.9 percent in the first quarter of 1997 to –2.9 percent in the same period of 1998.[29] Apart from wage settlements, delayed wage payments and unlawful labor practices such as arbitrary layoffs have become widespread since the economic crisis. But neither labor unions nor the government has been able to prevent them.

The most serious outcome of globalization and the economic crisis is workers' deteriorating quality of life. As table 3.2 illustrates, the unemployment rate rose from 2.2 percent in July 1994 to 7.6 percent in July 1998. The figure in July 1998 is the highest since 1966, when the rate of unemployment reached 8.4 percent. If the underemployed are included, the total number of unemployed is estimated to have reached 3–4 million as of July 1998. The worst is yet to come. Massive structural adjustments in progress could result in a greater number of unemployed in the latter part of 1998.

Along with the rising unemployment, there has been a sharp drop in workers' household income. As table 3.3 demonstrates, the lowest-income families experienced the largest reductions in household income. A group of households earning a monthly average of 800,000 won in the first three months of 1997 saw a 12 percent reduction in their income during the same period in 1998. The higher the income level, the less the loss of income. A group of households whose monthly average income was 4.41 million won in the first three months of 1997 saw a 0.9 percent increase in its income during the first three months of 1998. Since the

[27] *Hankyoreh*, 6 June 1998.
[28] Korea Labor Institute, "Nosa Kwangae" [Labor-business relations], *Quarterly Labor Review* 11, no. 2 (1998), 42.
[29] *Hankyoreh*, 5 June 1998.

Table 3.2   Trend of Unemployment Rates, July 1994–July 1998

	1994	1995	1996	1997	1998
Jobless rate (%)	2.2	1.8	1.8	2.2	7.6
Thousands of jobless	445	338	387	476	1,651

Source: Dong-A Ilbo, 27 August 1998.

Table 3.3   Rate of Income Increase by Class January–March 1998 Compared to January–March 1997

Average monthly income per household (KW 1,000)	Rate of increase
800	−12.0
1,430	−5.5
1,920	−4.4
2,580	−3.1
4,410	0.9

Source: Dong-A Ilbo, 28 August 1998.

economic crisis, reductions in income have been disproportionate to income level, implying the victimization of lower-income families.

The most striking result of the economic crisis is the weakening of the middle class. Not only has the economic crisis led to job loss and wage cuts but it has robbed the middle class of its wealth through asset deflation. In South Korea, middle-income families' savings are usually divested into real estate and stocks. Frozen real-estate markets and the stock-market crash critically undercut the wealth base of the middle class. The primary beneficiaries of the crisis proved to be wealthy families. High interest rates yielded additional windfall profits to the "haves."[30] According to a survey by the newspaper *Hankyoreh*, the ratio of those who perceive themselves as belonging to the low-income stratum has considerably increased since the economic crisis (see table 3.4). In December 1996, only 10.3 percent of respondents revealed that they belonged to the lowest class, but after the economic crisis the percentage rose to 22.2 percent. The percentage of respondents belonging to the upper middle class has also decreased, from 14.1 percent in December 1996 to 5.1 percent in July 1998. A positive outcome of South Korea's economic miracle was the expansion of the middle class. But the erosion of the middle class

[30] *Dong-A Ilbo*, 30 May 1998.

Table 3.4   Self-Perception of Social Stratification, December 1996 – July 1998 (in percent)

Class	Upper	Upper Middle	Middle	Lower Middle	Lower
December 1996	0.7	14.1	48.8	26.2	10.3
November 1997	1.0	11.9	44.3	25.3	17.5
July 1998	0.9	5.1	35.2	36.7	22.2

Source: Hankyoreh, 22 July 1998.

as a result of the economic crisis could damage not only the social foundation of South Korea but the very spirit of its economic miracle.

The economic crisis has led to a variety of other social problems. One is a sharp rise in the number of the homeless. During the economic heyday, the homeless were unheard of. Since February 1998, the number of homeless has increased exponentially. The number of homeless was estimated to be one thousand in February 1998, but it rose to two thousand in April and three thousand in June and is projected to increase to six thousand by the end of the year. According to a survey by *Chosun Ilbo*, those laid off as a result of the economic crisis make up 71 percent of the homeless.[31] The crisis has also been responsible for the spreading malaise of crime, divorce, and suicide.[32]

The economic crisis and the process of structural adjustment have entailed both opportunities and challenges to labor. As a result of the Tripartite Accord, the political status and organizational strength of workers have improved considerably. But weakened bargaining power, threats of joblessness, diminishing income and wealth, and extensive layoffs are severely undercutting the quality of workers' lives. Workers can be seen as the primary victim of the failure to cope with globalization and the economic crisis in this regard.

The Crisis of Workers and State Responses

Kim Dae Jung was the first president to form a political coalition with labor. His populist appeals, manifested in his *Daejung Kyungjaeron* (mass-participatory economics), inspired workers and mobilized their political support.[33] Despite his political debts to labor, however, Kim was obliged

[31] *Chosun Ilbo*, 18 May 1998.
[32] *Joongang Ilbo*, 16 July 1998.
[33] President Kim's *Daejung Kyungjaeron* reveals his earlier efforts to combine a market economy with democracy. Balancing efficiency through the market

to seek neoconservative reforms as dictated by IMF conditionalities. He has been struggling to juggle the two contradictory postures. His position is well reflected in the South Korean government's recent publication on DJnomics.[34] DJnomics attempts to balance his populist ethos with the neoconservative mandates. Labor policy constitutes the core of his populist ethos, and his preoccupation with labor was strongly expressed in his National Independence Day speech on 15 August, in which he declared the Second Nation Building (*Jeiui Konkuk*). The following passage from his speech epitomizes his labor policy:

> We are now at a historic crossroads where we have to create a constructive labor-management relationship conducive to the new age of harmony and cooperation. It is imperative that we put an end to the confrontation and animosity between two major sectors in society. A relationship of trust based on fair sharing of the burdens is the foundation of the second nation-building. It is my intention to strengthen the employee-stockholder and social security systems which will serve as a testing ground for the fair distribution of national wealth. Labor and management must negotiate a lasting settlement based on reconciliation and cooperation, reflecting other countries' experiences in recent years.... Protecting the lives of those citizens who are jobless will be my priority.[35]

His response to the crisis of workers focuses on three major policy initiatives.[36] First is the institutionalization of labor-market flexibility. Kim sees restructuring the labor markets as unavoidable if South Korea's international competitiveness is to be enhanced. Thus, in addition to flexible layoffs and hiring substitute workers, the government is seeking a variety of policy measures to ease the structural rigidity of the labor markets. They include diversification of job categories, flexible wage systems, strengthening job-placement efforts, improving efficiency in occupational training, and broadening the base of the labor supply.

The second major policy initiative is the creation of a viable and comprehensive social safety net. The government has identified four major areas of emphasis in this regard. They are the minimization of unemployment, creation of new jobs, occupational training and job placement, and construction of an extensive social safety net. About 10.2 trillion won

---

and equality through participation is its core idea. It can be seen as a Korean version of social democracy (see Dae Jung Kim, *Daejung Kyungjaeron* [Mass-participatory economics] [Seoul: Cheongsa, 1986]).

[34] Ministry of Finance and Economy and Korea Development Institute, *DJnomics: Kookminkwa Hamkkae Naeilul Yeonda* [DJnomics: open tomorrow with the people] (Seoul: Daehan Minkook Jungpu, 1998).

[35] *Korea Herald*, 15 August 1998.

[36] Ministry of Finance and Economy and Korea Development Institute, *DJnomics*, 181–208.

has been allocated for employment stabilization and construction of a social safety net. The creation of new jobs through public works and investment in venture firms have been given top priority, receiving 5.2 trillion won, more than half of the entire budget. A social safety net for the unemployed including unemployment benefits, minimum cost-of-living support for the destitute, and scholarships for children of the unemployed received the second largest share, 2.1 trillion won; 1.9 trillion was allocated for minimizing unemployment through financial support of small- and medium-sized firms; and 896 billion won was allocated for occupational training and job conversion.[37] The construction of a social safety net through fiscal stimulus is one of the boldest Keynesian initiatives in South Korea's history.

Finally, Kim Dae Jung's government is trying to institutionalize a new pattern of labor-management-government relationships in the wake of the current crisis. The tripartite council itself is a reflection of such a corporatist arrangement, in which the state plays the role of a neutral arbitrator between labor and business, while labor and business share the burden of structural adjustment equally. But as Western European experience shows, the success of social corporatism depends on at least three preconditions: an ideology of social partnership shared by business and labor, a system of centralized, concentrated top-level associations, and a voluntary, informal coordination of conflicting objectives.[38]

In the South Korean context, however, such an institutional arrangement may be premature. The Kim Young Sam government made several attempts to create such a corporatist arrangement but failed.[39] Several factors explain the failure. First, it is extremely difficult to forge a viable trust among the state, business, and labor. Social partnership is impossible without such trust. But authoritarian domination over labor by the coalition of the state and capital in the past hindered the formation of such trust. Second, the structure of organized labor also matters. Social

[37] Ibid., 193.
[38] Peter J. Katzenstein, *Small States in World Markets: Industrial Policy in Europe* (Ithaca, NY: Cornell University Press, 1985); Adam Przeworski, *Capitalism and Social Democracy* (Cambridge,UK: Cambridge University Press, 1985).
[39] Su-Jin Kim, "Hankook Nodong Chohapui Hyunhwangkwa Jeonmang" [The present condition and prospect of Korean labor unions], *Economy and Society* 25 (Spring 1995): 22–48; Yong Cheol Kim, "Industrial Reform and Labor Backlash in South Korea: Genesis, Process, and Termination of the January Strike" (paper presented at the XVII World Congress of the International Political Science Association, Seoul, Korea, 1997); Hyun-Seok Yu, "Moohan Kyungjaeng Sidaeui Hankook Nosakwangae" [Korean labor-business relations in the era of unlimited competitiveness], in Sejong Institute, *Asia wa Segyehwa: Dong Asia Kookgaui Daeung* [Asia and Globalization: Reactions of East Asian States] (Seoul, 1998), 163–215.

corporatism is not viable without strong top-level labor associations, but in South Korea labor unions are fragmented into company union shops, and most bargaining takes place at the company level. Thus, pattern bargaining may not be feasible in South Korea. Such weak top-level associations diminish the likelihood of social corporatism. Finally, social corporatism is predicated on institutional links between political parties and labor interests. Despite the lifting of the ban on workers' political activities, it seems quite unlikely that political parties will form explicit coalitions with labor. An alliance with labor at this point could turn out to be a liability not only because of the lingering legacy of the Cold War ideology but also because of the economic crisis and an image of labor militancy. Such barriers could prevent the Kim Dae Jung government from ensuring and sustaining industrial peace through the institutionalization of social corporatism.

Outcomes of the Kim Dae Jung government's labor policy are yet to be seen. But the beginning does not seem promising. As demonstrated by the labor dispute at Hyundai Motors, which was triggered by labor-management differences over flexible layoffs, pacifying labor in a time of economic hardship may not be easy. In fact, labor disputes over layoffs have been spreading. Disputes at such workplaces as Mando Machinery, Hyundai Aluminum, Hyundai Ribat, and Daewoo Shipbuilding have not been resolved. Acceleration of the structural adjustment was likely to intensify labor unrest in the latter part of 1998 and afterward.

Conclusion

Globalization has brought ambivalent outcomes to South Korean workers. It has not only fostered democratization of industrial labor relations through the amendment of the existing labor laws but also strengthened workers' political and organizational power by lifting bans on multiple unionism, unions' political activities, and third-party intervention in labor disputes. Equally important is workers' improved domestic and international status through the formation of a transnational coalition with international labor organizations. In this regard, globalization can be seen as a blessing to workers in South Korea.

But South Korean workers now see more evil in globalization. It is a curse to them. No matter how transitional it is, globalization, along with economic crisis and structural adjustment, is jeopardizing their social and economic foundation. While globalization and heightened international competition have fostered corporate bankruptcies and extensive unemployment, structural adjustments to cope with the failure of globalization have significantly weakened workers' bargaining power in the name of flexible labor-market conditions. The introduction of flexible

layoffs and hiring of substitute workers put an end to the lifetime employment system, a long-cherished tradition of industrial labor relations in
South Korea. The adoption of a merit system and flexible working hours
is also wiping out traditional workers' benefits, such as the seniority system and the additional income base. More importantly, the specter of
job loss and the drastic deterioration in quality of life is haunting South
Korean workers. Indeed, they are experiencing the brave and painful
new world of globalization.

South Korea's response to the workers' crisis reveals an interesting
contrast with the West. In the West, globalization brought about a fundamental transformation of labor management from the old form of social
corporatism into productive coalition at the company level.[40] The market-
adaptive mechanisms to deal with new technological innovation, flexible
working hours, and functional reorganization of workplaces were natural responses to the challenges of globalization. But facing globalization
and economic crisis, the political elite in South Korea has chosen a path
to social corporatism that is characterized by a uniform wage standard,
centralized wage negotiation, centralization of organized labor, and Keynesian full employment. It is ironic that South Korea has chosen the
failed path of the West as a new alternative for coping with challenges of
globalization. The social-corporatist option is likely to be traumatic not
only because the historical preconditions and social trust necessary for
its implementation are lacking but also because of its incompatibility
with the competitiveness mandate of globalization.

How can the dilemma be overcome? There are several possible solutions. First, the strategy of external numerical flexibilization based on
layoffs, downsizing of new employment, and forced retirement needs to
be replaced by internal numerical flexibilization based on flexible adjustment of working hours and co-sharing of jobs.[41] Second, a widely cast
social safety net cannot be the sole panacea for the dilemma of unemployment. There must be an ordering of priorities. In this regard, public
works, which can create jobs at the same time that it boosts the national

---

[40] Kathleen Thelen, "Beyond Corporatism: Toward a New Framework for the
Study of Labor in Advanced Capitalism," *Comparative Politics* 27, no. 1 (October
1994): 107–24; Paul Windolf, "Productivity Coalitions and the Future of Cor-
poratism," *Industrial Relations* 28 (Winter 1989), 1–20; Harry C. Katz, "The
Decentralization of Collective Bargaining: A Literature Review and Compara-
tive Analysis," *Industrial and Labor Relations Review* 47 (October 1993), 3–22;
Torben Iversen, "Power, Flexibility, and the Breakdown of Centralized Wage
Bargaining: Denmark and Sweden in Comparative Perspective," *Comparative
Politics* 28, no. 4 (July 1996), 399–436.

[41] See Bernard Brunhes, "Labor Flexibility in Enterprises: A Comparison of
Firms in Four European Countries," in OECD, *Labour Market Flexibility: Trends
in Enterprises* (Paris, 1989), 7–36.

economy, should be given the utmost attention. Third, there must be decentralization of industrial labor negotiations since a tripartite pact at the national level could entail a higher risk. Institutional arrangements to foster industrial-labor-government talks at the local level can be an effective way of cultivating trust and defusing labor volatility. Finally, there must be a genuine political engineering to consolidate social consensus among the state, business, and labor. It will be extremely difficult for the Kim Dae Jung government to implement labor reforms without such a consensus. A social consensus will in turn depend on political entrepreneurship, fair burden sharing, voluntary compliance with agreements, and, most importantly, patience and endurance on the part of all parties.

CHAPTER 4

Segyehwa *Reform of the*
South Korean Developmental State

C. S. Eliot Kang*

Globalization is a complex process that is intensifying the levels of interaction and interconnectedness within and between states and societies.
As Samuel Kim describes in the introduction to this volume, it is a multidimensional process that involves the intensification of economic, political, social, and cultural interconnectedness around the globe. Though
some remain unconvinced that this boundary-expanding and boundary-
penetrating process is something fundamentally new, few would dispute
that the sea change in technologies and the transformation of the international power structure that came with the end of the Cold War have
accelerated the pace of international commercial and financial transactions and, for better or worse, increased the interconnectedness of
markets throughout the world.

Economic globalization is not, however, a preprogrammed or determinative process. Chung-in Moon observes that its course and character
are shaped and reshaped by the dynamic interaction between spontaneous, developmental logic and the state's strategic choices and responses.[1]
It is also a disruptive process that creates new winners and losers, producing political conflict within and among nations.

By the time Kim Young Sam took the oath of office as president of the
Republic of Korea in early 1993, the South Korean economy, dominated
by the state and big business, was undergoing a transformation from
an export-oriented, newly industrialized economy to an advanced industrial one. The very same availability of international capital and technologies facilitating this transformation was also creating formidable

---

* The author acknowledges the invaluable research assistance of Yoshinori
Kaseda.
[1] See Chung-in Moon, "Globalization: Challenges and Strategies," *Korea Focus* 3,
no. 3 (May–June), 62–77.

new competitors from the developing world as well as reinvigorating established competitors in the increasingly globalized marketplaces of the world.

Under the banner of *segyehwa*, Kim Young Sam attempted a top-down reform of the South Korean political economy to meet the rapidly changing conditions of the world economy. Kim took office promising sweeping reforms to revitalize the country, not the least in the realm of economics. *Segyehwa*, as it applied to the economic challenge, was a set of reform measures as well as a good deal of political sloganeering to remake the Japan-inspired "developmental state" into a market-oriented information society ready for competition in the globalized marketplaces of the post–Cold War world.

Segyehwa was to transform the economy, which was still too export-oriented and ridden with inefficiencies as a result of years of a collusive relationship between the state and big business. It called for liberalization of trade, inward and outward foreign investment, and foreign exchange. It also called for reform of domestic institutions and practices in accordance with the rules of the Organization for Economic Cooperation and Development (OECD) and other international bodies.

Unfortunately, the external political and economic pressures were relentless, and, more importantly, the vested interests constituting the main pillars of "Korea Inc." proved formidable barriers to the restructuring of the South Korean political economy. The deteriorating state of trade and capital accounts made it clear that the much vaunted "tiger" economy was stumbling as globalization created new low-cost competitors and energized the information- and services-driven advanced economies of the West. According to one often cited index of national competitiveness, South Korea's position declined even as Kim Young Sam touted his *segyehwa* reform measures as a legacy (table 4.1).

In fact, the reform measures that the Kim administration did manage to push through only made the country more vulnerable to mass international capital movements, which perhaps more than anything else represent globalization. Indeed, the biggest victim of the Asian financial crisis that began in Thailand in the spring of 1997 is South Korea. The South Korean juggernaut, once the world's eleventh largest economy and ranked twelfth in trade, now lies prostrate. With the assistance of the International Monetary Fund (IMF) and its major trading partners, as well as the leadership of the new president, Kim Dae Jung, South Korea may yet rise again. However, the prognosis is still uncertain.

This chapter details South Korea's struggle to adjust to globalization. It examines first the legacy of the Korean developmental state that was responsible for South Korea's great export-driven growth in the 1970s and 1980s but now weighs heavily on the political economy, which must

Table 4.1 International Competitiveness Ranking, 1995–8 (Selected Nations by 1998 Ranking)

	1998	1997	1996	1995
United States	1	1	1	1
Singapore	2	2	2	2
Hong Kong	3	3	3	3
United Kingdom	12	11	19	15
Germany	14	14	10	6
Taiwan	16	23	18	14
Japan	18	9	4	4
France	21	19	20	19
China	24	27	26	31
Italy	30	34	28	29
Korea	**35**	**30**	**27**	**26**

Source: Institute of Management and Development, *The World Competitiveness Yearbook* (Lausanne, Switzerland, 1998). Rankings are as of 19 April 1998.

become more market-oriented and open to the world. It then examines in detail the external and internal factors that have inhibited this transition. It also discusses the sharp deterioration of South Korea's trade and capital account balances as the Asian financial crisis approached and the new reform effort being led by the newly installed Kim Dae Jung administration began to deal with the harsh realities of what South Koreans are calling the "IMF era."

The South Korean Developmental State

To be sure, the "miracle on the Han," the rapid economic takeoff of the South Korean economy during the late 1960s and early 1970s, was very much the achievement of the developmental state. Based on the Japanese example, Park Chung Hee created a state that played a central role in directly and indirectly mobilizing resources to achieve fast economic development and growth.[2] With the failure of the import-substitution policy pursued by the South Korean government since the end of the Korean War, Park Chung Hee pushed for industrialization and export promotion to obtain the foreign exchange necessary for economic development and national security.

In the early stage, the Park regime favored light industries as the

---

[2] For a full account, see Alice H. Amsden, *Asia's Next Giant: South Korea and Late Industrialization* (New York: Oxford University Press, 1989).

main beneficiaries of government support. However, in 1973 it began promoting heavy and chemical industries to give South Korea the capability of arming itself. Trying to achieve rapid development of the steel, petrochemical, shipbuilding, machinery, and electronics industries, the regime pursued policies favorable to large conglomerates, known in Korean as the *chaebol*. It directed scarce capital to these favored companies and suppressed labor activism.[3] This new strategy was quite successful, at least initially.

By the early 1980s, the limitations of the South Korean developmental state began to become clear. Whereas the trend toward liberalization of the domestic economy was beginning to gain steam elsewhere in the world, the South Korean government was deeply entrenched in an economy heavily dependent on exports. It controlled the allocation of capital in the economy, while its growing symbiosis with the *chaebol* allowed their unhealthy expansion. Indeed, the government-sanctioned heavy investment in capital equipment by the *chaebol* in favored export industries became a burden for the larger economy since it increased foreign debt. At the same time, the wage levels of workers began to climb with the increasing activism of unions and the tightening of the labor market, leading to deteriorating terms of trade.

The mid-1980s brought a period of relief in the form of low oil prices and low international loan rates. In addition, the Plaza Accord, in autumn 1985, led to the appreciation of the Japanese yen against the South Korean won, greatly improving South Korea's terms of trade as more and more of its exports began competing with Japan's. Unfortunately, the resulting rapid expansion of the economy only masked and later intensified the problems of the developmental state as the Cold War era was ending.

South Korea's trade balance deteriorated after this golden period, and the unfavorable trend continued into the Kim Young Sam administration. The positive trade balance of 1986–9 turned negative in 1990. The trade deficit reached $8.9 billion in 1995, and by 1996 it had almost tripled, reaching $23.7 billion. The current account balance deteriorated from, in terms of its percentage of the gross domestic product, a 2.3 percent surplus in 1989 to a 0.9 percent deficit in 1990 and a 4.9 percent deficit in 1996.[4] Unable to arrest this erosion, the Kim administration witnessed South Korea's becoming the biggest victim of the financial crisis that swept through Asia in 1997.

[3] On the South Korean government's control of the flow of capital, see Jung-en Woo, *Race to the Shift: State and Finance in Korean Industrialization* (New York: Columbia University Press, 1991).

[4] Keizai Kikaku-cho Chosa-kyoku, *Ajia Keizai 1997* [The Asian economy, 1997] (Tokyo: Okura-sho Insatsu-kyoku, 1997), 324, 328.

External Challenges Facing the Developmental State

Indeed, by the time Kim Young Sam became president, South Korea was facing a serious economic challenge. Globalization was on its doorstep, but South Korea was still the quintessential developmental state, dependent on exports for growth. As late as 1996, its export-dependency ratio was about 26.9 percent, making South Korea highly vulnerable to the changing conditions of the post–Cold War international political economy.[5]

Since the 1980s, South Korea has been subject to increasing protectionist pressure as well as demands that it open its market to high-end goods and services from its developed trading partners, especially the United States. At the same time, it has had to deal with the increased competition for low-end products from cheaper-wage developing countries.

America's New Crusade

As South Korea was trying to make the transition from a newly industrialized economy to a developed one, the Cold War was coming to an end. The United States, the triumphant leader of the Western alliance against communism, was becoming more free to pursue its own economic interests; and Washington emerged as the principal advocate and agent of "globalization," increasingly less inclined to view South Korea as an important military ally but more inclined to view the nation as a competitor and mercantilist state. Consequently, a major shift occurred in South Korea's economic relationship with the United States.

In its bilateral trade with the United States, South Korea enjoyed a surplus of $4.2 billion in 1985, reaching a peak of $9.6 billion in 1987. After that, however, the surplus began to shrink, turning to a deficit by 1991.[6] The deficit was $1 billion in 1994 and then skyrocketed to $11.5 billion by 1996. The deficit with the United States accounted for as much as 58 percent of South Korea's total trade deficit in 1996.[7]

These deficits occurred within the context of the sustained appreciation of the won against the dollar. This appreciation was, in fact,

---

[5] The formula for the export-dependency ratio is export/GDP x 100. The calculation is based on data in International Monetary Fund, *Direction of Trade Statistics Yearbook*, 1997 ed. (Washington, DC, 1997), and in Keizai Kikaku-cho, *Ajia Keizai 1997*, 298.

[6] International Monetary Fund, *Direction of Trade Statistics Yearbook*, 1991 ed. (Washington, DC, 1991).

[7] International Monetary Fund, *Direction of Trade Statistics Yearbook*, 1997 ed. (Washington, DC, 1997).

Table 4.2 Importers of South Korean Goods, 1970–97 (in Percent)

	1970	1980	1990	1993	1994	1995	1996	1997
United States	46.8	26.3	29.8	22.1	21.4	19.3	16.7	15.9
Japan	28.0	17.4	19.4	14.1	14.1	13.6	12.2	10.8
Europe*	5.8	11.2	9.9	8.2	8.2	9.1	7.7	8.3

Source: Keizai Kikaku-cho, *Ajia Keizai 1997*, 312 (data for 1970); Bank of Korea, *Monthly Statistical Bulletin*, July 1985, February 1998.
Note: *Germany, United Kingdom, Italy, and France.

encouraged by the United States in order to increase its exports to South Korea.[8] The U.S. Treasury Department was empowered by Section 3004 of the Omnibus Trade and Competitiveness Act of 1988 to apply sanctions against countries "manipulating" their currency for trade advantages, and it repeatedly put pressure on South Korea to appreciate the won.[9]

The inescapable reality for South Korea was that the United States remained the most important market for South Korea (table 4.2). Export to the United States has been the engine of South Korea's development. The South Korean economy grew particularly fast, increasing by 9.8 percent per year on average, during the 1983–90 period, when the country had a large trade surplus with the United States. In contrast, the growth slowed down to an annual average of 6.9 percent in 1991–6, when the large surplus disappeared and was replaced by an increasingly large trade deficit.[10]

In part, this deterioration is attributable to straightforward economic factors. However, the change was not simply due to a shifting comparative advantage; international power politics played a critical role. A large part of the trade balance shift was the result of increasing protectionism in the United States against South Korean products as well as pressure on South Korea to reduce and eliminate its barriers against U.S. goods and services.

[8] Kihwan Kim, "The Political Economy of U.S.–Korea Trade Friction in the 1980s: A Korean Perspective," in eds. Jongryn Mo and Ramon H. Myers, *Shaping a New Economic Relationship: The Republic of Korea and the United States* (Stanford, CA: Hoover Institution Press, 1993), 40.

[9] For details, see Yen-Kyun Wang, "Exchange Rates, Current Account Balance of Korea, and U.S.–Korea Negotiations on Exchange-Rate Policy," in eds. Mo and Myers, *Shaping a New Economic Relationship*.

[10] The calculation is based on the real GDP figures in Keizai Kikaku-cho, *Ajia Keizai 1997*, 298.

Of course, U.S. protectionism was nothing new. In the 1980s, however, it reached new heights as the expansionary economic policy of the Reagan administration led to huge U.S. trade deficits with East Asia. Because much of the expansion was attributable to its massive defense spending in order to leave the Soviet Union behind in the "dustbin of history," the Reagan administration put political pressure on its Asian allies to offset the cost of this effort to the United States. The U.S. pressure on South Korea only increased during the Bush administration. After all, the end of the Cold War did not lessen the military threat from Pyongyang.

The United States took an unprecedented number of trade actions against South Korean exports during the 1980s. For example, from 1980 to 1988 some fifty-seven non-Section 301 cases were filed against South Korean firms. Twenty-four of them resulted in findings against South Korea.[11] In addition, nontariff barriers (NTBs), such as antidumping actions and countervailing duties, were targeted against South Korean goods. These actions had serious consequences for South Korean exports. Wan-Soo Kim and Bokyeun Han note that "between 1989 and 1992, Korea's overall exports to the U.S. declined 12.4 percent, while its exports to the U.S. under NTBs fell 28.7 percent, implying that Korea's exports to the U.S. have been seriously affected by various forms of import restrictions by the U.S. in recent years."[12]

Then, of course, the United States used Section 301 of the Trade Act of 1974 and the Super 301 provisions of the Omnibus Trade and Competitiveness Act of 1988 to promote its exports. Particularly effective was the use of Super 301, which mandates that "the administration identify 'unfair traders' and negotiate elimination of the trade barriers in question, with automatic retaliation if progress were not satisfactory."[13]

In May 1989, wielding the "club" of Super 301, the United States began to pressure South Korea to take significant steps toward liberalizing its domestic markets and its foreign-investment regime. South Korea first agreed to the liberalization of its agriculture and fishery markets, and the average tariff rate on products from those markets dropped from 25.2 percent in 1988 to 18.2 percent in 1992.[14] It also agreed to modify domestic content and export requirements placed on products produced by

[11] Kihwan Kim, "Political Economy of U.S.–Korea Trade Friction," 44–5.
[12] Wan-Soo Kim and Bokyeun Han, "Trade Pressures in Korea's Foreign Economic Frictions," in IPE Program of the Sejong Institute, *Korea's Economic Diplomacy: Survival as a Trading Nation* (Seoul: Sejong Institute, 1995), 202–3.
[13] Jeffrey F. Frankel, "Liberalization of Korea's Foreign-Exchange Markets and the Role of Trade Relations with the United States," in eds. Mo and Myers, *Shaping a New Economic Relationship*, 122.
[14] Kim and Han, "Trade Pressures in Korea's Foreign Economic Friction," 204.

Figure 4.1 South Korea: Trade Balance with Major Industrial Countries
1973–97 (in Millions of U.S. Dollars)

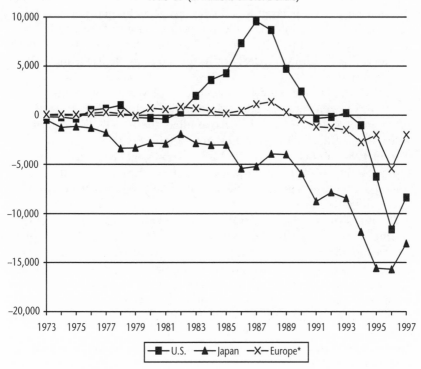

Source: Bank of Korea, *Monthly Statistical Bulletin* January 1982, June 1987, June 1993, February 1998.
* Germany, United Kindom, Italy, and France.

foreign subsidiaries operating in South Korea. Furthermore, it agreed to abolish all import restrictions aimed at promoting domestic production as well as to revise technical standards and testing procedures that impeded imports.[15] The result was a rapid shift in the balance of trade between the United States and South Korea (figure 4.1).

Other "Old Money" and New Competitors

The United States certainly was not the only country erecting barriers against South Korean goods and trying to pry open South Korean markets. Member countries of the European Community (EC) were doing the same. Of course, the EC has been a less important market for South

[15] Kihwan Kim, "Political Economy of U.S.-Korea Trade Friction," 49–50.

Korea than the United States or Japan (see table 4.2). Nonetheless, South Korea's trade with the EC has grown over the years, and increasing protectionism in this large market has also heightened South Korea's vulnerability in the international political economy. South Korea had a trade surplus with the EC from 1972 to 1990, reaching a peak of $2.1 billion in 1988.[16] However, the surplus turned to a deficit starting in 1991 (see figure 4.1).

As with the United States, protectionism played a role in this shift in South Korea's balance of trade with the EC. The EC as a whole, as well as its member countries individually, applied such NTBs as quantitative restrictions and antidumping measures against South Korean products. And in 1984 the EC adopted the New Commercial Policy Instrument to put pressure on foreign countries considered to be employing unfair trade practices. This policy tool was equivalent to Section 301 of the U.S. Trade Act of 1974.[17]

If South Korea's trade difficulties with the United States and the EC in recent years had political causes, the cause of South Korea's rapidly increasing deficits in trade with Japan was more economic in nature (see figure 4.1). Japanese officials point out that Japan's stance toward South Korea has been less protectionist than the United States' or the EC's.[18] In terms of formal barriers, the average tariff rate on all manufactured goods was lower in Japan (3.6 percent) than in the United States (5.5 percent) and the EC (5.6 percent) in 1991. Also, Kim and Han note that "fewer trade restrictions under NTBs are implemented in Japan than any other industrial countries."[19]

Japan certainly has many invisible barriers to trade, such as the complexity and rigidity of the distribution system and exclusionary business transactions related to *keiretsu* practices. They are formidable barriers, and they certainly have played a role in South Korea's perennial trade deficits with Japan. However, the recent dramatic increases appear to be related more to the structure of economic competition between South Korea and Japan than to the kind of overt political measures employed by other advanced industrial countries. As in other markets, South Korean exports to Japan have met with intense competition from cheaper goods from Southeast Asia and China. However, this competition has had more of an impact on the bilateral trade account; South Korea's major export items to Japan have been mostly labor-intensive

[16] Kim and Han, "Trade Pressures in Korea's Foreign Economic Friction," 212.

[17] Ibid., 213.

[18] Current and former officials of the Japanese Ministry of Foreign Affairs, Ministry of International Trade and Industry, and Ministry of Finance, interviews by author, Tokyo, February 1998.

[19] Kim and Han, "Trade Pressures in Korea's Foreign Economic Friction," 209.

goods since Japan is a more competitive producer of South Korea's high-end export items to other markets, such as automobiles, semiconductors, and steel.[20]

The sharply increasing deficits have also been the result of South Korea's dependence on Japan for capital and intermediate goods and other high-end products. With its attempt to move into the ranks of advanced industrial countries, South Korea's dependence on Japanese imports increased only because of the former's lagging indigenous technologies and skills.[21] Caught in a vise between low-wage and high-tech competition, South Korea has been unable to curtail the importation of critical capital and intermediate goods needed by its big businesses.

Indeed, the stark reality of low-wage competition from new competitors is central to South Korea's predicament in the new international political economy. The sharp increase in wage levels in South Korea (discussed in detail below) has severely eroded the competitiveness of its labor-intensive industries against East Asian countries with lower wage levels, particularly China.

What was happening to South Korea's footwear export market in the United States is illustrative of what was happening to its labor-intensive industries. As late as 1991, footwear was South Korea's largest export item to the United States. However, its market share plunged sharply in the face of low-wage competition from China (table 4.3). The entrance of some 1.2 billion Chinese into the international market system since the late 1970s has had an enormous impact not just on South Korea but on the entire world. When China, without much protest from others, devalued its currency in 1993 and again in 1994, many South Korean goods instantly lost their ability to compete in the world market.

Segyehwa *as a Response*

Segyehwa dealt with the external challenges discussed above in several ways. In response to market-opening measures targeting South Korea, *segyehwa* as a rhetoric served to give some political cover to Kim Young Sam's government, which was unable to resist the United States' arm twisting. *Segyehwa* was used as a slogan enabling South Korea to acquiesce to market openings as part of its larger globalization drive. That is, *segyehwa*

[20] In 1992 the shares of products exported to Japan were as follows: textiles, 24.3 percent; primary goods, 17.4 percent; electric and electronic goods, 16.1 percent; iron and steel, 12.2 percent (ibid., 207).

[21] When Kim Young Sam became president, the products South Korea imported from Japan were machinery and heavy capital equipment (34.7 percent), advanced electric and electronic goods (27.8 percent), and chemical materials and other intermediate goods (20.4 percent) (ibid.).

Table 4.3   U.S. Footwear Imports from South Korea and China, 1991–7
(in Millions of U.S. Dollars)

	1991	1992	1993	1994	1995	1996	1997
Korea	1,988	1,527	1,053	681	515	340	235
China	2,532	3,403	4,520	5,259	5,824	6,392	7,415

Source: National Trade Data Bank and Economic Bulletin Board, STAT-USA,
U.S. Department of Commerce, Washington, DC.

was a useful, if uncertain, psychological tool that helped the nationalistic
South Koreans accept a measure of reciprocity in international trade.[22]
More to the point, it was used to persuade those affected by market-opening measures that their jobs could not be shielded from foreign competition forever and that this reality was part of the process of South Korea's
gaining the respect of the industrial countries.

In many ways, Kim Young Sam's drive to gain membership in the
Organization for Economic Cooperation and Development (OECD)
exemplifies this kind of psychological use of *segyehwa*. South Korea's
achievement of this goal in December 1996 helped South Koreans deal
with economic liberalization and protected the government against protectionist and nationalistic pressures both at home and abroad. To be
sure, the policy component of OECD membership cannot be over-
looked: In deciding to join the OECD, South Korea committed itself to
formal obligations to other members of the elite organization, among
them accelerating implementation of various market-opening plans.
However, South Korea's membership in the prestigious OECD was critical in helping South Koreans to deal with trade liberalization.

More proactive were various measures adopted by Kim's government
to encourage South Korean investments abroad and to find new markets
as part of the effort to deregulate domestic capital and financial markets.
These measures, outlined in the Five-Year New Economic Plan for
1993–7 and the Long-Term Economic Design for the 21st Century, of
1996, dramatically increased direct overseas investment by South Korean
enterprises. South Korea's annual outward foreign direct investment
between 1990 and 1993 was $1.2–1.8 billion, and it swelled to $3.6 billion
in 1994 and $4.9 billion in 1995. More than half of this investment went
to Asian countries with lower wage costs.[23]

---

[22] See Lee Hong Koo, "Attitudinal Reform toward Globalization," *Korea Focus* 2,
no. 2 (March–April 1994), 85–94.

[23] Kayoko Kitamura and Tsuneo Tanaka, eds., *Examining Asia's Tigers: Nine
Economies Challenging Common Structural Problems* (Tokyo: Institute of Developing Economies, 1997), 6.

Such was the rush to invest abroad in countries paying cheaper wages that South Korean firms borrowed money from domestic and overseas sources to carry out their projects. As a result, foreign indebtedness had increased to $93 billion by July 1996, and it increased even further as the country headed for the financial crisis of 1997.[24] At the same time, as the South Korean firms became more multinational, their activities became less transparent and more difficult to monitor, which exacerbated the problem of overborrowing and overinvestment as well as risky financial operations by some firms.

Indeed, investment abroad in low-wage countries and liberalization of markets may be good in themselves, but the large foreign debt and the sharp deterioration of the terms of trade made South Korea more vulnerable to external shocks and signaled the increasingly fragile status of the South Korean economy. These were made worse by the uneven deregulation occurring in the domestic financial and capital markets. All these factors contributed to the balance-of-payments problem that destabilized the South Korean won in the fall of 1997.

Internal Challenges Facing the Developmental State

Even before the pundits and editorialists began writing about the origins of the financial crisis of 1997, there was a clear understanding among many thoughtful South Koreans that their country's economic advancement was burdened by the developmental state, in which government, big business, and, increasingly, big labor had become colluding partners. Hence, the intent of Kim Young Sam's *segyehwa* reform program was a thorough deregulation of the domestic economy aimed at transforming the developmental state into a market-oriented one better equipped to take South Korea to the next level of development.

Unfortunately, the sclerosis affecting the South Korean economy was difficult to clear. To make the situation worse, the reform program itself introduced instability into the rigid system while making South Korea's deep problems only too transparent for the international financial community to see as the reform measures allowed greater participation of foreign financial institutions in the domestic economy.

Expensive Labor

For some, the obvious and immediate source of South Korea's deteriorating terms of trade is the high wage levels in South Korea. During the authoritarian period, organized labor was repressed by the government to keep wage levels down. The resulting cheap labor helped South

---

[24] Ibid., 7.

Korean firms find a place in the world economy and fueled the rapid economic growth of the late 1960s and 1970s. As late as the first half of the 1980s, South Korean wage levels increased by only 5.5 percent per annum, in line with the 5.5 percent annual increase in productivity.[25]

However, political liberalization during the latter half of the 1980s was accompanied by intensified labor activism. For example, there were more labor disputes in the two months between 4 July and 4 September 1987 than had taken place in the previous ten years.[26] That year, a presidential election year, the number of labor disputes reached a peak at 3,749.[27]

The democratic election in 1987 did not result in much improvement in labor rights: The repression, though not as blatant as before, continued during the presidency of Roh Tae Woo, increasing the militancy of the South Korean unions. However, the frequent strikes and work stoppages did have a major impact on domestic wage levels as well as job security for unionized workers. The *chaebol*, with the acquiescence of the government, bought temporary labor peace with rapid pay increases and an implicit guarantee of "lifetime" employment for those working for them. In the 1987–9 period, wages increased by as much as 45 percent.[28]

Wages in South Korea, in fact, grew much faster than in Japan and Taiwan. During 1986–95, the average annual wage increase was 15.3 percent in South Korea, 9.85 percent in Taiwan, and 2.7 percent in Japan, whereas the annual increases in productivity were 9.2 percent, 6.4 percent, and 3.1 percent, respectively. This faster increase in the cost of labor in South Korea narrowed the wage gap between South Korea and the other two countries. In 1985 South Korea's labor cost was equal to Taiwan's and 4.1 times as cheap as Japan's. However, by 1995 it was a bit more expensive than Taiwan's and only 2.8 times as cheap as Japan's.[29]

The workers were helped by the fact that South Korea was suffering from a growing labor shortage. In 1980, for example, laborers in primary industries constituted 34 percent of the labor force, but their percentage decreased to 24.9 in 1985 and 17.9 in 1990.[30] Indeed, by the latter half of the 1980s, South Korea was importing laborers from abroad. With full

---

[25] *Asiaweek*, 25 January 1987, 67.
[26] Stephan Haggard and Chung-in Moon, "The State, Politics, and Economic Development in Postwar South Korea," in ed. Hagen Koo, *State and Society in Contemporary Korea* (Ithaca, NY: Cornell University Press, 1993), 90.
[27] Kitamura and Tanaka, *Examining Asia's Tigers*, 5.
[28] Robert Bedeski, *The Transformation of South Korea: Reform and Reconstruction in the Sixth Republic under Roh Tae Woo 1987–1992* (London: Routledge, 1994), 85.
[29] Keizai Kikaku-cho, *Ajia Keizai 1997*, 58.
[30] Kitamura and Tanaka, *Examining Asia's Tigers*, 3.

employment prevailing into the Kim Young Sam presidency, the average monthly wage for workers in South Korea's manufacturing sector rose from about 590,000 won in 1990 to around 1.12 million won in 1995. The problem was that productivity rose by only 65.5 percent in those five years, whereas wages rose by almost 90 percent.[31]

The Twin Pillars

The high-wage problem was in part a result of the disproportionate and distorting role the *chaebol* played in the South Korean economy. Wage increases by the *chaebol* became the benchmark for pay increases throughout the economy. However, this was the least of the problems caused by the domination of the South Korean economy by a handful of giant enterprises.

By the early 1990s, the *chaebol* had become so huge that the combined revenue of the top ten conglomerates equaled three-quarters of the country's gross national product.[32] This concentration of wealth had worked well earlier; however, in the globalized marketplaces of the 1990s, marked by short product cycles, it made the South Korean economy inflexible and inefficient.

For example, the *chaebol* became a serious threat to fair competition between affiliates of the *chaebol* and nonaffiliates, small and medium-sized businesses. The *chaebol* presented formidable entry barriers that discouraged competition from newcomers. In short, behaving in an oligopolistic manner, they skewed the economy to favor their own interests and impeded free competition.

One specific area in which the distorting effect of the *chaebol* on the South Korean economy can be seen is real-estate speculation. In the period 1985–95, land prices increased by 250 percent, with industrial land prices increasing even more, by 310 percent. This rapid increase in prices was driven largely by investments by the *chaebol*, which could not find a more productive use for their money, much of it borrowed. The *chaebol* bought land to use as collateral and a hedge against inflation. Indeed, they bid up the land prices to offset the interest rates on their bank loans.[33]

Although such speculation benefited the *chaebol* in the short run, it was a great burden to small and medium-sized businesses because it drove up the price of office space, commercial and industrial land, and so on. It

[31] Ibid., 4.
[32] *International Herald Tribune*, 24–5 December 1997.
[33] Chi Tong Uk, *Kankoku no Zokubatsu, Gunbatsu, Zaibatsu* (South Korea's kin groups, military groups, and business groups) (Tokyo: Chuo Koron, 1997), 154–5.

also led to a credit crunch since the *chaebol* used borrowed money for their speculation.[34] However, in the long run it was also damaging to the *chaebol* themselves because they too were adversely affected by increased production costs attributable to high land prices. The speculation also contributed to the demand for high wages by workers trying to keep up with the increased cost of living.

Modeled on the pre–World War II Japanese *zaibatsu,* the *chaebol* are the creation of the Park regime and were useful when the government was trying to jump-start industrialization. Through the *chaebol,* the South Korean government was able to target and build specific industries by allocating cheap credit to them and protecting their franchises. However, by the 1980s, when South Korea was on the brink of joining the advanced industrialized economies, this system had become a serious liability.

Many years of cozy relations between the state bureaucracy and the *chaebol* politicized the investment environment, with banks acting as cash boxes for targeted projects. Inevitably, corruption became a serious problem, and without the discipline of market forces guiding investment decisions, there was much waste. Furthermore, believing that the government would somehow guarantee their survival, big businesses kept adding to their debt. The encouraged export orientation of these giants also led to the neglect of, and imbalances in, the domestic economy. The negative effect on consumption standards is well known, but the practice of favoring *chaebol* often resulted in excess capacity, the neglect of small and medium-sized industries, and other distortions already discussed.

Some argue that had the "strong state" of the Park Chung Hee era survived into the 1980s, neither militant labor nor the oligopolistic *chaebol* would have become a problem in the 1990s. Whatever the antidemocratic demerits of such wishful thinking, there is something to the argument that the South Korean state of the 1980s and 1990s was no longer the autonomous creature of the idealized Park era that could rise above particularistic interests. It was instead deeply implicated in the corruption and inefficiencies of self-dealings of an advanced stage of developmental capitalism.

The loss of autonomy and power was positive to the extent that it was a sign of South Korea's growing economic (as well as political) maturity. As the South Korean economy became more and more sophisticated, it became increasingly impossible for the state to command the economy. This was particularly true of the state bureaucracy's relations with the big conglomerates.

The loss, however, was also negative. It amplified the conglomerates'

---

[34] In June 1995 the five largest *chaebol* accounted for 12 percent of the total bank loans, while the share of the thirty largest *chaebol* was 24 percent (ibid., 154).

antimarket impact on the South Korean political economy. The growing indispensability of the *chaebol* to the political circles that controlled the machinery of the state ensured that the oligopolistic power of the big conglomerates would continue.

Even under the semiauthoritarian governments of Chun Doo Hwan and Roh Tae Woo, the balance of power between the state and the *chaebol* was slipping in favor of the latter. When Chun and Roh attempted, each in his own way, to check the abuses of the *chaebol* in response to public resentment, they found it difficult to do. For instance, when Roh launched an anti–big business campaign, Koo Ja-kyung, chairman of the Lucky-Goldstar Group and of the Federation of Korean Industries (FKI), "warned politicians – both ruling and opposition – of potential retaliation through the discretionary use of political contribution" and "declared that the FKI would henceforth provide donations only to politicians willing to support and protect business freedom." Eventually, Roh had to abandon the anti *chaebol* campaign.[35]

This symbiosis of those who controlled the state bureaucracy and the *chaebol* inevitably led to regulatory failure and corruption, especially in the financial sector. It nurtured a large-scale underground economy that facilitated political corruption and market manipulation. Indeed, the state's contribution to South Korea's economic problems was not so much the mountain of regulations and rules it generated over time to micromanage the economy; rather it was its intimate complicity with the *chaebol* in distorting market forces when the economy had evolved beyond government guidance.

Unfortunately, Kim Young Sam's reform measures could not break this web of power and money. In fact, Kim himself was deeply mired in this web. In the Hanbo scandal, in which the conglomerate Hanbo borrowed from a government-controlled bank a huge sum of money that it could not pay back, Kim Young Sam's son and aides were implicated in influence peddling and money laundering involving funds supposedly left over from Kim's presidential campaign. It remains to be seen whether the current president, Kim Dae Jung, can fundamentally transform the collusive arrangement between government and big business.

Segyehwa *as a Response*

To the extent that *segyehwa* reforms tried to address the domestic structural problems, they focused mainly on deregulation. In Kim Young

[35] Chung-in Moon, "Changing Patterns of Business-Government Relations in South Korea," in ed. Andrew MacIntyre, *Business and Government in Industrializing Asia* (Ithaca, NY: Cornell University Press, 1994), 154–5.

Sam's announcement of his "New Economy" policy three weeks after his inauguration on 19 March 1993, he promised that he would drastically curtail the role of government and encourage participation and creativity in the economy. These goals were further clarified in the already mentioned five-year economic plan released in the summer of 1993 and other subsequent pronouncements and directives. The 1993 plan detailed tax, financial, monetary, and administrative reforms leading to the lifting of the onerous regulatory burden on businesses and the end of the government's domination of the domestic financial system.

As a package, these reform proposals were impressive, but they were pursued in an uncoordinated way and unevenly applied. Some of these measures made South Korea more vulnerable to the financial firestorm that swept through East Asia in 1997: They accelerated the kinds of deregulation demanded by the *chaebol* without promoting real competition and efficiency.

In fact, many reform measures targeting the *chaebol* were without "teeth" and ambiguous, making it easy for big conglomerates to ignore or circumvent them. For example, the 1993 plan called for many spending and production targets for the private sector and voluntary limits on business expansion plans. At the same time, it announced that eventually conglomerates would no longer be subject to restrictions on the kinds of businesses they can enter. Only a little later, however, a variety of limits to which the *chaebol* would be expected to adhere, such as the kinds of industries in which they could specialize, were listed.

Kim's attempt to streamline the government turned out to be largely cosmetic. It did not address the fundamental dilemma of advanced developmental capitalism, in which the state still has enormous power but exists in a collusive arrangement with big businesses.

Take, for instance, what happened to the effort to create a small but efficient administration better suited to the challenges of globalization. With much fanfare, Kim merged some government ministries and reorganized their functions.[36] Included in this effort was the merger of the Economic Planning Board (EPB) and the Ministry of Finance (MOF) into the Ministry of Finance and Economy (MOFE). However, this created a superagency combining the government's fiscal, budgetary, and other important economic functions, which made accountability even more problematic.

In the name of deregulation and government downsizing, the EPB, perhaps the least corrupt and most independent institution of the

---

[36] For more details on government reorganization, see Sanghyun Yoon, "South Korea's Kim Young Sam Government: Political Agendas," *Asian Survey* 36, no. 5 (May 1996), 513.

developmental state, was merged with the MOF in 1994.[37] The move was justified as a way to reduce the power of the MOF, which wielded a disproportionate amount of influence over banking, finance, and other economic matters and was closely linked to the *chaebol*. The merger was, in fact, more of an absorption of the smaller and more autonomous EPB by the larger and more politicized MOF.

The reforms that did take hold were the ones that caused the least amount of pain – at least in the implementation phase – to the privileged constituents of the developmental state. The most notable example is Kim's acceleration of the deregulation of the financial system. The "success" in this area was aided by the fact that South Korea's admission into the OECD – a highly valued political goal with symbolic importance to the South Korean electorate – required drastic reforms. It also helped that the United States had been pushing hard to have the South Korean financial system liberalized while the *chaebol* sought access to international capital to maintain their expansionist course.

In June 1993 the Kim administration unveiled the Financial Liberalization and Market Opening Plan. A year and half later it announced the Foreign Exchange Reform Plan. These plans focused on liberalizing interest rates and reducing the scope of the government's intervention in the financial sector.[38] They also encouraged greater foreign participation in the South Korean financial and capital markets, though, fatally, they allowed for faster portfolio than direct investment inflows.

Many of the measures carried out under these plans only made the Achilles heel of the South Korean developmental state – the highly politicized financial system that allowed those controlling the government to direct easy money to favored enterprises and projects – more vulnerable. The measures were promoted as a way to foster a more independent and professional role for banks in allocating credit, but true independence was impossible to achieve because no real progress was made in severing the collusive ties between government and business leaders.

The immediate effect of Kim's measures was to introduce more liquidity into the state- and *chaebol*-dominated economy by allowing easier access to the international financial system. At the end of 1991, the total

---

[37] During the early days of economic takeoff, the EPB's institutional autonomy and strong power enabled it to make effective economic policies and implement them. However, over time its power was weakened by rival ministries and agencies seeking greater independence from the EPB as well as by political leaders increasingly dependent on the *chaebol* for political contributions as democratization began to take hold (see Bedeski, *The Transformation of South Korea*, 81–2; see also Stephan Haggard, *The Pathways from Periphery: The Politics of Growth in the Newly Industrializing Countries* [Ithaca, NY: Cornell University Press, 1990]).

[38] *Far Eastern Economic Review*, 20 June 1996, 46–8.

portfolio investment in South Korea was $2.5 billion; by the end of 1994, it was $29.7 billion, an increase of some 1,088 percent. And South Korean banks' international liabilities increased by 49 percent, from $21.7 billion at the end of 1991 to $32.4 billion at the end of 1994.[39]

This allowed even more excessive expansion and wasteful investment by big businesses in new shipyards, semiconductor and auto production plants, and so on. That is, deregulation led to a massive domestic lending spree that encouraged further investment in risky and speculative ventures. For a time, the lending and spending spree raised the collateral values of assets, encouraging misplaced confidence in the appropriateness of these values.

The problem was not liberalization as such but the absence of effective prudential regulation and supervision of the financial system. As Catherine Mann points out, "The pace of liberalization of international capital flows outpaced the reforms to the domestic financial sector so that rather than complementary domestic reform development, international capital flows exposed and exacerbated vulnerabilities inherent in the 'silent partner' domestic financial system."[40] The fact is that key aspects of bank supervision and regulation lagged in part because they were not consistent with the needs of the *chaebol* (operating their own banks as "cash windows") or the government.

Opening the South Korean economy to a massive inflow of portfolio investment without fundamentally reforming the twin pillars of the developmental state made the weak domestic banking system a conduit for external shocks. If the *chaebol* were eager to tap foreign capital, foreign investors were just as eager to oblige. Kim's "reform" measures caused large capital inflows to be both "pulled" in and "pushed" in. High domestic interests rates, largely the result of an uncompetitive banking system, encouraged foreign borrowing. At the same time, foreign capital, mostly short-term, came in seeking these higher yields.[41] This was a recipe for a disaster.

The IMF Era

As little progress was being made in fixing the fundamental problems of the South Korean political economy, South Korea's trade and capital

---

[39] International Monetary Fund, *International Financial Statistic Yearbook*, 1997 ed., 519.
[40] This discussion on financial and capital markets deregulation follows from Catherine Mann's speech at the Tokyo American Center on 9 March 1998.
[41] For example, the rates on commercial promissory notes were 12.6 percent in 1993, 12.9 percent in 1994, 13.8 percent in 1995, and more than 12 percent in 1996 (Kitamura and Tanaka, *Examining Asia's Tigers*, 5).

account balances slipped further into the red. When the financial storm broke out in Southeast Asia in the spring of 1997, there was much denial from many informed South Koreans that South Korea would be seriously affected, but, in hindsight, there was little hope that South Korea was going to be spared from the wrath of market forces.

Toward the Fall

Without effective reform, South Korea experienced a significant deterioration of its trade balance in the last years of Kim's presidency. Its deficit of $6.3 billion in 1994 increased to $10 billion in 1995 and doubled to 20.6 billion in 1996.[42] There were three immediate causes of this sharp deterioration: the appreciation of the won against the yen, the declining prices of dynamic random access memories (DRAMS), and the increase in domestic nonresidential capital investment. The latter two factors were direct products of the structural flaws of the South Korean economy exacerbated by *segyehwa* "remedies."

The average value of the won against the dollar was 803.5 in 1994, 771.3 in 1995, and 804.5 in 1996.[43] The increase in the trade deficit in 1995 can be attributed to the won's appreciation in that year, but the deficit increase in 1996 cannot be explained by the depreciation in 1996, something that should have increased South Korean exports.

The problem was that the won was effectively rising against the yen as the yen fell against the dollar in 1996; the average exchange rate between the yen and the dollar fell from 102.2 yen to the dollar in 1994 to 94.1 in 1995 but rose to 108.8 in 1996. Calculated from the exchange rates between the won and the dollar and between the yen and the dollar, the average exchange rate between the won and 100 yen was 785.9 in 1994, 819.7 in 1995, and 739.4 in 1996.[44] From 1995 to 1996, the won appreciated nearly 10 percent against the yen. Given that many South Korean goods – electronics, automobiles, steel, ships, and so on – were competing with Japanese goods based more on price than on quality, the result was a predictable unattractiveness of South Korean goods in the international markets.

Another blow to South Korea was the sharp price decline in DRAMS prices in the world market. The leading South Korean *chaebol* had become overdependent on this product. In 1996, for example, semiconductors accounted for 18 percent of total South Korean exports.[45]

---

[42] Keizai Kikaku-cho, *Ajia Keizai 1997*, 324, 328.
[43] Ibid., 340.
[44] Ibid., 340–1.
[45] *Far Eastern Economic Review, 1996 Asia Yearbook* (Hong Kong, 1997), 153.

However, the price of 16-megabit DRAMS plunged nearly 80 percent from January 1996 to the end of the year.[46] As a result, DRAMS sales fell from about $42 billion in 1995 to about $25 billion in 1996.[47] Obviously, this price drop was a severe blow to South Korean electronics firms; and since their main competitors were again Japanese, the exchange rate factor also severely squeezed the South Korean firms.[48] The DRAMS price collapse and the depreciation of the yen resulted in a 22.1 percent decline in the dollar value of South Korean electronics exports in 1996 despite a 62.4 percent increase in volume.[49]

The DRAMS price drop was in part caused by overinvestment by South Korean firms trying to grow their way out of their problem. This was the case with other industries as well, both low- and high-tech. Caught in the vise between high- and low-tech competition, South Korean *chaebol*, with the government's complicity, desperately threw more and more borrowed money on new production lines and plants. With new money made available through the deregulation of the financial market, the *chaebol* increased their purchase of sophisticated capital goods that South Korea could not produce. Compared to its negative growth in the 1991–3 period, nonresidential capital investment increased by 15.8 percent in 1994, 12.9 percent in 1995, and 8.2 percent in 1996.[50] This increase, however, worsened the trade balance.

Given what was happening to South Korea's trade account, and given its massive borrowing and spending spree, it was just a matter of time before the financial crisis that hit Southeast Asia reached South Korea. Indeed, there was a run on the South Korea won when the international financial community lost faith in the "miracle on the Han"; and in December 1997 South Korea had to sign a deal with the IMF to stabilize its currency. The $58 billion bailout organized by the IMF was the largest in the IMF's history. In order to receive this aid, South Korea had to accept the demands of donor institutions and countries. South Korea had to agree, first, to strengthen its fiscal and monetary policies; second, to implement far-reaching fiscal reform; third, to liberalize trade and capital-flow laws; and, fourth, to reform the structure of South Korean corporations, particularly the *chaebol*.[51] The irony, of course, is that most

---

[46] *Nikkei Weekly News*, 2 June 1997.

[47] *Wall Street Journal*, 10 October 1997.

[48] The three major South Korean electronics firms suffered a dramatic drop in net profit from 1995 to 1996: Samsung Electronics suffered a 93 percent drop; Hyundai Electronics, a 91 percent drop; and Lucky-Goldstar (LG) Semiconductor, an 88 percent drop (see Hasegawa Keitaro, *Ajia Daitenkan to Nippon* [The shift of the Asian MEGA trend] [Tokyo: Kobun-sha, 1997], 31).

[49] Keizai Kikaku-cho, *Ajia Keizai 1997*, 12.

[50] *OECD Economic Outlook* 62 (December 1997).

[51] *New York Times*, 4 December 1997.

of these reforms were the ones Kim Young Sam was trying to carry out under the banner of *segyehwa*.

Kim Dae Jung's Election

The failure of reforms and the "IMF crisis" brought about the election of Kim Dae Jung as the fifteenth president of South Korea in December 1997. The unprecedented transfer of power to an opposition candidate may represent the end of the collusive arrangement between the *chaebol* and politicians. Indeed, the crisis could provide Kim Dae Jung with a unique opportunity to liberalize the South Korean political economy and succeed where Kim Young Sam failed. To be sure, Kim still needs to overcome many formidable barriers and rearguard actions by players with vested interests in the developmental state while navigating the treacherous and uncertain currents of the international financial system stirred up by the 1997 crisis.

Kim Dae Jung has won much praise and respect from those at home and abroad who would like to see the liberalization of the South Korean political economy. Despite his populist past and his skeptical comments about the proposed IMF austerity measures during the electoral campaign, Kim immediately embraced the Kim Young Sam administration's agreement with the IMF. When he became president in February 1998, Kim Dae Jung promised liberalization – even if it caused severe pain in the short run – as one of the most important goals of his presidency, and he reaffirmed his commitment as he headed into his second year in office.[52]

Taking charge of crisis management even before he was inaugurated, Kim Dae Jung has been pushing hard for needed reforms in government and business while trying to tame the militant South Korean unions. While it is premature to pass judgment, his effort, which is very much in line with Kim Young Sam's *segyehwa* reform attempt, shows limited signs of progress.

With regard to governmental reforms, Kim Dae Jung's goal of limiting government intervention in the economy has been tempered by the emergency situation facing the South Korean economy. While he pledged to transform the government's role in business activities from that of meddler to that of arbiter, the sheer necessity of managing the IMF crisis has increased the government's command authority in the economy.

For example, Kim Dae Jung has reduced the power of the MOFE by curtailing its responsibilities and abolished the post of vice prime minister for the economy. At the same time, he has established a number of ad

---

[52] *Chosun Ilbo*, 15 August 1998.

hoc organizations, such as the Planning and Budget Commission (EPBC) and the Financial Supervisory Commission (FSC), to deal with the economic emergency and carry out reforms. Although these entities are meant to bypass entrenched interests in government bureaucracies, some argue that these new entities, with sweeping powers, may actually end up reinforcing a key pillar of the developmental state.[53] They also predict the reconstitution of much of MOFE's authority in one institutional guise or another.[54]

Indeed, some habits are hard to break. The government has selected ten major industries for extensive reorganization, arguing that strong government intervention is needed for their efficient restructuring. In the case of aircraft and parts manufacturing, for example, the Ministry of Commerce, Industry, and Energy launched a consortium with private firms, including creditor banks.[55] The danger is that this kind of sectoral policy will create new monopolies and oligopolies supported by banks operating under even tighter political supervision than before. It is not at all clear, given the demands of emergency economic management, that one of the key lessons of the Asian financial crisis, that government should refrain from picking winners and losers, has any practical meaning for the Kim administration.

Kim Dae Jung is also making limited progress with the reform of the *chaebol*, reducing their dominance in the economy. Much of the government reform effort has gone into getting the *chaebol* to consolidate their far-ranging and disparate operations to some coherent core business lines to reduce their debt burden and increase profitability. After many threats and counterthreats, a nine-point agreement was reached in July 1998 between the Kim administration and the FKI. They agreed that the government will not force the *chaebol* to shed and consolidate operations through "big deals," but the *chaebol* will be expected to do so on their own. At the same time, the *chaebol* agreed to divest themselves of marginal businesses and stop engaging in intersubsidiary trading and making cross-payment guarantees. In turn, Kim pledged to expedite the financial restructuring and to continue with the deregulation of government controls on business.[56]

It is too early to assess accurately the *chaebol* reform program, but the present reality is that the *chaebol* domination of the domestic economy continues and the self-reform program by big business has been marked by foot-dragging and superficial fixes. Of course, the continuation of

[53] Former senior ROK officials, interview by author, Seoul, April 1998, and Tokyo, June 1998.
[54] Ibid.
[55] *Korea Herald*, 13 August 1998.
[56] *Korea Times*, 6 July 1998.

chaebol domination in the economy is understandable given that there has been a huge number of bankruptcies among small and medium-sized businesses resulting from the IMF austerity program. This is a legacy of the developmental state, not necessarily the result of neglect or failure on the part of the Kim Dae Jung administration.

The real concern is that, without changes in the modus operandi of the *chaebol*, the "big deals" will only lead to reduced domestic competition and reinforcement of the oligopoly in order to make the surviving *chaebol* more competitive in the international markets. There is limited indication that the *chaebol* are really serious about fundamental reform. For example, they have reduced their high debt-to-equity ratio, but only on paper. The five biggest *chaebol* have lowered the ratio from 470.1 percent in 1997 to 285.4 percent at the end of 1998.[57] However, this was accomplished in good part through revaluing old assets to reflect current values and adding the gain to the equity base and engaging in inter-subsidiary in-kind investments where gains from sales of patents and other non-cash assets are used to acquire equity. They have avoided divestitures and have failed to attract new capital, particularly foreign capital.

Perhaps Kim Dae Jung has been more successful in dealing with South Korea's notoriously militant labor unions, long-time Kim Dae Jung supporters, for they have not engaged in any large-scale, economy-crippling strike. Kim Dae Jung has established a tripartite commission made up of representatives from unions, management, and the government to negotiate on labor matters.

The first tripartite negotiation attempt failed, but the Second Labor-Management-Government Commission is operating as well as can be expected. To be certain, it is constantly under the threat of a walkout by one of the parties. At one point or another, the Federation of Korean Trade Unions (FKTU), the Korean Confederation of Trade Unions (KCTU), and the Korea Employers Association (KEA) have all threatened to leave the arrangement; even government bureaucrats have attempted to undermine the commission.[58] In February of 1999, the KCTU, the more militant of the two unions, did leave the commission; however, its half million members have not triggered a new round of labor actions that would cause other unions to follow. If there is a general strike, it could throw a monkey wrench into the recovery of the South

---

[57] *Korea Herald*, 3 March 1999.

[58] Recently, a senior Labor Ministry official challenged the legality of the presidential advisory panel, questioning the 23 July accord between the committee and the nation's two labor federations. This is not surprising given that the commission has undercut the authority of the Labor Ministry (ibid., 4 August 1998).

Korean economy. Nonetheless, to its credit, this mechanism has avoided, at least up to this point, a massive layoff of unionized workers. The ranks of the record-level unemployed are, of course, made up of nonunion workers from small and medium-sized businesses. By the end of 1998, the unemployed numbered some 1.67 million or 7.9 percent of the workforce.[59]

It is difficult to judge at this point what will be the result of Kim Dae Jung's reform effort and crisis management. However, it is already clear that he is being hampered by difficulties similar to those faced by Kim Young Sam. Given the emergency situation facing South Korea, Kim Dae Jung could take Draconian measures to achieve reforms, but he wants to leave behind a strong legacy of democracy, and has made it difficult for his government to use the kind of authoritarian tools available to his predecessors. However, he has shown – out of necessity – his willingness to violate the free-market principles in which he professes to believe and some of the key lessons of the Asian financial crisis concerning government-industry relations and work with the entrenched interests of the developmental state.

Whither the South Korean Developmental State?

In this stage of globalization, and an eddy of Korean history called the IMF era, the fate of South Korea will depend just as much on what happens outside of South Korea as on what happens within. To be fair, it was not for the lack of effort and foresight that Kim Young Sam's reform measures failed to transform the South Korean developmental state into a more liberal political economy. From his inauguration, Kim Young Sam pressed for liberalizing reforms. The problem was that globalization – especially the economic processes – is unforgiving and has a logic of its own, while Kim Young Sam himself turned out to be a cog in the machinery of the developmental state that became stuck in the Hanbo scandal, taking the steam out of the reform campaign. It remains to be seen whether Kim Dae Jung, an outsider coming to power in a midst of a severe crisis, can replace the developmental state with a new political economy better equipped for survival in an increasingly globalized world.

The immediate obstacle for Kim Dae Jung and South Korea is the continuing slide of the South Korean economy. At the end of 1998, South Korea had foreign-exchange reserves of $48.5 billion, up from about $8.9 billion at the end of 1997.[60] In 1998 South Korea tallied a record trade surplus of $39.0 billion on a customs-cleared basis. However, this

[59] *Far Eastern Economic Review*, 4 February 1999.
[60] Ibid.

is not all good news. With plunging domestic demand and corporate investment, customs-cleared imports dropped some 35.5 percent from 1997 to $93.3 billion in 1998. Exports actually fell 2.8 percent in dollar terms to $132.3 billion due to deflating prices and slow demand abroad.[61] The trade surplus and the resulting buildup of foreign-exchange reserves are largely due to the collapse of imports. In essence, South Korea is having a giant bankruptcy sale to increase its cash flow while buying very little from its suppliers.

Severely impacted by the massive deflation of the regional economy, South Korea is only one of many East Asian countries now engaged in a price war in international markets. The Japanese, caught in their own web of internal structural problems, are signaling that a major slide in the yen is on the way. Although the yen recovered after a sharp drop in value in the spring and summer of 1997, Eisuke Sakakibara, Japan's vice minister of finance and an outspoken advocate of a strong yen, has acknowledged that a weaker yen would be in Japan's interest.[62] Of course, if the yen does fall significantly and stays low, there is the danger that the Chinese yuan will be devalued as well. This would mean cheaper competition, from the high end as well as the low end, which could stop the South Korean export-led recovery effort in its tracks and trigger another run on the won.

Once again, the Koreans are running against time.

[61] *Korea Herald*, 27 February 1999.
[62] *New York Times*, 11 March 1999.

CHAPTER 5

Globalization of the
South Korean Chaebol

Eun Mee Kim

Huge electronic advertisements for the South Korean *chaebol* have adorned New York City's Times Square for some time. Visitors to major international airports throughout the world are greeted by luggage carts adorned with advertisements for the South Korean *chaebol.* These advertisements are for the *chaebol*'s export products. However, not only the *chaebol*'s products but the *chaebol* themselves have "gone global" in the 1990s.

The South Korean *chaebol* have become globetrotting enterprises. They no longer simply export cheap products to the global market; they set up subsidiaries and joint ventures around the world. Their presence has been noted with fanfare by the host governments. For example, hosting the dedication ceremony of the Uzbekistan Daewoo Motors on 19 July 1996 was none other than the president of Uzbekistan,[1] who decorated Kim Wu Chung, the president of Daewoo, with Uzbekistan's highest honor. The president of Indonesia attended the opening of LG's television-monitor factory in Indonesia. It was not just in developing countries that the South Korean *chaebol* received such royal treatment. At the opening ceremony of Samsung's electrical-appliance factory in England, the queen herself was present.[2]

* The author gratefully acknowledges the research assistance provided by Jiyoung Kim, Nahee Kang, and Sunduk Jeong of the Graduate School of International Studies of Ewha Womans University. The research was conducted with a research grant from the university's Institute for International Trade and Cooperation.

[1] Eui Chul Yi, "The Big Business Group's Overseas Investment Boom" (in Korean), *Monthly Chosun,* 1996, 9.
[2] "The 21st Century Vision of the South Korean Corporations" (in Korean), *Seoul Kyungje Shinmun,* 29 December 1996, 7.

This chapter focuses on the South Korean *chaebol*'s "globalization," and in particular, outward foreign direct investment (OFDI). The *chaebol* are family-owned and -managed business conglomerates, which have dominated the South Korean economy since the 1960s. Their dominance in the market as well as in society in general has increased tremendously, and it is virtually impossible to understand the South Korean economy without a careful evaluation of their role in it. The South Korean government identifies thirty business groups (*chaebol*) each year based on total assets. In 1999, the minimum total assets were $2.0 billion. The thirty business groups are subject to the Fair Trade Commission's policies, which prohibit cross-debt guarantees among *chaebol* member firms and place stringent credit controls.

The *chaebol* have spearheaded South Korea's OFDI. Globalization of the *chaebol* includes inward foreign direct investment (IFDI) and/or technology transfer from multinational corporations to the *chaebol*; OFDI from the *chaebol*; global competitiveness; and global management practices. Of these, OFDI is the most recent phenomenon, occurring to a great extent in the 1990s, and thus is the least studied. OFDI has also become a thorny issue in light of the financial crisis, which has swept through Asia since the latter half of 1997. Some argue that the *chaebol*'s OFDI was based on excessive borrowing from international financial institutions, and brought financial drains on the *chaebol* as well as the domestic financial institutions. Thus, this chapter examines critically the *chaebol*'s OFDI in the 1990s as a means for understanding one important dimension of South Korea's corporate globalization.

The goal of this chapter is to examine one of the least understood but crucial dimensions of corporate globalization – i.e., OFDI. The emphasis will be on the *chaebol*'s OFDI since it dominated South Korea's outward investment. As noted above, this research took on added urgency since there is speculation that the *chaebol*'s OFDI is partly to blame for the financial crisis. Thus, this chapter also examines the Kim Dae Jung administration's (1998–) corporate restructuring policies, which aim to control the management practices of the *chaebol* in general, and their OFDI in particular. The restructuring policies have been influenced by the International Monetary Fund's (IMF) conditions for the bailout loan package and give us an opportunity to examine the role of the IMF for future OFDI. We will examine how corporate restructuring has thus far affected the *chaebol*'s OFDI, and provide projections for OFDI.

This chapter is organized into four main parts: the political economy of globalization of the Kim Young Sam administration (1993–8); the overall pattern of OFDI; the *chaebol*'s OFDI; and corporate restructuring and globalization of the Kim Dae Jung administration (1998–).

The Political Economy of Globalization and the
Kim Young Sam Administration (1993–8)

Globalization differs from internationalization in that the former refers to a new global system in which "national cultures, national economies, and national borders are dissolving."[3] In a globalized economy, national strategies for economic development, national regulations for investment and trade, and national enterprises are less significant than in an internationalized economy.[4] In contrast, internationalization refers to a system in which international transactions continue to be performed largely at the national level; in other words, national cultures, national boundaries, and national economies matter. One of the most noteworthy trends in the global economy is the globalization of production.[5] Increasingly, transnational corporations have become significant players in the global economy because they are the ones who coordinate production across national borders.

As discussed in Chapter 1 in this volume, the concept of globalization is still being hotly debated by scholars and policymakers. Depending on one's theoretical perspective as well as one's assessment of the utility of "globalization," the arguments vary widely. In this chapter, I use the "alternative conceptualization" of globalization suggested by Samuel S. Kim in Chapter 1, and define globalization as a multidimensional "process" in which "interconnectedness" in economic, political, social, and cultural dimensions extends and intensifies across the globe. I focus on the globalization of enterprises.

Although Paul Hirst and Grahame Thompson are quite critical of globalization, arguing that globalization, in which global corporations move freely around the world, is simply a myth, their definition of transnational corporations (TNCs) provides a useful heuristic device for analysis. Globalized enterprises are TNCs, which differ from multinational corporations (MNCs). Hirst and Thompson define TNCs as "footloose capital, without specific national identification and with an internationalized management," that is at the least "potentially willing to locate and relocate anywhere in the globe."[6] On the other hand, MNCs are based in "one predominant national location." Thus, the former are

---

[3] Paul Hirst and Grahame Thompson, *Globalization in Question: The International Economy and the Possibilities of Governance* (Malden, MA.: Polity Press, 1996), 1.
[4] Ibid., 7.
[5] See John H. Dunning, *Alliance Capitalism and Global Business* (New York: Routledge 1997); Gary Gereffi and Miguel Korzeniewicz, eds., *Commodity Chains and Global Capitalism* (Westport, CN.: Greenwood Press, 1994).
[6] Hirst and Thompson, *Globalization in Question*, 1.

not wholly controlled by the policies and regulations of any one nation, while the latter are constrained by those of the home government.[7]

The late 1980s saw an increase in foreign direct investment in the world economy and a rise of MNCs and TNCs from developing nations, in particular from East Asia. John Dunning argues that the determinants of foreign direct investment (FDI) also changed in the late 1980s. While the traditional FDI was mainly from advanced industrialized nations to developing ones seeking markets, resources, or efficiency, the new forms of FDI sought to "acquire new competitive, or ownership-specific, advantages." He observes that this new type of FDI occurred often in firms that produced "technology-intensive and branded goods in oligopolistic industries" and took the form of acquisitions, mergers, or nonequity alliances with competitors, suppliers, or customers.[8] Dunning and others have argued that MNCs from developing countries are different from those from developed countries, since the former must deal with two sets of countries, which are either more or less developed than their own. This changes the dynamic of FDI, since traditional OFDI by MNCs and TNCs from developed nations simply sought investment sites based on the host country's positive pull factors, including resource endowments and demand conditions, as well as the home country's push factors, including higher wages, and firm-specific advantages. However, MNCs and TNCs from developing countries such as South Korea seek relatively cheap input costs, better endowment of resources, and demand conditions in less developed countries, as well as access to advanced technology and management know-how in advanced nations. The following provides a partial list of factors in the domestic and global economic and political conditions, which may affect OFDI decisions. While the domestic factors for OFDI may not differ for MNCs and TNCs from developed and developing nations, the global factors are quite different for the two groups of countries. For example, MNCs and TNCs from countries such as South Korea will seek positive global political factors, and low transaction costs in the global economic conditions. On the other hand, MNCs and TNCs from the U.S. may not necessarily seek these advantages since they already possess them. This chapter will use these factors to assess whether South Korea's OFDI patterns are more similar to those of the advanced countries or are more indicative of developing nations.

Domestic political:
1. Government initiatives and incentives, that promote globalization and OFDI

---

[7] Ibid., 11.
[8] Dunning, *Alliance Capitalism and Global Business*, 8–10.

2. Relaxation of governmental regulations, which obstruct OFDI

Domestic economic:
1. High input costs: wages, labor shortage, material (raw and processed), etc.
2. High transaction costs: access to markets, communication, transportation, and shipment

Global political:
1. Creation of regional economic blocs, e.g., North American Free Trade Agreement (NAFTA), European Union (EU)
2. Protectionism

Global economic
1. Low input costs: wages, labor surplus, material (raw and processed), royalty payments, etc.
2. Low transaction costs: access to markets, communication, transportation, and shipment

The Globalization Drive of the Kim Young Sam Administration (1993–8)

An important factor in South Korea's OFDI in the 1990s was the intensive and extensive globalization drive of the Kim Young Sam administration. At President Kim Young Sam's inauguration, on 25 February 1993, he pledged to create a New Korea through changes and reforms, the main theme of his election campaign. In order to pursue the New Korea policy, the Kim Young Sam administration set four policy goals: a clean government, a sound economy, a healthy society, and peaceful unification. Based on these principles, President Kim initiated political and social reforms, economic renewal, and cultural development.[9] Political and social reforms focused on curing the "Korean disease," characterized by widespread misconduct and corruption in politics and officialdom, lax social discipline, breakdowns in authority, regional animosity, excessive consumption by the newly rich, and a faltering economy. Kim sought to eradicate these symptoms by reducing political funds, disclosing personal and family assets of high government officials and politicians, and revising the laws having to do with public officials' ethics, elections, political funds, and local autonomy. The latter laws were aimed at breaking the collusive ties among politicians, civil servants, and business leaders.

Economic renewal and reforms were concentrated on the liberalization

---

[9] Gerardo Ungson, Richard M. Steers, and Seoung-Ho Park, *Korean Enterprise: The Quest for Globalization* (Cambridge, MA: Harvard Business School Press, 1997), 6.

of the South Korean markets through an open trade policy under "internationalization and globalization." More radical initiatives included the introduction of real-name systems for all financial and real-estate transactions to guarantee transparency in financial dealings, which reduced the underground economy and contained nonproductive land speculation.

In his second year in office, President Kim announced that implementing globalization, or *segyehwa*, would be his administration's main priority. This new policy, envisaged in November 1994, was aimed at preparing the nation to meet the challenges of an increasingly globalized world and to play a central role in international affairs. Under the globalization program, all sectors of society – political, economic, social, and cultural – were to become competitive at the international level.[10] Nationally, *segyehwa* aimed to (1) create a first-rate nation; (2) rationalize all aspects of life; (3) maintain national unity by rising above class, regional, and generational differences; (4) strengthen Korea's national identity as the basis for successful globalization; and (5) enhance a sense of community with all humanity. President Kim outlined six main areas for reform: (1) the education system, to prepare citizens to be leaders in a globalized world; (2) the legal and economic systems, to meet global standards of excellence; (3) politics and the press, to ensure that they would meet the challenges of globalization; (4) national and local governments, to make them more efficient and more geared toward globalization[11]; (5) environmental policies, to enable the nation to take a more active part in global environmental protection; and (6) the Korean culture and the Korean way of thinking (consciousness), so that Koreans could contribute to global culture and go out into the world with pride in themselves and respect for others.[12] The government also formed the Presidential *Segyehwa* Promotion Committee (PSPC), a high-profile panel made up of senior administration officials, academics, and specialists. This committee had formulated strategic policies for reform in fifty-one projects in diversified fields as of December 1997.[13]

The *segyehwa* policy included four phases of business globalization;

[10] Information in this paragraph is mainly drawn from the website of the Korean Embassy in Washington, D.C., at http://korea.emb.washington.dc.us/.

[11] As a result of government reorganizations, about one thousand civil-service jobs were cut almost overnight. Among those displaced were two cabinet ministers, three vice ministers, four assistant ministers, and twenty-three director-generals. Four ministries were made into two: the Economic Planning Board and the Ministry of Finance became the Ministry of Finance and Economy, and the Ministry of Construction and the Ministry of Transportation became the Ministry of Construction and Transportation.

[12] "President Kim Young Sam's First Three Years in Office: A New Era of Change and Reform" (in Korean), *Korea Update* 7, no. 4 (4 March 1996).

[13] Office of the Prime Minister website, http://202.30.75.2/DATA/m5main.htm.

businesses were to move from phase one to phase four: (1) domestic
company with a domestic market orientation; (2) domestic company
with an international market orientation; (3) foreign local company; and
(4) finally, global company.[14] The vision and basic principles of the initiative for economic globalization focused on achieving world-class competitiveness and establishing a sound economy.[15] In order to attain these
goals, it was necessary to enhance economic efficiencies by promoting
autonomy, competition, and liberalization. The Kim administration
devised such strategies as reducing governmental intervention, promoting economic deregulation, and revising laws and regulations for ensuring fair competition in order to achieve a market economy based on
advanced capitalism.

Thus, the vision and goals of economic globalization can be summa-
rized as the establishment of an economic system and operation led by
the private sector and a market economy driven by (fair) competition.[16]
The strategies for implementing these policy goals were to improve operations for macroeconomic policies, restructure directions for microeconomic policies, and efficiently implement foreign economic policies.
The first strategy, that of improving operations for macroeconomic policies, was a response to the rapidly changing environment of the global
market and an attempt to adapt to the market-opening, liberalization,
and internationalization trends in the financial markets through an
optimal policy mix of efficient fiscal and financial policies. The second
strategy, of restructuring directions for microeconomic policies, focused
on reforming government regulations, strengthening procompetitive
policies, changing industrial policies, reforming corporate and labor
policies, and establishing consumer-protection policies. The restructuring of corporate policies was aimed at promoting deregulation so that
individual enterprises could be autonomous with respect to management. However, policies aimed at preventing economic concentration,
such as dispersion of ownership and regulation of total capital investment, were to be maintained for the time being. In addition, policies and
systems governing corporate activities and operations were to be revised
to enhance the transparency, rationality, efficiency, and responsibility of
corporate management.[17]

In sum, the Kim Young Sam's globalization policy toward the businesses was more passive than active. The policy was to remove obstacles
for overseas investment, and to allow and encourage the private sector
to take initiative in the globalization drive. The government's role was

[14] Ungson, Steers, and Park Korean Enterprises, 114
[15] Office of the Prime Minister website.
[16] Ibid., 145–6.
[17] Ibid.

minimal and reactive, since it was to remove regulations and to help facilitate corporate globalization. Thus, this policy was different from the prodevelopment industrial policies of the past, which directed the private sector to invest in certain industrial sectors by providing low-interest-rate loans, industrial licenses, and other subsidies. The globalization of the private sector was left to the private sector, and therefore only a handful of the wealthiest *chaebol* could do so. These *chaebol* also had to rely on international financial institutions to fund their OFDI projects, since the government was not prepared to provide low-interest-rate loans for OFDI.

The Overall Pattern of OFDI

South Korea's OFDI outpaced its IFDI in 1990, making the country a net exporter of direct investment. After years of constraining OFDI because of a small foreign-currency reserve and concerns about capital flight, the South Korean government relaxed its policy on OFDI in 1986, following the country's first trade surplus in its modern economic history. In 1994 several OFDI-related policies were introduced to ease regulations and decrease the number of sectors prohibited from OFDI. Finally, in 1996 the negative list for sectors and regions for OFDI was completely abolished, regulations on foreign real-estate acquisitions were relaxed, and the upper limit on OFDI by private enterprises was raised.[18] Although the South Korean government's OFDI policies did not provide subsidies to promote OFDI, they removed barriers to overseas investments and allowed private enterprises to more or less freely invest in overseas markets. Boosted by the Kim Young Sam administration's globalization policy and favorable economic conditions, OFDI has increased sharply since 1994.

A comparison of IFDI and OFDI figures puts the OFDI in perspective. As figures in table 5.1 show, both IFDI and OFDI have increased rapidly in the 1990s. Considering the more recent involvement of the South Korean enterprises in OFDI, the large number and size of OFDI are particularly noteworthy. OFDI has outpaced IFDI since 1990, and the gap between the two has widened quickly. OFDI increased nearly sixty-fold between 1981 and to a peak in 1996, from $109 million to nearly $6.2 billion.[19] During the same period, IFDI increased from $152 million to $3.2 billion. OFDI figures in the 1990s show that South Korea was no

[18] Ministry of Finance and Economy, "Statistical Data on Foreign Direct Investment" (in Korean) (Seoul, 1996).

[19] Bank of Korea, *Economic Statistical Yearbook* (Seoul, 1997); International Economic Policy Bureau, Ministry of Finance and Economy, *Economy's Trends in Foreign Investment and Technology* (in Korean) (Seoul, 1997).

Table 5.1   Inward Foreign Direct Investment and Overseas Foreign Direct
Investment, 1990–8 (in Thousands of U.S. Dollars)

	IFDI		OFDI	
	Total		Total	
	Permission/Notification		Permission/Notification	
Year	Cases	Amounts	Cases	Amounts
1990	482	802,635	515	1,610,563
1991	509	1,395,996	527	1,510,690
1992	444	894,476	631	1,206,155
1993	458	1,044,274	1,049	1,875,711
1994	646	1,316,505	1,947	3,580,992
1995	872	1,941,423	1,561	4,912,114
1996	968	3,202,646	1,797	6,174,881
1997	1,055	6,971,000	1,591	5,654,000
1998	831	8,852,356	685	5,109,782
Total	6,265	26,421,311	10,303	31,634,888

Note: Statistics for 1990-98 are based on approved cases.
Source: Bank of Korea, *Economic Statistics Yearbook* (1997); Ministry of Finance and
Economy (MOFE), *1997 International Investment Trends* (1998) and   *Trends in
International Investment and Technology Inducement* (1998, 1999).

longer just a recipient of foreign capital and technology but an active
global investor.

The financial crisis that has swept through Asia influenced the figures
for 1997, and 1998, in which IFDI outpaced OFDI.[20] The OFDI figure for
1998 was 9.6 percent lower than in 1997. On the other hand, the IFDI
figures showed strong progress since the financial crisis. Although the
number of cases decreased to 831 in 1998 from 1,055 in 1997, the year of
the largest recorded level in South Korea's recent history, over $ 8.8 bil-
lion. It is noteworthy that the bulk of IFDI in 1998 and 1999 is in services,
which reached 67 percent of total IFDI. And the majority of IFDI was
made by acquiring stocks.[21]

[20] Starting in the spring of 1997, several Southeast Asian economies experienced
currency crises when their currencies fell sharply against the U.S. dollar. The
first country hit by the crisis was Thailand, in May 1997. Thailand's currency
crisis sent shock waves to the Philippines, Singapore, Hong Kong, Indonesia,
and then to East Asian nations, including South Korea, Taiwan, and even
Japan. What began as a currency crisis quickly became an overall financial crisis in Thailand, Indonesia, and South Korea and resulted in these nations seeking massive financial bailout packages from the IMF.
[21] Ibid., 3; Economic Cooperation Bureau, Ministry of Finance and Economy,
"Trends in International Investment and Technology Inducement" (in
Korean) (Seoul, 1999).

Regional variations of OFDI and IFDI patterns in the 1990s are presented in table 5.2. They show a clear pattern of OFDI concentration in Asia and North America. The recent surge of OFDI in North America was most likely in response to the NAFTA. Thus, OFDI in this region represented the efforts of the South Korean corporations to penetrate the North American market. Investment in Asia continued to be high, which most likely represented the efforts to seek lower wages and to increase market shares in the burgeoning Southeast Asian and Chinese markets.

According to a study conducted by the Korea Institute for International Economic Policy (KIEP), the single most important motive for OFDI in 1994 was to seek new overseas markets followed by the motive to utilize lower wages in host nations.[22] This differed from another survey done in 1987 which showed that the two most important reasons for OFDI were to utilize lower wages and to sidestep trade barriers. As shown in our present study, OFDI in recent years reflects the *chaebol*'s aggressive overseas market expansion strategy (e.g., Eastern Europe), and their low-wage strategy in response to rising wages in South Korea (e.g., Southeast Asia, China). This trend shows that OFDI from South Korea is not very different from that of advanced countries.

The *Chaebol*'s OFDI

The involvement of the *chaebol* in OFDI was quite impressive. As in the past, when the large *chaebol* were the major recipients of IFDI and technology transfers, they were also the leaders in OFDI, spearheading the South Korean economy's globalization drive. At the end of 1995, the total accumulated amount of OFDI of all South Korean enterprises was more than $10 billion.[23]

The largest *chaebol*, in particular Daewoo, Hyundai, and Samsung, had the largest OFDIs.[24] In 1994 the total OFDI (actual investment figures) of the largest five *chaebol* was nearly $1.4 billion,[25] accounting for almost 70 percent of all OFDI. The same five *chaebol* plan to invest more than $60 billion in the next ten years.[26] It is particularly noteworthy that in 1994,

[22] KIEP, *Policy Debate on Problems and Management of OFDI* (in Korean), KIEP, 24 March 1998.

[23] "Overseas Investment Pitch" (in Korean), *Seoul Kyungje Shinmun*, 17 September 1996.

[24] Eui Chul Yi, "The Big Business Group's Overseas Investment Boom"; "Overseas Investment Pitch"; "The Korean Corporations' Globalization" (in Korean), *Seoul Kyungje Shinmun*, 28 December 1996, 19.

[25] Bank of Korea, "Current Status of Overseas Investment Enterprises" (in Korean), in *ODI Statistical Yearbook* (Seoul, 1994, 1995).

[26] Eui Chul Yi, "The Big Business Group's Overseas Investment Boom"; *Seoul Kyungje Shinmun*, "Overseas Investment Pitch."

Table 5.2 Regional Variations of OFDI and IFDI Patterns, 1990–8

Overseas Foreign Direct Investment (OFDI) of South Korea
(Based on Invested Cases)

Year	Asia			Middle East			North America		
	Cases	Amount	Ratio	Cases	Amount	Ratio	Cases	Amount	Ratio
1990	321	797.083	49.5	2	564	0.0	111	588,251	36.5
1991	350	630,644	41.7	0	202,780	13.4	93	518,012	34.3
1992	487	700,011	58.0	2	570	0.0	64	249,090	20.7
1993	870	966,645	51.5	6	6,996	0.4	85	423,324	22.6
1994	1,656	1,724,288	48.1	5	164,904	4.6	149	824,820	23.0
1995	1,266	2,533,616	51.2	1	3,591	0.1	161	1,438,999	29.1
1996	1,391	3,201,609	51.5	7	41,462	0.7	229	1,195,755	19.2
1997	1,147	21,748,686	47.0	4	49,323	0.8	258	1,208,973	20.7
1998	457	2,378,757	46.6	1	6,540	0.1	145	1,226,410	24.0
Total	7,945	15,681,339	49.1	27	476,730	1.5	1,300	7,673,634	24.0

Inward Foreign Direct Investment (IFDI) in South Korea
(Based on Invested Cases)

Year	Asia			Middle East			North America		
	Cases	Amount	Ratio	Cases	Amount	Ratio	Cases	Amount	Ratio
1990	164	257,009	32.1	–	42	0.0	86	325,661	40.7
1991	131	248,214	17.9	1	3,341	0.2	89	300,188	21.6
1992	87	170,472	19.1	1	4,279	0.5	73	389,477	43.7
1993	141	391,583	37.5	1	87	0.0	73	342,587	32.8
1994	207	569,061	43.4	1	10,715	0.8	119	312,530	23.9
1995	300	791,159	40.9	–	1,600	0.1	167	646,646	33.4
1996	303	1,217,650	38.0	5	1,100	0.0	172	877,163	27.4
1997	320	1,137,282	16.3	2	3,225	0.0	193	3,372,888	48.4
1998	358	2,014,213	23.0	8	19,774	0.2	274	3,037,888	34.6
Total	1,651	6,796,643	25.8	19	44,163	0.2	1,246	9,605,028	36.5

Note: Asia is comprised of all Asian countries, including Southeast Asia and Oceania.
Source: Ministry of Finance and Economy, *Trends in International Investment Technology Inducement* (1998, 1999).

Table 5.2 (cont)

Overseas Foreign Direct Investment (OFDI) of South Korea
(Based on Invested Cases) (in Thousands of U.S. Dollars)

Latin America			Europe			Africa			
Cases	Amount	Ratio	Cases	Amount	Ratio	Cases	Amount	Ratio	OFDI-Total
40	85,918	5.3	36	122,074	7.6	5	16,659	1.0	1,610,549
39	43,858	2.9	41	112,592	7.5	4	12,808	0.2	1,510,694
31	69,959	5.8	42	184,590	15.3	5	1,926	0.2	1,206,146
33	47,231	2.5	49	346,545	18.5	6	84,486	4.5	1,875,227
40	96,208	2.7	84	638,676	17.8	13	132,186	3.7	3,581,082
42	246,179	5.0	82	705,754	14.3	9	20,448	0.4	4,948,587
49	421,578	6.8	109	1,322,526	21.3	12	37,325	0.6	6,220,255
48	627,805	10.7	108	1,028,744	17.6	21	184,201	3.1	5,847,732
19	378,667	7.4	46	930,389	18.2	17	189,018	3.7	5,109,781
341	2,017,403	6.3	597	5,391,890	16.9	92	669,095	2.1	31,910,053

Inward Foreign Direct Investment (IFDI) in South Korea
(Based on Invested Cases) (in Thousands of U.S. Dollars)

Latin America			Europe			Africa			
Cases	Amount	Ratio	Cases	Amount	Ratio	Cases	Amount	Ratio	IFDI-Total
1	10,060	1.3	54	206,963	25.9	–	–	0.0	799,735
2	11,970	0.9	73	824,358	59.4	–	–	0.0	1,388,071
10	44,214	5.0	65	282,218	31.7	1	127	0.0	890,787
3	1,248	0.1	60	307,424	29.5	–	–	0.0	1,042,929
8	10,874	0.8	89	406,681	31.0	–	–	0.0	1,309,861
8	19,213	1.0	103	475,164	24.6	1	66	0.0	1,933,848
8	47,898	1.5	124	1,058,318	33.1	–	–	0.0	3,202,129
16	45,267	0.6	131	2,409,440	34.6	2	1,014	0.0	6,969,116
22	732,817	8.4	158	2,968,387	33.8	8	315	0.0	8,773,394
78	923,561	3.5	857	8,938,953	34.0	12	1,522	0.0	26,309,870

Daewoo was the largest overseas investor with almost $450 million, when it was only the fourth largest *chaebol.*

The *chaebol*'s recent OFDI has often been large in scale. Daewoo opened a major automobile company in Uzbekistan with $3.2 billion on 19 July 1996.[27] OFDIs of more than $100 million from the leading South Korean *chaebol* have not been unusual. Although the figures will undoubtedly be adjusted as a result of the financial crisis, the fact remains that OFDI has become an important activity of the top *chaebol* (see table 5.3). In fact, the financial crisis intensified the OFDI activity of the largest *chaebol.* In 1998, the largest thirty *chaebol* accounted for over 92 percent of total OFDI, which was much higher than in recent years (see table 5.3).

Regional investment patterns of the largest five *chaebol* show that the top five *chaebol* have quite different regional investment patterns. Daewoo, as noted in the South Korean press, has invested heavily in the former Soviet-bloc nations in Eastern Europe. Automobiles have been an important OFDI project for Daewoo. On the other hand, Hyundai has significant OFDI projects in North America, including automobile plants and semiconductor factories. Samsung also has plans for globalization, although its OFDI operations are smaller than those of its rivals, Hyundai and Daewoo. For the largest three OFDI investors, assembly manufacturing accounted for the largest share of OFDI. In comparison, Sunkyung and LG concentrated their OFDI in petrochemicals and had an overall less diversified investment structure. The largest OFDI investors showed a much wider range of business activities, which was quite similar to their investment patterns in the domestic South Korean market. In sum, the larger the *chaebol*, the more diversified they were in terms of OFDI.

Case Studies

The history of OFDI is relatively short in South Korea. Although the first overseas investment was made in 1968, substantial OFDI did not begin until the late 1980s. Thus, it is not surprising that just three of the largest *chaebol* – Daewoo, Hyundai, and Samsung – account for most of South Korea's OFDI. The most important reason for the concentration of OFDI activity in the largest *chaebol* is the government's corporate globalization policy, which does not provide incentives for OFDI and leaves it up to the private sector to take initiative. Thus, it is not surprising that the largest *chaebol* are the largest investors of OFDI, especially in its early stage. Many smaller *chaebol*, and independent small and medium-sized enterprises, cannot readily engage in OFDI even though the obstacles

[27] Seoul Kyungje Shinmun, "Overseas Investment Pitch," 3.

Table 5.3   OFDI of the Top Thirty South Korean *Chaebol,* 1981–97
(in Thousands of U.S. Dollars)

Year	Top 30 Chaebol	Ratio	Total OFDI
1981	27,007	95.7	28,211
1982	35,876	35.6	100,837
1983	69,900	64.2	108,917
1984	34,540	68.8	50,186
1985	84,423	74.9	112,775
1986	171,467	93.9	182,649
1987	385,941	94.2	409,708
1988	182,196	84.4	215,861
1989	494,609	86.8	569,589
1990	788,114	82.2	958,935
1991	919,051	82.4	1,115,468
1992	969,169	79.5	1,219,430
1993	932,398	73.9	1,262,118
1994	1,738,725	75.6	2,298,623
1995	2,393,022	78.0	3,066,924
1996	3,410,406	80.8	4,219,990
1997	2,346,911	79.3	2,960,742
1998	3,482,900	92.2	3,777,486
Total	18,466,655	81.5	22,658,449

Note: Statistics for OFDI are based on approved cases.
Source: Ministry of Finance and Economy, *Trends in International Investment Technology Inducement* (1998, 1999).

for OFDI have been removed since OFDI projects require large sums of capital. In other words, the large *chaebol* are the only ones that could take advantage of the favorable changes in the domestic political factors for OFDI. Had the government provided positive incentives to non-*chaebol* firms, the OFDI may have been less concentrated in the largest *chaebol.*

Hyundai was the first company to take its construction business abroad. The Hyundai Motor Company and Hyundai Heavy Industries Company, Ltd., were key companies that led the OFDI in Hyundai. In the case of Hyundai Electronics, the establishment of Hyundai Electronics America in 1969 and the export of semiconductors and personal computers to the United States added to Hyundai's international strategic management. Hyundai Engineering and Construction also entered the Thai market through a joint-venture housing project worth $3.3 billion, and Hyundai has joint-venture plants in China worth $100 million.[28]

---

[28] Ungson, Steers, and Park, *Korean Enterprise,* 120.

Hyundai announced plans for globalization that included building plants in the United States and hiring local employees. On 21 May 1995, Hyundai announced its plan to construct the world's largest semiconductor manufacturing plant in Eugene, Oregon, worth $1.3 billion. In the same year, Hyundai acquired AT&T's NCR electronics business for $340 million, and in the following year it acquired Maxtor, a U.S.-based disk-drive manufacturer, for $150 million.[29] Hyundai Auto Canada's Bromont Plant and Hymex-Hyundai de Mexico were established in 1989 and 1991, respectively. Overall, $348 million of Hyundai's total OFDI of $405 was directed toward North America. In the case of Hyundai Motor Company, investments made in the United States were geared toward automobile sales. Hyundai Corporation maintained trade businesses, and Hyundai Electronics Industries Company, Ltd., invested mainly in the manufacture of electronic products, such as semiconductors and video and CD players.

Daewoo is in automobiles, electronics, and financial services worldwide. The diverse companies of the Daewoo Group are bound by a collective faith in the "Daewoo Spirit" and by the common goal to successfully bring about globalization for mutual prosperity, which represents the essence of Daewoo's management philosophy. This unity has created a natural synergy among member companies, which collectively generated total sales of $65 billion in 1996 and placed the Daewoo Group twenty-fourth among *Fortune* magazine's "Global 500 Businesses."

As of June 1997, Daewoo had investments in 380 projects in eighty-five different countries. Many of Daewoo's overseas investments were concentrated in the emerging market nations, which have the greatest potential for growth in the coming century. By localizing operations in foreign nations, Daewoo hoped to fully realize the benefits of its commitment to mutual prosperity. Daewoo has substantial investments in major motor vehicle and components production plants in Poland, Romania, the Czech Republic, Uzbekistan, India, China, the Ukraine, Vietnam, the Philippines, Iran, and Indonesia. Other fully operational investment programs have been established for manufacturing electronics and home appliances in the United Kingdom, France, Spain, Poland, Mexico, Vietnam, and Uzbekistan. Daewoo also has been providing telecommunications equipment and services in China, Uzbekistan, the Ukraine, and Kazakhstan.

Daewoo launched the Daewoo Global Management Plan in 1990 to meet the challenges of, and to better cope with, the changing international business environment. The plan involves restructuring Daewoo's management and business operations to adapt to a rapidly maturing

---

[29.] Hoover's Online, "Hoover's Company Profile."

domestic market and a world market that combines free trade with protectionism in the form of regional trade blocs. The goals underlying globalization at Daewoo were (1) to develop new markets, (2) to access lower cost-factor inputs, (3) to acquire new technology, and (4) to overcome trade barriers. Daewoo's globalization efforts were in large part a response to its poor international market presence in the early years but also included a concerted drive to open new markets.[30] Daewoo's path toward globalization differed from that of the other *chaebol* in that it sought to hone its advantage in traditional products, but with an eye to unexplored markets, as witnessed in its presence in Eastern Europe, Central Asia, and Latin America. This, however, also caused the near collapse of Daewoo in July 1999.

Samsung, which was the largest South Korean *chaebol* in 1996,[31] invested 600 billion Korean won in OFDI in that year. Although its OFDI was only the third largest among the leading *chaebol*, Samsung has pursued a vigorous OFDI strategy since 1993, when its top management launched the "new strategic management" initiative and made OFDI one of its top priorities.[32] Samsung established a comprehensive manufacturing complex, which put all the components of production in one location in each of its Third World OFDI sites in order to minimize transaction costs and increase synergy between processes. In 1982, Samsung was the first South Korean corporation to establish an overseas production line in Portugal, where its average annual revenue increased to $29.4 billion in 1997. Samsung Electronics has been Samsung's most active company in terms of OFDI. In 1993, Samsung Electronics established a joint-venture manufacturing plant for a telecommunication switching system in Shandong Province in China and expanded its products to include fiber-optic cables, transmission equipment, and headsets.[33] By the end of 1996, Samsung Electronics owned twenty overseas plants.

Critical Assessment

The OFDI of the *chaebol* is not without its critics. The fact that the *chaebol*'s unprofitable OFDI has in part caused the financial crisis brought to the fore the *chaebol*'s heavy reliance on foreign loans for corporate expansion, and unsound investment decisions. OFDI would not have

[30] Ungson, Steers, and Park, *Korean Enterprise*, 123.
[31] The rank is based on total sales in 1996. Hyundai was first, followed by LG and Daewoo.
[32] Samsung Group, "Samsung's Global Strategy and Operation" (in Korean), *Samsung Strategic Report* (Seoul, 1997).
[33] Ed Parsely and Terrence Clernan, "Reforms Boost Capital Flows," *Far Eastern Economic Review*, 26 May 1994.

come under such close examination had it not been for the financial crisis, since OFDI was not under the direct control of the South Korean government.

A report prepared by KIEP in 1998 shows that much of OFDI since 1994, which was encouraged by the globalization drive of the Kim Young Sam administration, was ridden with financial problems.[34] The research findings showed that in 1995, among large investments – i.e., investments over $50 million – the equity capital ratio was 12.5 percent and the debt/equity ratio was over 927 percent. These figures showed that large investments were financed heavily by debt. These investments were also the least profitable. In fact, the profit ratios compared to total assets, equity capital, and total sales, respectively, showed that they were all in the red. This was in contrast to comparable domestic firms, which made net profits in 1995 as well as 1994. Although these statistics were not broken down in terms of *chaebol* and non-*chaebol* firms, we know from other sources (see table 5.2) that the former dominated the large overseas investments made in the 1990s. According to the report, the reason for the extremely high debt/equity ratio was that the large investors preferred the relatively low-interest-rate loans offered in the host country, compared to the high-interest-rate loans they had to pay to receive loans from domestic financial institutions. Thus, the large-scale OFDI was dependent on foreign debt, and thus when these investments were unprofitable, the entire *chaebol* suffered.

An evaluation of South Korea's competitiveness shows that its ranking has gone down from twenty-seventh in 1996 to thirty-fifth in 1998, partly as a result of the financial crisis.[35] Among the six input factors for calculating the competitiveness ranking, South Korea showed the lowest rankings in internationalization (rank forty-sixth), and finance (rank forty-fifth). Such low rankings correspond to the IMF directives, which urge the South Korean economy to open up to investments and products from other nations, as well as to restructure the financial institutions to meet international standards.

In addition, as noted above, the *chaebol*'s OFDI was brought under more careful scrutiny so that their management was to become more transparent and internationally competitive. D. M. Leipzinger argued that South Korea's financial crisis was in large part due to the moral hazard of the *chaebol*.[36] He asserted that the *chaebol* made reckless investments and hid such investments from the public in general, and from the shareholders in particular, through opaque management practices. Other critics have

---

[34] KIEP, "Policy Debate on Problems and Management of OFDI."

[35] The World Competitiveness Online website, http://www.imd.ch.

[36] D. M. Leipzinger, "Public and Private Interests in Korea: Views on Moral Hazard and Crisis Resolution," EDI discussion paper, May 1998.

pointed to Daewoo's OFDI as a prime case of reckless investment. Daewoo has made several large-scale automobile OFDIs in Eastern Europe with much fanfare, as noted in the introduction of this chapter. The goals of Daewoo's OFDI strategy were to expand the market into new areas, which have been neglected by MNCs from other nations. The idea was that Daewoo would not wait until the citizens were rich enough to purchase cars, but help develop the economy and build the infrastructure, so as to create demand. Moreover, this strategy would give Daewoo the advantage for being there first. However, critics from abroad and in South Korea pointed out that this strategy was based on extremely long-term projections and was highly risky. Taking Leipzinger's point of view, we can argue that Daewoo made such an unsound investment decision because its management was not transparent. In other words, Daewoo did not have to worry about satisfying its shareholders or improving short-term profits in making such a decision. However, such practices became subject to strict governmental control. Finally, in July 1999 Kim Woo Choong, the chair of Daewoo, declared that he would relinquish his control of Daewoo and agreed to the government's and debtor's committee's control of Daewoo. This is the problem of South Korea's corporate management. Thus, it is important to evaluate the management decisions of OFDI of the *chaebol* critically in order to improve the efficiency and competitiveness of South Korean corporations as they embark on future OFDI projects.

The Future of OFDI: Corporate Restructuring and Globalization of the Kim Dae Jung Administration (1998–)

The Kim Dae Jung administration (1998–) inherited the financial crisis from the Kim Young Sam administration. The financial crisis, which began with the currency crisis of Thailand's baht in May 1997, quickly spread to other Asian economies including Indonesia and South Korea. By early November 1997, South Korea's stock market began to fall sharply while its won kept losing value against the U.S. dollar. On 8 November 1997, foreign investors sold $71 million of shares in the half-day trading, causing speculation that South Korea's financial turmoil would surpass that of Thailand and Indonesia.[37] By the end of 1997, South Korea sought assistance from the IMF, and finally signed a letter of intent covering an international accord to be provided with a $57 billion

---

[37] The information provided is based on various news sources, including Reuters, *Wall Street Journal, New York Times,* CNN, and the *Financial Times,* as found on the website http://www.stern.nyu.edu/~nroubini/asia/AsiaChronology 1.htm for chronology of 1997 and http://www.stern.nyu.edu/~nroubini/asia/AsiaChronology1998.html for chronology of 1998.

loan package from the IMF. Under the watchful eye of the IMF, the South Korea government has undertaken major restructuring programs in the following areas: corporate sector; labor market; financial institutions; and the public sector. Having resolved, in large measure, South Korea's external liquidity problems with assistance from the IMF, the World Bank, and the Asian Development Bank, the Kim Dae Jung administration is now focusing on structural reforms in the financial and corporate sectors.

Here, we focus on the Kim Dae Jung administration's corporate restructuring plans, which affect the *chaebol*'s OFDI. The Kim Dae Jung administration is aware of the fundamental causes of the crisis, and recognizes that a "band aid" solution will be insufficient to achieve durable economic growth. Restructuring the *chaebol* based on market principles focuses on the following five measures: (1) enhanced transparency; (2) resolution of cross-debt guarantees; (3) improvement of financial structure; (4) streamlining business activities; and (5) strengthening accountability.[38] Enhanced transparency requires adopting new accounting and auditing rules in line with internationally accepted standards as well as the establishment of an external auditors' committee. It also involves strengthening the legal protection for the rights of minority shareholders and compulsory appointment of outside directors.

One of the major reasons for the *chaebol*'s financial weakness is the cross-debt guarantees among member firms. Thus, the *chaebol* are prohibited from issuing new guarantees between subsidiaries and required to eliminate their existing cross-debt guarantees by the end of March 2000. Furthermore, financial institutions have been prohibited from demanding cross-debt guarantees.[39]

Improvement of financial institutions concerns mainly the reduction of corporate debt/equity ratios (which has been pointed out as being one of the main causes of the financial crisis) to internationally accepted levels within two years. Companies are required to reduce their debt/equity ratios to below 200 percent by the year 2000. For this purpose, corporations are required to submit blueprints of their restructuring plans to the Financial Supervisory Commission (FSC). If they do not comply, they are subject to financial constraints.[40] This has been agreed to in principle by the *chaebol* and their main banks. As a means of raising capital, restrictions on capital infusion with consideration were lifted, and to discourage debt financing, interest payment on excessive borrowing will not be deducted from taxable income as of the year 2000. For corporate

[38] "Challenges and Changes: Korea's Response to the New Economic Reality," Korean Ministry of Finance and Economy, June 1998, 21–8.
[39] Ibid.
[40] "Daewoo Will Take FDI Amounting to $8 bil. This Year," (in Korean), *Maeil Kyungje Shinmun*, 1 April 1999.

debt reduction, the legal basis for the establishment of equity funds was completed on 16 September 1998, and asset-backed-securities (ABS) will be issued.[41]

The *chaebol* were strongly urged to focus on core businesses and to sell nonviable businesses. Out of the fifty-two corporations classified as nonviable, twenty were affiliated with the five largest *chaebol*.[42] In order to facilitate streamlining the business activities, three major bankruptcy-related laws were amended in February 1998, and the merger and acquisition process has been liberalized to include foreign takeovers.

Measures to improve corporate governance, or more specifically, to strengthen accountability of owners/managers, are also in the works. This task involves increasing legal liabilities of controlling owners and introducing a de facto directors' system as well as a cumulative voting system. In addition, institutional investors are expected to take the role as monitors of corporate management with the newly given voting rights.[43]

Such restructuring measures are consistent with the IMF program that places strong emphasis on enhancement of transparency, improvement of capital structure (financial structure), enforcement of minority shareholders' rights (strengthening accountability), facilitation of merger and acquisition, and realignment of bankruptcy-related laws (streamlining business activities).

The corporate sector is expected to take a dramatically different shape as "Big Deals" – an integral part of the streamlining the *chaebol* – finalizes. The first "Big Deal" agreement reached between the top five *chaebol* on six major industries was announced on 7 October 1998, and the details are as follows:[44]

1. Semiconductors: Joint venture of Hyundai Electronics and LG Semiconductors
2. Train Car Manufacturing: Consortium of Hyundai Precision and Industries and soon-to-be-merged Daewoo Heavy Industries and Hanjin Heavy Industries
3. Power Plant Equipment: Consortium of Hyundai power generation division and Korea Heavy Industries
4. Petrochemicals: Consortium of Samsung Chemical, Hyundai Petrochemicals, and a possible foreign partner

[41] Bank of Korea, "Introduction of Laws Related to Liquid Assets and Mutual Funds,"(in Korean) in *Monthly Economic Indicators* (January 1999), 54-61.
[42] "Korea's Economic Reform Progress Report," press release, Ministry of Finance and Economy, 2 October 1998.
[43] Ministry of Finance and Economy, "Challenges and Changes."
[44] "The First 'Big Deal' Agreement Reached" (in Korean), *Chosun Ilbo*, 7 October 1998.

5. Aerospace: Consortium with equal ownership of Hyundai, Daewoo, and Samsung
6. Vessel Engines: Consortium of Korea Heavy Industries, Samsung, and Daewoo

On 24 March 1999, the leaders of the corporate sector publicly pledged to implement the Big Deals in seven industries (semiconductors, airplanes, oil emulsification, oil refinery, trains, and so on) as well as the swap of Samsung Motor and Daewoo Electronics.[45] Most of the big five will downsize into almost half of their pre-IMF size, SK with plans of selling off approximately 75.6 percent of its companies. Such effort is to streamline their business activities to core industries, thereby increasing competitiveness, reducing the debt/equity ratio, and increasing foreign capital.[46] The *chaebol*'s restructuring plans versus actual progress as of 30 April 1999 are presented in table 5.4. The table shows that Samsung, LG, and SK have made significant progress, and moreover, LG and SK have exceeded their goals for 1998. Hyundai and Daewoo, on the other hand, have been problematic, and in particular, Daewoo's debt/equity ratio increased in 1998. This was a strong warning sign for Daewoo's current plight of near bankruptcy due to massive foreign debt.

However, both the government and the *chaebol* expressed dissatisfaction concerning the final agreement, the government because of existing overlapping and excessive investment, and the *chaebol* due to the presence of the government's strong hand in restructuring processes.[47] The implications of corporate restructuring on future OFDI is that the *chaebol*'s net-profit-oriented business management has changed to strong emphasis on cash-flow-oriented business strategy. In addition, the *chaebol* is pursuing not quantitative, but qualitative OFDI by both limiting future OFDI projects and reviewing the existing ones to increase productivity and efficiency in its OFDIs.[48]

Conclusion

Globalization, or *segyehwa*, was an important policy objective of the Kim Young Sam administration. Although the Kim administration did not provide large subsidies and incentives for businesses to engage in OFDI,

---

[45] "The Train Named the Big Deals Is Arriving at a Terminus" (in Korean), *Hankuk Ilbo*, 24 March 1999 .
[46] "The Big Five's Corporate Restructuring Plans" (in Korean), *Hanguk Kyungje Shinmun*, 9 September 1998.
[47] *Chosun Ilbo*, "The Big Five's Corporate Restructuring Plans."
[48] The information is drawn from the Korean Ministry of Finance and Economy website: http://www.mofe.go.kr.

Table 5.4 Corporate Restructuring Plan (1998) and Progress (1999)* of the Five Largest *Chaebol*

		Main Industries	Member Firms	Debt/Equity Ratio—%	IFDI (in Millions of U.S. Dollars)
Hyundai	plan	Automobiles	62→32 (Nov. '98)	553→194	8,484 (until 2002)
		Construction	79→26 (April '99)		
		Heavy and chemical			
		Electronics			
		Financial institutions and services			
	progress	Sold shares of 8 firms			
Daewoo	plan	Trade	36→10	572→449	7,000 (until 2000)
		Automobiles		474→199.5	
		Heavy			
		Electronics			
		Securities and investment			
	progress	Sold Seoul Hilton Hotel and shipbuilding		474→527	
Samsung	plan	Electronics	66→40	370→197	5,000 (until late 1998)
		Trade			
		Financial institutions and services			
	progress	Sold part of electronics		366→276	
LG	plan	Chemical and energy	53→38	505→199	6,500 (until late 1999)
		Electronics and telecommunications			
		Financial institutions and services			
	progress	77% of IFDI received ($160 million)		508→341	
SK	plan	Energy and chemicals	41→22 (until 2002)	466→200	2,000 (until late 1999)
		Information and telecommunications			
		Construction			
		Transporation and distribution			
	progress	Debt/equity ratio improved		466→355	

Note: Restructuring plans as of November 1998, and progress as of 30 April 1999.
Sources: Ministry of Finance and Economy, *Korea's Economic Reform Progress Report* (1998); KIEP, *Status Report of Restructuring of the Five Business Groups* (website information, 30 April 1999).

it eliminated government restrictions, which had prohibited OFDI in the past. However, such a passive policy did not provide the environment for all businesses to engage in OFDI. In South Korea, where the wealth has been heavily concentrated in a handful of large *chaebol*, the outcome was not surprising. The largest investors of OFDI were found among the largest five *chaebol*, and in particular Daewoo (rank four), Hyundai (rank two), and Samsung (rank one).[49]

An investigation of the OFDI patterns of South Korea in general and the *chaebol* in particular shows that, as Dunning and others have argued, the *chaebol* were seeking the host nation's location-specific advantages, as well as access to advanced technology. However, the majority of OFDI from South Korea's leading *chaebol* was in the former, which suggested that the latter might still appear too costly an investment for research and development. The study's findings imply that Daewoo is the only *chaebol* to have become a truly global enterprise, while Hyundai and Samsung are still more firmly rooted in South Korea, and their management styles reflect strong control from their headquarters. However, Daewoo's local autonomy of its OFDIs has a darker side. A more critical evaluation of its OFDIs reveals that although Daewoo was successful in incorporating local employees into management, it suffered from a weak financial condition. Daewoo's OFDIs were based largely on debt from international financial institutions, and moreover did not show short-term profits. Thus, the evaluation of Daewoo's OFDIs is mixed at best. An aggressive pioneer in overseas markets, whose investments are not sound, may be only short-lived if external economic conditions deteriorate or if transparency in management is actively pursued. All this came to the fore in July 1999, when Daewoo was forced to present its plans to break up the group into several sections, and to actively seek buyers for them. Excessive foreign debt and the inability of Daewoo to repay it were seen as the main cause of Daewoo's collapse. Daewoo was under the control of the debtors' committee as of the end of July 1999.[50]

The 1997 financial crisis and the subsequent IMF Stand-By Agreement package project economic hardship in the near future. The Kim Dae Jung administration has been promoting corporate restructuring plans as part of broader economic restructuring to conform to the IMF's conditions for the loan, and to revitalize the economy. According to Standard & Poor's report announced on October 1998, corporate restructuring lags behind other restructuring plans such as those of financial

---

[49] Ranking is based on the total assets in 1997.
[50] "'Global Management' of Daewoo on the Operating Table" (in Korean), *Kyung Hyang Shinmun*, 27 July 1999.

institutions.[51] Thus, corporate restructuring is far from over. The ongoing negotiation for "Big Deals" among the largest five *chaebol* needs to be successfully completed. These Big Deals should not only help reduce the number of business sectors for each *chaebol*, but should accompany transparency in management and an overall improvement in efficiency. Without the latter two, corporate restructuring will simply change the map of the *chaebol* without significantly upgrading its management to meet international standards.

Continued expansion of OFDI (successful OFDI, of course) and transformation of domestic enterprises into TNCs will determine the prospects for South Korea's economy in the next century. Although the recent financial crisis has negatively affected OFDI at least in the short term, globalization is a trend that will be difficult to overturn. In fact, the rapid rise of IFDI and stabilization of OFDI figures in 1998 suggest that globalization efforts have restarted since the financial crisis. Globalization, which is more than the politically motivated agenda of the Kim Young Sam administration, will be an important tool of survival for relatively small economies such as South Korea. Therefore, although the *chaebol*'s OFDI is smaller than before the financial crisis, OFDI will inevitably become important in the twenty-first century. Corporate globalization involves increased IFDI and OFDI, and internationally competitive management practices. It appears that in this globalized economy and this globalized world, the South Korean enterprises have no choice but to go global.

[51] The information is drawn from *Joong Ang Ilbo*, 16 November 1998.

CHAPTER 6

Overcome by Globalization: The Rise of a Women's Policy in South Korea*

Seungsook Moon

Globalization has emerged as a key word in contemporary discourse on social change since roughly the second half of the 1980s.[1] This recent attention paid to globalization reflects multiple and complicated processes of transformation that have uneven impacts on the lives of hundreds of millions of women and men in different societies. In the United States we are bombarded by commercial and policy rhetoric about a "global village." This rhetoric, however, is more than empty prolixity in that more and more people live with an increasingly heightened awareness of the world as a whole as a consequence of the accelerated development of the global market and the proliferation of the consumer culture, which has been made possible by technological advances in telecommunications and transportation. The effect has been a compressed world.

By the summer of 1995, the term *segyehwa* (globalization) was in vogue in the local discourse on national development represented by the South Korean mass media. Since the postmilitary civilian regime under President Kim Young Sam introduced the term when it announced it as its policy goal in November 1994, globalization has been generally used to suggest the nationalist imperative to develop South Korea as one of the leading countries in the world. In this regard, it resonates such precedent slogans as "national modernization" and "creation of an advanced nation," widely circulated during Park Chung Hee's and Chun Doo Hwan's regimes, respectively. Indeed, some argue that like the "new Korea" of 1993 and "internationalization" of 1994, *segyehwa* is an updated

* Research for this chapter was made possible by Vassar College Faculty Research Grants and a General Research Grant from the American Philosophical Society.
[1] Roland Robertson, *Globalization: Social Theory and Global Culture* (London: Sage, 1992), 8.

version of a manipulative political slogan to obfuscate urgent problems, namely, the escalation of American pressure to open domestic markets for agricultural commodities and the rush-hour collapse of the Great Songsu Bridge in Seoul, which left scores of people dead.[2] In line with this criticism, it is necessary to point out that the South Korean regime produced the discourse of *segyehwa* around when the Uruguay Round (1986–95) was completed by the formation of the World Trade Organization (WTO) and ratification of the series of free-trade agreements among nation-states.

This chapter examines the relationship between globalization, including the local discourse of *segyehwa* on the one hand, and women's policy as an institutionalized mechanism for promoting gender equality and women's welfare on the other hand. The emergence since the mid-1980s of the women's policy deserves attention because it demarcates the shifting relationship between women and the state in South Korea from one characterized by dominance and manipulation to one potentially based on negotiation. First, it is necessary to clarify what globalization means because it involves intricate and multiple processes of transformation that increase not only homogeneity, through global capitalism and consumer culture, but also heterogeneity and complexity through international migration.

This discussion is followed by an analysis of certain aspects of globalization relevant to the rise of the women's policy in South Korea. This policy emerged in the context shaped by economic, political, and sociocultural globalization, which has engendered positive and negative consequences for the empowerment of women as a social group and as political actors. Economic globalization tends to have mixed, but largely negative, effects on women. On the one hand, it has incorporated a large number of women, predominantly as production workers, into highly exploitative global factories and subcontracting workshops. This type of employment is characterized by not only low pay but also extreme insecurity in that women workers may lose their jobs at any moment when transnational capital moves elsewhere in search of cheaper and unorganized labor. On the other hand, economic globalization is accompanied by the relative decline of the nation-state's sovereignty, which can create space for the emergence of nonstate actors, including women. In association with the current milieu of political democratization in South Korea, the decline of the state's power contributes to the rise of women as a significant electoral power and thereby enables them to demand the state's commitment to gender equality and women's welfare through a

---

[2] Jun-man Kang, *Kim Young Sam ideologi* [Kim Young Sam's ideology] (Seoul: Kaimagowon, 1995), 144, 158.

women's policy. Sociocultural globalization also enhances the demand for a women's policy by popularizing the universalistic notion of women's human rights.

Yet, the viability of the women's policy as an institutionalized vehicle of women's empowerment is contingent upon several factors, among which the development of grassroots-based women's movements and economic globalization are particularly significant. The first decade of the women's policy in South Korea testifies that its substance would have been lost were it not for a vibrant women's movement with feminist consciousness capable of making use of new space opened up by globalization. At the same time, the current Asian economic crisis suggests that economic globalization poses a big challenge to the fledgling women's policy by temporarily reducing resources and escalating the trend toward privatization in the long run. It is the argument of this chapter that economic globalization has exerted ambivalent effects on the development of the women's policy, whereas the effects of political and sociocultural globalization have been largely positive.

Conceptualizing Globalization

Globalization may be conceptualized in terms of the processes of societal transformation shaped by "a shift in the spatial form and extent of human organization and interaction to a transnational or interregional level."[3] It involves not only an economic dimension but political and sociocultural dimensions as well. It consists of complicated processes that simultaneously homogenize and heterogenize the world. For instance, while global capitalism spreads consumer culture throughout the world, or at least throughout certain regions,[4] increasing transnational migration generates multicultural and multiethnic societies within nations. Similarly, while multinational corporations and transnational agencies play conspicuous roles in trade, finance, and international relations, there is no evidence of nation-states withering away.[5]

---

[3] David Goldblatt, David Held, Anthony McGrew, and Jonathan Perraton, "Economic Globalization and the Nation-State: Shifting Balances of Power," *Alternatives* 22 (1997), 271.

[4] There are growing studies of the urban middle class in rapidly industrializing Asian societies. See Richard Robison and David S. G. Goodman, ed., *The New Rich in Asia: Mobile Phones, McDonalds' and Middle-class Revolution* (New York: Routledge, 1996), and Denise Potrzeba Lett, *In Pursuit of Status: The Making of South Korea's "New" Urban Middle Class* (Cambridge, MA: Harvard University Press, 1998).

[5] See Saskia Sassen, "Toward a Feminist Analytics of the Global Economy," in *Globalization and Its Discontents* (New York: The New Press, 1998). She argues globalization has transformed the nation-state by eroding its sovereignty as a

Economic globalization, advocated by neoliberal economic theory, is arguably the most conspicuous aspect of globalization that can be traced back to the emergence of modern capitalism in the period of the decline of feudalism in Europe.[6] A crucial event that shaped recent economic globalization was the Uruguay Round, which resulted in the formation of the WTO and a series of regional free-trade agreements.[7] The Uruguay Round was initiated by the United States under the auspices of the General Agreement on Trade and Tariffs (GATT) in 1986 and lasted until 1995. It was an attempt to establish a set of rules for world trade characterized by "freedom" of investment and trade in all industrial sectors and the protection of intellectual property rights. It has generated the impetus for opening domestic markets in banking, insurance, and telecommunications, in which First World countries have unequivocal advantages over Third World countries.

In fact, discourse on globalization tends to reduce it to economic liberalization that sanctifies the "free" flow of capital and commodities.[8] Along with "free" trade and finance, multinational corporations and foreign direct investment epitomize the tendency to cross territory-based national boundaries.[9] Although it has lifted the standard of living of tens of millions of people in Asia, neoliberal economic globalization has generally produced negative impacts upon the livelihoods of a far larger number of workers and peasants.[10] In particular, the undermining of daily

political and economic unit and therefore the territory-based nation-state constitutes a strategic site where the impacts of (economic) globalization are acutely observed.

[6] Immanuel Wallerstein, The Modern World System (New York: Academic Press, 1974).

[7] The WTO, a major outcome of the ten years of the Uruguay Round, is composed of 117 voting members with power to enforce General Agreement on Trade and Tariffs (GATT) provisions. Like the U.N., it has independent jurisdiction to oversee trade in agriculture, manufacturing, services, investment, and intellectual property protection. That is, it has global governing powers and its rules are binding on all members. The Uruguay Round has also led to regional free-trade agreements – e.g., the North American Free Trade Agreement (NAFTA); the Mercosur Treaty signed among the Southern Cone countries of Latin America; trade agreements by the South African Development Community, the European Community, and the Asian Pacific Economic Community. See Philip McMichael, *Development and Social Change: A Global Perspective* (Thousand Oaks, CA: Pine Forge Press, 1996), 162–9.

[8] Richard Falk, "Resisting 'Globalization-from-above' through 'Globalization-from-below'," *New Political Economy* 2 (1997), 17–24; Barry K. Gills, "Editorial: 'Globalization' and the 'Politics of Resistance'," *New Political Economy* 2 (1997), 11–5.

[9] Goldblatt et al., "Economic Globalization and the Nation-State." 269–85.

[10] Negative effects of global capitalism on lives of women in many Third World countries are well documented by feminist studies of economic development. See Lynne Brydon and Sylvia Chant, ed., *Women in the Third World: Gender Issues*

subsistence and the environment by economic liberalization has generated locally based resistance movements and growing transnational net-
working among them.[11]

The spread of grassroots movements leads to the discussion of a political aspect of globalization, that is, democratization. As the growing body
of literature on popular social movements and civil society documents, a
global grassroots struggle for democratization has revived the discourse
on civil society in many parts of the Third World and the former Second
World.[12] Latin America witnessed the spread of popular movements
against military regimes throughout the 1980s.[13] Similarly, in the former
Eastern Bloc countries there were rising popular protests against totalitar-
ian states throughout the 1980s.[14] Since the 1980s, Asia also has witnessed
growing popular movements – in China, South Korea, Taiwan, and the

in Rural and Urban Areas (New Brunswick, NJ: Rutgers University Press, 1989);
Bina Agarwal, ed., *Structures of Patriarchy: State, Community and Household in
Modernizing Asia* (London: Zed Press, 1988), Gita Sen and Carol Grown, *Devel-
opment, Crises, and Alternative Visions: Third World Women's Perspective* (New York:
Monthly Review Press, 1987); Eleanor Leacock, Helen Safa, and contributors,
eds., *Women's Work: Development and the Division of Labor by Gender* (South
Hadley, MA: Bergin & Garvey Publishers, Inc., 1986); June Nash and Maria P.
Fernandez-Kelly, eds., *Women, Men, and the International Division of Labor*
(Albany, NY: State University of New York Press, 1983); Kate Young, Carol
Wolkowitz, and Roslyn McCullagh, eds., *Of Marriage and the Market: Women's
Subordination Internationally and Its Lessons* (London: CES Books, 1981); Lour-
des Beneria, ed., *Women and Development: The Sexual Division of Labor in Rural
Societies* (New York: Praeger, 1982); Esther Boserup, *Women's Role in Economic
Development* (New York: St. Martin's Press, 1970).

[11] See Falk, "Resisting 'Globalization-from-above' through 'Globalization-from-
below,'"; Donna Dickenson, "Counting Women In: Globalization, Democratization and the Women's Movement," in ed. Anthony McGrew, *The Transformation of Democracy? Globalization and Territorial Democracy* (London: Polity Press in
association with the Open University, 1997); Jeremy Brecher and Tim Costello,
Global Village or Global Pillage: Economic Reconstruction from the Bottom Up (Boston:
South End Press, 1994).

[12] See Robert Fine, "Civil Society Theory, Enlightenment and Critique," *Democratization* 4 (1997), 7–28; John A. Hall, ed., *Civil Society: Theory, History and Comparison* (Cambridge, UK: Polity Press, 1995); David L. Blaney and Mustapha
Kamal Pasha, "Civil Society and Democracy in the Third World: Ambiguities
and Historical Possibilities," *Studies in Comparative International Development* 28
(1993), 3–24; Andrew Arato and Jean Cohen, *Civil Society and Political Theory*
(Cambridge, MA: MIT Press, 1992).

[13] Arturo Escobar and Sonia Alvarez, eds., *The Making of Social Movements in Latin
America* (Boulder, CO: Westview Press, 1992); Jane Jaquette, ed., *The Women's
Movement in Latin America: Feminism and the Transition to Democracy* (London:
Unwin Hyman, 1989).

[14] John Keane, ed., *Civil Society and the State: New European Perspectives* (London:
Verso, 1988).

Philippines.[15] Although these movements are heterogeneous in terms of their development and influence and by no means guarantee the advent of more democratic societies, they signify an unmistakable global trend.

This aspect of globalization is influenced by a consciousness of the world as a single whole, especially the universalistic notion of a collective humanity mirrored in the ideas of human rights and women's rights. In this regard, political globalization is closely intertwined with sociocultural globalization. As shown below, U.N.-sponsored women's conferences and related attempts to eliminate discrimination against women have produced a global milieu favorable to the activation of a women's movement in South Korea since the mid-1980s.

However, grassroots movements are not uniformly a democratizing force. The rise of religious fundamentalism as a social and political movement in various regions of the world points to the opposite, particularly for women. Religious fundamentalism in India and the Middle East has risen partly in response to the failure of modernization to bring about comfortable and secure lives for the masses. In parallel, Christian fundamentalism in the United States has developed partly in response to marginalization within or alienation from what significant segments of the lower middle class perceive as a materialistic world.[16] As Donna Dickenson argues, these strands of religious fundamentalism tend to share the emphasis on patriarchal families and women's domestic responsibilities as the linchpins of society.[17]

To be certain, this discussion of the major dimensions of globalization cannot be exhaustive. Rather, it is an attempt to map the contour of the complicated processes of societal transformation. Suffice it to mention here that globalization, to use Roland Robertson's idea, is best understood as "contested" processes. The trajectory of globalization is not

[15] For the development of civil society in China, see Gordon White, *In Search of Civil Society: Market Reform and Social Change in Contemporary China* (Oxford, UK: Clarendon Press, 1996), and Thomas Gold, "The Resurgence of Civil Society in China," *Journal of Democracy* 1 (1990), 18–31. For the South Korean case, see Jang Jip Choi, "Political Cleavages in South Korea," in ed. Hagen Koo, *State and Society in Contemporary Korea* (Ithaca, NY: Cornell University Press, 1993), and Hagen Koo, "Strong State and Contentious Society," in *State and Society in Contemporary Korea*. For the Taiwanese case, see Hun-han Chu, "Social Protests and Political Democratization in Taiwan," in ed. Murray A. Rubinstein, *The Other Taiwan: 1945 to the Present* (Armonk, NY, and London: M. E. Sharpe, 1994). For the Filipino case, see G. Sidney Silliman and Lela Garner Noble, *Organizing for Democracy: NGOs, Civil Society, and the Philippine State* (Honolulu, HI: University of Hawaii Press, 1998).

[16] See Justin Watson, *The Christian Coalition: Dreams of Restoration, Demand for Recognition* (New York: St. Martin's Press, 1997).

[17] Dickenson, "Counting Women In."

predetermined by the inner logic of capitalism. Nor is it a mere extension of a "Western project of modernity."[18] This notion of the contested nature of globalization is well reflected in the complicated interplay between certain aspects of globalization and the development of the women's policy discussed below. It is also mirrored in the South Korean discourse of *segyehwa*, in which globalization is interpreted as raising the status of the nation to put it on a par with the world's "advanced" nations.

The Making of the Women's Policy

In December 1983 the South Korean government officially used the term *women's policy* when it inaugurated the Deliberatory Council for the Women's Policy as a mechanism to mediate policies concerning women to promote gender equality.[19] This new council came under the direct authority of the prime minister. The emergence of the women's policy was harbingered by the establishment in April 1983 of the Korean Women's Development Institute (KWDI), a research center collecting data on women's lives, analyzing problems of discrimination against women, and assessing their needs as potential and actual mothers. The KWDI drafted the Basic Plan for Women's Development and the Guidelines for Improving Sexual Discrimination, later adopted by the Deliberatory Council for the Women's Policy. These two documents became the basis for a women's development plan and were integrated into the Sixth Five-Year Economic Development Plan (1987–91). In March 1988 the government created the Ministry of Political Affairs to arbitrate policies promoting gender equality and protecting maternity. Yet, this new ministry lacks the political power to formulate, implement, and enforce a women's policy on its own.

The first decade of the women's policy in South Korea has been characterized by negotiation and bargaining between the state on the one hand and the women's associations on the other hand. In this inchoate stage of development of the women's policy, the major site of struggle and negotiation has been the enactment of laws and their revision for the

[18] Robertson, *Globalization*, 182.
[19] Such countries in Latin America as Argentina, Brazil, Chile, Costa Rica, Paraguay, Peru, Uruguay, and Venezuela have developed state policies to promote gender equality by addressing short-term and long-term issues affecting women. See Ann Matear, "'Desde la protesta a la propuesta': The Institutionalization of the Women's Movement in Chile," in ed. Elizabeth Dore, *Gender Politics in Latin America: Debates in Theory and Practice* (New York: Monthly Review Press, 1997), 92, and Sonia Alvarez, "The (Trans)formation of Feminism(s) and Gender Politics in Democratizing Brazil," in ed. Jane S. Jaquette, *The Women's Movement in Latin America: Participation and Democracy*, 2nd ed. (Boulder, CO: Westview Press, 1994).

effective elimination of discrimination against women in employment and family/kinship, as well as social life in general. Women working within and outside of the state have managed to legislate the following laws and their revisions: the Equal Employment Act, the Infant and Child-care Act, the Special Law on Sexual Violence, and the Domestic Violence Prevention Act, enacted in 1988, 1991, 1993, and 1997, respectively.[20]

Without an active and dedicated women's movement, the women's policy would have remained melodious rhetoric without any substance. Despite the government's fanfare about the women's policy, the Ministry of Political Affairs has suffered from the lack of a budget, personnel, and decision-making power. In 1997 the women's policy budget represented 0.23 percent of the total government budget.[21] It is noteworthy that this picayune proportion was allocated two years after President Kim Young Sam's pledge to "globalize the quality of life" by establishing the Women's Policy Subcommittee within the Presidential *Segyehwa* Promotion Committee in 1995. Even within the Ministry of Health and Welfare, the budget for women's welfare represented only 0.48 percent of the ministry's budget for 1997.[22] The Ministry of Political Affairs had a staff of thirty-four persons, including the minister and the deputy minister,[23] a grossly inadequate number for a ministry responsible for the nation's women's policy. As mentioned above, this ministry was not given decision-making power. It was allowed to suggest women's policy issues and deliberate women's policy proposals drafted by other ministries at cabinet meetings. Therefore, it was forced to wait without making decisions, when there was a conflict of interests between two or more ministries concerning women's policy issues.

Despite the limitations of the women's policy in terms of organizational resources, its emergence in South Korea symbolizes a significant change in the relationship between women and the state. The conscious focus on gender equality as a policy goal demarcates the rise of women as a potential political force. In the context of electoral democracy, this

[20] This overall assessment is based on the author's four-hour-long conversation with Ms. Han, Myong-suk on 30 April 1998. Ms. Han is the former chairperson of the Korean Women's Associations United, which is a ten-year-old umbrella organization of movement-oriented associations, representing middle-class, working-class, and rural women. It has played a major role in enacting and reforming the four laws during the past decade.

[21] *Yosong Sinmun* (Seoul), 14 November 1997.

[22] Ibid., 4 October 1996. In September 1996, the first postmilitary, civilian government of Kim Young Sam announced an increase in the defense budget and a decrease in the welfare budget. See Korea Women's Association United, *KWAU Newsletter*, 3 (January 1997), 7.

[23] Korean Women's Development Institute, *Yosong Baiksô* (White papers on women) (Seoul, 1991), 317.

means that women are viewed as exercising electoral power. In other words, women are no longer merely the object of state mobilization or the tools to be used to implement a particular policy. This shift heralds a complicated relationship between women and the state in the decades to come.

"Women's welfare projects" and "family planning" policy are two policies that illustrate the old relationship of dominance and mobilization between the state and women. The former has dealt with such under-privileged or stigmatized categories of women as prostitutes, unmarried mothers, female heads of households, and women who left their families. Basically, women's welfare projects have offered temporary residence, minimum living expenses, and job training in conventionally feminine occupations, such as sewing, embroidery, cooking, typing, and so on. Their professed intent is to protect those women who are needy and do not have stable employment to support themselves and their children or other dependents. Yet, this does not directly apply to prostitutes, who are able to make ends meet by performing sex acts. Moreover, job training offered to these women is largely inadequate because it fails to provide independent living. It is noteworthy that these women are considered deviants from the middle-class norm of femininity centering around the role of full-time housewife contained within marriage and the nuclear family. Regardless of the professed goal, those welfare projects have functioned to prevent "deviant" women from going further astray and to redeem their fallen or lost femininity by having them perform feminine tasks.[24]

Family-planning policy initially was directed to far broader categories of women than women's welfare projects, although it has affected lower-class women in rural and urban areas more adversely than it has their upper-class counterparts. Prior to the emergence of the women's policy, family planning (or population control) was the single most important policy directed at women in that it had been officially incorporated into the five-year economic development plans since the early 1960s.[25] As feminist analyses of this policy in various countries have documented,[26] family-planning policy in South Korea was aimed at the drastic reduction

[24] Seungsook Moon, "Economic Development and Gender Politics in South Korea, 1963–1992" (Ph. D. dissertation, Brandeis University, 1994).

[25] Ibid., 233.

[26] For feminist analyses of family planning in Third World countries, see Betsy Hartmann, *Reproductive Rights and Wrongs: The Global Politics of Population Control and Contraceptive Choice*, rev. ed. (Boston: South End Press, 1995). For a comparative collection of case studies, see Faye D. Ginsberg and Rayna Rapp, eds., *Conceiving the New World Order: The Global Politics of Reproduction* (Berkeley, CA: University of California Press, 1995).

of the aggregate birthrate by means of intrusive and often coercive birth control, namely the use of IUDs and sterilization.[27] Under this policy, women's bodies, especially those of lower-class women, were reduced to sites of technocratic control and manipulation. Consequently, in the absence of the idea of women's empowerment, both women's welfare projects and the population-control policy tended to cast women as passive recipients or instruments of patriarchal control.

In sum, mapping the women's policy in the past decade in comparison with earlier policies concerning women highlights two related points. The women's policy remains more rhetoric than substance in the male-dominated structure of institutionalized politics. Nevertheless, it symbolizes the shifting relationship between women and the state, from that of dominance and mobilization to negotiation and exchange.

Aspects of Globalization and the Women's Policy

What are the aspects of globalization that contribute to the emergence and development of the women's policy in South Korea? As argued below, this policy has emerged in the space created by economic, political, and sociocultural globalization. The connection between economic globalization and the emergence of the women's policy can be described as circuitous. As the body of literature on gender and development studies demonstrates, the conditions under which women are integrated into the global economy are far from those promoting women's empowerment. In particular, women's massive incorporation into manufacturing industries has exposed them to extremely exploitative and vulnerable situations.[28] In hiring workers, both global factories and subcontractors working for the former tend to make active use of patriarchal ideologies in local societies. As ethnographic studies illustrate, global factories employ predominantly young single women, whose labor is culturally depreciated and whose employment will not continue after marriage or childbirth.[29] This turnover determined by women's life cycle obviates those firms' paying more for low-skilled tasks performed by workers with seniority. In contrast, subcontractors operating in the informal sector

[27] Mi-Kyoung Lee, "Kukgaui ch'ulsan chongch'aik" [A feminist analysis of the state policy on birth], *Yosonghak Nonjip* 6 (1989), 49–76.

[28] Although agribusiness is a crucial site where large numbers of women are incorporated, I am here focusing on export-oriented manufacturing industries because South Korea has pursued this pattern of economic development.

[29] Seung Kyong Kim, *Class Struggle or Family Struggle? The Lives of Women Factory Workers in South Korea* (Cambridge, UK: Cambridge University Press, 1997); Diane Wolf, *Factory Daughters: Gender, Household Dynamics, and Rural Industrialization in Java* (Berkeley, CA: University of California Press, 1994); Lydia Kung, *Factory Women in Taiwan* (Ann Arbor, MI: UMI Research Press, 1983).

tend to prefer married women who because of their domestic responsibilities are willing to accept piece-rate payment with no benefits.[30] In the period of accelerated economic globalization, a similar type of gender politics in global assembly lines is also observed in the United States. Electronics companies in the Silicon Valley hire immigrant women of color as "cheap" production workers. In their attempt to keep their wages low, these companies exploit a cultural perception among some immigrant communities that factory jobs are not "feminine." These companies encourage women to see their factory work as secondary to their identity as women, and therefore accept it as merely a secondary source of income.[31] In all cases, employers exploit the patriarchal ideology that women are primarily housewives whose earning is supplemental to that of husband-providers. In a nutshell, economic liberalization capitalizes on women's subordination as the second sex.[32]

However, economic globalization can produce an opening for women's empowerment. This type of unintended consequence is observed in the rise of the women's policy in South Korea. In order to trace this link, we need to look at the relative decline of the "developmental state" in South Korea since the late 1970s.[33] Although the Korean

---

[30] See Seung Kyong Kim, *Class Struggle or Family Struggle?*; Ping-Chun Hsiung, *Living Rooms as Factories: Class, Gender, and the Satellite Factory System in Taiwan* (Philadelphia: Temple University Press, 1996).

[31] See Karen J. Hossfeld, "'Their Logic against Them': Contradictions in Sex, Race, and Class in the Silicon Valley," in ed. Kathryn Ward, *Women Workers and Global Restructuring* (Ithaca, NY: Cornell University Press, 1990).

[32] Although it is beyond the scope of this chapter, it is important to recognize that these women are not merely vulnerable victims. They develop various strategies to fight against oppressive working conditions, ranging from labor organizing and collective struggle to individual resistance embedded in daily routine. (See Seung Kyong Kim, *Class Struggle or Family Struggle?*; Ping-Chun Hsiung, *Living Rooms as Factories*; Diane Wolf, *Factory Daughters*; Hwa- Soon Cho, *Let the Weak Be Strong: A Women's Struggle for Justice* [Bloomington, IN: Meyerstone Books, 1988]; Aihwa Ong, *Spirits of Resistance and Capitalist Discipline: Factory Women in Malaysia* [Albany, NY: State University of New York, 1987]; Lydia Kung, *Factory Women in Taiwan*).

[33] The relative decline of state's power vis-a-vis business is well illustrated by the problem of excessive investment in heavy and chemical industries in the late 1970s. The problem of excessive investment in capital-intensive heavy and chemical industries stemmed from the state's failure to control big business. During the second half of the 1970s, economic conglomerates competitively expanded into the strategic industries that the state fostered for economic and military reasons. Since both these conglomerates and the state relied heavily upon foreign loans to develop the strategic industries, the inefficient overlapping of investment led to a major debt crisis. See Jong-Chan Rhee, *The State and Industry in South Korea: the Limits of the Authoritarian State* (New York: Routledge, 1994), 3–4.

state has played the central and directive role since the inception of economic development in 1962, its ability to preside over the national economy, especially big business, has gradually dwindled over time. As Eun Mee Kim argues, the relationship between the state and big business, which was initially fostered by the state, has shifted from dominance through symbiosis to competition. Furthermore, the state itself has undergone transformation from a comprehensive developmental state to a limited developmental state.[34]

This relative decline in the state's ability to intervene in the economy generated an impetus for the state to modify its economic policy and look for a new policy area where it could maintain or even expand its sovereignty. Chun's regime, which followed the sudden collapse of Park's regime in 1979, discovered economic liberalization as a stone that could kill three birds at once. First, economic liberalization could be used to weaken the ascending power of big business. Second, the regime could distance itself from the previous military regime, which was deeply tainted by its favoritism toward, and collusive alliance with, big business by curbing big-business monopoly. This could ameliorate the government's tenuous legitimacy as a coup d'Ttat regime. Third, it could secure support from the Reagan administration by complying with the latter's economic principles. Therefore, Chun's regime initially embraced the mantra of economic liberalization. It appointed proponents of economic liberalization to major posts on the Economic Planning Board (EPB) and in the Ministries of Commerce and Industry and Finance. The emphasis on economic liberalization was well reflected in the revised Fifth Five-Year Economic Development Plan (1982–6).[35]

This attempt to liberalize the economy was not free from opposition and trouble. Strong resistance came from both the Ministry of Commerce and Industry and the Ministry of Finance, which had vested organizational interests in extensive state intervention in the economy. However, the exposure of the colossal curb-market loan scandal in May 1982, known as the Chang Young-ja incident, played an instrumental role in muffling resistant voices.[36] Kim Jai-ik, the first secretary of the Presidential Economic Secretariat, utilized this scandal to convince President Chun to pursue economic liberalization.[37] Nor did economic

---

[34] Eun Mee Kim, *Big Business, Strong State: Collusion and Conflict in South Korean Development, 1960–1990* (Albany, NY: State University of New York Press, 1997).

[35] Rhee, *The State and Industry in South Korea*, chapter 7.

[36] Chang Young-ja and her husband, former deputy chief of the KCIA, fraudulently manipulated almost $1 billion worth of commercial papers, which represented roughly 17 percent of the total money supply in South Korea at the time, to lend huge loans to big-business corporations.

[37] Rhee, *The State and Industry in South Korea*, 192–5.

liberalization last throughout the entire period of Chun's regime. For-feiting legitimacy since the 1979 coup d'etat, this military regime could not afford to alienate big business for very long. Although it tried to appease the populace by relaxing its grip over the civil society, it failed to gain its support. In preparation for the 1985 National Assembly election, it allowed student activism on campuses and reinstated professors and journalists dismissed for their dissident activities. It also lifted the ban forbidding opposition politicians to participate in political parties. Nev-ertheless, it failed to secure a majority in the Assembly. Facing mounting resistance from labor, students, opposition politicians, intellectuals, and religious activists, the regime resorted to a collusive alliance with big busi-ness. During the second half of its rule, it catered to big business interests by providing favorable loans and business deals in exchange for political donations.[38]

The significance of economic liberalization for the emergence of the women's policy lies in the fact that it forced the South Korean state to look for a new policy area and thereby modify its role by facilitating its decline as a developmental state. In its earlier pursuit of economic liber-alization, Chun's regime stressed for the first time issues of social welfare. It was precisely during the period of economic liberalization between 1981 and 1984 that the organizational skeleton for the women's policy appeared. In the transitional milieu of emphasizing the welfare function of the state, the Korean Women's Development Institute and the Delib-eratory Council for the Women's Policy were formed. The women's policy under presidents Roh and Kim continued to build upon gradually altering the role of the state from that of economic commander-in-chief to that of provider of social welfare. During the period between 1988 and 1989, Roh's administration tried again to pursue economic liberalization by regulating big business as a way to ensure "fair" market competition.[39] In this context, it created the Ministry of Political Affairs, whose main function would be to propose and mediate women's policy issues at cabi-net meetings.

Under Kim Young Sam's rule, the new view of the state as the provider of social welfare continued to play an important role. Moreover, his administration's women's policy was far more affected by economic glob-alization than the previous two regimes. With the escalation of economic globalization after the Uruguay Round, President Kim proclaimed the *segyehwa* project by establishing the Presidential *Segyehwa* Promotion Committee in 1995. Soon the committee formed the Women's Policy Subcommittee and announced the Ten Tasks for the Expansion of

[38] Ibid., 205–7.
[39] Ibid., 234.

Women's Social Participation, whose goal was to realize the three major conditions necessary for women's participation in larger society – provision of accessible childcare, promotion of women's employment, and elimination of sexism in convention and law.[40]

The decline of state power caused by economic liberalization in itself, however, does not automatically lead the limited developmental state to identify a women's policy as its new policy area. There are other contributing factors, and political democratization constitutes a significant impetus for the emergence of the women's policy in South Korea. Unlike the economic development policy, the women's policy deals directly with issues of inequality and discrimination. In comparison with social-welfare policy, which tends to be paternalistic at best, the women's policy is oriented toward the empowerment of women through promotion of equality and maternity protection. This justice-oriented nature of the women's policy suggests that it emerges and continues to develop when women's movements are an essential part of an activated civil society. As mentioned above, in the absence of an active women's movement, a women's policy would have been mere rhetoric or propagandistic display to mislead international communities.[41]

A close examination of the process by which specific women's policy issues are generated reveals the significance of the rise of women's electoral power. In association with economic liberalization, political democratization reduces the relative autonomy of the state in the presence of augmenting popular demands articulated by various social groups, including women. From the point of view of candidates running for high positions in state bureaucracies, women can be an appealing power bloc

---

[40] The ten tasks consist of the following commitments by the government: (1) the expansion and improvement of childcare facilities by sponsoring civilian participation, (2) the introduction of an after-school-hour childcare system, (3) the expansion of the provision of school meals, (4) the use of a quota system to increase women's representation in public-sector employment, (5) the introduction of an incentive system to hiring women in public corporations, (6) the establishment of the social system to pay maternity protection, (7) the expansion and improvement of the occupational training system for women workers, (8) the establishment of a women-related information network, (9) the enactment and enforcement of the women's development law, and (10) the elimination of sexism in mass media. See Eun Cho, *Cholbanui kyonghom cholbanui mosori: yosong choch'aikui hyonjang* [Experience of the half voice of the half: a scene from the women's policy] (Seoul: Miraimidio, 1996), 161–2.

[41] In the absence of active grassroots women's movements, women's policy would have been a contemporary version of the Bengali nationalist discourse on women in colonial India at the turn of the century generated by the male elite. See Partha Chatterji, "The Nation and Its Women," in *The Nation and Its Fragmentations: Colonial and Postcolonial Histories* (Princeton, NJ: Princeton University Press, 1993).

since they make up half of the voters. In order to attract their support, candidates need to identify common interests shared by women of various social groups. Indeed, presidential candidates included a women's policy in their campaign pledges during elections in 1987, 1992, and 1997.

The Equal Employment Law (EEL) enacted in 1988 is the earliest example of this trend. Its enactment appeared as a potential women's policy issue in 1985 when the Ministry of Labor announced its plan to improve employment discrimination against women in hiring, promotion, and retirement. This attention was in response to persistent demands for equal employment voiced by women's associations since the mid-1970s. Soon, the KWDI began to study equal-employment laws of other countries in preparation for an equal-employment bill. However, Chun's regime did not allow the result of this study to be made public, presumably because it was "too early" for Korean society to enforce such a law. In contrast to this dismissal, in December 1986 the ruling Democratic Justice Party (DJP) picked up the issue of equal employment and monopolized the drafting of the bill without extensive consultation with various social groups. The DJP intended to use it as election bait.[42] While this incident reveals the regime's politically expedient use of a women's policy, it also suggests women's emergence as an electoral power.

It was not until the 1997 presidential election, however, that candidates showed visible interest in a women's policy. Throughout the election year, presidential candidates mentioned women's policy issues in their campaign pledges in order to appeal to women voters. Four major political parties – the New Korea Party (NKP), the National Congress for New Politics (NCNP), the New National Party (NNP), and the Democratic Party (DP) – crafted their own women's policy by organizing public discussions and consultation with professional groups.[43] All of them addressed the following items: establishment of a ministry of women, a quota system to increase women's representation in politics and employment, a housewives' pension program, school meals in junior high and high schools, allocation of 6 percent of the GNP for the education budget, free education for preschool children, and a domestic-violence prevention law. They differed from one another in terms of the specific structure of a ministry of women, the quota percentage, and whether and how soon to eliminate the household-head system propped up by family law.[44] Furthermore, the ruling NKP drafted a revision of the EEL and specified a 20 percent quota for women representatives in the party

[42] *Dong-A Daily* (Seoul), 11 January 1989.
[43] *Yosong Sinmun* (Seoul), 7 March, 19 September 1997.
[44] Ibid., 14 November 1997.

constitution.[45] In alliance with women politicians, women's associations made serious efforts to consolidate women's voting power. They organized street campaigns to encourage women to vote for candidates committed to implementing specific women's policies.

The growth of the women's movement, particularly the emergence of educated middle-class women working within or closely with the state, is crucial to the making of the women's policy in South Korea and benefits significantly from the sociocultural globalization, characterized by the growing awareness of the world as a whole in general and the increasing acceptance of gender equality as a measure of social development in particular, propagated by U.N.-sponsored global conferences on women and related activities. Discourse on the women's policy generated by mass media, women's associations, and the state tends to make frequent reference to Korean women's status measured in terms of certain global standards. For instance, the local discourse on *segyehwa* stresses the elevation of the quality of life in Korean society to meet global standards. The Women's Policy Subcommittee of the Presidential *Segyehwa* Promotion Committee argues that a women's policy is necessary in order to raise the status of Korean women to a global level. Although standardized categories devised to measure women's status may not be accurate indicators of empowerment of women of different socioeconomic backgrounds, ranking is frequently used in the highly status-conscious Korean society as a convenient way to locate South Korean women in the world. The discourse points out the imbalance between the nation's economic standing and its social standing measured in terms of women's status. As a result of three decades of compressed industrialization, prior to the current economic crisis South Korea was the twelfth-largest trading country, ranked twenty-seventh in terms of GNP, and thirty-eighth in terms of the per-capita income among 132 nations. Yet, according to the *World Competitiveness Report* prepared by the International Management Development and the World Economic Forum, South Korea was lowest in terms of sexual equality in employment. It ranked last among forty-one countries in 1994 and among forty-eight countries in 1995.[46] According to the *1995 U.N. Human Development Report*, South Korea ranked ninetieth among 116 nations in terms of the "Gender Empowerment Measure" (GEM), based on women's representation in parliament, administrative and managerial positions, and professional and technical positions and on their share of earned income.

Since its inception in the mid-1980s, the women's policy in South Korea has been influenced by the perception of the nation's status in the

[45] Ibid., 6 June 1997.
[46] Eun Cho, *Cholbanui kyonghom cholbanui mosori*, 31.

pecking order of nation-states in the world. The growing awareness of the
status of Korean women in the world is facilitated by Korea's membership
in transnational or regional agencies. After South Korea became a member of the Organization for Economic Cooperation and Development
(OECD) in 1997, considered to be a passport to the pantheon of "developed" or "advanced" nations, women's associations aptly publicized that
the overall percentage of economically active women in South Korea
(47.9 percent in 1994) was below the average among OECD members
(59.8 percent in 1994), and the unemployment rate among college-
educated women under twenty-five in South Korea was far higher than in
other member countries.[47] The 1997 International Parliamentary Union
(IPU) convened in Seoul also highlighted the extremely low representation of Korean women in the National Assembly. According to the *U.N.
Human Development Report*, women occupied 1 percent of parliamentary
seats in South Korea in 1994, making it 109th among 116 countries. Similarly, it ranked nineteenth among twenty-two Asian countries.[48]

The growing concern with Korean women's status in the world has
been enhanced by a series of global or regional conferences on women
held in South Korea or elsewhere. In particular, the U.N. initiatives on
gender equality since the late 1970s have created a global milieu favorable to the emergence of the women's policy in South Korea. In 1979, the
U.N. General Assembly adopted the Convention on the Elimination of
All Forms of Discrimination against Women, which recommended that
national governments establish a professional organization to conduct
research on women's issues. Following this advice, at the Copenhagen
Conference in 1980 the South Korean government announced its plan
to establish a research center for women's development studies. The
opening of the KWDI and the establishment of the Deliberatory Council
for the Women's Policy in 1983 occurred in response to the global
emphasis on gender equality propagated by the United Nations. In
December 1984 South Korea ratified the convention and thereby
became obliged to develop a women's policy to eliminate discrimination
against women.[49] No Sin-yong, the prime minister in 1985, commented
that this direction was intended to be an "adjustment to the global
trend."[50]

[47] *Yosong Sinmun* (Seoul), 5 September 1997.
[48] Ibid., 18 April 1997.
[49] In 1996, the majority of nations in the world signed and ratified this con-
    vention. Interestingly, the United States, with Afghanistan, is one of the two
    countries which signed it but did not ratify it. There are a handful of countries
    which neither signed nor ratified it. See Joni Seager, *The State of Women in the
    World Atlas*, 2nd ed. (New York: Penguin Reference, 1997), 14–5.
[50] KWDI, *Yosong baikso* [White paper on women] (Seoul, 1985), 570.

It is noteworthy that the state and the women's movement, represented by educated, middle-class women working within the state, define global standards for women's status differently. For the political elite, living up to these standards is a way to achieve international recognition and prestige. As a latecomer to the pantheon of modern nation-states, South Korea has always been concerned with emulating institutional standards set by First World countries. The best example of this is the pursuit of rapid national development through capitalist industrialization and urbanization. However, the national prestige sought by the elite cannot be achieved by economic growth alone. There must also be improvements in the culture and social spheres. Women's status has become another criterion for recognition and prestige. The women's movement, on the other hand, uses global standards to justify its reform movements. For example, women's associations have proposed legal and policy reforms to promote gender equality and the protection of motherhood in the name of a "global trend."

The South Korean government's involvement in the U.N. initiatives on gender equality appears to have been consistent for the past decade. South Korea participated in the U.N. Council on Women's Status as an observer in 1986, was elected to the council in 1993, and was reelected in 1997. Months after the Fourth World Conference on Women in Beijing in 1995, the government enacted the Women's Development Law.[51] Based on this law, the government recently launched the First Five-Year Women's Development Plan (1998–2002) which comprises twenty women's policy issues in six areas.[52]

A word of caution is needed here to avoid a possible misconception about the U.N.'s role in empowering women. It is crucial not to overemphasize the significance of the U.N. initiatives to the growing trend toward gender equality in South Korea because they are deeply enmeshed in political and economic interests of countries controlling the United Nations.[53] Moreover, South Korean women, especially the majority of lower-class women, have little institutional power to challenge them. This is why the sustainable development of grassroots-based women's movements is essential to the success of the women's policy beyond the inchoate stage of establishing an institutional base within the state.[54]

---

[51] KWAU, *KWAU Newsletter*, 2 (August 1996), 2.

[52] *Yosong Sinmun* (Seoul), 24 October 1997.

[53] U.N. conferences on women and development have been criticized for this problem. See Sabine Haüsler, "Women and the Politics of Sustainable Development," in ed. Wendy Harcourt, *Feminist Perspectives on Sustainable Development* (London: Zed Books Ltd., 1994).

[54] The significance of local grassroots women's movements to viability of feminist politics incorporated in the state cannot be overemphasized. There are always

Similarly, the South Korean government's apparent concern with gender equality, reflected by its positive responses to a series of the U.N. initiatives, does not guarantee its continued commitment to the women's policy as an institutionalized vehicle to achieve gender equality and women's welfare. Like any other government, it is largely motivated by political rationality to maintain or expand its power. In the current context of political democratization, this tendency makes it willing to negotiate with various social groups, including women. The success of the women's policy in the near future is contingent upon various factors, ranging from the strength of local women's movements to the vicissitudes of the global economy. In particular, the unexpected turn of the Korean economy as part of the current Asian economic crisis deserves attention since it poses a major challenge to the fledgling women's policy in South Korea.

Ramifications of the Current Economic Crisis for the Women's Policy

In December 1997 the global mass media reported the collapse of the South Korean economy stemming from an enormous corporate debt of more than $120 billion, most of which was due in 1998. The Korean currency and stock market plummeted as the foreign currency reserve in the Bank of Korea was being depleted and the *chaebol* were on the verge of failure to repay the interest on foreign loans. Apparently, the IMF emergency bailout fund was the band-aid solution to this seemingly sudden disaster. The timing of this crisis was quite ironic in that it roughly coincided with the election of Kim Dae Jung, who professedly aspired to become "the first President eradicating sex discrimination." Regardless of his good intentions and his personal commitment to gender equality, the women's policy faces a daunting challenge under the IMF regime, which requires a radical restructuring of the Korean economy to make it a full-blown market economy based on competition and privatization.

With the election of Kim Dae Jung in December 1997, women's associations and women's policy bureaucrats expressed high hopes for the establishment of a ministry of women or its equivalent since as a presidential candidate Kim had repeatedly pledged to promote women's

dangers of cooptation of middle-class feminists working within the state and their separation from local movements. See Ann Matear, "'Desde la protesta a la propuesta': The Institutionalization of the Women's Movement in Chile," in ed. Elizabeth Dore, *Gender Politics in Latin America: Debates in Theory and Practice* (New York: Monthly Review Press, 1997) and Sonia Alvarez, "The (Trans) formation of Feminism(s) and Gender Politics in Democratizing Brazil," in ed. Jane S. Jaquette, *The Women's Movement in Latin America: Participation and Democracy,* 2nd ed. (Boulder, CO: Westview Press, 1994)

welfare and gender equality.[55] In particular, he had given priority to the creation of an upgraded ministry of women in his women's policy. However, by late January 1998 the new regime had announced the replacement of the Ministry of Political Affairs with the Special Council on Women, which would report directly to the president.[56] Despite persistent demand and much protest from women's associations, the Special Council was officially launched with fifteen standing members and a staff of forty-one in March 1998. Like its predecessor, this council is not granted power to initiate and formulate policy or to implement and enforce it.[57]

The disappointing development described above results largely from the economic crisis that has jettisoned the hope and the plan for establishing and expanding welfare services in the midst of massive bankruptcies and layoffs. Prior to the crisis, women's policy bureaucrats in collaboration with women's associations struggled to secure resources to implement women's policy. The crisis debilitates their leverage in this negotiation and thereby hampers their ability to make the best use of the space created by economic, political, and sociocultural globalization. The entire women's policy budget, including monies of the Ministry of Health and Welfare and the Ministry of Labor to be used for programs related to women, fell from 0.23 percent of the total government budget in 1997 to 0.22 percent in 1998.[58] Although this may be viewed as a slight decrease, it portends a possibility of cutbacks in the near future as the economy is being contracted for some time before its recovery.

In particular, the economic crisis has aggravated the problems of women's employment and unemployment because women are the last hired and the first fired in the patriarchal society, in which the man, as husband, is supposed to be the head of the family and its provider. In response to the soaring number of women workers first laid off since December 1997, the Equal Employment Promotion Headquarters of the Women's Democratic Friend Association started a movement to advocate women workers.[59] As the protesting voice of women's associations became louder, the government adopted some punitive measures against employers who violated the Equal Employment Law, but it could not monitor underhand practices of laying off women.[60]

---

[55] In November 1997, eighty-eight women's organizations coordinated televised discussions of four presidential candidates on women's policy issues under the auspices of the Women's Newspaper Company. Kim Dae Jung appeared best informed on women's issues and showed most sympathy to them in these discussions.

[56] *Yosong Sinmun*, 6 February 1998.

[57] Ibid., 13 March 1998.

[58] Ibid., 14 November 1997, 10 July 1998.

[59] See its house organ, *Pyongdung* (Equality) 9 (January/February 1998), 25–9.

[60] Yosong Sinmun, 23 October 1998.

The crisis may lead to increased resistance to the women's goal of revising the EEL, which has been the most contentious women's policy. This reflects the fact that the economy presides over other areas of social life in a modern capitalist society and therefore economic interests are often the most fiercely protected and contested. Since its enactment in 1988, the EEL was partially revised in 1989 and 1995. The women's movement has attempted to revise it because it still contained inadequate or ambiguous clauses. For instance, the law fails to address equal pay for work of equal worth, covert forms of discrimination, and sexual harassment as a form of employment discrimination. Moreover, it lacks punitive measures grave enough to deter practices of discrimination against women in employment. Attempts by the women's movement to revise the law have met with strong resistance and opposition from the powerful Board of Economy and Finance, business owners, and sometimes the Ministry of Labor.[61] In the presence of strong resistance, revised bills drafted by political parties in collaboration with women's associations have been overshadowed by other bills, and their discussion in the National Assembly sessions has currently been postponed.[62]

In the long run, the economic crisis can dismantle the women's policy by accelerating privatization, which tends to undermine the state's capacity to provide welfare services. In the West, we have seen shrinking welfare states in the process of economic globalization since the 1980s.[63] This tendency portends a tortuous path for the women's policy in South Korea. It also suggests a complex relationship between globalization and women's empowerment. On the one hand, women have benefited from political and sociocultural globalization, identified respectively with grassroots movements for democratization and the popularization of universalistic ideas of human rights and women's rights. On the other hand, as argued above, economic globalization has had largely negative effects on the development of the women's policy as an institutionalized mechanism for women's empowerment. While it indirectly generated an opening for the women's policy by undermining the state's sovereignty over the national economy, this very decline has harnessed the state's ability to pursue the women's policy by shrinking the resources available for this new policy area. Absent radically altered priorities in terms of the allocation of public resources, the future of the fledgling women's policy does not seem very bright.

[61] Ibid., 8 August, 4 July 1997.
[62] Ibid., 28 November 1997.
[63] V. Spike Peterson, "The Politics of Identification in the Context of Globalization," *Women's International Forum* 19 (1996), 5–15.

CHAPTER 7

Strangers in the Midst of Globalization: Migrant Workers and Korean Nationalism

Katharine H. S. Moon

The jury is still out on whether globalization is a step away from or toward nationalism. The process of globalization appears to be a dualistic process; while bringing markets, firms, and peoples together, it also provokes "defensive and exclusionary nationalism."[1] Korea is no exception. Hyun Ok Park characterizes *segyehwa* as a "new language of nationalism," a call for a "de-territorialized national community among Koreans" in order to "gain leadership in the international community."[2] On the other hand, Lee Hong-koo decries Koreans' tendency toward economic and cultural nationalism and exhorts Koreans to "accept that national, racial, cultural and religious pluralism is the fundamental principle of globalization."[3] Globalization is introducing new economic actors from different countries and cultures to Koreans and challenging Koreans' self-identity as a homogeneous people. Since the early 1990s, migrant workers who come mostly from China and South and Southeast Asia have been visible in the workplaces and streets of Korea. Even in the face of the Asian financial crisis and the Korean government's measures to expel them, there were an estimated 370,000 migrant workers in Korea in February 1998.[4] Their legal status and civil rights as foreigners and workers have been hotly debated in Korea, and their presence in general

---

[1] David Goldblatt, David Held, Anthony McGrew, and Jonathan Perraton, "Economic Globalization and the Nation-State: Shifting Balances of Power," *Alternatives* 22 (1997), 270.

[2] Hyun Ok Park, "Segyehwa: Globalization and Nationalism in Korea," *Journal of the International Institute* (Internet version), 4, no. 1 (1996).

[3] Hong-koo Lee, "Attitudinal Reform toward Globalization," *Korea Focus* 2, no. 2 (1994), 87.

[4] *Migration News* 5 (March 1998). See the following internet site to access each month's report: http://migration.ucdavis.edu/By-Month/By_Month.html.

has raised questions about what constitutes the Korean workforce and nation and who is a Korean.

There is no doubt that globalization – namely, the increased and intensified movement of capital, goods, and information across national borders – has generated the demand for and movement of foreign workers into South Korea. The literature on globalization says little about the migration of peoples, but Pang Eng Fong and Linda Y. C. Lim point out that "market forces, policy liberalisations, information flows and technological developments are causing labour markets in Asia to become increasingly internationalised on a global as well as regional basis."[5] In Korea's case, internal changes resulting from the last four decades of rapid economic growth – near full employment, high wages and education levels, industrial restructuring – have helped create the demand for imported labor since the late 1980s, particularly in the "3D" (dirty, dangerous, and difficult) jobs. The shortage of workers has been most severe in labor-intensive sectors such as construction and small-sized, low-skilled manufacturing, such as garment and shoe manufacture. In 1990 a Ministry of Labor survey revealed that only eight out of ten jobs were filled in manufacturing establishments with ten to twenty-nine employees. A Korea Labor Institute survey of 240 firms in and around Seoul in October 1993 found an overall vacancy rate of 9 percent. The same survey found that while fewer than 5 percent of larger firms (200 or more workers) employed foreign workers, the smallest firms (fewer than 30 workers) tended to depend on the migrants, who constituted about 25 percent of the workforce.[6]

Most of the migrant workers have come from other Asian countries, such as China, the Philippines, Malaysia, Thailand, India, Pakistan, Bangladesh, Myanmar, and Nepal. The majority are illegal residents, having entered on tourist visas and overstayed their time limits or having abandoned their designated job places as "industrial trainees." Only those who have been allowed into the country as trainees since 1992 have limited legal status. By June 1996, Korea had hosted about 57,000 such trainees.[7]

[5] Pang Eng Fong and Linda Y. C. Lim, "Structural Change in the Labour Market, Regional Integration, and International Migration," in Organization for Economic Cooperation and Development (OECD), *Migration and the Labour Market in Asia: Prospects for the Year 2000* (Paris, 1996), 67. See also P. J. Lloyd, "Globalisation, Foreign Investment, and Migration," in eds. P. J. Lloyd and Lynne S. Williams, *International Trade and Migration in the APEC Region* (New York: Oxford University Press, 1996).

[6] Young-bum Park, "Labour Market Developments and Foreign Worker Policy in the Republic of Korea," in OECD, *Migration and the Labour Market in Asia*, 171–2.

[7] Hye-kyung Lee, "The Employment of Foreign Workers in Korea: Issues and Policy Suggestions," *International Sociology* 12, no. 3 (1997), 353.

This program, which the government hoped would alleviate the labor shortage and offer skill training to workers already employed by Korean companies overseas, has fallen short of meeting the original goals. For one thing, since large companies tended to have overseas activities, most of the trainees tended to be placed in large companies in Korea, where demand has not been high. To address this problem, in 1994 the government established a recruitment program, administered by the Association for Small Businesses, to meet labor needs for small and medium-sized enterprises. But despite the productive intentions of the government and businesses, employers often have been left stranded since trainees have tended to desert their officially sanctioned workplaces in search of higher pay; their basic monthly wage in 1994 was between U.S. $200 and $260, while that of illegal workers was about $500.[8] On the other hand, while working for substantially less than a Korean counterpart in the same job, the trainees had few employee benefits and little protection. But the primary structural shortcoming was that the limitations of the trainee program helped generate a large population of illegal workers, a population the government was unable to control. According to the Labor Ministry, by 1 October 1997, 34 percent of trainees had abandoned their authorized place of employment, and 26,600 of the 78,000 trainees admitted since 1993 had reneged on their work contracts.[9]

Illegal workers have fared poorly in Korea. Although they are usually offered more money than trainees and make more than they would in comparable jobs in their home countries, because of their illegal status they are easy targets of employer abuse. The most widely reported problem is that employers withhold workers' pay and/or passports in order to keep them tied to the shop beyond their desired stay. Human rights groups in Korea, such as the Joint Committee on Migrant Workers in Korea (JCMK), the umbrella organization for migrant workers' advocacy groups, have referred to such practice as a modern form of slave labor.[10] A 1996 report on human rights in South Korea compiled by Sarangbang (Center for Human Rights in South Korea) adds that "escaped trainees when caught are put in chains and handcuffed, starved and usually, severely treated."[11] Moreover, until late 1993, they were not eligible for industrial-accident insurance. (There are numerous accounts of such workers losing a limb or experiencing some other sort of injury or illness owing to poor work conditions but not receiving proper medical treatment because they feared deportation and/or lacked money.) In

---

[8] *Business Korea* (Internet version), September 1994.
[9] *Migration News* 4 (November 1997).
[10] See http://kpd.sing/kr.org/jcmk/situation/situation_eng.html.
[11] *Sarangbang* (Center for Human Rights in South Korea), *Human Rights in South Korea – A Perspective from within* (Seoul: Korea Human Rights Network, 1996).

addition, foreign workers, both legal and illegal, ethnic Korean or not, have confronted social discrimination in the workplace and the general public.

Korea is not the only Asian nation faced with deciding how to treat migrant workers. Japan, Taiwan, Singapore, Malaysia, and Thailand also have been dealing with new strangers in their midst since the late 1980s to early 1990s. But each state has different policies and enforcement patterns, influenced by their respective historical legacies in dealing with foreigners and their domestic politics in general. Although Singapore's official policy toward unskilled foreign workers – the granting of work permits and therefore the legal right to work and maintain residence – is considered less restrictive than those of South Korea and Japan, Gary Freeman and Jongryn Mo deem Singapore's control of foreign workers, both legal and illegal, and their employers most severe. In addition to steep fines and prison terms, "since 1989 employers who knowingly hire five or more illegals, and illegal workers themselves, have been subject to caning."[12] This is not surprising given Singapore's insistence on law and order for all people within its borders, nationals as well as foreigners, both Asian and Western. And given Southeast Asian nations' colonial and post-colonial history of ethnic tension and competition, it is not hard to understand why Malaysia was not alarmed by the presence of illegal foreign workers from Indonesia until the economic crisis of 1997: "It is commonly believed that Indonesians make up the bulk of illegal entries since the religion, customs and language that they share with Malays makes detection more difficult. One estimate is that illegal migration adds about 1 per cent annually to the total population and that the Malay-dominated government is hesitant to impede such a politically useful flow."[13]

Among receiving Asian countries, South Korea stands out as the country with the most aggressive democracy movements and labor unrest during the recent decades of Asian ascendance. Japan has no comparable movement for democracy, human rights, and labor rights during these years, and Japanese repression of civil society has been of a softer version compared to Korea's "hard authoritarianism."[14] Taiwan's contemporaneous democratization process was directed more by factions within the Kuomintang than by street fighting between the masses and the police,

---

[12] Gary Freeman and Jongryn Mo, "Japan and the Asian NICs as New Countries of Destination," in eds. Lloyd and Williams, *International Trade and Migration in the APEC Region*, 166.

[13] Ibid., 167.

[14] Chalmers Johnson, "Political Institutions and Economic Performance: The Government-Business Relationship in Japan, South Korea, and Taiwan," in ed. Frederic C. Deyo, *The Political Economy of the New Asian Industrialism* (Ithaca, NY: Cornell University Press, 1987).

as in Korea.[15] It was more about power sharing between different elites – namely, between the aging elites born on the mainland and those born on Taiwan and coming of political age – than about resisting state-capital collusion against labor.[16]

In Korea, however, movements for democracy and labor rights have held hands, albeit somewhat uncomfortably, since the 1960s. Activists in the Urban Industrial Mission (UIM) infiltrated factory floors and dormitories to help raise consciousness and organize workers around the issues of labor exploitation and government repression.[17] After the Kwangju massacre in 1980, the increasingly radical student movement emphasized the ideological and practical need to join forces with labor interests.[18] And the minjung movement, of the same period, highlighted the working class as the primary victims of Korea's oppressive political and economic order.[19] In so doing, major proponents of minjung politics "rationalized, legitimized, and even radicalized the opposition movement . . . in their struggle for democracy."[20] And in the late 1980s, labor played a decisive role in paving the road to democracy. Given the history of democracy movements' incorporation of labor interests and labor movements' pressures for democratization, we need to consider whether and how this legacy affects the contemporary movement for labor and human rights of foreign workers in South Korea in the context of democratization and globalization.

The legacy of democracy movements and the contemporary process of democratization in Korea can serve as interpretive filters for

[15] See Ambrose King, "State Confucianism and Its Transformation: The Restructuring of the State-Society Relation in Taiwan," in ed. Tu Wei-Ming, *Confucian Traditions in East Asian Modernity* (Cambridge, MA: Harvard University Press, 1996), 237–41.

[16] Yun-han Chu, "The Realignment of Business-Government Relations and Regime Transition in Taiwan," in ed. Andrew MacIntyre, *Business and Government in Industrializing Asia* (Ithaca, NY: Cornell University Press, 1994).

[17] See George Ogle, *South Korea: Dissent within the Economic Miracle* (London: Zed, 1990), 86–9; and Wha Soon Cho, *Let the Weak Be Strong: A Woman's Struggle for Justice* (New York: Crossroad, 1988).

[18] Wonmo Dong, "University Students in South Korean Politics: Patterns of Radicalization in the 1980s," *Journal of International Affairs* 40, no. 2 (1987).

[19] See Man'gil Kang, "Contemporary Nationalist Movements and the Minjung," trans. Roger Duncan, in ed. Kenneth Wells, *South Korea's Minjung Movement* (Honolulu, HI: University of Hawaii Press, 1995). Kang distinguishes the different historical and ideological influences on the evolution of the minjung movement. He notes that compared to the emphasis on the colonized peoples of Asia as the oppressed subjects of history during Japanese colonial rule, the post-1950s minjung "shifted decidedly toward a worker-centered constituency" (38).

[20] Hyung-A Kim, "Minjung Socioeconomic Responses to State-led Industrialization," in Wells, *South Korea's Minjung Movement*, 54.

globalization. The Korean experience helps us address the question of how immature democracies adopt, spread, and affect the process of building cosmopolitan institutions, laws, and norms. Relatedly, we can learn how globalization affects the way forces of democratization interpret and shape democratic politics and government. In contrast, most theorists of democracy and globalization, or cosmopolitanism in the case of Immanuel Kant, have tended to focus their analysis on democracy as a form of government rather than on democratization. Kant argued that the proliferation of democratic governments leads to the generation of cosmopolitan values and peace among nations. For David Held, globalization necessitates a new model of democratic government based on "cosmopolitan democratic law."[21] Neither says much about the relationship between the *process of democratization* and globalization.

Some hope that globalization will help forge multilayered cooperative interactions among states and people based on democratic values, including human rights and the rule of law.[22] On the other hand, Held reminds us of the possible threats to, and limitations of, state-based democracy in the age of globalization: "As substantial areas of human activity are progressively organized on a global level, the fate of democracy, and of the independent democratic nation-state in particular, is fraught with difficulty." His caution stems from the fact that the increasing permeability of borders raises questions about the "nature of a constituency, the meaning of representation ... and the proper form and scope of political participation."[23] The flow of foreign workers into Korea is one example of such a need for defining who has what kind of rights in a democratizing and globalizing society. In the following section, I argue that the interaction between globalization and democratization as social and political forces has direct bearing on the status and plight of foreign workers in South Korea and on how Koreans envision or revise their nation.

The Foreign Workers' Movement

Every man has the sacred right of labor and the right is equal.... *Segyehwa* (globalization) movement is a perfect lie, without the equal guarantee of the right to labor and human rights.

Joint Committee on Migrant Workers in Korea (JCMK),
"Message to Korean Government and People."

[21] David Held, *Democracy and the Global Order: From the Modern State to Cosmopolitan Governance* (Stanford, CA: Stanford University Press, 1995).
[22] See Kwame Anthony Appiah, "Cosmopolitan Patriots," in ed. Pheng Cheah and Bruce Robbins, *Cosmopolitics: Thinking and Feeling beyond the Nation* (Minneapolis, MN: University of Minnesota Press, 1998), 91–114.
[23] Held, *Democracy and the Global Order*, 21, 18.

It is striking that foreign workers from South and Southeast Asia and the Korean activists advocating on their behalf explicity frame their call for justice in the normative language of globalization, that is, human rights and democracy. The message from which the above quotation is taken accuses the Korean government and people of treating foreign workers "just as slaves" and "criminals" and therefore not living up to the new moral standards that accompany globalization.[24] In a statement entitled "Our Position on the Police Intrusion on a Migrant Workers' Counseling Office," the JCMK targets the Ministry of Justice in particular: "The Government and the Ministry of Justice should not overemphasize their Globalization motto to go out of control, but should consider working for an end to discretionary crackdown and a just solution to the problems."[25] In decrying a police raid of the Songnam Migrant Workers' House on 3 June 1996 and the ensuing arrest of two illegal workers from Nepal and the head of the Songnam Center, Pastor Hae Song Kim, the JCMK announced that it was "disturbed by the behaviour of the officials and the incredible situation where 500 armed police came to be involved in a situation of this kind, all this despite the Government's call for Globalization and Internationalisation."[26]

The rhetoric employed by the foreign workers' movement calls for the elevation of Koreans' moral character from parochialism to something akin to global citizenship. For example, a JCMK report entitled "The Situation of Foreign Workers in Korea and Measures to Ensure Their Protection" argues that Koreans must recognize the fact that migrant workers have "become our neighbors" and "must find ways to live together harmoniously and overcome the existing system that unfairly persecutes and oppresses migrant workers." And they deliver the exhortation in the name of globalization: "Such steps will ensure better ties with foreign nations and contribute to a smooth globalization process already in the making."[27]

The advocacy movement also links the situation of migrant workers to Korea's commitment to democracy in two ways. First, the JCMK emphasizes that only a public's enlightened attitude toward the human rights of all and subsequent demonstration of its views can motivate the government to take steps toward futher respect of the democratic process. For example, the JCMK reported that as a result of the public's outcries over the mistreatment of foreign workers, "the government implemented a positive measure for the first time in February, 1992 by

[24] Joint Committee of Migrant Workers in Korea (JCMK), http://kpd.sing-kr.org/jcmk/issue/law/law3_2_eng.html.
[25] JCMK, http://kpd.sing-kr.org/sniwh/overseas1.html.
[26] JCMK, http://kpd.sing-kr.org/sniwh/overseas2.html.
[27] JCMK, http://kpd.sing.kr.org/jcmk/situation/situation_eng.html.

granting industrial accident insurance to illegal foreign workers. By September of 1994, the government not only decided to compensate for those who left the country with industrial accidents, but also ordered [the] Department of Labor to take charge in monitoring violations of labor laws."[28] The lesson such activists are communicating is that to speak out against abuses of foreign workers is a way to empower the civil society and to make the government accountable to democratic politics in Korean society. It is significant that such exhortations seem to reflect actual public concern and not just movement rhetoric. Chae Young Ki, a research fellow at the government-funded Korea Labor Institute, stated that "Koreans were shocked when they heard that [foreign] workers had their passports taken from them, and hadn't been paid, and had been beaten.... I think the Korean people felt humiliated."[29]

Second, the advocacy movement for foreign workers has cast the government's treatment of the foreign worker movement and the foreign workers themselves as a form of political repression. Their depiction of the government's crackdown on escaped trainee-workers and illegal workers reminds the observer of police and military violence against antigovernment activists in the democracy movements of the 1970s and 1980s. In a statement entitled "Our Position on the Police Intrusion on a Migrant Workers' Counseling Office," the activists claim,

> The Ministry of Justice is applying a heavy-handed crackdown in order to solve the rising number of escaping industrial trainee-workers.... Outside the Shiwa Industrial Complex a foreign worker jumped from the second floor of a building to evade arrest from Immigration Officials.... The violence of the Immigration Officials is indiscriminate [sic], they continue to harass churches, shelters for workers, and human rights supporters who help those workers who do not receive their salaries and are victims of factory accidents. Recently at the Protestant Foreign Workers Counseling Center in Ansan, 10 Immigration Officials threatened to arrest [anyone] who came to the Center.[30]

In the aftermath of the police raid on the Songnam counseling center, the demands the JCMK had made to the government concerning foreign workers expanded to include the rights of advocacy groups to counsel individuals and carry out public campaigns.[31] In short, the call was for the government to observe democratic practice by leaving civic organizations alone to do their work.

The foreign workers' movement has also adopted some symbolic and coalitional patterns that characterized democracy movements of the

---

[28] Ibid.
[29] *Far Eastern Economic Review*, "Help Wanted," 2 February 1995, 36.
[30] http://kpd.sing-kr.org/sniwh/overseas1.html.
[31] Ibid.

past. For starters, the first public protest (called a strike by the *Far Eastern Economic Review*) by foreign workers and their Korean advocates, which lasted for nine days in January 1995, took place in front of Myongdong Cathedral, the traditional stage and refuge of antigovernment protesters in the era of military rule.[32] What started as a demonstration by thirteen Nepalese trainees led to a meeting of more than thirty-eight grassroots and labor organizations to form "an association for the human rights protection of foreign industrial trainees."[33] And as in the democracy, labor, and human-rights movements of the 1970s and 1980s, Christian churches have stepped into the activist fray. The Conference of Protestant Churches and the National Conference of Pastors and the Committee for Human Rights have joined the JCMK's fight.[34] In 1995 the Korean National Council of Churches, the umbrella organization for Christian churches in South Korea, awarded Pastor Hae Song Kim, who had been seriously injured in the police raid on the Songnam Center, that year's Human Rights Award.[35] In addition, migrant workers from the Philippines have used Catholic churches as both meeting places and moral agents through which to mobilize their forces in challenging abuse and mistreatment. Mainstream Christian churches have stepped into the civic action on this issue at the initial stage of organization and protest – quite a contrast to their relative quiescence and inaction in the earlier movements for democracy and labor rights. Whereas earlier church activism was limited to radical, fringe segments, such as the Protestant-based UIM and the Catholic-based Young Christian Workers, or JOC,[36] many mainstream church leaders today accept taking a political role on behalf of those oppressed by labor and human-rights abuses as integral to their mission.

Globalization and Nationalism

Depending on the nature and scale of the oppositional term, the national self contains various smaller "Others" – historical others that have effected an often uneasy reconciliation among themselves and potential others that are beginning to form their differences. And it is these potential others that are most deserving of our attention because they reveal the performative principle that creates nations – the willing into existence of a nation which will choose to privilege its difference and obscure all of the cultural bonds that had tied it to its sociological kin.

Prasenjit Duara, "Historicizing National Identity, or Who Imagines What and When"

---

[32] *Far Eastern Economic Review*, "Help Wanted," 2 February 1995, 36.
[33] JCMK, http://kpd.sing.kr.org/jcmk/situation/situation_engl.html.
[34] JCMK, http://kpd.sing-kr.org/sniwh/overseas2.html.
[35] JCMK, http://kpd.sing-kr.org/sniwh/overseas1.html.
[36] Ogle notes that the total number of clergy affiliated with the UIM "probably did not exceed twenty five over the decade" of the 1960s (see Ogle, *South Korea*, 87).

We think of Korea as our second homeland. Help us love the country. We are waiting for a time of peace and an equal chance of labor. We have [done] our best to make a sacrifice of ourselves for our poor fatherlands and also to do a certain role for the development of Korean economy. And we will continue to do this. A world in which everyone can be happy, isn't it the purpose of a true democracy?

JCMK

The statement in the second epigraph above appears in the JCMK's "Message to Korean Government and People," dated 26 April 1996. In it, foreign workers link their call for better treatment with the purpose and future of Korean democracy. They also identify themselves as outsiders who contribute to the development of the Korean economy and consciously or subconsciously raise the issue of their relationship to the Korean nation. This is a strange predicament for Koreans to consider. The Korean "miracle" was built on the myth and reality of self-sacrificing Korean nationalism[37]: through their willpower and blood, sweat, and tears, hard-working South Koreans themselves rebuilt Korea out of its tragic past. But is there room today for *foreign* blood, sweat, and tears in the Korean "miracle"? Who can take credit for future successes? Who will be held responsible for the setbacks and failures? What is the meaning and content of the Korean nation if foreigners purport to claim Korea as their "second homeland"? Does Korea's pursuit of democracy and globalization require that it alter its definition of *nation*?

The status and treatment of foreign workers in Korea is inherently related to the idea of nation and qualifications for citizenship, not only because of the presence of different faces and ethnicities from South and Southeast Asia but also because of the entry of ethnic Koreans from China and the possible influx of North Korean migrants to the South. Heh-Rahn Park has made the following observation regarding migrant Korean Chinese in South Korea: "Without subtlety these migrants delineated their identity as Koreans, no different from any South Korean in South Korea; the only difference is the legalistic significance defining them as Chinese citizens ... in their Chinese passports." Like the non-Korean foreign workers who assert their valuable contribution to the Korean economy, "Mr. Jang," a Korean Chinese interviewed by Park, claimed his affinity to the Korean nation: "I came here in order to 'develop' Korea ... rather than China." But whereas the Southeast and South Asian migrants tend to appeal to human-rights and democratic norms under globalization, Park's interviews suggest that "Korean Chinese believe that claiming 'Korean sentiments' is an effective way to

---

[37] See G. Cameron Hurst III, "*URI NARA-ISM*": *Cultural Nationalism in Contemporary Korea*, Universities Field Staff International (UFSI) Reports, no. 33 (Indianapolis IN, 1985).

attain Korean civil rights."[38] Hyun Ok Park has remarked that "the relationship between ethnicity and national membership in South Korea is multifaceted and contradictory." On the one hand, "the previous anticommunist, anti-North Korean nationalism . . . has begun to be replaced with a new language of nationalism, *segyehwa*," which "represents . . . a deterritorialized national community among Koreans." Yet, "in the 1990s, the rights of Korean Chinese are no better than those of other foreign migrant workers; they have been denied residential rights and they are subject to penalties if they overstay their visas in South Korea."[39]

But Korean Chinese do have advantages over non-Korean migrants. Despite some variations in language, food, and customs, they share significant commonalities with Koreans, including physical features, that make them stand out less than their South Asian counterparts. In the early stages of Korea's search for foreign workers, the government and employers favored the entry of Korean Chinese into Korea because they would least disturb Korean homogeneity. In 1992 the Korea Apparel Manufacturers' Association recommended to the Ministry of Trade and Industry that "priority . . . be given to ethnic Koreans from China and the Commonwealth of Independent States, in light of language problems."[40] In commenting on segregation in the foreign labor market, Hye-kyung Lee states that "Korean Chinese tend to work in various industries and in better-paying jobs relative to other Asians" and that these jobs are not always characterized by the "3Ds."[41] For example, Korean Chinese men tend to congregate in construction and higher forms of manufacturing work, whereas their South Asian counterparts tend to work in 3D sweatshops. Similarly, in Japan, ethnic Japanese from Brazil and Peru have tended to be favored by Japanese businesses and find themselves in jobs of higher status and pay than nonethnic Japanese in low-skilled or unskilled work. In a report written for the Carnegie Endowment for International Peace, Takashi Oka states that "employment brokers say they have been asked to supply Japanese-Brazilians who look as much like the Japanese as possible"[42] and that they have more work security and

---

[38] Heh-Rahn Park, "Narratives of Migration: From the Formation of Korean Chinese Nationality in the PRC to the Emergence of Korean Chinese Migrants in South Korea" (Ph.D. dissertation, University of Washington, 1996), 152, 168, 175.

[39] Park, "Segyehwa."

[40] *Korea Economic Daily*, 15 September 1992.

[41] Lee, "Employment of Foreign Workers in Korea," 363.

[42] Takashi Oka, *Prying Open the Door: Foreign Workers in Japan* (Washington, DC: Carnegie Endowment for Peace, 1994), 43. Oka observes, regarding the intensity of race consciousness among Japanese, "Japanese-Peruvians, who tend to be more racially mixed than Japanese-Brazilians, complain of job discrimination, with some saying that they receive 30 percent less pay than Japanese-Brazilians." (43)

benefits than illegal Asian workers. For example, ethnic Japanese are the only group of legal, unskilled foreign workers allowed into Japan, and they usually receive renewable one-year contracts. Unlike unskilled laborers who are not ethnically Japanese, they "are paid close to comparable wages ... and are eligible for national health insurance."[43] A 1991 survey by the Overseas Japanese Association found that 79.9 percent of ethnic Japanese worked in factories and 7 percent in offices, and "only 5.3 percent worked in construction, where so many illegal Asians work. In factories, 33.5 and 19.9 percent worked in electric and electronics companies. Only 10 percent were in the tough and dirty metalworking industries."[44] Despite the significant forms of discrimination against ethnic Japanese from South America, analysts note the primacy of maintaining some degree of ethnic and cultural homogeneity, which is reflected in Japan's foreign worker policies.[45]

In contrast to the ethnically oriented policies in Japan, the Korean government does not have any official preferential policy toward Korean Chinese[46] even though they make up the largest single group of foreign workers. I believe the reason lies in the more complicated nature and politics of Korean nationalism and national membership. To welcome diasporic Koreans from China with open arms is to establish a precedent for other would-be entrants of Korean descent, namely, those from North Korea. The South Korean government is extremely nervous about the possible influx of millions of refugees either through the collapse of the Pyongyang regime or through reunification, and knows that Northeast China (the ethnic Korean region) serves as a gateway. According to the June 1994 issue of *Migration News*, recent defectors had reported that owing to food shortages, the Pyongyang government was loosening restrictions on people's movement to allow them to search for food. As a consequence, "experts say that 2,000 North Koreans are hiding in China," although 80 percent are returned to North Korea. (Currently an estimated 150,000 such "food migrants" reside in China.) The article added that thousands of North Koreans were working in Siberia as contract loggers. The implication is that North Koreans would be poised to move to the South via third countries, either China or Russia. South Korea would then be in an awkward position to block Koreans from the North if it had officially opened its door to Koreans from China or Eastern Europe.

Heh-Rahn Park points out that indeed the South Korean government

[43] Ibid., 44.
[44] Ibid.
[45] See Oka, *Prying Open the Door*; Freeman and Mo, "Japan and the Asian NICs"; and Piyasiri Wickramasekara, "Recent Trends in Temporary Labour Migration in Asia," in OECD, *Migration and the Labour Market in Asia*, 108.
[46] Freeman and Mo, "Japan and the Asian NICs," 166.

and people began changing their tune regarding their kin from China starting in the early 1990s. The timing coincides not only with the normalization of relations with the People's Republic of China (PRC) but also with the first presence of foreigners in the workplaces and streets of Seoul. Whereas the Korean government and media had welcomed Korean Chinese as long-lost kin when they visited South Korea in the context of family reunions in the 1980s – Park recounts the *Seoul Sinmun*'s reference to the "call of *hyoruk* ('flesh and blood': literally, bloodshared family)"[47] – the welcome had soured by 1990. From then on, the government and media depicted Korean Chinese as illegal migrant workers and criminals (e.g., fraudulent peddlers of Chinese herbal medicine).[48] With regard to Korean Chinese women who had married South Korean farmers when the Seoul government initiated its policy, Park points out that the Korean public portrayed them as "women obsessed with material wealth who are willing to transgress all moral principles and threaten the very basis of Korean identity."[49] It appears that when Korean Chinese no longer resigned themselves to what Ernest Renan called the "spiritual family" of the past[50] and ventured into the everyday economic and social life of South Korea, they became unwanted strangers.

The possibility of reunification or collapse also affects the government's and businesses' policies toward all foreign workers in Korea because the North represents a large source of labor power that the South could use. Young-bum Park, of the government-sponsored Korea Labor Institute, recommended in a report commissioned by the Organization for Economic Cooperation and Development that "Korea should not open its labour market on a large scale," partly because since "in North Korea, about 50 per cent of the labour force is still employed in the agricultural sector, it could be a major source of unskilled labour when Korean reunification occurs."[51] In a similar vein, the Federation of Korean Industries, which represents *chaebol* businesses, together with the Korea Federation of Small Businesses, opposed the legalization of

---

[47] *Seoul Sinmun*, 24 September 1983.

[48] Park, "Narratives of Migration," 196–201.

[49] Ibid., 222.

[50] In the late nineteenth century, Renan posed, "a nation is a soul, a spiritual principle. Two things, which in truth are but one, constitute this soul or spiritual principle. One lies in the past, one in the present. One is the possession in common of a rich legacy of memories; the other is present-day consent, the desire to live together, the will to perpetuate the value of the heritage that one has received in an undivided form" (Duara Prasenjit, "Who Imagines What and When," in eds. Geoff Eley and Grigor Suny, *Becoming National* (New York: Oxford University Press,1996), 52.

[51] Young-bum Park, "Labour Market Developments and Foreign Worker Policy," 179.

foreign workers through an employment-permit system on the grounds
that it would jeopardize reunification efforts. The *Korea Herald* of 2 June
1997 reported:

> The guarantee of the same labor conditions for foreigners may also pose a
> burden on the government in its push for joint economic projects with North
> Korea or after national reunification.... The employment permit system is
> expected to make it difficult for the government to send foreign workers
> back to their countries when there arises the need for Seoul to hire a massive
> number of North Korean workers after Korean reunification, the federation
> statement said.

In this view, belonging to a nation is defined by (expanded) territorial
boundaries and not just ethnicity or economic contribution.

Through the contemporary movement of diasporic Koreans inside its
borders and the possible integration with the North, South Korea faces a
challenge in (re)defining the nation. It is not clear whether ethnicity,
ideology around division and reunification, or potential economic contribution – what Aiwa Ong calls "Homo economicus" in reference to
wealthy Chinese who are permitted to buy their legal residence abroad[52]
– will determine legal residency or citizenship status. Korea also con-
fronts a challenge to its familiar form of nationalism, one that is derived
from a sense of victimization by and defensiveness toward threatening
powers. G. Cameron Hurst remarks that Korean nationalism exhibits "a
xenophobia that relishes the image of Korea, past and present, as victim
of an outside world intent only upon its exploitation."[53] But with the
presence of foreign workers, especially those from South and Southeast
Asia, Koreans are for the first time being charged with a xenophobic
nationalism that is offensive and oppressive toward others, especially
those who are poorer and weaker. That is, South Koreans, as a people
and a government, are being identified as racists, exploiters, and arro-
gant human-rights abusers intent on using foreigners only for economic
gain. How, then, can Korea distinguish its conduct from that which it
found offensive and abrasive of its former colonizer, Japan, and its "big
brother" *qua* bully, the United States?

During Kim Young Sam's presidency, South Korea's legacy of movements for democracy and human rights dove-tailed the normative
aspects of globalization – pluralism and cross-culturalism – publicized by
Korean elites. The rhetoric of both activists and elites catered to a more
progressive, less parochial conceptualization of nation and relationship

---

[52] Aiwa Ong, "Flexible Citizenship among Chinese Cosmopolitans," in Cheah
and Robbins, *Cosmopolitics*, 144.
[53] Hurst, "*URI NARA-ISM*," 1.

with foreigners. Lee Hong-koo, senior vice president of the Advisory Council on Democratic and Peaceful Unification in 1993, and the current ambassador to the United States, described the need for Koreans to adopt a more cosmopolitan identity for the sake of national survival and power:

> World history teaches us that those who embrace heterogeneous cultures and civilizations have proved to be much more creative, resourceful and reform-minded. As we enter the information age, it is obvious that such culturally adaptive or flexible societies will be able to develop new technologies and innovations at a far more rapid pace. In this regard, we should be worried about the possibility that the myth of national homogeneity might foster cultural and psychological inflexibility, which would be detrimental to our efforts to enhance our technology and knowledge in this era of harsh international competition.[54]

Similarly, advocating "managed globalization" that focuses on individuals' enlightenment, Chung-in Moon states that "inward-looking and xenophobic biases cannot cope with the challenges of spontaneous globalization. Peace education, education for human capital formation and cross-cultural education constitute critical components of managed globalization.... [C]ross-cultural education assists individuals in transforming themselves into citizens of the world. Individuals are the ultimate agents of globalization."[55]

Korean media have been cautious about advocating an open-door policy toward migrant foreign workers, noting that their presence creates "social problems." Yet, they have emphasized the need for better treatment of foreign workers in order to maintain South Korea's "image" as a candidate for membership in the advanced industrialized club in the context of globalization. For example, on 3 May 1994, the *Korea Economic Daily* called for the "gradual legitimization of illegal workers from abroad," and on 9 June it reminded readers that the "official endorsement of manpower import ... is tantamount to accepting the responsibilities as a nation that has come to be widely regarded to have reached beyond its developing phase. As such it is expected to live up to what is right in dealing with migrant workers." The *Korea Herald* on 8 March 1997 expressed this point more explicit in terms of moral outrage and political expedience:

> Protecting the basic human rights of these visitors as well as supplying worker's benefits [are] primary considerations. Some disturbing reports regarding the unfair and inhumane treatment of foreign workers have attracted the concern

[54] Lee, "Attitudinal Reform toward Globalization," 87.
[55] Chung-in Moon, "Globalization: Challenges and Strategies," *Korea Focus* 3, no. 3 (1995), 66.

of international labor organizations as well as misgivings from their respective home governments. The unacceptable conditions that many guest laborers find themselves in should be corrected. While this is clearly a moral issue, the unethical practices of some employers reflect poorly on Korea's international reputation regarding its dealings with alien nationals.... These unfortunate developments have served to fuel anti-Korean sentiment in several Southeast Asian countries such as Nepal and the Philippines.

Although domestic political pressures such as concern over crimes committed by foreigners, small businesses' complaints about trainees who escape in search of higher-paying jobs, and confusion about legal accountability and statistical tracking of migrants undoubtedly influence government policies and actions, the concern over Korea's international recognition and reputation has significantly shaped the governnment's response to foreign workers. Specifically, the government has sought to avoid being seen as repressive or irresponsible. In the fall of 1994 Seoul announced that it would offer assistance to foreign workers who had been deported without being paid back wages or worker's compensation and "requested that the governments of the Philippines, Nepal, Bangladesh and other Asian nations compile complaints from their nationals who were exploited by South Korean employers." The hope was that "these steps will curtail criticism from developing countries about worker exploitation."[56] The concern with international cooperation was also a reflection of Korea's increasing efforts to join international organizations and assert its newfound power. On 3 May 1994, the *Korea Economic Daily* urged greater attention to the human rights of foreign workers, "especially pertinent now that the new World Trade Organization appears to be poised to make an important trade issue of outrageously low wages." Indeed, "France and the US [had] led a drive to insist that the WTO address the issue of 'social dumping,' the notion that trade agreements should include clauses that require trading partners to observe at least minimum worker rights if they want to export their goods."[57]

In a positive sense, the state has been attempting to establish the rule of law more firmly and widely in accordance with international standards. According to *Business Korea*, Supreme Court Judge Lee Kon Ung, ruling in favor of a Filipino citizen who had filed a suit challenging the nonapplicability of industrial-accident insurance to illegal foreign workers, stated, "Under relevant laws, foreign workers must be provided with the same protection that is afforded to Korean workers." The same article remarked, "Observers said the ruling will not only affect [foreign

[56] *Migration News* 1 (October 1994).
[57] Ibid., 1 (May 1994).

workers] from the perspective of health care benefits but in terms of protection of their human rights."[58] This ruling spurred other progressive policies. The Korea Labor Welfare Corporation sponsored a measure that would designate six general hospitals throughout Korea to prepare beds "exclusively for foreign laborers, along with a task team of medical doctors and nurses either versed in foreign languages or experienced in overseas assignment," beginning on 15 August 1994.[59] Beginning in March 1995, the government extended (optional) medical-insurance coverage to its 32,000 legal foreign industrial trainees on a par with the coverage for Korean nationals.[60] And in September 1997, the government revised the Immigration Control Law to grant legal foreign workers the right to organize, bargain collectively, and strike (effective 1 January 1998). Under the revision, foreign workers would gain the right to join unions after completing two years as industrial trainees and would be covered by the Labor Standard Law.[61]

The recent revision of the 1948 citizenship law is the most striking example of the government's (legalistic) responsiveness to the economic realities and normative challenges of globalization. In tracing evolutions of identity as a consequence of migration, Benedict Anderson commented, "As they [migrants] follow in the wake of grain and gold, rubber and textiles, petrochemicals and silicon chips, they carry with them memories and customs, beliefs and eating habits, musics and sexual desires."[62] It is a poignant reminder that the most mundane aspects of human existence become ever more complex and politicized through the mix of new peoples and cultures. According to a Korean YMCA survey of 299 foreign workers conducted in late 1996 and early 1997, 5.7 percent of the males reported having Korean girlfriends.[63] The *Chungang Ilbo* reported on 22 September 1997 that each year between seven thousand and ten thousand Korean women "are choosing foreign men as their lifetime partners."

Such mingling of foreigners and natives has engendered what the *Chungang Ilbo* calls "epoch-making" (*hoekgijok*) change from patrilineage to bilineage in determining nationality.[64] In late September 1997, the Ministry of Justice revised the citizenship law so that any child born in marriage to a Korean citizen, man or woman, would be entitled to Korean

[58] *Business Korea* (Internet version), December 1993.
[59] *Korea Economic Daily*, 13 August 1994.
[60] Xinhua News Agency, 16 February 1995.
[61] *Migration News* 4 (October 1997).
[62] Benedict Anderson, "The New World Disorder," *New Left Review* 193 (May/June 1992), 8.
[63] *Asia Pulse* (Internet version), 18 February 1997.
[64] *Joong Ang Ilbo*, 21 September 1997.

citizenship.[65] It also established gender equality in citizenship requirements for foreign-born spouses of South Koreans by mandating that any such foreigner who has resided in Korea for two years or more can qualify for Korean citizenship. Prior to this change, foreign women who had married Korean men automatically qualified for citizenship, whereas foreign men married to Korean women had to reside in Korea for at least five years before they qualified.[66]

Korean newspapers viewed the revision as a function of "changing times" and globalization. For example, the *Hankyoreh* described it as the "government's attempt to modernize the Korean legal order in accordance with the era of globalization" (*segyehwa sidae e matge uri pobjerul kundaehwaharyonun noryokuro pyongadoenda*)[67]. It saw such actions as part of the Korean government's recent attempts to become part of international organizations and regimes. The *Chungang Ilbo* stated that the revised law was a "reflection of the government's attempt to observe the provisions against the discrimination of women ... as stipulated in the UN Convention for the Elimination of Discrimination Against Women and the International Covenant on Human Rights, which the ROK adopted respectively in 1984 and 1990." Clearly, the presence of foreign workers and the suffering they and their new Korean families have experienced owing to their legal and social marginality spurred such changes. Through this reality and legal recognition, the *Chungang Ilbo* claimed, "the systematic obstacles to international [and interracial] marriage are eliminated and the diversification of the people's blood lineage [*hyoltong*] inevitable."[68]

Upon learning of the revision, Paek Misuk, wife of a Pakistani migrant worker and mother of two Korean-Pakistani girls, elatedly exclaimed, "We want to rear our two daughters as respectable Koreans."[69] Given the history of legal and social discrimination against interracial marriages and children of mixed Korean heritage that ensued from the presence of U.S. soldiers since the Korean War, such an about-face regarding the desirability and legitimacy of ethnic and racial purity is without doubt revolutionary. It is also a reflection of the growing power and voice of the civil society in defining nation and citizen. *Chungang Ilbo* (9/21/97, p. 22) reported that women's groups and human-rights organizations were using the "momentum" of the revision to pressure the government to go beyond the recent revisions and make children born out of wedlock to a

---

[65] See ROK Ministry of Justice, Revised National Citizenship Law, Amendment 5431, 13 December 1997.
[66] *Hankyoreh*, 20 September 1997.
[67] Ibid.
[68] *Joong Ang*, 21 September 1997.
[69] *Joong Ang*, 20 September 1997, 23.

Korean parent and foreign worker eligible for Korean citizenship and its attendant benefits. The rationale is that most foreign workers, who are illegal, have little incentive to register their marriage and children officially because they fear being fined and deported. Another commentary in *Chungang Ilbo* sympathized with the unfortunate plight of such children and also urged that the new citizenship entitlements apply to them. "After all, our blood flows in such children as well," the writer reminded readers.[70]

The Asian financial crisis and the response of the International Monetary Fund (IMF) have triggered renewed nationalist sentiments among many Koreans. Once again the fear of being dictated to and controlled by more powerful foreign nations and organizations has been asserted and articulated in the press and in ordinary conversations. In contrast to the Kim Young Sam regime, which created and led the drive for globalization, Kim Dae Jung's new regime has been put on the defensive regarding its interactions with foreigners. It is accused of serving as a lackey to the IMF, being weak in disciplining the almighty *chaebol* businesses, and reneging on its commitment to democracy. The government is in the position of having to decide which aspects of globalization it will pursue and justify its decisions both to the outside world and at home. For the current Kim regime, pursuing economic liberalization no longer is a matter of joining the forces of globalization to build a stronger, wealthier, more cosmopolitan Korea (as rationalized by Kim Young Sam). It also means putting people out of work, at least in the short run, and accepting more foreigners to influence the economy. Opening Korea's borders and workplaces to migrant workers can no longer be advocated loftily as part of the trend toward economic and cultural globalization; if it is to be successfully defended, it must be promoted as necessary for the survival of the Korean economy. But the government has not taken this approach. Rather, its policy toward migrant workers since the crisis has been characterized by the question, "How can we provide for others when we can't provide for our own?" On 27 December 1997, the Justice Ministry announced that all illegal foreign workers must leave the country by the end of March 1998. As an incentive, it offered a no-fine policy – the Korean government has imposed monetary fines on those foreign workers who have overstayed their visas or entered illegally – for those leaving voluntarily.

Without doubt, this policy was aimed against unskilled foreigners, targeting them as an economic burden rather than a boon, and the rationale was that Koreans could fill the jobs once held by the migrants. In the spring of 1998, the Ministry of Commerce, Industry, and Energy

[70] Ibid., 21 September 1997, 6.

announced its intention to reduce the number of industrial trainees in order to free up jobs for Koreans. In order to facilitate the localization of labor, the government vowed to offer low-interest loans of up to 300 million won to small businesses that replaced foreign workers with domestic workers.[71]

But this apparently nationalistic move by the government – kicking out foreigners to save Koreans – has not received widespread support. Small businesses have voiced opposition to the government's policy of reducing the number of foreign workers in Korea because of the continuing labor shortage in textile, dyeing, metal, and other 3D industries. Despite the rapidly rising unemployment rate in Korea, small businesses have not been able to fill jobs. According to the Central Employment Information Center of the Ministry of Labor, only 6,860 of the 23,084 jobs offered through the center in the first three months of 1998 were filled.[72] The reason was that Koreans were not willing to work for low wages and in "inferior labor conditions." Moreover, improving working conditions and attracting local labor through the use of cheap government loans may also miss the mark. Most of the small and medium-sized firms surveyed by the Korea Labor Institute in October 1993 were found to "shy away from" automation not only because of the large investments involved but also because "their production processes do not lend themselves easily to the change."[73] In addition, Young-bum Park notes significant biases against the hiring of housewives and the elderly, the "reserve" labor force who some believe should be put on payrolls. "Of the responding firms," says Park, "two-thirds claimed that older workers and housewives did not have the stamina for the intense physical labour which younger foreign workers were able to do. About one out of every six claimed that they did try to get older workers but found them unwilling to work for the wages offered."[74]

If the demand for foreign workers continues in Korea even in the context of the crisis, so does the supply. In the first three months of 1998, about 46,569 illegal workers took advantage of the government's no-fine policy and left Korea.[75] But an estimated 100,000 to 150,000 undocumented workers remained. According to interviews with advocates for migrant workers conducted in March 1999, many such workers went

[71] *Korea Herald*, 20 May 1998.
[72] Ibid., 2 May 1998; *Korea Economic Weekly*, 6 April 1998.
[73] Young-bum Park, "Labour Market Developments and Foreign Worker Policy," 175.
[74] Ibid., 174.
[75] Jae-Hyup Lee, "Controlling Foreign Migrant Workers in Korea," *Korean Journal of International and Comparative Law* vol. 26 (December, 1998), 137. Lee cites the Republic of Korea Ministry of Justice, *Statistical Report*, 1998.

into hiding, fearing deportation and subjection to steep fines. Many also lost their jobs or found their wages severely reduced. And these advocates also remarked that they are witnessing increasing flows of foreign workers in 1999. As Reverend Kim Hae Song of the Songnam Migrant Workers' House and Korean-Chinese House commented, on 25 March, 1999 "If the situation for Koreans has been hard because of the economic crisis, the conditions for other Asians (from poorer countries) have been tougher. They still come, thinking they can do better here."

Second, organized labor has refrained from casting migrant workers as the culprits for the growing unemployment problem. Before the crisis, the two major labor unions, the Federation of Korean Trade Unions (FKTU) and the Korean Confederation of Trade Unions (KCTU), had viewed foreign workers as a possible threat to wage stability and the upgrading of technology and environment in workplaces.[76] They were opposed to the rapid increase in the number of illegal workers hired, and preferred to see a limited but regulated importation of foreigners. Benedict Anderson noted that "workers who used to be faithful supporters of the French Communist Party but whose rundown neighborhoods are exactly where the poor immigrants are compelled to cluster" serve as a strong support base for Le Pen's neofascist movement in France.[77] Korean labor movements might similarly cast off their historical identity as proponents of democracy and narrow their vision of political and economic change, advocating gains for themselves at the expense of foreign workers.

The cautious and suspicious attitude toward foreign workers remains, but the crisis and the IMF response seem to have helped identify all laborers, Korean and foreign, as common victims of abusive business practices, government-business collusion, and Western neoimperialism. The FKTU, in its assessment of the status of labor in the crisis, described the difficulties foreign workers had since the government's December call for migrants to leave Korea: "Some ... employers have made use of the forced departure policy of the government and they have delayed wage payment intentionally, dismissed unfairly, and unpaid [sic] the compensation of occupational diseases." The report states that "this matter should be treated [the same as] domestic labour issues" and that the FKTU "has cooperated with the Joint Committee of Migrant Workers in Korea to protect migrant workers' rights." It adds that the FKTU, on behalf of migrant workers, will take legal action "against any companies who took unfair labour practices."[78]

---

[76] *Business Korea* (Internet version), December 1993.
[77] Anderson, "The New World Order," 9.
[78] Pong-Sul Ahn, "Case Study on Employment and Social Safety Nets in Korea," (Seoul, 1998). Ahn wrote the report as director of the International Relations Bureau of the FKTU.

And contrary to the more explicit xenophobia expressed against foreign workers in Malaysia and Indonesia since the crisis, the KCTU's position paper on the IMF bailout strongly warns against blaming migrant workers for Korean labor's troubles:

> There is a danger of a synergy effect between pseudo-nationalism drummed up by chaebol forces and the innocent nationalistic sentiments of ordinary people that may develop into . . . ultra-rightist hysteria. As can be seen from the talk of banning or expelling migrant workers and [an] indiscriminate import boycott campaign, there [are] already some signs of these dangers surfacing. We must remember the historical fact that the German nationalist reaction to foreign intervention following the currency crisis in [the] 1930s led to the growth of Nazism.[79]

The rhetoric employed by organized labor in response to the crisis and the IMF echoes the us-against-them mentality of the 1980s movement for labor rights and democracy. Once again the government is not to be trusted, and once again big business is protected from fully paying for its errors. And once again the dangers to Korea and to Korean labor come from powerful foreigners – the IMF and, by extension, the West. Korean nationalism still seems to be more about resisting the power of the already powerful rather than about beating up on the poor and powerless.

Organizations for migrant workers' rights are echoing Korean labor's sentiments. The JCMK also blames industrialized countries and international organizations like the IMF, the World Bank, and the World Trade Organization for "dominating their neo-colonies." In its call for solidarity to Korean workers and all Koreans on May Day 1998 – to rally together with migrant workers at the May Day rally at Myongdong Cathedral – the JCMK blamed Western-led globalization for the negative consequences to workers' rights and welfare. Specifically, it named businesses' preference for flexibilization of labor as the main threat to workers' rights, job security, and social benefits.[80] The FKTU and the KCTU are also strongly opposed to the Korean government's proposals for labor flexibilization, which has been urged by Korean big businesses and the IMF.[81] The JCMK

---

[79] Korean Confederation of Trade Unions, "IMF Bailout and Employment Crisis: The Labour Response" (Seoul, 11 December 1997). The report was written by Jin-Ho Yoon, adviser to the KCTU IMF Taskforce.

[80] JCMK, "A Solidarity Message for Korean Workers and for All Koreans," 1 May 1998, http://labournet.org.uk/1998/May/jcmk.html.

[81] The Korean government and big businesses have argued that labor market rigidity is an obstacle to the restructuring of the Korean economy. Therefore, they have advocated the creation of a contingency workforce, promotion of fixed contract employment and part-time and at-home work, as well as increased flexibility in the wage structure.

is emphasizing the common interests of domestic and foreign workers rather than their differences. In its May Day solidarity message, the JCMK reiterated the sufferings of migrant workers and reminded Korean workers that "like you and so many oppressed and exploited peoples throughout the world we are determined to forward the struggle against so-called Globalization." They reminded Koreans that the forces of globalization, not migrant workers, are to blame for "taking jobs away from the host people."[82]

The financial crisis aside, the question remains whether foreign workers in Korea will continue to be temporary guestworkers or whether the increasing competitive pressures of globalization and the permeability of borders will make them more long-term inhabitants of the Korean Peninsula. Even with the possible southward flow of migrants from North Korea, the question remains whether and for how long the "backward" northern cousins would endure the second-class status that menial jobs would confer on them. And if talks of Asian integration bear fruit as the forces of regionalism and globalization march onward, then intra-Asian migration will leave lasting marks on the ethnic and cultural histories of Northeast Asian countries such as Korea, as Western colonialism has in Southeast Asia.

It is possible that Korea, like Germany, France, Britain, and the United States, will witness the emergence and stridency of antiforeigner, anti-immigrant, and anti-"other" political groups. But it seems likely that in the short term the legacy of the democracy movements, including organized labor, will temper excessive nationalism aimed against foreign workers from poorer countries. Moreover, the civic movements' adoption of the normative aspects of globalization – human rights and democratization – as a form of resistance to the elite-directed forms of economic globalization may also help thwart nationalistic abuses toward migrant workers.

[82] JCMK, "A Solidarity Message for Korean Workers and for All Koreans."

CHAPTER 8

South Korean Foreign Relations
Face the Globalization Challenges

Chae-Jin Lee

It is indisputable that all nation-states, big and small, are confronted with the pervasive and irreversible process of globalization. *Foreign Policy* asserted in 1997 that "globalization . . . is not a passing phenomenon that affects only international money managers, CNN viewers, or Internet surfers. It represents a profound redefinition of roles, possibilities, and risks around the world that is altering the very nature of international relations and, therefore, the nature of foreign policy. It is taking place at a speed that overwhelms the capacities of most individuals and institutions to grasp all of its implications or realize all of its interconnections."[1] This assertion becomes increasingly important to the specialists and practitioners of contemporary foreign policies.

Moreover, the dynamics of globalization call into question the classic realist paradigm that in an essentially anarchic and conflictual world, the nation-state (which remains the basic unit of analysis in international relations) should pursue the primary goals of its egoistic national interests, protect its sovereign independence, and jealously guard the integrity of its territorial boundaries. This contrasts sharply with another influential view that the intensification of global interconnectedness poses a crisis for the modern nation-state, which is "increasingly unable to fulfill its core functions without recourse to international coopera-tion." For the modern state is trapped within "an extensive web of global interdependence, heavily permeated by international networks and forces."[2] From this perspective, today's market operations have over-shadowed the nation-states' traditional capacities and have forced them to become more cooperative.

[1] *Foreign Policy* 107, Summer 1997, 5.
[2] David Held, *Democracy and the Global Order* (Stanford, CA: Stanford University Press, 1995), 25.

Globalization is manifested in a variety of ways, explains David Held:

> Goods, capital, people, knowledge, images, communications and weapons, as well as crime, culture, pollutants, drugs, fashions and beliefs, readily flow across territorial boundaries. Transnational networks, social movements and relationships extend through virtually all areas of human activity. The existence of global systems of trade, finance and production binds together the prosperity and fate of households, communities and nations across the world. Territorial boundaries are therefore arguably increasingly insignificant in so far as social activity and relations no longer stop – if they ever did – at the "water's edge."[3]

In this era of globalization, the Republic of Korea (South Korea) faces a challenge as well as an opportunity in its foreign relations – a challenge to its realist predilections and highly nationalistic mindset and an opportunity to advance by adapting to the pressures and advantages of complex international interdependence. Yet South Korea's foreign relations in the decade since the Seoul Olympic Games have met with only limited success as Seoul struggled to come to terms with a rapidly changing international reality. Although South Korea has cultivated a generally positive, assertive, and successful diplomatic posture, its failure to respond to the political economy of globalization became all too apparent when the recent financial crisis required massive rescue efforts led by the International Monetary Fund (IMF). The most daunting task faced by South Korea is to go beyond traditional concepts and attitudes and strike a judicious balance between realist imperatives and liberal policy prescriptions. Since this dilemma cuts across a number of specific issue areas, especially diplomatic activities, national security, and economic relations, each issue area will be examined in the context of the globalization challenges.

The Globalization of Diplomatic Activities

If linking a nation-state's public policy with the international community is in fact an important part of globalization, South Korea has already taken purposeful steps, at least for a decade, to lay the foundation for diplomatic globalization. No doubt the Seoul Olympic Games marked a turning point in the unfolding of South Korea's vigorous activities in the world community. The two previous games, in Moscow in 1980 and in Los Angeles in 1984, having been marred by politically motivated boycotts, it was indeed no small feat for South Korea to host the largest-ever international sports event in 1988. It attracted 161 of the 167 members

3 Ibid., 121.

of the International Olympic Committee (including the Soviet Union
and China, with whom South Korea had no diplomatic relations) as participants, the notable exceptions being North Korea, Cuba, Albania,
Nicaragua, Ethiopia, and the Seychelles.

This event provided the South Koreans with an opportunity to engage
in the sensitive diplomacy of international sports programs and to show
their economic, technological, cultural, and social achievements to a
global audience. On the eve of the games, President Roh Tae Woo ebul-
liently called the Olympiad a "grand festival of global harmony" that
transcends differences in race, language, culture, religion, ideology, and
political persuasion. He declared:

> On the rubble of war, our people have worked an economic miracle that has
> astonished the world. They have overcome a national crisis by creating a demo-
> cratic political miracle. Now our people are about to achieve a cultural miracle
> on the Han River by staging a more magnificent Olympic Games than any
> previous ones, most of which were hosted by industrially advanced nations.
> With the Seoul Olympics, we will arrive at the threshold of the developed
> world, the entry to which has been our long-standing national goal. The Seoul
> Games will also provide a powerful impetus to improving our relations with all
> the nations of the world, and especially with North Korea, thereby opening the
> door to unification.[4]

The success of the Olympiad inculcated the populace with a sense of
national pride and a heightened awareness of internationalism. In particular, South Korea set forth a new national image – that of a vibrant,
competent, and efficient modern state – and its leaders developed confidence in their ability to manage domestic and foreign affairs. The
momentum from this "sports diplomacy" helped to accelerate South
Korea's ambitious "northern diplomacy" (*pukbang oegyo*), which aimed at
normalization of its diplomatic and economic relations with the Soviet
Union, China, and other socialist countries. This amounted to a South
Korean attempt to break out of the Cold War system and to overcome its
ideological and security constraints.

The aggressive thrust of South Korea's northern diplomacy made significant inroads in Hungary and other Eastern European countries in
the late 1980s and in the Soviet Union in 1990. In line with his "new
thinking" and *perestroika* and *glasnost* policies, Mikhail Gorbachev was
favorably inclined toward South Korea's diplomatic initiatives and economic promises, and a major breakthrough took place in a brief summit
meeting between Presidents Roh and Gorbachev in San Francisco on 4

---

[4] Roh Tae Woo, *Korea: A Nation Transformed* (Oxford, UK: Pergamon, 1990), 41.

June 1990.[5] At a press conference following the meeting, Roh explained:

> The northern policy of the Republic of Korea will serve to convince socialist countries of the effectiveness and efficiency of freedom and democracy and help them carry out reforms. The ultimate objective of our northern policy, however, is to induce North Korea to open up and thus to secure stability and peace on the Korean Peninsula. The road between Seoul and Pyongyang is now totally blocked. Accordingly, we have to choose an alternative route to the North Korean capital by way of Moscow and Beijing. This may not be the most direct route, but we certainly hope it will be an effective one.[6]

In spite of North Korea's unmistakable warnings and protests, South Korea and the Soviet Union agreed to normalize diplomatic relations in September 1990. This accord immensely satisfied the South Koreans and enabled them to expand their diplomatic horizons and economic operations abroad. South Korea agreed to provide $3 billion in economic assistance to the Soviet Union. In December 1990 Roh triumphantly visited Moscow and held a second summit meeting with Gorbachev. The two agreed that their countries would respect each other's sovereign equality, territorial integrity, and political independence, renounce the threat or use of force, and settle international conflicts and controversies by peaceful means.[7] They also stated that the Moscow-Seoul rapprochement was a step toward eliminating the Cold War in the Asian Pacific region and removing their longstanding confrontational mentality.

The making of Seoul's northern diplomacy with the Soviet Union boosted South Korea's efforts to enter the United Nations, to sign the "Agreement on Reconciliation, Nonaggression and Exchanges and Cooperation" (the Basic Agreement) with North Korea, and to normalize diplomatic relations with China. In addition to making its peaceful overtures toward China, South Korea mobilized its national resources to the maximum extent in an effort to gain China's acceptance of Seoul's diplomatic objectives. South Korea launched an economic offensive toward China when China experienced diplomatic isolation and economic difficulties following the Tiananmen Square incident. Seoul sent large numbers of tourists to China, imported Chinese goods to gain political advantages, and provided financial support for the Asian Games held in Beijing in the fall of 1990. The South Koreans demonstrated a willingness to facilitate China's four modernization programs and open-door policy – perhaps more effectively than Japan or the United States could – and

---

[5] For a discussion of this summit meeting, see Don Oberdorfer, *The Two Koreas: A Contemporary History* (Reading, MA: Addison-Wesley, 1997), 204–12.
[6] Roh Tae Woo, *Korea*, 49.
[7] For the joint statement, see the *Korea Herald*, 15 December 1990.

argued that there was no substitute for full ambassadorial relations to legalize the growing economic linkage between the two countries. The economic imperative was a crucial factor in the Chinese decision to shift to a policy of diplomatic flexibility toward South Korea.

Moreover, the South Koreans persistently argued that China, by normalizing its diplomatic relations with South Korea, would be assuming a genuine role of leadership in Asia and that it was in China's best interests to recognize the importance of the Beijing-Seoul relationship for its own intrinsic merits.[8] A variety of government leaders and discreet emissaries from each country visited the other's capital to pave the way for diplomatic reconciliation.

Compared to the complex diplomatic issues that China had negotiated with Japan (Japanese aggression in China, the state of war, war reparations, the Japan-Taiwan peace treaty) or the United States (the U.S.-Taiwan security treaty and the U.S. military presence on Taiwan and in the Taiwan Straits), China's negotiations with South Korea went smoothly. The South Korean negotiators, newcomers on the Chinese diplomatic scene, enjoyed the distinct advantage of understanding the cumulative record of China's earlier diplomatic negotiations. The South Koreans successfully negotiated with their Chinese counterparts without assistance from America or Japan.

On 24 August 1992 Foreign Ministers Lee Sang Ok and Qian Qichen signed a joint communiqué in which China and South Korea agreed to establish diplomatic relations and to develop "the enduring relations of good neighborhood, friendship and cooperation on the basis of the principles set forth in the Charter of the United Nations and the principles of mutual respect for sovereignty and territorial integrity, mutual nonaggression, noninterference in each other's internal affairs, equality and mutual benefit, and peaceful coexistence."[9] The communiqué declared that the government of the Republic of Korea "recognized" the government of the People's Republic of China as the sole legal government of China and "respects the Chinese position that there is but one China and Taiwan is part of China." On signing the joint communiqué, Lee announced that South Korea would immediately sever diplomatic relations with Taiwan. The communiqué settled on the mild term *respect* in regard to the Taiwan question and incorporated both China's adherence to the Five Principles of Peaceful Coexistence and South Korea's emphasis on the principles of the United Nations Charter.

The consummation of Seoul's northern diplomacy toward the Soviet

[8] For a survey of South Korea's diplomatic relations with China, see Chae-Jin Lee, *China and Korea: Dynamic Relations* (Stanford, CA: Hoover Institution Press, 1996).

[9] *Korea Herald*, 25 August 1992.

Union and China enhanced South Korea's diplomatic status (especially compared to that of North Korea, which had failed to normalize its diplomatic relations with the United States and Japan), prompted its new economic expansion abroad, and assisted its national security interests (see table 8.1). The northern diplomacy weakened the political basis of North Korea's military alliance with the Soviet Union and China and enabled South Korea to enter into a peaceful, friendly, and cooperative relationship with North Korea's two major allies. And the overall regional security environment on the Korean Peninsula was relaxed.

If northern diplomacy epitomized President Roh's foreign relations, President Kim Young Sam championed a "new diplomacy" (*sin oegyo*) that explicitly referred to globalization. In his speech before the Korean Council on Foreign Relations in May 1993, Minister of Foreign Affairs Han Sung Joo placed globalization first when he identified the five fundamentals of President Kim's "new diplomacy": globalization, diversification, multidimensionalism, regional cooperation, and futuristic orientation.[10]

He argued that a new diplomacy must pay greater attention to such global issues as democracy, freedom, human rights, world peace, arms control, poverty, and environmental protection, issues that extend across national and regional boundaries. He proposed that South Korea diversify its diplomatic activities toward all nations, serve as an intermediary between developed and developing nations, and overcome its "one-dimensional preoccupation" with national security issues. Despite Han's sophisticated advocacy of globalization, however, he found it difficult to steer the conservative bureaucracy toward his diplomatic vision. On the first anniversary of his presidency, in February 1994, President Kim said:

> I am chagrined to find that the importance of internationalization is yet to be generally well understood and thus a solid public consensus has yet to be formed on this task. A century ago, we failed to internationalize on our own initiative and were thus forced by others to open up our country. This was why Korea remained backward, soon to be reduced to a colony of a foreign power. If we are not to repeat the mistakes we made 100 years ago at the time of Korea's first opening, we must actively endeavor to accomplish Korea's second opening on our own initiative. We must learn the lessons of history. Instead of deploring the fact that our doors are unlocking, we should ourselves throw open our doors and march out into the wide world. We no longer have any reason to feel inferior to or be afraid of others.[11]

[10] For Han's policy pronouncement, see *Kim Young Sam: Creating a New Korea* (Seoul: Korean Overseas Information Service, 1993).

[11] For President Kim's press conference on 25 February 1994, see *President Kim Young Sam's First Anniversary Press Conference* (Seoul: Korean Overseas Information Service, 1994).

Table 8.1   South Korea's Diplomatic Establishments, 1990 and 1997

	Embassies		Consulates-General		Missions	
	1990	1997	1990	1997	1990	1997
Asia	18	21	13	16	0	2
America	22	20	16	16	1	1
Europe	21	28	6	5	3	4
Middle East	17	14	2	1	0	0
Africa	17	17	0	0	0	0
Total	95	100	37	38	4	7

Source: Ministry of Foreign Affairs.
Note: The figures in the table are from April 1990 and December 1997.

In a 1997 *Oegyo Paekso* [diplomatic white paper], the Ministry of Foreign Affairs renewed its pledge to work toward "globalization diplomacy"
(*segyehwa oegyo*) so that the government could more effectively respond
to fluctuating international situations and make South Korea a "first-rate
advanced nation."[12] As an important part of its globalization diplomacy,
Seoul practiced a "summit diplomacy" when President Kim visited a wide
range of nations during his tenure, attended multilateral meetings
such as the Asia Pacific Economic Cooperation (APEC) meeting and the
Asia-Europe Meeting (ASEM), and hosted a stream of high-level foreign
visitors to Seoul.

Another aspect of its globalization diplomacy concerned the United
Nations and other international organizations. The Ministry of Foreign
Affairs emphasized the growing importance of the United Nations:
"As the U.N. is expected to play a greater role in dealing with such global
issues as disarmament, environment, human rights, and narcotics in the
post–Cold War period, our nation should pursue an active U.N. diplomacy to secure the maximum level of our national interests and to
assume a role commensurate with our position in the international community."[13] This U.N.-oriented global diplomacy enjoyed broad popular
support in South Korea. When polled in May 1995 as to the most important areas of international cooperation for South Korea to pursue in the
United Nations, South Koreans responded with "Preserve international
peace and prevent war" (70.2 percent), "Enhance environmental protection" (45.5 percent), "Emphasize nuclear non-proliferation and disarmament" (43.5 percent), and "Promote science, technology, and space

[12] Ministry of Foreign Affairs, *Oegyo Paekso* [diplomatic white paper] (Seoul,
1997), 108.
[13] Ibid., 109.

programs" (24.9 percent).[14] Only a small number of the respondents mentioned "Solve narcotics problems" (6.6 percent) or "Assist refugees" (4.5 percent).

Even though South Korea had remarkable success in economic development and expressed a desire to become an intermediary between developed and developing countries, it was not a generous donor to the Official Development Assistance (ODA) program. As table 8.2 demonstrates, in 1997 South Korea provided only $185.8 million in ODA, which amounted to a mere 0.04 percent of its GNP.[15] This percentage fell far short of the average ODA given by all members of the Organization for Economic Cooperation and Development (OECD) (0.25 percent) and of the ODA offered by other countries whose economies were comparable to South Korea's – such as Spain, Austria, and the Netherlands. The grant-in-aid administered by the Korea International Cooperation Agency increased from $50 million in 1995 to $53.4 million in 1996 and $54.7 million in 1997. By the end of 1997, South Korea had extended about $1.1 billion in government loans to more than twenty countries, with special emphasis on China, Vietnam, Indonesia, the Philippines, Sri Lanka, Rumania, and Poland. Yet South Korea was not ready to use economic assistance as an effective method for its global diplomacy.

In order to meet the challenge of globalization, the South Korean government organized an intensive English-language program for its personnel, recruited overseas Koreans for its agencies, and set up about a dozen graduate schools specializing in international relations. For the most part, however, the South Koreans often looked upon diplomacy merely as an instrument to protect their country against the encroachments of globalization pressures. They probably agreed with Strobe Talbott's admonition that "global interdependence is affecting the way virtually all governments think about international relations and practice diplomacy. The more engaged in and affected by the process, the more they must change."[16] In spite of the saliency of globalization, however, a large number of career bureaucrats were reluctant to change their entrenched realist or state-centric outlook, and they settled for marginal or incremental improvements when more substantive conceptual and attitudinal transformations were called for. Now that a severe financial crisis has eroded the sanctity of those realist orientations, the shock of the IMF's stipulations may induce paradigmatic changes in their narrow international outlook and orientations.

[14] For a survey conducted by the Ministry of Information on 29 May 1995, see *Chongbu Yoronchosa Charyojip* [A Collection of Government Opinion Surveys] (Seoul: Ministry of Information, 1996).

[15] See *Oegyo Paekso* (diplomatic white paper) (Seoul, 1998), 224–8.

[16] Strobe Talbott, "Globalization and Diplomacy," *Foreign Policy*, Fall 1997, 72.

Table 8.2   South Korea's ODA, 1991–7 (in Millions of U.S. Dollars)

	1991	1992	1993	1994	1995	1996	1997
Bilateral Aid	31.52	45.22	60.12	60.07	71.46	123.31	111.34
Grant-in-Aid	25.04	30.99	32.68	38.45	50.11	53.41	54.77
Loans	6.48	14.23	27.44	21.62	21.35	69.90	56.57
Multilateral Aid	25.96	31.58	51.44	80.15	44.35	35.84	74.48
Contributions to international organizations	5.78	8.01	10.25	12.88	14.82	30.08	29.27
Expenditures to international organizations	11.82	21.47	25.67	62.27	29.71	5.76	35.53
Total	57.48	76.80	111.56	140.22	115.99	159.15	188.82
% GNP	0.02	0.03	0.03	0.04	0.03	0.03	0.04

Source: Ministry of Foreign Affairs.

In his inaugural address in 1998, President Kim Dae Jung stated that "diplomacy in the age of globalization will require a change in ways of thinking. The new ways of thinking must be different from those prevailing during the Cold War. Diplomacy in the 21st century will center around the economy and culture. We must keep expanding trade, investment, tourism and cultural exchanges in order to make our way in the age of boundless competition, which will take place against a backdrop of cooperation."[17] In an attempt to strengthen his government's role in economic diplomacy, he decided to change the Ministry of Foreign Affairs into the Ministry of Foreign Affairs and Trade; the ministry is entrusted with a preeminent role in dealing with international economic issues. President Kim's initial policies show a clear resolve to forgo the realist framework for a more effective liberal approach toward South Korea's external challenges. It remains to be seen how skillfully he can use the IMF system to improve South Koreans' attitude toward globalization diplomacy.

The Security Domain

In contrast to the imperative for globalization inherent in its recent diplomatic and economic activities, South Korea still views the goals and means of its national security primarily in local rather than regional or

---

[17] For the text, see the *Korea Herald*, 26 February 1998.

global terms. The primacy of local considerations is dictated by the legacy of the Korean War and by the existence of a hostile rival – North Korea. The relationship between globalization and national security is complex and fluid, as Wolfgang H. Reinicke suggests:

> As for the security ramifications of the now largely interdependent and rapidly globalizing world, it will no longer suffice for the architects of international security to view international relations along traditional lines. The coexistence of interdependence and globalization places new demands on international security.... The shifting demands on international security will also transform the domestic politics of security policy. The challenges emanating from globalization do not usually threaten a country's overall security or territorial integrity.[18]

Yet the cross-border movement of capital, technology, intelligence, and weaponry and the erosion of a sovereign and territorial nation-state undermine the conventional framework of geostrategic determinism. No responsible managers of national security issues can afford to underestimate the spillover effects of globalization.

The South Korean *Defense White Paper, 1995–1996* defines the goal of its security policy as "to defend the nation against external military threats and aggressions, to support the peaceful unification of Korea, and to contribute to regional stability and world peace." It further states that "globalization in the field of national defense is to implement faithfully the basic duties of our military of safeguarding national territory and national sovereignty by strengthening self-defense capabilities and expansion of the foundation of friendly international cooperation."[19]

This statement is indicative of the South Koreans' continuing allegiance to a realist perspective when it comes to national security requirements. They are not yet prepared to accept the liberal assumption that "economic interdependence would discourage states from using force against each other because warfare would threaten each side's prosperity" or that international institutions such as the United Nations, the International Atomic Energy Agency (IAEA), and the IMF could help overcome selfish state behavior, mainly by encouraging states to forgo immediate gains for the greater benefits of enduring cooperation.[20] Likewise, they do not subscribe to the thesis that military conflicts are less likely now that the Cold War is over, precisely because the Korean Peninsula remains a concrete remnant of Cold War confrontations.

[18] Wolfgang H. Reinicke, "Global Public Policy," *Foreign Affairs*, November–December 1997, 134.

[19] Ministry of National Defense, *Defense White Paper, 1995–1996* (Seoul, 1996).

[20] For the liberal view, see Stephen M. Walt, "International Relations: One World, Many Theories," *Foreign Policy*, Spring 1998, 32.

In fact, the zero-sum mentality and neorealist view still dominate South Korean leaders' perception of their security environment. They take the North Korean threat seriously and are convinced that the Korean Peninsula is one of the world's potential military flashpoints. They surmise that North Korea has substantial critical military capabilities, such as ground troops, jet fighters, bombers, tanks, artillery, armored personnel carriers, attack submarines, amphibious craft, and commando forces. They also conclude that North Korea poses an especially serious threat to South Korea by deploying its forces offensively near the demilitarized zone (DMZ), by developing weapons of mass destruction and missiles, and by basing its aircraft less than six minutes' flight time from Seoul. And they have a lingering fear of North Korea's nuclear ambitions, despite the Geneva Agreed Framework. *The Defense White Paper, 1998* states,

> North Korea's military strategy toward the South is short-term blitzkrieg, which aims at creating great panic in the South in the early stage of a war by launching simultaneous attacks in the forward and rear areas, plunging quickly and deeply into the South with maneuver forces armed with tanks, armored vehicles and self-propelled artillery to take the initiative in the war, thus sweeping the entire South before USFK reinforcements come. Considering the US military capability, South Korea's human and material potential, the ROK-US alliance and their joint military posture, and the sentiment of the UN and the international community, blitzkrieg is regarded as the only strategy it could use for a war.[21]

In order to protect South Korea's vital security interests against any North Korean blitzkrieg, Seoul has adopted several protective measures: modernizing the South's self-defense capabilities (see table 8.3), upholding the mutual security treaty with the United States and maintaining a bilateral deterrent system (the Combined Forces Command), and reducing or eliminating the sources of North Korea's aggressive temptations. Contrary to the government's preoccupation with a threat from North Korea, however, the overwhelming majority of South Koreans were not overly concerned about the national security issues, even if they did believe that North Korea possessed nuclear weapons. In response to a question about what was most important for South Korea's national security and independent defense, they mentioned the need for political stability (38.6 percent), economic prosperity (23.2 percent), citizens' security consciousness (25.1 percent), increased military capabilities (7.9 percent), and expanded diplomatic relations (4.1 percent).[22]

[21] Ministry of National Defense, *Defense White Paper, 1998* (Seoul, 1999), 56.
[22] For a survey conducted by the Ministry of Information on 10 June 1995, see *Chongbu Yoronchosa Charyojip.*

Table 8.3 South Korea's Defense Budget, 1990–8

	1990	1991	1992	1993	1994	1995	1996	1997	1998
Amount (in billions of won)	6,637.8	7,452.4	8,410.0	9,215.4	10,075.3	11,074.4	12,243.4	13,786.5	13,800.0
% Increase	10.4	12.3	12.8	9.6	9.3	9.9	10.6	12.6	0.1
% GNP	4.35	4.01	3.57	3.46	3.48	3.26	3.1	3.2	3.1
% Budget	29.3	27.6	25.3	24.2	23.3	22.1	21.1	20.4	20.0

Source: Ministry of National Defense.

In an effort to promote globalization in the area of national security, the South Korean Ministry of National Defense identified three major tasks: (1) to foster powerful first-rate armed forces, (2) to develop international military relations, and (3) to improve international competitiveness. More specifically, South Korea attempted to gradually reduce its military dependency on the United States and to increase its military interactions with Japan, Russia, China, Poland, and other countries. To the chagrin of the United States, South Korea diversified the foreign sources for its military procurements: It purchased an increasing amount of military hardware from France, Britain, and other Western countries and acquired Russian weapons as repayment for outstanding loans. And South Korea cautiously, but deliberately, initiated limited high-level military exchanges with China.

The South Korean armed forces actively participated in U.N. Peace-Keeping Operations (UNPKO), sending a medical unit to Western Sahara, an engineering unit to Angola, military observers to Georgia and the Indo-Pakistani border, and an officer to the UNPKO office. They accepted the UNPKO "Stand-by Agreement." Hence, South Korea's military personnel contributed to the maintenance of worldwide peace and security and gained valuable experience in international security management.

In addition to its own military posture, South Korea has drawn upon both bilateral and multilateral methods as well as international organizations to resolve its national security problems with North Korea in recent years, particularly the gnawing question of nuclear nonproliferation, the North Korean submarine incident, and the Four-Party Talks for a peace mechanism in Korea.

In view of the passing of the Cold War, the two Korean governments reached a historic milestone in December 1991, when their prime ministers signed the comprehensive Basic Agreement and the Joint Declaration for the Denuclearization of the Korean Peninsula. This declaration stated that the South and the North would not possess facilities for nuclear reprocessing and uranium enrichment and would conduct reciprocal nuclear inspections under the auspices of the South-North Joint Nuclear Control Commission.

The euphoria accompanying both agreements was short-lived, however; in March 1993 North Korea announced its intention to withdraw from the Nuclear Non-Proliferation Treaty (NPT). Since South Korea had no direct channel for managing this nuclear crisis with North Korea, it relied upon the IAEA and the U.N. Security Council to request North Korea's compliance with the NPT regime and then upon the United States to negotiate with North Korea. After a lengthy round of meetings, the United States and North Korea at last signed an Agreed Framework in Geneva on 21 October 1994.[23] In return for the North Korean pledge to freeze its nuclear programs, to remain in the NPT regime, and to resume inter-Korean talks, the United States promised to provide alternative energy supplies (light-water nuclear reactors and heavy oil) to North Korea, to exchange liaison offices between Washington and Pyongyang, and to reduce barriers to trade and investment with North Korea. Even if the South Koreans were not entirely satisfied with the manner in which the Geneva Agreed Framework was ironed out, they accepted its terms and agreed to join the Korean Peninsula Energy Development Organization (KEDO), a multinational consortium to construct two light-water nuclear reactors in North Korea. Hence, South Korea is willing and able to deal with the North Korean nuclear issue in the context of a global nonproliferation regime.

South Korea's role in the KEDO operations did not diminish even when a North Korean submarine with armed commandos ran aground near the eastern coast of South Korea in September 1996. The South Korean government declared it an act of military provocation in violation of the Korean Armistice Agreement and decided to internationalize the inter-Korean rivalry. It brought the matter before the U.N. Security Council and hammered out a statement to be issued by its president. The statement read,

> The Council expresses its serious concern over this [submarine] incident. The Council urges that the Korean Armistice Agreement should be fully observed and that no action should be taken that might increase tension or undermine peace and stability on the Korean Peninsula. The Council stresses that the Armistice Agreement shall remain in force until it is replaced by a new peace mechanism. The Council encourages both sides of the Korean Peninsula to settle their outstanding issues by peaceful means through dialogue, so the peace and security on the peninsula will be strengthened.[24]

Meanwhile, South Korea let the United States negotiate an appropriate resolution with North Korea. Accordingly, the North Korean Ministry of Foreign Affairs issued a statement toward the end of December in which it expressed "deep regret" over the submarine incident and promised to ensure that "such an incident will not recur." In response, South Korean Minister of Foreign Affairs Yoo Chong Ha announced that "the North Korean statement is one that the people of the Republic of Korea can

---

[23] See Leon V. Sigal, *Disarming Strangers: Nuclear Diplomacy with North Korea* (Princeton, NJ: Princeton University Press, 1997).
[24] United Nations Security Council, S/PRST/1996/42, 15 October 1996.

accept, because it recognizes the incident, apologizes and promises to prevent a recurrence."[25] Thus ended the first submarine crisis.[26]

More important than this incident, however, was the question of how to transform the Korean Armistice Agreement into a permanent system of peace on the Korean Peninsula. In the absence of any meaningful regional or global collective security systems, the South Koreans would have preferred to preserve the status quo in the armistice arrangements with their northern counterparts. However, the North Koreans intended to nullify the Korean Armistice Agreement altogether by deactivating both the Military Armistice Commission (MAC) at Panmunjom and the Neutral Nations Supervisory Commission and by requesting a recall of Chinese representatives from the MAC. They wanted to conclude a peace treaty with the United States without South Korea's participation on the grounds that South Korea was not a signatory to the Korean Armistice Agreement.

In order to counter North Korea's maneuver and to prevent U.S.-North Korean negotiations over Korean security questions, South Korea shelved its earlier argument that the two Koreas must decide to convert the Korean Armistice Agreement into a new peace system and took the initiative in advancing a multilateral approach toward Korean peace. At the Cheju summit meeting on 16 April 1996, Presidents William Clinton and Kim Young Sam reconfirmed "the fundamental principle" that "establishment of a stable permanent peace on the Korean Peninsula is the task of the Korean people" and that "separate negotiations between the United States and North Korea on peace-related issues cannot be considered."[27] However, they proposed to convene a four-party meeting of representatives of South Korea, North Korea, China, and the United States, as soon as possible and without preconditions, for the purpose of starting a process aimed at achieving a permanent peace agreement. It was a serious attempt to bring North Korea to the conference table with South Korea. Unlike the tripartite conference Presidents Jimmy Carter and Park Chung Hee had proposed in their joint communiqué of 1979, South Korea and the United States wished to solicit China's participation in a new meeting so that China, as a signatory to the Korean Armistice Agreement, could exert a moderating influence over North Korea and help bring about a satisfactory implementation of any agreement that might be concluded.

[25] *New York Times*, 30 December 1996.
[26] When the second North Korean submarine incident occurred in June 1998, President Kim Dae Jung decided not to refer the matter to the United Nations but to resolve it in a conciliatory manner at Panmunjom.
[27] See *Korea Herald*, 17 April 1996.

Since North Korea continued to insist on peace negotiations only with the United States, it did not initially welcome China's or South Korea's participation in the negotiations. Even though North Korea had been persuaded to accept South Korea's participation, it was clearly reluctant to have China play a direct role in the peace process even though China had saved the North Korean regime by massive military intervention during the Korean War and had signed the Korean Armistice Agreement. North Korea was suspicious of China's ultimate objectives in Korea and apprehensive of the possibility that China would cooperate with the United States and South Korea and take a position contrary to Pyongyang's vital security interests.

Hence, North Korea suggested a "three-plus-one" formula: The three principal parties (both Koreas and the United States) would conduct the peace negotiations, and China would endorse the outcome. The United States was initially amenable to this formula, but South Korea opposed it and supported China's full participation in the peace negotiations. South Korea was concerned about the ominous implications of tripartite peace talks (akin to the Paris negotiations on Vietnam) and hoped that China would play a constructive role in the negotiations.[28] After preparatory meetings in New York led to an agreement on the agenda, time, and venue for formal peace negotiations, the first full session of the Four-Party Talks began in Geneva in December 1997. At the fourth full session held in January 1999, the participants agreed to form two subcommittees to discuss the relaxation of tensions and to establish a peace system. It remains unclear, however, whether the Four-Party Talks can ever produce a new and viable structure for peace in Korea.

Meanwhile, the South Koreans are interested in exploring other multilateral modalities for creating a peaceful external environment conducive to their national security interests. They used the Association of Southeast Asian Nations (ASEAN) Regional Forum (ARF) to obtain international support for their efforts to preserve the Korean Armistice Agreement (until it is replaced by a new peace mechanism), to realize the goal of nuclear nonproliferation on the Korean Peninsula, and to implement the Geneva Agreed Framework and the KEDO agreements. They also proposed a Northeast Asia Security Dialogue (NEASED), in which the two Koreas would join the United States, China, Japan, and Russia in promoting confidence-building measures on the peninsula. Although South Korea hoped that the NEASED would become a Korean functional equivalent of the Conference on Security and Cooperation in Europe (CSCE), it failed to make progress because North Korea, and to a lesser extent China, opposed it.

---

[28] Senior South Korean diplomat, interview by author, Seoul, November 1997.

Ultimately, however, South Korea continues to emphasize the paramount importance of its own armed forces and to regard the United States, the United Nations, and other international organizations and modalities as principally supportive of Seoul's national security. In his inaugural address, President Kim Dae Jung declared, "Our national security has to be independent collective security. Based on the unity of the people and strong armed forces with high morale, we must keep strengthening our independent security capabilities. At the same time we will never neglect collective security, but further reinforce the ROK-U.S. security arrangement. For the establishment of peace on the Korean Peninsula, we will make utmost efforts to bring the four-party meeting to success."[29] As long as the hostility in inter-Korean relations remains unabated, South Korea's realist military leaders are likely to remain skeptical about the prospect that regional or collective security systems or international arms control regimes can guarantee their national security even in the post–Cold War period.

Foreign Economic Relations

The development of South Korea's assertive diplomatic activities and strong self-defense capabilities was closely linked with and inevitably based upon its economic performance. Until recently the South Korean model for economic development was widely heralded as an exemplary case of rapid industrialization in a relatively short time span. In assessing South Korea's economic growth, Ezra F. Vogel concluded that "no nation has tried harder and come so far so quickly, from handicrafts to heavy industry, from poverty to prosperity, from inexperienced leaders to modern planners, managers, and engineers."[30] And Alice H. Amsden praised South Korea as "Asia's next giant."[31]

As a developmental state, South Korea had successfully moved from an import-substitution policy to an export-led growth policy. The government adopted a series of highly centralized five-year economic plans and pursued a neomercantilist policy to protect domestic industries and to expand foreign trade. For this purpose, South Korea encouraged the *chaebol*'s expansionist operations at home and abroad and used its foreign policy as a key instrument for directing its international economic activities.[32] In fact, the South Korean economy expanded at an average rate of 9 percent between the early 1960s and the early 1990s. In 1996

---

[29] *Korea Herald*, 26 February 1998.
[30] Ezra F. Vogel, *The Four Little Dragons* (Cambridge, MA: Harvard University Press, 1991), 65.
[31] Alice H. Amsden, *Asia's Next Giant: South Korea and Late Industrialization* (New York: Oxford University Press, 1989).

Table 8.4 South Korea's Foreign Trade, 1991–7 (in Billions of U.S. Dollars)

	1991	1992	1993	1994	1995	1996	1997
Exports	71.9	76.5	82.2	96.0	125.1	129.8	136.2
% Increase	10.5	6.4	7.5	16.9	30.3	3.8	4.9
Imports	81.5	81.5	83.8	102.4	135.1	150.2	144.6
% Increase	16.7	0	2.7	22.2	32.0	11.2	-3.7
Total							
(exports + imports)	153.4	158.0	165.9	198.3	260.1	280.0	280.8
Balance							
(exports – imports)	–9.6	–5.0	–1.6	–6.4	–10.0	–20.4	–8.4

Source: Ministry of Foreign Affairs.

South Korea became the twelfth largest trading nation (with $280 billion) and had the eleventh largest economy (with $480 billion GNP) in the world; its per capita GNP reached $11,000 (see table 8.4). The rate of unemployment remained below 3 percent, and the rate of inflation was under 5 percent. And the debt service ratio was manageable.

In response to the pressures of liberalization and globalization, the South Koreans advocated a gradual and incremental approach to long-term free trade and grudgingly offered significant concessions to the United States and other industrialized countries in the late 1980s and early 1990s. They insisted that their domestic industries were not yet prepared to confront the sudden challenge of unrestricted international competition and that they had the enormous burden of increasing self-defense capabilities against the North Korean security threat. They also argued that South Korea had experienced a rapid increase in labor wages in the context of political democratization, imported almost all of its crude oil and other essential raw materials for its industrialization, and incurred a chronic trade deficit with Japan. Furthermore, they contended that the appearance of submitting to external pressures might undermine the viability of South Korea's fledgling democratic institutions and fuel a nationalistic backlash.[33]

South Korea's agricultural policy provides a good example of this line of reasoning. Although the relative importance of agriculture declined in terms of its share of the GDP (from 46 percent in 1963 to 6.6 percent in 1995) and its share of the labor force (from 60 percent in 1963 to

[32] For the *chaebol*'s growth, see Eun Mee Kim, *Big Business, Strong State* (Albany, NY: State University of New York Press, 1997).

[33] For South Korea's arguments, see Chae-Jin Lee, "U.S. Policy toward South Korea," in ed. Donald N. Clark, *Korea Briefing, 1993* (Boulder, CO: Westview Press, 1993), 68.

12 percent in 1995), the government continued to allocate handsome subsidies to farmers and to restrict imports of inexpensive agricultural goods.[34] As a result, South Korean consumers paid inflated prices for agricultural products (three times world prices on the average), and the international competitiveness of South Korea's export-oriented manufacturing sectors deteriorated. Even though the situation ran counter to the principles of comparative advantage and fair trade, the South Korean government used its foreign policy to resist growing international pressure for agricultural liberalization and to negotiate an agreement favorable to its farmers. When the South Korean delegation finally had no alternative at the Uruguay Round negotiations in 1993 but to accept a gradual long-term liberalization plan for agricultural imports, the minister of agriculture, forests, and fisheries was forced to resign because of emotionally charged nationalistic protests. The global and regional free-trade regimes – the World Trade Organization (WTO) and the Bogor Declaration (1994) of the APEC – will severely limit Seoul's ability to protect its domestic agricultural interests.

Another example of Seoul's nationalistic economic policy was restrictions on foreign direct investment (FDI) in South Korea. Although South Korea was heavily dependent upon external borrowings and domestic savings to finance its industrial projects, it failed to recognize fully FDI's importance in a globalized economic order. As Sakong Il (a former minister of finance) explains,

> The relatively minor role FDI played in Korea's development can be explained by various factors. First of all, from the suppliers' point of view, Korean policies throughout most of the period were not accommodating enough for foreign management to gain control or exercise autonomy over firms in which they invested. The general fear of foreign domination of Korean industries was too widespread for the government to be accommodating on this matter. This fear is rooted in Korea's history of Japanese colonization. Koreans still tend to cast a suspicious eye on FDI as a means of once again exerting foreign (especially Japanese) domination of Korean industries. It is no secret that Koreans remain highly sensitive to the potential domination of Japanese industrial power within their own country.[35]

Only in the 1980s did the government overcome its fear of foreign domination and adopt a series of laws and regulations to induce FDI in South Korea. It offered attractive incentives (tax holidays, profit remittances, investment protections), removed the limit on foreign ownership of industries in South Korea, and used a negative list system for

---

[34] David P. Vincent and Honggue Lee, *Benefits and Costs of Agricultural Liberalization in Korea* (Seoul: Korea Institute for International Economic Policy, 1997).

[35] Il Sakong, *Korea in the World Economy* (Washington, DC: Institute for International Economics, 1993), 119.

FDI.[36] Moreover, in 1995 it introduced a "one-step" service system for FDI. A year later it announced a five-year foreign investment liberalization plan to reduce the number of restricted business categories from fifty-seven in 1996 to eighteen (e.g., fishing, broadcasting, banking, telecommunications, postal service, railroad, and tobacco manufacturing). From 1992 to 1996 Japan was the largest foreign direct investor with $5,566 million, followed by the United States ($5,091 million), the Netherlands ($1,420 million), Malaysia ($895 million), and Germany ($720 million). Yet FDI played only a marginal role in South Korea: It constituted less than 1 percent of total domestic fixed capital formation in 1996. The continuing apprehension of foreign domination and remaining restrictions, coupled with frequent labor disputes, wage increases, and high real-estate costs, made South Korea less than attractive to foreign direct investors. The conservative bureaucrats in South Korea tended to cling to the old notions of direct market intervention and industrial policy even in the new era of "borderless" global economies. They sought to maintain control over the economy and to regulate the processes of investment, trade, loans, joint ventures, technology transfer, mergers and acquisitions, and other external financial transactions.

On the other hand, the top 30 *chaebol*, which accounted for about 45 percent of the country's total sales, attempted to assert a degree of independence from the government and to exercise freedom of activities and decisions in the global economy. Even though the *chaebol* were overly leveraged and excessively diversified with few competitive advantages, they preferred to use short-term commercial borrowings to finance long-term projects, in part because South Korea's nominal interest rates were much higher than those of its trading partners. And the *chaebol* moved overseas in the 1990s to expand the geographical range of their operations, to achieve economies of scale, to reduce production costs (especially in China, Southeast Asia, and Eastern Europe), and to acquire new ideas and technology.

South Korea's OECD membership led the international financial community to assume that bank loans to South Korea carried no risk of default.[37] The amount of South Korea's foreign borrowings doubled from 1994, when South Korea received its first informal signal to become an OECD member, to 1996, when its membership was officially granted; South Korea's total foreign debts stood at $157.5 billion (33 percent of its GDP) by the end of 1996.[38] In addition, the South Korean banking

---

[36] June-Dong Kim, Impact of Foreign Direct Investment Liberalization: The Case of Korea (Seoul: Korea Institute for International Economic Policy, 1997). A negative list system specifies those industries in which FDI is not permitted.
[37] *New York Times*, 22 December 1997.
[38] *Joong Ang*, 11 April 1998.

system assumed as much as $500 billion in soured loans.[39] Since the OECD membership required open financial markets, the government's regulatory capacity over commercial borrowings and other financial operations decreased in the face of market liberalism and global interconnectedness.

Sakong Il attributes international investors' loss of confidence in the South Korean economy to four factors.[40] First, the South Korean commercial banks' lack of experience in sophisticated modern banking techniques led them to overextend credit to the *chaebol*, which then overinvested primarily through borrowing. As Paul Krugman explains, banks, depositors, lenders, and shareholders in South Korea suffered from "extreme moral hazard," hoping that the government would bail them out in the event of trouble.[41] Without a prudent regulatory and supervisory mechanism, the banks failed in their domestic and international operations. Former Prime Minister Nam Duck-Woo commented that structural flaws in South Korea's financial system surfaced in the course of democratization and globalization.[42]

Second, even though many business firms, particularly *chaebol*, became deeply indebted, they were more interested in expanding their market shares in diversified fields than in maximizing profits through specialization and globalization. The total debts incurred by the top 30 *chaebol* increased by 32.4 percent from the end of 1996 (269 trillion won) to the end of 1997 (357 trillion won); the average debt/equity ratio grew from 386.5 percent to 518.9 percent during the same period.[43] The *chaebol* exemplified the nontransparent nature of the decision-making process and the lack of financial disclosure requirements. In this age of "borderless" economies, the *chaebol*, driven by a desire for empire-building, were bound to encounter difficulties. Third, the government's crisis management capability during Kim Young Sam's presidency was lacking: When he replaced the chief economic planner (the deputy prime minister) seven times and the senior economic secretary to the president six times in five years, confusion, inconsistency, and unpredictability ensued. And rampant corruption, particularly government-business collusion, undermined rational economic decisions.

Fourth, the escalating financial and currency crisis in Southeast Asia during the summer of 1997 prompted anxious international investors to adjust their risk exposure to emerging Asian markets as a whole. South

[39] *New York Times*, 30 June 1998.
[40] Discussion with Sakong Il, Los Angeles, March 1998.
[41] See *Fortune*, 16 February 1998, 86.
[42] Duck-Woo Nam, "The Financial Crisis in Korea," *Korea Economic Update*, January 1998.
[43] *Chosun Ilbo*, 16 April 1998.

Korea's credit standing suffered accordingly, and foreign capital flowed out of South Korea. The rapid exodus of capital dramatically devalued the local currency against the dollar, caused stock prices to nose-dive, and substantially drained foreign exchange reserves. Yet bureaucratic inertia prevailed in South Korea. In November 1997, when IMF Managing Director Michel Camdessus secretly visited Seoul and informed South Korean economic officials that South Korea's crumbling finances required the IMF's intervention, they flatly responded, "You're crazy; our system works."[44] This response betrayed either overconfidence or blind nationalistic pride. Only a few days later, a newly appointed deputy prime minister desperately appealed for the IMF's immediate rescue efforts.

In return for its massive bailout package, the IMF stipulated a set of tough conditions. The South Korean government was required to execute a disciplined fiscal and monetary policy, to restructure financial institutions, to manage the labor market, which might generate high unemployment rates, and to make the *chaebol* more transparent, productive, and responsible. The IMF's "trusteeship" repudiated the classic realist principle of sovereign independence and the sanctity of territorial boundaries. This external pressure accelerated South Korea's adaptation to the challenges of economic globalization.

In the aftermath of South Korea's financial crisis, President Kim Dae Jung unabashedly embraced liberalization and globalization as the only way out of South Korea's serious predicaments: "I am going to practice the free market system ... I shall guarantee the safety of foreign investment in Korea. I wish to encourage and induce [foreign investors] to continue their investment in Korea. Foreign banks are being similarly encouraged by me to provide us with long- and short-term loans."[45] In his inaugural address, he declared that the "inducement of foreign capital is the most effective way to pay back our foreign debts, strengthen the competitiveness of businesses and raise the transparency of the economy."[46] He opened the door widely for FDI and even allowed foreign investors' hostile mergers and acquisitions of South Korean companies; however, a number of foreign businessmen in South Korea continued to complain about the government's unrealistic and inconsistent FDI policy.[47] For domestic political reasons, President Kim was not willing to lift the remaining restrictions on agricultural imports. In the name of "agricultural security," he promised to achieve a 100 percent self-sufficiency in grain production.[48]

[44] *Wall Street Journal*, 2 March 1998.
[45] *Los Angeles Times*, 11 January 1998.
[46] *Korea Herald*, 26 February 1998.
[47] See survey in *Chungang Ilbo*, June 3, 1998.
[48] Korean Broadcast Station (KBS) News (Seoul), 16 April 1998.

The IMF-imposed "cold wind" (*hanpa*) bifurcates the popular and the bureaucratic attitudes toward economic globalization in South Korea. While President Kim is determined to undertake sweeping structural reforms in line with the imperatives of globalization, a strong nationalistic or even xenophobic backlash is emerging in South Korea. A writer for the *Los Angeles Times* reported,

> The economic crisis in South Korea has triggered anti-foreign sentiment that has sent sales of imported products plummeting and prompted fears among foreigners that such economic nationalism could spin out of control.... Faced with mounting unemployment and rising prices, South Koreans are rallying against the forces perceived to be the chief cause of their woes: the International Monetary Fund, U.S. bankers and foreign goods. Rather than accepting that South Korea's own policies caused its woes, many Koreans blame their current misery on the IMF's tough prescriptions for reform.[49]

The same writer also observed that the country's "Buy Korean" campaign was so successful that it was having a devastating effect on the sales of imported products in a country that was just beginning to open its trade doors; U.S. companies were particularly hard-hit because they were viewed as the real power behind the IMF's stiff conditions. Robert Manning asserted that the financial crisis was making South Korea "tumultuous, inward-focused, resentful and economically nationalistic as it copes with the pressures of globalization."[50] In this context, Kim Kyung Won, former ambassador to the United Nations and the United States, who served as chairman of the Globalization Promotion Council that advised the prime minister, lamented that even though the government's official policy was an open-door one, the bureaucrats who were entrusted with its implementation could not rid themselves of their "anachronistic exclusive nationalism."[51]

Asked about the xenophobic nature of South Koreans, Kim Dae Jung responded, "I also aim to persuade the Korean people that the world has changed. We are living in a globalized economy. We must begin to compete with foreign companies; even the small mom-and-pop store in Korea must compete with the huge American grocery stores."[52] Kim Dae Jung is faced with the difficult tasks of reassuring the uneasy international financial community that South Korea faithfully adheres to the standards of a globalized economic order and persuading the worrisome populace that the IMF system could become an opportunity to rejuvenate South Korea's international competitiveness in the long run. He

[49] *Los Angeles Times*, 17 January 1998.
[50] Ibid., 4 January 1998.
[51] *Chungang Ilbo*, 16 March 1998.
[52] *Los Angeles Times*, 11 January 1998.

energetically conducted an "invest-in-Korea" campaign during his nine-day state visit to the United States in June 1998. It is ironic that despite his public espousal of liberal economic policy and free-market princi-ples, he may be tempted or expected to rely upon statist means and pop-ulist tactics so that he can implement South Korea's economic reforms, especially the restructuring of *chaebol*.[53] He ordered the top five chaebol to liquidate twenty nonviable subsidiaries and put strong pressure on them to swap firms to achieve specialization and efficiency.[54]

The foregoing demonstrates that South Korea responded differently to globalization in three key foreign policy spheres – diplomacy, national security, and economic relations – and that the government-led cam-paign to advance globalization was hampered by several constraining factors, the most apparent being the pervasive influence of Korea's national division. Han Sung Joo points out that although this national division, coupled with the dynamics of external power politics, has ren-dered South Korea "highly sensitive to foreign influence," it has taken "such a toll on the sentiment, temperament and emotion of the Koreans as to impede their capacity to adopt to the imperatives and opportunities of time."[55] Since the South Koreans have passionately defended "the inviolability" of their borders along the demilitarized zone for almost half a century, it is understandably difficult for them to embrace readily the concept of a "borderless world," even in an economic sense. Espe-cially with respect to issues of national security, they have been unable to go beyond the limitations of their realist and neorealist paradigms. They show an unmistakable preference for what James Rosenau calls "boundary-strengthening" over "boundary-eroding."[56]

Another major constraining factor is the legacy of Korea's historical experience. As a small state coveted by larger neighboring countries, the "Hermit Kingdom," of necessity, became highly nationalistic and isola-tionist. The long record of Korea's international victimization serves as a potent antidote to the trend of global interdependence. South Koreans are instinctively fearful of foreign domination and big power diplomacy. As illustrated in the initial phase of Japan's FDI, they are extraordinarily sensitive about the possibilities of Japanese economic and cultural encroachments mainly because of the latter's past colonialism.

---

[53] For a policy difference between President Kim and the *chaebol*, see *Hanguk Ilbo*, 17 April 1998.

[54] See *Korea Herald*, 17 and 19 June 1998.

[55] Han Sung Joo, "The Future of the World, the Region and Korea," in ed. Han Sung Joo, *The New International System* (Seoul: Ilmin International Relations Institute, 1996), 359.

[56] See James N. Rosenau, *Along the Domestic-Foreign Frontier* (Cambridge, UK: Oxford University Press, 1997), 79–83.

In view of their strong nationalistic sentiments, South Koreans are loath to accept universalistic norms and cosmopolitan attitudes. Han Sung Joo, who initiated and spearheaded President Kim Young Sam's globalization policy, revealed frustration with this reluctance when he characterized South Korea as a "parochial society" with particularistic proclivities.[57] A homogeneous cultural entity, South Korea has had little experience with cultural or ethnic diversity. The concepts "global culture" and "global citizen" are largely alien to South Koreans, who jealously maintain a clear distinction between their Korean "in-group" and foreign "out-groups" and resist the influx of external influences.[58] This attitude prevents South Korea from taking advantage of the benefits of globalization.

It is particularly important for South Koreans to recognize the necessity of developing a more cosmopolitan orientation because presently there is only a weak and dissonant popular basis in South Korea for globalization efforts in foreign relations. In a national survey in May 1995, South Koreans responded that the primary purposes of globalization policy are to "achieve economic development through trade" (38.3 percent), "make the first-rate state in all areas" (28.1 percent), "exercise international leadership for world peace" (16.6 percent), "enhance the international reputation of our culture and art" (9.8 percent), and "open exchanges with foreign countries" (6.6 percent).[59] Asked about the extent of South Korea's globalization, they answered "very much" (2.4 percent), "somewhat" (42.1 percent), "not much" (50.6 percent), and "not at all" (4.4 percent). They identified the most underdeveloped areas of South Korea's globalization as "political culture" (44.1 percent), "social welfare" (37.2 percent), "administrative services" (23.2 percent), "environmental protection" (22.4 percent), "popular consciousness" (19.5 percent), "labor-management relations" (12.2 percent), "women's social participation" (12.1 percent), "social infrastructure" (11.5 percent), "mass media" (8.4 percent), and "international competitiveness of industries" (8.1 percent). This survey indicates that the South Korean leaders responsible for political culture, social welfare, administrative services, and environmental protection are well advised to perform well in their globalization efforts. They are also expected to moderate the

---

[57] Han Sung Joo, address to the conference "Democratization and Globalization in Korea: Assessments and Prospects" in conjunction with the Seventeenth World Congress of the International Political Science Association, Seoul, Korea, 19 August 1997.

[58] For a discussion of "global culture," see Mike Featherstone, *Undergoing Culture: Globalization, Postmodernism, and Identity* (London: Sage, 1995).

[59] Survey, 29 May 1995.

effects of realism, nationalism, and parochialism and to overcome isola-tionist impulses and cultural exclusivity.

If the process of globalization does require South Koreans to make a fundamental conceptual and attitudinal shift, such a change will take a long time and demand a concerted effort. Globalization, according to Strobe Talbott, is neither inherently good nor inherently bad,[60] but the future of South Korea as a strong, prosperous, and influential country will depend largely upon its success in dealing with a globalizing world order. If the current financial crisis is successfully managed, it may actually prove to be a "blessing in disguise" in the long run for serving to promote South Korea's globalization in foreign relations.

[60] Talbott, "Globalization and Diplomacy," 71.

CHAPTER 9

Segyehwa, *the Republic of Korea,*
and the United Nations

B. C. Koh

Even though the word *segyehwa* is consistently – and officially by the
Republic of Korea (ROK) government – translated as "globalization,"
the two terms are by no means synonymous. A brief review of the ways in
which the two terms are defined must therefore precede a substantive
discussion of how the ROK has pursued and is pursuing *segyehwa* through
the United Nations.

Taking globalization first, its single most important index is the growing interdependence of the world in economic transactions. G. John
Ikenberry thus identifies "three dimensions or processes of globalization" as "market globalization, production globalization, and information globalization." One of its notable consequences, he argues, is the
production of "increasingly strong pressures for states to be of a certain
sort – open, democratic, flexible, and respectful of the rule of law."[1]

James Mittelman sees globalization as a concept that encompasses
"varied phenomena ... [and] interrelates multiple levels of analysis: economics, politics, culture, and ideology." It is "a coalescence of varied
transnational processes and domestic structures, allowing the economy,
politics, culture, and ideology of one country to penetrate another....
[It] is a market-induced, not a policy-led process."[2]

David Bobrow and James Na stress, however, that there is a notable
"lack of consensus among world and Korean policy analysts and policy

[1] G. John Ikenberry, "Patterns and Theories of the Globalization Paradigm"
(paper presented to the conference "Democratization and Globalization in
Korea: Assessments and Prospects" in conjunction with the Seventeenth World
Congress of the International Political Science Association, Seoul, Korea, 18–9
August 1997, 1–2).

[2] James H. Mittelman, ed., *Globalization: Critical Reflections* (Boulder, CO: Lynne
Rienner, 1997), 2–3.

elites about the nature and consequences of globalization." In their words, "For some in the advanced industrialized countries it holds out the prospect of a golden age ... and for others the opposite, 'a euphemism for American decline and even for colonization.' ... As for developing countries, it poses the prospect of 'the international transmission of inequality' and at the same time 'an unprecedented expansion of world trade and world output and ... an unprecedented improvement in the human condition in developing countries.'"[3]

Given all this, one must ascertain exactly what Kim Young Sam had in mind when he decided to make *segyehwa* the centerpiece of his administration. He first revealed his intention to do so on 17 November 1994, at a breakfast meeting in Sydney, Australia, with South Korean journalists covering his tour of the Philippines, Indonesia, and Australia. Saying that his visits to foreign countries and his participation in Asia Pacific Economic Cooperation (APEC) summits, the most recent of which had been held in Jakarta a few days earlier, had made him acutely aware of the need for *segyehwa*, Kim told the reporters that his government would soon begin work on formulating a long-range plan for globalization. He also mentioned several goals, including turning South Korea into a center of global management and reforming institutions and people's thinking in order to promote globalization.[4]

Presiding over the first meeting of an extensively reshuffled cabinet a month later, Kim told his cabinet ministers that their first task would be to promote *segyehwa*, which he called the "main pathway to [our] country's development and national prosperity."[5] In his New Year's message in January 1995, Kim sounded a clarion call for making 1995 the "first year of globalization," the year in which both the government and the people would vigorously pursue *segyehwa*.[6]

Finally, on 25 January 1995 Kim Young Sam unveiled his globalization

[3] David B. Bobrow and James J. Na, "Korea's Affair with Globalization: Deconstructing Segyehwa" (paper presented to the conference "Democratization and Globalization in Korea: Assessments and Prospects" in conjunction with the Seventeenth World Congress of the International Political Science Association, Seoul, Korea, 18–19 August 1997, 1).

[4] *Hanguk Ilbo* (Korea Daily), Seoul (18 November 1994), 1.

[5] Ibid., 27 December 1994, 1. All but four of the nineteen cabinet ministers were newly appointed. Observers noted that the new cabinet consisted predominantly of those with academic or technocratic backgrounds, seeing it as evidence that Kim Young Sam was serious about pursuing globalization. The appointment of Lee Hong-koo as prime minister illustrated this nicely. Lee, a former professor at Seoul National University with a Ph.D. in political science from Yale, had served as unification minsiter twice and as the ROK ambassador to the United Kingdom. He thus seemed particularly well qualified to lead a globalization drive (ibid., 1–5).

[6] Ibid., 3 January 1995, 1.

priorities at a luncheon with twenty-seven members of the newly inaugurated Committee to Promote Globalization. Making plain that he
intended *segyehwa* to make Korea a "unified state playing a central role in
the world," a truly world-class state, Kim specifically identified six areas
that required globalization: (1) education, (2) the legal and economic
order, (3) politics and the press, (4) public administration, (5) the environment, and (6) culture and attitudes.[7]

Segyehwa as understood by Kim Young Sam, then, is different from
globalization expounded by Ikenberry, Mittelman, Bobrow, and others.
The principal common denominator is their multifaceted nature; both
are concepts that have multiple dimensions, encompass "varied phenomena," interrelate "multiple levels of analysis," and embody "a coalescence
of varied transnational processes and domestic structures." Whereas Mittelman sees globalization as a market-induced process, however, Kim
Young Sam envisions *segyehwa* as a process that can and ought to be accelerated by the combined efforts of the state and the civil society.

What of *segyehwa*'s linkage to foreign policy? It was Han Sung-Joo, Kim
Young Sam's first foreign minister (March 1993–December 1994), who
listed *segyehwa* as a key component of the Kim government's "new diplomacy." Han, in fact, had used the term long before it became a virtual
emblem of the Kim Young Sam administration. In a speech at a luncheon
hosted by the Korean Council on Foreign Relations (*Hanguk Oegyo
Hyophoe*) on 31 May 1993, Han said that "Korea's new diplomacy" would
comprise five basic themes: (1) *segyehwa*, which he translated as "globalism," not "globalization," (2) diversification, (3) multidimensionalism,
(4) regional cooperation, and (5) future-orientation.[8]

"With the advent of the era of globalism," Han declared, "Korea's
diplomacy needs to pay more attention to such universal values as freedom, justice, peace and welfare." He added, "We will take an active part
in international efforts to tackle global issues such as international peace
and security, disarmament and arms control, eradication of poverty, protection of environment, and efficient utilization of natural resources.
Through such engagement, we will play our due part in making a more
just, safe, and prosperous world."[9]

---

[7] Ibid., 26 January 1995, 1; see also the editorial "'Segyehwa' ui chongnip" (Clar-
ifying "globalization"), ibid., 3.

[8] Taehan Minguk Oemubu, *Oegyo paekso, 1994* [diplomatic white paper, 1994]
(Seoul: Oemubu, 1994), 15–8; for an English text of Han's speech, see Han
Sung-Joo, *Segyehwa sidae ui Hanguk oegyo: Han Sung-Joo chon oemujanggwan yon-
sol kigomun-jip* [Korean diplomacy in an era of globalization: Collection of
speeches and essays by former foreign minister Han Sung-Joo] (Seoul: Chisik
Sanopsa, 1995), 73–103.

[9] Ibid., 77–8.

Han then turned his attention to the United Nations. In his words, "One of the most noteworthy changes in the aftermath of the Cold War is the strengthened role of the United Nations in the international arena, particularly, in the fields of peace-making and peace-building." He noted that since its admission to the world organization in 1991, the ROK had "steadily increased its participation in the activities of the United Nations." "We will," he said, "contribute to UN Peace Keeping Operations and international peace and security, thereby also securing our place in the international community." In such other fields as arms control, particularly curbing the proliferation of weapons of mass destruction, and the eradication of poverty, Han pledged his country's active support as well. As the "world's 13th-ranking economy in trade volume and 15th in GNP," he said, the ROK planned to "assume responsibilities commensurate with our standing in the international community. An increase in aid to the developing world and in contributions to relevant international organizations is the very first step we have to take towards this end."[10]

In short, the Kim Young Sam government's *segyehwa* envisaged a more active role for South Korea in the international arena, including the United Nations. South Korea would markedly increase its participation in U.N. activities with the aim of making a genuine contribution to the solution of global problems. In what specific ways did the ROK try to attain its goal in the United Nations? To what extent did it succeed? These are the questions I propose to explore in this chapter.

Implicit in this approach is the assumption that the best way to assess the effectiveness of South Korea's globalization is to use its *own* definition of the goal. The extent to which the available evidence suggests that the goal or its more concrete indicators in specific areas, such as political and diplomatic globalization, are being attained will become the main basis of my assessment.

ROK Participation in the United Nations: Key Indicators

Although the ROK did not become a full-fledged member of the United Nations until 1991, when its status, along with that of the Democratic People's Republic of Korea (DPRK), was upgraded from observer to member status, its participation in international organizations, both governmental and nongovernmental, had grown steadily over the years. As table 9.1 shows, between 1960 and 1977 the number of intergovernmental organizations (IGOs) in which the ROK participated doubled, while its membership in international nongovernmental organizations

[10] Ibid., 78–80.

Table 9.1 ROK Participation in International Organizations Compared to That of Eight Other Countries, 1960–98

	1960	1977	1984	1985	1987	1989	1994	1995	1996	1997	1998
ROK	**19**	**39**	**37**	**36**	**39**	**41**	**47**	**48**	**50**	**51**	**52**
	102	371	642	686	761	820	1,034	1,072	1,138	1,200	1,250
DPRK	**2**	**12**	**17**	**16**	**22**	**20**	**20**	**18**	**18**	**18**	**18**
	22	63	113	137	155	141	175	179	186	185	187
China	**2**	**21**	**29**	**32**	**35**	**37**	**50**	**49**	**51**	**52**	**52**
	30	71	355	403	504	677	955	1,013	1,079	1,136	1,191
Taiwan	**22**	**10**	**6**	**6**	**6**	**6**	**7**	**8**	**10**	**11**	**10**
	108	239	429	419	464	554	775	809	865	908	932
Japan	**42**	**71**	**60**	**58**	**60**	**58**	**62**	**61**	**63**	**63**	**63**
	412	878	1,296	1,222	1,420	1,583	1,863	1,889	1,970	2,019	2,059
France	**90**	**104**	**93**	**67**	**81**	**83**	**85**	**88**	**87**	**86**	**88**
	886	1,457	2,227	1,704	2,264	2,598	3,038	3,127	3,255	3,327	3,440
UK	**76**	**91**	**79**	**63**	**72**	**71**	**71**	**74**	**71**	**72**	**72**
	742	1,380	2,021	1,607	2,091	2,416	2,846	2,918	3,031	3,125	3,227
USA	**59**	**78**	**65**	**33**	**59**	**64**	**62**	**64**	**64**	**65**	**64**
	612	1,106	1,593	804	1,579	1,933	2,273	2,327	2,418	2,490	2,560
USSR/Russia	**29**	**43**	**73**	**69**	**69**	**61**	**48**	**58**	**62**	**61**	**63**
	179	433	668	646	714	806	822	1,092	1,300	1,462	1,582
Global total	**154**	**252**	**365**	**369**	**311**	**300**	**263**	**266**	**260**	**258**	**254**
	1,255	2,502	4,615	4,649	4,235	4,621	4,928	5,121	5,472	5,585	6,020

Source: Adapted from Union of International Associations, *Yearbook of International Organizations 1985/86,* vol. 2 through 1998/9, vol. 2 (Munich: K.G. Sauer, 1995–8).
Note: In each cell, the upper number (in bold) is the number of intergovernmental organizations (IGOs), while the lower number is the number of international nongovernmental organizations (INGOs).

(INGOs) nearly quadrupled. By the 1990s South Korea's level of participation in international organizations was on a par with China's, and as
far as IGOs were concerned, only slightly below that of Japan. In other
words, South Korea was well connected globally.

Against this backdrop, let us now examine several indicators of ROK
participation in the United Nations. They include (1) actively taking part
in U.N. proceedings by cosponsoring resolutions and making statements
during deliberations in both the plenary sessions and committee meetings, (2) seeking membership in various U.N. bodies and being elected
to leadership positions in them, (3) participating in U.N. peacekeeping
operations, and (4) making financial contributions to the United
Nations and related organizations and programs.

Active Participation in U.N. Proceedings

The United Nations offers its member states and, to a limited degree,
observers a forum for articulating their views as well as an arena for international cooperation. The degree to which states make use of these
opportunities varies. At a minimum, states participate in the general
debate that occurs during the first few weeks of each General Assembly
session by having their representatives make statements. The representatives may range from a state's permanent representative to the United
Nations to its head of government or state. Cosponsoring resolutions
and making statements in committees and plenary sessions of the General Assembly during deliberations of agenda items, on the other hand,
represent more active forms of participation.

South Korea invariably dispatched its foreign minister to the United
Nations to participate in the general debate. Speeches made by ROK
foreign ministers during the Kim Young Sam administration clearly
addressed major global issues and articulated Seoul's position thereon. A
few examples may be worth noting. In his statement before the forty-
eighth session of the General Assembly on 29 September 1993, ROK
Foreign Minister Han Sung-Joo spoke of "an age of historic transition,"
"a new world order," and "a trend toward peace, cooperation and interdependence, instead of conflict, confrontation and ideological bigotry."
Han pledged that his government would continue to participate in
"efforts to translate into a meaningful reality initiatives such as 'preventive diplomacy' and 'post-conflict peace-building.' "[11]

He also expressed South Korea's strong support for "the efforts to stop
nuclear weapons proliferation beyond 1995 through the extension of
the Nuclear Non-Proliferation Treaty [NPT] and for "the strengthening

[11] Ibid., 437, 439.

of IAEA [International Atomic Energy Agency] safeguards as the central device to ensure the effectiveness of the NPT." Han touched on such other global issues as development, trade, the environment, and human rights. Regarding development, although he welcomed "the recent initiatives to restructure and revitalize the UN system in the economic and social field," Han underscored the need for "a substantial increase in development resources" and encouraged developed countries to "enhance their efforts in this area."[12]

On human rights, Han reaffirmed South Korea's "firm support for the international movements to promote human rights," saying that "human rights have finally come of age in [South] Korea." Although he refrained from mentioning the human-rights situation in North Korea, he did express his government's concern over the North's nuclear program and urged the North to "comply with its safeguards agreement with the IAEA" in conformity with a Security Council resolution to that effect. Han also called on the DPRK "to cooperate with us in implementing the inter-Korean Joint Declaration of 1991 on the denuclearization of the Korean peninsula."[13] Finally, Han told the General Assembly that "globalism is at the core of the New Diplomacy" his government was pursuing and that "through ... engagement in global affairs ... [South] Korea seeks to play its due part in the works of the United Nations to make the world a safer, just and prosperous place."[14]

The most noteworthy aspect of the statement made to the fiftieth session of the General Assembly on 28 September 1995 by Gong Ro-Myung, Han's successor as foreign minister, was his explicit reference to the human-rights situation in the North. Expressing his government's deep concern, Gong called on North Korea to heed the demands of the world community for the protection of human rights. Gong also expressed the hope that the world community and the United Nations would lend their support to paving the way for an exchange of information and correspondence between family members separated by the Korean division with the ultimate aim of realizing their reunion.[15]

Apart from the above, Gong followed the practice of briefly commenting on such key global issues as peacekeeping operations, development assistance, arms control, and U.N. reform. Citing the need to strengthen and restructure U.N. peacekeeping operations in order to deal with new forms of conflict, Gong reaffirmed South Korea's support for the U.N.

---

[12] Ibid., 443–4.
[13] Ibid., 442–3, 445.
[14] Ibid., 448.
[15] Oemubu, Kukje Yonhap-guk, *Che 50 ch'a Yu-en ch'onghoe kyolgwa 1996, 9* [The results of the fiftieth U.N. General Assembly, September 1996] (Seoul, 1996), 20–1.

Standby Arrangement System and readiness to commit an eight-hundred-person military unit to it. He revealed that South Korea was prepared to increase its voluntary contributions to the operational activities of the United Nations by 65 percent the following year. On arms control, Gong announced his government's one-year moratorium on the export of antipersonnel land mines. He also called on North Korea to implement faithfully the NPT, its safeguards agreement with the IAEA, the Agreed Framework signed by the United States and the DPRK in October 1994, and the North-South denuclearization declaration.[16]

The statement by Yoo Chong-Ha, Gong's successor and Kim Young Sam's third and final foreign minister, to the fifty-second session of the General Assembly on 29 September 1997 emphasized U.N. reform. Yoo recalled that his country had joined the Group of sixteen in issuing a statement on 10 August endorsing Secretary-General Kofi Annan's reform initiatives. He then underscored the importance of "reliable financial support" for the organization. "Only when Member States discharge their financial obligations in full, on time and without conditions," he added, "will the United Nations safely and smoothly reach its ultimate destination of ensuring a better future for humankind." He pointed out that "[South] Korea has made it a firm policy to pay its assessed dues in full and on time."[17]

Regarding Security Council reform, Yoo counseled that it "must be handled with utmost prudence and seriousness." "Every effort should be made," he said, "to work out a consensus formula, while bearing in mind that 'haste makes waste.'" Noting the "emergence of a considerable number of medium-powered countries with the capability to make meaningful contribution to the cause of international peace and security," Yoo stated that "any plan to reform the Council should provide those countries with opportunities to serve in the Council with reasonable frequency commensurate with their capabilities and contributions." Finally, Yoo expressed reservations about the "systems of permanent membership and the right of veto," saying that "more can be done to make the Security Council a more representative, efficient and democratic body."[18]

Consistent with previous practice, Yoo also covered other global issues, such as the nonproliferation of weapons of mass destruction, antipersonnel land mines, terrorism, development, human rights, and humanitarian assistance. While expressing Seoul's "full support [for] the noble crusade to protect innocent civilians from anti-personnel land-mines,"

[16] Ibid., 20–2.
[17] Embassy of the Republic of Korea, *Issues and Policies: Official Speeches* (Washington, DC, 29 September 1997), 1.
[18] Ibid., 1–2.

Yoo asserted that "a sweeping ban cannot be a satisfactory answer to a country like the Republic of Korea, which faces the real and present risk of a recurrence of all-out war, and whose heavily populated capital is only twenty-five miles from the military demarcation line." "In our view," he added, "the draft convention adopted in Oslo two weeks ago fails to reflect the exceptional nature of the security situation on the Korean Peninsula."[19]

On human rights, Yoo echoed the concern first expressed by Gong Ro-Myung in 1995 over the situation in the North, saying that "we truly hope that, in the not-too-distant future, our compatriots in the North will come to enjoy basic human rights and freedoms, as other people do around the world." Yoo also noted that "the plight of innocent civilians in the North and, in particular, vulnerable groups such as malnourished children, is a matter of serious concern" for both the government and the people of the South. He said that his government would place a priority on providing assistance to the vulnerable children in close cooperation with international humanitarian agencies, stressing the "vital importance of transparency in the distribution process."[20]

South Korea manifested an activist approach to U.N. deliberations by cosponsoring resolutions and making statements in both committees and plenary sessions of the General Assembly. During the fiftieth session (19 September–23 December 1995), for example, South Korea cosponsored thirty-five resolutions and made statements on forty-six occasions. The fiftieth session approved a total of 218 resolutions; thus, the rate of South Korean cosponsorship was 16 percent.[21] During the fifty-first session (17 September–18 December 1996), South Korea cosponsored fifty-one resolutions and made statements on forty-one agenda items. Its cosponsorship rate in that session was 19.2 percent (51 out of 265), a slight increase over the previous session.[22]

Election to U.N. Bodies and Leading Positions

South Korea sought and attained membership in a wide array of U.N. organs and programs, ranging from the Security Council to the Commission on the Status of Women (see table 9.2). Of the thirteen organs and programs listed in the table, the most important is the Security Council. South Korea set its sights on the Security Council soon after it was admitted to the United Nations. As early as 1993, Foreign Minister Han

[19] Ibid., 2.
[20] Ibid., 3–4.
[21] Oemubu, Kukje Yonhap-guk, *Che 50 ch'a Yu-en ch'onghoe kyolgwa*, 5.
[22] Oemubu, Kukje Yonhap-guk, *Che 51 ch'a Yu-en ch'onghoe kyolgwa* [the results of the fifty-first U.N. General Assembly] (Seoul, 1997), 5.

Table 9.2 ROK Membership in U.N. Bodies

U.N. Organization	Term of Membership
Security Council	1996–7
Economic and Social Council	1993–5, 1997–9
U.N. Children's Fund	1988–91, 1991–3, 1994–7
Commission on Narcotic Drugs	1963–8, 1982–5, 1992–5, 1996–8
Commission on Crime Prevention and Criminal Justice	1992–4, 1995–7, 1998–2000
Committee on Human Rights	1993–5, 1996–8
Committee for Program and Coordination	1993–5, 1996–8
Committee on Information	1993–5, 1996–8
Committee on the Peaceful Uses of Outer Space	1995–6
U.N. Development Program	1993–5, 1996–8
Commission for Social Development	1996–9
Commission on Population and Development	1994–7, 1998–2001
Commission on the Status of Women	1994–7, 1998–2001

Source: Permanent Mission of the Republic of Korea to the United Nations, *Korea and the UN* (New York, 1999).

Sung-Joo told the General Assembly that his country "hopes to better contribute to the maintenance of international peace and security by having an opportunity to serve in the Security Council in the near future." He added, "We hope to receive the encouragement and support of the world community in these efforts."[23]

Since nonpermanent members of the Security Council are elected on the basis of regional quotas, South Korea needed to compete first within the Asian Group, to which two seats are allocated, with one being filled for a two-year term every year. A break came in May 1995, when Sri Lanka decided to withdraw from the race, thus enabling South Korea to win the support of the Asian Group as its "sole candidate."[24] When the General Assembly held elections on 8 November 1995, South Korea received 156 out of 177 votes cast. Eight countries were ineligible to vote because they had failed to pay U.N. dues for two years in a row. North Korea requested a "point of order" before the balloting took place, lodging a "strong protest" against the declaration by the Asian Group's chairperson – the permanent representative of Brunei – that the ROK was the group's "endorsed and sole candidate." DPRK permanent representative Pak Gil

---

[23] Han, *Segyehwa sidae ui Hanguk oegyo*, 448.
[24] Oemubu, Yu-en Chongchaek-kwa, *Yu-en kaeyo mit urinara waui kwangye* [An overview of the United Nations and our country's relations with the U.N.] (Seoul, 2 March 1999), 13.

Yon called the characterization "inaccurate," adding that South Korea lacked the ability to contribute to the maintenance of peace and security on the Korean Peninsula, in the Asian region, or in the world. Since a state of war existed on the peninsula, Pak warned, South Korea's election to the Security Council would actually aggravate the situation there.[25]

South Korea regarded its election to the Security Council as a major achievement, noting that it occurred only four years after its admission to the United Nations. During its two-year term, South Korea played an active role, earning, according to its own assessment, recognition as a "responsible member" of the international community. The ROK Foreign Ministry lists the following among the noteworthy results of its stint in the council.[26]

South Korea helped to adjust the diverse interests and points of view within the Security Council on the Cambodian issue, joining Friends of Cambodia, a group of concerned states formed in September 1997, and supporting the Secretary-General's efforts to resolve the problem. In May 1997, when South Korea was serving as the president of the Security Council, such developments as a coup d'etat in Sierra Leone and an escalation of the fighting in Afghanistan required immediate council attention, and such other issues as alleged violations by U.N. member states of sanctions against Libya and the collapse of the Mobutu regime in Zaire necessitated action. South Korea performed the role of a mediator and succeeded in forging a consensus among council members. During the same month, South Korea took the lead in organizing the first open debate in the council's history on the refugee issue, guiding the adoption of a presidential statement on "the protection for humanitarian assistance to refugees and others in conflict situations."[27]

With a view toward increasing transparency and democracy in the Security Council's modus operandi, South Korea voluntarily drafted and circulated among all U.N. member states a report on its stint as the council president in May 1997. Before its term in the council expired, South Korea collaborated with Egypt in guiding the production of a joint statement on the council's internal management by all ten nonpermanent members.

South Korea itself gained much from its two-year stint in the Security Council. When North Korea precipitated such incidents as the penetration of armed soldiers into the joint security area in the demilitarized zone (DMZ) in April 1996 and the infiltration of a submarine with armed

[25] Oemubu, Kukje Yonhap-guk, *Che 50 ch'a Yu-en ch'onghoe kyolgwa*, 40–1.
[26] Oemubu, *Chuyo oegyo munje haesol: Yu-en anbori isaguk hwaltong pyongka* [Major foreign-policy issues: An assessment of the activities as a member of the Security Council] (Seoul, 1998).
[27] Ibid.

agents in September 1996, South Korean presence in the council proved to be a major factor in persuading it to adopt presidential statements. South Korea also took advantage of IAEA executive director Hans Blix's briefings in the council on two occasions, in November 1996 and November 1997, to highlight North Korea's failure to fully implement its safeguards agreement with the IAEA and its failure to make information about its past nuclear activities available.

South Korea benefited from the opportunities to work closely with the five permanent members of the Security Council, to deal with international problems firsthand, and to forge close ties with nonaligned council members. The last-mentioned factor was largely responsible for South Korea's receiving an invitation to attend as a guest the conference of the foreign ministers of the Non-Aligned Movement in New Delhi in April 1997. According to Seoul, the ROK's two-year term in the Security Council proved to be a truly globalizing experience.

South Korea was elected to leadership positions in U.N. bodies a number of times. In June 1992 it was elected a vice-chairman of the U.N. Conference on Environment and Development. In September of the same year, it was elected the chairman of the Asian Group, the regional bloc to which both the ROK and the DPRK belong. In December of that year, South Korea was elected to one of the two vice-chairmanships in the First Committee (Disarmament and International Security) of the General Assembly. In September 1993 it was elected one of the twenty-one vice-presidents of the General Assembly. In October 1998 South Korea won a vice-chairmanship in the Fourth Committee (Special Political and Decolonization) of the General Assembly.[28]

Additionally, South Korean citizens were elected to serve in important positions, such as the special rapporteur on the human-rights situation in Afghanistan for the U.N. Commission on Human Rights, a member of the executive board of the U.N. Commission on the Status of Women, a member of the U.N. Committee on Human Rights, and a judge of the International Tribunal for the Law of the Sea. As of February 1999, 215 South Korean citizens were serving in twenty-four international organizations, seventeen in the U.N. Secretariat. The highest-ranking ROK citizen at the United Nations is Choi Young-jin, who is an assistant secretary-general in the Department of Peacekeeping Operations. A member of the ROK foreign service since 1972, Choi served as a deputy executive director of the Korean Peninsula Energy Development Organization (KEDO), an international consortium set up to oversee the construction of two light-water nuclear reactors in North Korea.[29] Finally, in March

---

[28] Oemubu, Yu-en Chongch'aek-kwa, *Yu-en kaeyo mit urinara wa ui kwangye*, 14.
[29] Ibid., 16; *Korea Herald*, 16 April 1998.

1998 a South Korean diplomat – a minister-counselor at the ROK embassy in Saudi Arabia – was chosen as "one of the two senior diplomats included in the special group which will inspect Iraqi presidential palaces suspected of housing stockpiles of weapons of mass destruction." This operation was based on an agreement between U.N. Secretary-General Kofi Annan and Iraqi President Saddam Hussein signed in February 1998.[30]

Participation in U.N. Peacekeeping Operations

As table 9.3 shows, South Korea began participating in U.N. peace-keeping operations (PKOs) during the first year of its membership. The operations listed in the table constitute two broad categories: those pertaining to political transitions, elections, or referenda and those pertaining to actual peacekeeping. South Korea dispatched observers or administrative personnel to the first type of operations and contributed army engineers or army medical personnel to the second type.

About 40 percent of U.N. member states contribute personnel to U.N. peacekeeping operations. In the U.N. Mission for the Referendum in Western Sahara, which consisted of 202 persons from twenty-six countries, the South Korean contingent was the third largest. In the U.N. Military Observer Group in India and Pakistan, a relatively small operation consisting of forty-five observers from eight countries, South Korea was both the largest and the only Asian participant.[31]

Overall, South Korea is not a major player in the U.N. peacekeeping operations; such countries as Poland, India, Bangladesh, Finland, Ghana, Austria, and Ireland each currently contribute more than seven hundred troops. When the *quality* of contributions is taken into account, however, South Korean participation in PKOs can be rated as above average, for an overwhelming proportion of South Korean participants has been either engineers or medical specialists, whose work is undoubtedly many times more valuable than that of mere foot soldiers.

Financial Contributions

In a strict sense, paying assessed contributions to the United Nations may not have anything to do with globalization. Nor can it be viewed as a special contribution. In the context of the chronic financial crisis bedeviling

---

[30] "Korean Diplomat to Joint U.N. Iraq Weapons Inspection Team," *Korea Herald* (Seoul), 24 March 1998.
[31] United Nations, Department of Public Information, *Current United Nations Peacekeeping Operations, as of November 30, 1998* (New York: 11 December 1998).

Table 9.3   ROK Participation in U.N. Peacekeeping Operations, 1992–8

Operation	ROK Participation	Period
UNTAC	5 observers	July 1992–May 1993
UNOSOM II	250 army engineers	July 1993–March 1994
UNOMSA	6 observers	April 1994
MINURSO	42-person army medical unit*	September 1994–present
ONUMOZ	6 observers	October 1994
UNOMIG	3 military observers	October 1994–present
UNMOGIP	9 military observers	November 1994–present
UNAVEM III	204 army engineers	October 1995–December 1996

Source: Oemubu, Kukje Yonhap Chongch'ae-Kwa, *Yu-en p'yonghwa yuji hwaldong (PKO)* (The Republic of Korea and U.N. Peacekeeping Operations) (Seoul: Oemubu, March 1999).
Note:
  UNTAC: U.N. Transitional Authority in Cambodia
  UNOSOM II: U.N. Operations in Somalia II
  UNOMSA: U.N. Observer Mission in South Africa
  MINURSO: U.N. Mission for the Referendum in Western Sahara
  ONUMOZ: U.N. Operation in Mozambique
  UNOMIG: U.N. Observer Mission in Georgia
  UNMOGIP: U.N. Military Observer Group in India and Pakistan
  UNAVEM III: U.N. Angola Verification Mission III
* As of March 1999, the size of the ROK medical unit in MINURSO had been reduced to 20 persons.

the world organization, however, South Korea's record of paying its assessed contributions on time and in full is well worth noting. What is more, South Korea makes voluntary contributions to U.N. bodies and programs as well. Although the total amount may not be large, South Korean contributions are by no means negligible. Moreover, as can be seen in table 9.4, they have steadily increased until 1998, when the effects of the currency crisis that hit Seoul in late 1997 led to a decrease in the total, though not in South Korea's contribution to the regular U.N. budget. The total contributions to U.N. bodies in 1996 were 23 percent above those in 1995, and they increased another 15 percent in 1997. Note that the figures for U.N. specialized agencies and other U.N. bodies include both assessed and voluntary contributions.

It should be stressed that South Korea's share of the regular U.N. budget compares favorably to the shares of other countries. As table 9.5 shows, only in 1992–4 was South Korea assessed less than China, Denmark, Mexico, and Saudi Arabia. In subsequent years, South Korea either matched or surpassed these countries. Actually, in 1995 only Saudi Arabia was assessed the same rate as South Korea. In 1998 South Korea's

Table 9.4 ROK Contributions to International Organizations, 1995–8
(in Thousands of U.S. Dollars)

Organization	1995	1996	1997	1998
U.N. regular budget	8,750	8,910	9,200	10,180
U.N. PKO budget	5,261	5,500	5,000	3,750
U.N. specialized agencies	13,097	16,573	17,325	13,201
Other U.N. bodies	3,759	7,216	9,837	7,573
Subtotal	30,867	38,199	41,362	34,704
Other IGOs	6,990	8,448	12,851	9,702
NGOs	380	—	—	—
APEC	180	180	180	135
Other	2,000	3,000	3,000	2,375
Grand total	40,417	49,827	57,393	46,916

Source: Oemubu, Kukjegigu Chongch'aekgwan-sil, *Kukje kigu pundamkum naeyok*
(Itemized Contributions to International Organizations) (Seoul: Oemubu,
February 1999).

assessment exceeded those of all of the countries listed in table 9.5,
including Austria. In 2000, moreover, South Korea's share of the regular
U.N. budget will surpass the 1 percent mark for the first time. South
Korea's rank among U.N. member states in terms of assessed contributions to the regular budget climbed from twentieth to fifteenth in 1995
and has remained in the fifteenth to seventeenth range ever since.

Before the currency crisis and ultimately the economic crisis hit South
Korea, the United States tried to persuade it to increase its contributions.
In August 1997, only three months before the crisis erupted, the U.S.
permanent representative to the United Nations, Bill Richardson, visited
Seoul to urge the ROK government to double its contributions to the
United Nations. "In light of Korea's economic success and its growing
political influence around the world, we think Korea should do more in
the United Nations," Richardson said. He stated at a press conference at
the ROK Foreign Ministry that the "United States supports increased
South Korean participation, profile and personnel in UN organizations."
His comment was in response to ROK Foreign Minister Yoo's statement
indicating Seoul's willingness to make contributions to the United
Nations commensurate with South Korea's economic capability, provided
that increases in its contributions be "gradual and matched with increase
in the number of high-level Korean officials at the UN Secretariat."[32]

In the wake of the economic crisis, South Korea indicated that it might

[32] "Ambassador Richardson Asks Seoul to Double Financial Contributions to
U.N.," *Korea Herald*, 15 August 1997.

Table 9.5   ROK Percentage of the Regular U.N. Budget Compared to That of Six Other Member States, 1992–2000 (in Percent)

Country	1992–4	1995	1996	1997	1998	1999	2000
ROK	0.69	0.80	0.8175	0.82	0.955	0.994	1.006
Austria	0.75	0.85	0.8650	0.87	0.935	0.941	0.942
China	0.77	0.72	0.7350	0.72	0.901	0.973	0.995
DPRK	0.05	0.04	0.0500	0.05	0.031	0.019	0.015
Denmark	0.65	0.70	0.7175	0.72	0.687	0.691	0.692
Mexico	0.88	0.78	0.7875	0.79	0.941	0.980	0.995
Saudi Arabia	0.96	0.80	0.7200	0.71	0.594	0.569	0.562
ROK's rank	20	15	17	17	15	16	16

Source: Oemubu, Yu-en Chongch'aek-kwa, *Kukje kigu pundamkum naeyok* (Seoul, 2 March 1998) and United Nations, *Scale of Assessments for the Apportionment of the Expenses of the United Nations*, A/RES/52/215 (New York, 20 January 1998).

freeze its financial contributions to the United Nations at the 1997 level for the next three years. Ambassador Park Soo Gil, the ROK permanent representative to the United Nations, said on 11 December 1997 that he had informed U.N. member states that as a recipient of emergency assistance organized by the International Monetary Fund, South Korea was in no position to increase its assessed contributions to the United Nations.[33] As will be noted below, however, the Seoul government that assumed power in February 1998 decided not to carry out the implied threat.

Voting in the U.N. General Assembly

Does South Korea's voting record in the United Nations provide any clues to how it is conducting itself as a global citizen? A detailed analysis of South Korea's voting record in the U.N. General Assembly is beyond the scope of this chapter; however, a brief look at one aspect of the record may be in order. Table 9.6 presents some data on how South Korea's voting record compares to those of selected U.N. member states. The numbers in the cells indicate the degree to which voting by the ROK and other countries coincided with that by the United States during the 1991–7 period.

The most interesting revelation of the table is that although the rate of the ROK's coincidence with the United States is consistently above the average for all U.N. member states, it is nonetheless lowest among the U.S. allies. Except in 1996 and 1997, moreover, the ROK's coincidence

---

[33] *Chungang Ilbo* (Seoul), 12 December 1997.

Table 9.6   Voting Coincidence with the United States in the U.N. General Assembly: The ROK and Selected U.N. Member States, 1991–7 (in Percent)

	1991 46th	1992 47th	1993 48th	1994 49th	1995 50th	1996 51st	1997 52nd
ROK	35.3	36.2	44.2	55.9	64.3	60.0	62.5
DPRK	15.5	12.9	7.8	9.0	8.7	13.0	4.3
Canada	69.5	60.0	66.7	74.5	73.5	73.0	71.7
China	16.4	16.4	10.6	22.8	21.5	29.7	27.6
France	70.5	63.8	71.0	75.8	76.9	77.8	78.3
Germany	71.3	63.8	74.4	77.8	76.9	74.2	73.8
Japan	61.7	53.7	65.8	78.4	75.4	72.4	67.3
Russia[a]	41.9	59.5	68.6	66.6	73.1	59.3	58.6
U.K.	79.6	73.5	80.0	84.3	85.1	79.1	79.4
Average[b]	27.8	31.0	36.8	48.6	50.6	49.4	46.7

Source: Samuel S. Kim, "North Korea and the United Nations," *International Journal of Korean Studies*, 1, no. 1 (Spring 1997), 91; U.S. Department of State, *Voting Practices in the United Nations–1997* (Washington, DC, 1998), 23–37.
Note: [a] The figure for 1991 is for the former Soviet Union.
[b] Average coincidence for all U.N. member states.

percentages are lower than those of even the former Soviet Union and Russia. A major reason for this is that South Korea tends to side with the developing countries on many issues. When it does not actually vote with the Group of Seventy-Seven, South Korea frequently abstains from voting. One manifestation of South Korea's globalization at the United Nations, then, is its support, either active or passive, of the aspirations of Third World countries, which constitute an overwhelming majority of the U.N. membership.

To no one's surprise, the DPRK has the lowest rate of coincidence with the United States. Despite gradual improvement in their bilateral relations in recent years, the two countries remain adversaries. Nor have they attained their shared objective of diplomatic normalization. The situation, in short, is unlikely to change until and unless there is a breakthrough in their relations, which most probably will require a marked improvement in inter-Korean relations as well.

Segyehwa and the United Nations under Kim Dae Jung

Although one of the first acts of the Kim Dae Jung government was to abolish the Committee to Promote Globalization established by its predecessor, that did not mean that the new administration intended to jettison the goal of *segyehwa* altogether. Significantly, Kim Dae Jung mentioned the word *segyehwa* twice in his inaugural address, delivered on 25 February 1998. First he spoke of the need to globalize Korean culture, adding, "We must embrace and develop the high values that are contained in our traditional culture." Later he referred to the "era of *segyehwa*," asserting that diplomacy in the new era "will center around the economy and culture." "We will," he said, "keep expanding trade, investment, tourism and cultural exchanges in order to make our way in the age of boundless competition which will take place against a backdrop of cooperation."[34]

Although Kim Dae Jung failed to mention the United Nations in his inaugural address, he made clear the importance he attached to the world organization by appointing Lee See Young, a career diplomat with long experience in U.N. affairs, as the ROK's permanent representative to the United Nations. A thirty-six-year veteran of the ROK Foreign Ministry, Lee is reputed to be its top expert on the United Nations. He previously served as the vice-minister for foreign affairs and the ROK ambassador to France.

During his state visit to the United States in June 1998, moreover, Kim Dae Jung made a point of meeting U.N. Secretary-General Kofi Annan. In addition to explaining his government's policy toward the North, Kim discussed with Annan such global issues as "the recent underground nuclear tests conducted by India and Pakistan" and their effects on international peace and security.[35]

Notwithstanding its economic difficulties, the Kim Dae Jung government decided not only to pay its U.N. dues in full but also to increase its contributions to the United Nations and related programs. In a report released in June 1998, the ROK foreign ministry admitted that the level of South Korea's voluntary contributions to the United Nations and other international organizations – which averaged 0.16 percent of all voluntary contributions to the latter – was inadequate and indicated Seoul's readiness to increase it to 0.95 percent, the level of the U.N. assessment for the ROK in the 1998 U.N. regular budget.[36]

The Kim Dae Jung government also sponsored an award for human-resource development under the U.N. Economic and Social Commission

---

[34] Ch'ongwadae, *Che 15-dae taet'ongnyong ch'wi'imsa: kungnan kukbok kwa chaedoyak ui sae sidae rul yopsida* [The inaugural address of the fifteenth president: Let us open a new era in which we overcome national difficulties and make a leap anew] (Seoul, 25 February 1998); Embassy of the Republic of Korea, "President Kim Addresses Inaugural Ceremony," *Current Topics* (Washington, DC, 25 February 1998).

[35] "S. Korea's Kim Discusses North with UN Chief," *Reuters* (New York), 7 June 1998.

[36] Oemubu, Kukjekigu Chongch'aekgwan-sil, *Yu-en kaeyo mit uri nara waui kwangye*, 26 June 1998, 17.

for Asia and the Pacific (ESCAP). The theme was "empowering the urban poor," and South Korea entrusted an ESCAP jury to select the winner, which was the Human Development Center of Thailand. ROK Foreign Vice-Minister Sun Joun-yung presented the award at an ESCAP-organized ceremony in Bangkok on 20 April 1998.[37]

Finally, the Kim Dae Jung government began exploring ways to increase ROK participation in U.N. peacekeeping operations. It informed the United Nations that it was willing to dispatch about eight hundred soldiers, police officers, and civilians upon the United Nations's request. Since under current laws the National Assembly must approve any dispatch of ROK personnel to PKOs on a case-by-case basis, the Kim government was studying a proposal to enact a new law on PKOs that would grant blanket authorization.[38]

Not enough time has passed to allow an assessment of the actual effects of the Kim Dae Jung government's words and deeds relating to *segyehwa* in general and its manifestation in U.N. policy in particular. What is nonetheless clear is that although it gives top priority to economic recovery, the government in Seoul is determined to shoulder its share of the burden in global cooperation. Nor is it any less eager than its predecessor to make South Korea a world-class country, one that is truly globalized.

Conclusion

Have South Korean activities in the United Nations contributed to the discussion and amelioration, if not the solution, of global problems? Inasmuch as global problems by definition have a global impact in an increasingly interdependent world, any contribution to their solution, however modest, will benefit South Korea as well. South Korea's stakes are especially large in issues related to international security, notably the proliferation of weapons of mass destruction.

In both words and deeds alike, South Korea did make a special effort to fulfill its responsibilities as a global citizen in the United Nations. The statements its representatives have made to the General Assembly during the general debate have been devoted overwhelmingly to global issues, with about two-thirds of the space in the statements being allocated to such discussion each year. One may legitimately question the value of

---

[37] ROK Ministry of Foreign Affairs and Trade, *Speech by H. E. Mr. Sun Joun-yung at the Presentation Ceremony for the 1998 ESCAP HRD Award*, 20 April 1998, Bangkok, Thailand (Seoul, 20 April 1998). See also Sun's statement at the fifty-fourth session of Economic and Social Commission for Asia and the Pacific (ESCAP) on 20 April 1998 in idem, *Asia and the Pacific into the 21st Century: Prospects for Social Development* (Seoul, 20 April 1998).

[38] *Choson Ilbo*, 1 July 1998.

such statements per se. For *general debate* is a misnomer par excellence. What happens during that period is not really a debate but a series of unilateral statements that typically attract scant attention. There are exceptions, of course, for U.N. rules of procedure permit the exercise of a right of reply. North Korea, in fact, did just that after ROK Foreign Minister Gong Ro-Myung raised the issue of human rights in the North for the first time in September 1995, which in turn prompted South Korea to exercise a right of reply.[39]

By gaining membership in selected U.N. bodies, South Korea succeeded in increasing both the quantity and the quality of its contributions to the United Nations's handling of global issues. Of particular value was South Korea's two-year stint in the U.N. Security Council. Not only did South Korea's election to the council signify a diplomatic coup, but its own assessment that it had discharged its responsibilities as a nonpermanent member of the council creditably is not entirely self-serving. The ROK's voluntary submission of a report on its tenure as president of the council (an office that rotates monthly among all council members) set a precedent worth emulating.

Although neither South Korea's track record in PKO participation nor its financial contributions to the United Nations can be rated as extraordinary, they are nonetheless noteworthy. Qualitatively South Korea is an important participant in PKOs. South Korea's assessed contributions to the U.N. regular budget, which are based on a complicated formula designed to measure each member state's ability to pay,[40] place it in the top eighth or ninth percentile among the 185 member states. South Korea's share of the PKO budget, however, by Seoul's own admission, has been much lower than its economic capability would warrant. Nor have South Korea's voluntary contributions to U.N. programs been generous by any measure. Until South Korea manages to overcome its current difficulties and regain a momentum for growth, however, its financial contributions to the United Nations will remain modest at best.

All in all, the United Nations has provided the Republic of Korea with an important arena in which to make globalization a reality. The record thus far suggests that Seoul has made significant headway toward realizing its laudable goal, a goal that is likely to benefit all the parties concerned – the Republic of Korea, the United Nations, and all humankind.

What, if any, are the larger implications of the South Korean experience? For one thing, it demonstrates that globalization in a broad sense is not merely a market-driven but a policy-induced process. The Kim

[39] Oemubu, Kukje Yonhap-guk, *Che 50 ch'a Yu-en ch'onghoe kyolgwa*, 23.
[40] United Nations, "Assembly to Consider Scale of Assessments for 1998–2000, Budget for 1998–1999, at Conclusion of Current Segment Tonight," U.N. Press Release GA/9389, 22 December 1997, 2.

Young Sam government's decision to give it top priority was clearly a pivotal factor in the equation. To put it differently, political leadership can exert a potent influence on a state's pursuit of globalization.

Another lesson of the South Korean experience borders on the trite: The attainment of globalization hinges not only on the availability of financial and human resources but also on political will. South Korea's financial contributions to the United Nations, its participation in U.N. peacekeeping operations, and its success in winning seats in a number of U.N. bodies for both itself and its citizens all support this interpretation. Finally, the South Korean record suggests that in the context of the United Nations, the benefits of globalization may well eclipse its costs.

Looking to the future, South Korea will continue to rely on the United Nations to pursue *segyehwa* – to increase the level of its contributions, both quantitative and qualitative, to help solve global problems and in so doing to raise its standing in the global community. Inasmuch as globalization, even in the narrow sense in which it is understood in South Korea, is a two-way process, all this will ineluctably lead to the globalizaton of South Korea itself – in the sense of moving South Korean thinking and behavior, both at the individual and the collective level, in the direction of meeting global standards. Slowly but surely, then, the gap between *segyehwa* and globalization will be bridged.

CHAPTER 10

The Security Domain of
South Korea's Globalization

Victor Cha

The Republic of Korea's (ROK) democratization, economic achievements, hosting of gala international events, membership in the Organization for Economic Cooperation and Development (OECD), and
enthusiasm for participation in regional and global institutions attest to
its internationalist outlook. However, on closer analysis, a number of
anomalies become apparent. While Korea highlights multilateralism in
its foreign policy, it also stresses its bilateral alliance with the United
States as a security priority not only today but even after unification. Even
though Korean explications of the Northeast Asian region in the
post–Cold War era are peppered with the language of cooperative security communities and interdependence, balance-of-power suspicions
become clear in Seoul's procurement and force modernization patterns.
Although Korea is a member of the elite, cosmopolitan OECD, it still
holds to antiquated policies such as banning the import of Japanese
popular culture. One noted Korean scholar and practitioner questioned
how far globalization processes can have permeated a country in which
the following questions would draw ambivalent responses: "How many
foreign residents does Seoul have among its population of 10 million? Or
how would most of your neighbors react if a foreigner moved into your
neighborhood? Finally, how would you answer if someone asked you why
Seoul does not even have a Chinatown?"[1]

The existing literature on globalization helps to explain some but not
all of these anomalies. Globalization studies have been almost entirely
in the economic arena, with little attention given to the security effects
of this process. Consequently, the literature on globalization and Korea

[1] Lee Hong-koo, "Attitudinal Reform toward Globalization," *Sasang Quarterly*,
Winter 1993, reprinted in *Korea Focus* (March–April 1994), 86.

also has been devoted largely to the economic domain, neglecting the political-military dimension. Furthermore, scholarship is lacking on the interaction between globalization and domestic-ideational determinants of foreign policy. This chapter attempts to address some of these voids.

We need first to understand in general terms globalization's security effects and then to determine how these security effects translate in terms of a state's foreign policy. In other words, globalization's imperatives permeate the domestic level and are manifested in certain behavioral attributes or traits of policy. In this sense, globalization is both a top-down and bottom-up process. I apply these propositions to the Korean case with special reference to relations with the United States. In the end, the Korean case shows how the process of globalization is far from a homogenizing one, always refracted through the prism of national identity.

The Security Effects of Globalization

Globalization is best understood as a spatial phenomenon.[2] It is a process rather than an event. It is a gradual and ongoing expansion of interaction processes, forms of organization, and forms of cooperation outside of the traditional spaces defined by sovereignty. Activity takes place in a less localized, less insulated way as transcontinental and interregional patterns crisscross and overlap one another.[3] In short, the nation-state

[2] David Held, "Democracy and Globalization," *Global Governance* 3, no. 3 (1997), 253. As James Rosenau says, "It refers neither to values or structures but to sequences that unfold either in the mind or behavior, to interaction processes that evolve as people and organizations go about their daily tasks and seek to realize their particular goals." "The Dynamics of Globalization: Toward an Operational Formulation," *Security Dialogue* 27, no. 3 (1996), 251.

[3] Contrary to popular notions of globalization, this does not mean that sovereignty ceases to exist in the traditional Weberian sense (i.e., monopoly of legitimate authority over citizens and subjects within a given territory). Instead, globalization is a spatial reorganization of production, industry, finance, and other areas that causes local decisions to have global repercussions and daily life to be affected by global events (James Mittelman, "The Globalisation Challenge: Surviving at the Margins," *Third World Quarterly* 15, no. 3 [1994], 427). Or as David Goldblatt et al. note, "Globalization denotes a shift in the spatial form and extent of human organization and interaction to a transcontinental or interregional level. It involves a stretching of social relations across time and space such that day-to-day activities are increasingly influenced by events happening on the other side of the globe and the practices and decisions of highly localized groups and institutions can have significant global reverberations." David Goldblatt, David Held, Anthony McGrew, and Jonathan Perraton, "Economic Globalization and the Nation-State: Shifting Balances of Power," *Alternatives* 22 (1997), 271.

does not end; it is just less in control as activity and decisions for the state increasingly take place in a postsovereign space.[4]

Much of the literature on globalization has focused on its economic rather than its security implications.[5] In part this is because the security effects of globalization often get conflated with changes to the international security agenda accompanying the end of Cold War superpower competition. It is also because unlike the economic effects, which are manifested and measured every day in terms of activities such as international capital flows and Internet use, the security effects are inherently harder to conceptualize and measure.[6]

The Agency and Scope of Threats

The most far-reaching security effect of globalization is that both the agency and the scope of "threat" in international relations become more complex. Not only states but also nonstate groups or individuals can be agents of threat. Whereas the vocabulary of conflict in international security traditionally centered on interstate war (e.g., between large set-piece battalions and national armed forces), with globalization the fight is between irregular substate units – ethnic militia, guerrillas, and terrorists – and terms such as *global violence* and *human security* have become common. Increasingly targets are not opposing force structures or even cities but local groups and individuals.[7] Providers of security are still nationally

[4] See Samuel Kim's contribution in this volume (Chapters 1 and 11). See also Wolfgang Reinicke, "Global Public Policy," *Foreign Affairs*, November–December 1997, 127–38; and Rosenau, "Dynamics of Globalization," 247–62.

[5] Examples of the nonsecurity bias in some of the more prominent works on globalization include: Mittelman, " The Globalisation Challenge"; Goldblatt et al., "Economic Globalization and the Nation-State"; Reinicke, "Global Public Policy"; Rosenau, "Dynamics of Globalization"; Joseph Nye and William Owens, "America's Information Edge," *Foreign Affairs*, March–April 1998, 20–36; Strobe Talbott, "Globalization and Diplomacy: A Practitioner's Perspective," *Foreign Policy*, Fall 1997, 69–83; Richard Falk, "State of Siege: Will Globalization Win Out?" *International Affairs* 73, no. 1 (1997), 123–36; Kenichi Ohmae, "The Rise of the Region State," *Foreign Affairs*, Spring 1993; and Held, "Democracy and Globalization."

[6] As far as possible, the ensuing analysis tries to differentiate globalization from post–Cold War effects on security. For example, the notion of selective engagement or intervention as a viable security strategy is predominantly a security effect deriving from the end of bipolar competition rather than from globalization. Similarly, the notion of rogue or pariah states is also more a function of the end of the Cold War than of globalization (although the latter's effects in terms of information and technology can raise the danger of these threats).

[7] Michael Klare, "The Era of Multiplying Schisms: World Security in the Twenty-First Century," in eds. Michael Klare and Yogesh Chandrani, *World Security: Challenges for a New Century*, 3rd ed. (New York: St. Martin's Press, 1998), 66.

defined in terms of capabilities and resources; however, increasingly they apply these capabilities and resources in a postsovereign space whose spectrum ranges from nonstate to substate to transstate arrangements. For this reason, security threats become inherently more difficult to measure, locate, monitor, and contain.[8]

Globalization widens the scope of security as well. States define security as more than national military security.[9] This is because some of the basic transaction processes that globalization engenders – instantaneous communication and transportation, exchanges of information and technology, capital flows – catalyze certain dangerous phenomena or empower certain groups. Disease, global warming, ozone depletion, acid rain, biodiversity loss, and radioactive contamination are health and environmental problems that have intensified as transnational security concerns precisely because of increased human mobility and interaction.[10] Globalization also has given rise to a "skill revolution" that enhances the capabilities of such groups as drug smugglers, political terrorists, criminal organizations, and ethnic insurgents to carry out their agendas more effectively than ever before.[11] Moreover, the national or unilateral solutions to these problems are increasingly ineffective.[12]

Identity and Nonphysical Security

Globalization has made identity a source of conflict. The elevation of regional and ethnic conflict as a top-tier security issue has generally been viewed as a function of the end of the Cold War. However, it is also a

[8] Lawrence Freedman, "International Security: Changing Targets," *Foreign Policy*, Spring 1998, 56; Reinicke, "Global Public Policy," 134.

[9] On the issue of security conceptions, see Richard Haas, "Paradigm Lost," *Foreign Affairs*, January–February 1995, 43–58; and Victor Cha, "Realism, Liberalism, and the Durability of the U.S.-South Korean Alliance," *Asian Survey* 37, no. 7 (July 1997), 609–22.

[10] Richard Matthew and George Shambaugh, "Sex, Drugs, and Heavy Metal: Transnational Threats and National Vulnerabilities," *Security Dialogue* 29, no. 2 (1998), 30.

[11] James Rosenau, "The Dynamism of a Turbulent World," in Klare and Chandrani, *World Security*, 21–3; Klare, "The Era of Multiplying Schisms," 67–8; James Shinn, ed., *Weaving the Net: Conditional Engagement with China* (New York: Council on Foreign Relations, 1996), 38; Roy Godson, "Criminal Threats to U.S. Interests in Hong Kong and China" (testimony before the Senate Foreign Relations Committee, East Asian and Pacific Affairs Subcommittee, 10 April 1997); and Seyom Brown, "World Interests and the Changing Dimensions of Security," in Klare and Chandrani, *World Security*, 4–5.

[12] As Matthew and Shambaugh argue, it is not the luxury of the Soviet collapse that enables us to elevate the importance of transnational security but the advances in human mobility, communication, and technology that force us to elevate it ("Sex, Drugs, and Heavy Metal," 29).

function of globalization. The process of globalization is characterized by implicit homogenization tendencies and messages, for example, the diffusion of standardized consumer goods generally from the developed North, Western forms of capitalism (and not Asian crony capitalism), and Western liberal democracy (not illiberal democracy). As Richard Falk observes, these homogenization impulses, in combination with the "borderlessness" of the globalization phenomenon, elicit a cultural pluralist response: "The rejection of these globalizing tendencies in its purest forms is associated with and expressed by the resurgence of religious and ethnic politics in various extremist configurations. Revealingly, only by retreating to pre-modern, traditionalist orientations does it now seem possible to seal off sovereign territory, partially at least, from encroachments associated with globalized lifestyles and business operations."[13]

Finally, globalization has anointed the concept of nonphysical security. Traditional definitions of security in terms of protection of territory and sovereignty, while certainly not irrelevant in a globalized era, have been expanded to include protection of information and technology assets. For example, Joseph Nye and William Owens expect "information power" to increasingly define the distribution of power in international relations in the twenty-first century. In a similar vein, the revolution in military affairs highlights not greater firepower but greater information technology and "smartness" of weapons as the defining advantages in future warfare.[14] These nonphysical security aspects have always been a part of the traditional national defense agenda, manifest in Cold War technonationalist institutions mandated with preventing the unauthorized transfer of sensitive technologies (i.e., Coordinating Committee for Export to Communist Countries, or COCOM). However, in a globalized world, the nation-state can no longer control the movement of such information assets.[15] Privatization and transnationalization of defense production have made firms, individuals, and other nonstate groups the primary producers, consumers, and merchants of a $50 billion-per-year global arms market.[16] Moreover, globalization of information and

[13] Falk, "State of Siege," 131–2; and Mittelman, "The Globalisation Challenge," 432.

[14] These capabilities are defined in terms of ISR (intelligence collection, surveillance, and reconnaissance), C4I, and precision force that can provide superior situational awareness capabilities (e.g., dominant battlespace knowledge, "precrisis transparency") (see Nye and Owens, "America's Information Edge"; and Eliot Cohen, "A Revolution in Warfare," ibid., 37–54).

[15] See Denis Fred Simon, ed., *Techno-Security in an Age of Globalization* (Armonk, NY: M. E. Sharpe, 1997).

[16] As Goldblatt et al. point out, multinational corporations (MNCs) now account for a disproportionately large share of global technology transfer as a result of FDI, joint ventures, international patenting, licensing, and know-how agreements. This means that they are more in control of transferring dual-use

technology has lowered barriers to nonstate entry into indiscriminate
profit-based weapons proliferation and raised detection costs.[17]

Propositions for Security Behavior

How might nonphysical security, diversification of threats, and the salience
of identity, the primary security effects of globalization, affect a state's
foreign policy? Or as Samuel Kim puts it, how might globalization
processes' permeation of a state's security agenda be manifested? Put
another way, in what ways might we observe globalization changing the
payoff structures of a state's security behavior?[18]

Intermestic Security

The first manifestation is an acknowledgement in statements and
rhetoric that security decisions increasingly take place outside the traditional purview of sovereignty. Globalization creates an interpenetration
of foreign and domestic issues that national governments must recognize in developing policy. One example of this "intermestic" approach to
security policy might be to accept that the transnationalization of threats
has blurred traditional divisions between internal and external security.[19]
The obverse would be the frequency with which a state adheres to "delimiting" security, formulating and justifying policy on the basis of "national
security" interests rather than universal or global interests.[20] Examples of
the former are European institutions such as Interpol, TREVI, and the
Schengen Accord which represent an acknowledgement that such
domestic issues as crime, drug trafficking, terrorism, and immigration
increasingly require transnational cooperation.[21] In Asia one might see

technologies than are traditional states. (Goldblatt et al., "Economic Global-
ization and the Nation-State," 277–9; see also Michael Klare and Lora Lumpe,
"Fanning the Flames of War: Conventional Arms Transfers in the 1990s," in
Klare and Chandrani, *World Security*, 160–79).

[17] For example, the Internet, the global positioning system (GPS), and the borderless movement of capital probably disproportionately benefit those players
in the global arms market over the enforcers.

[18] See Chapter 1 in this volume.

[19] On internal and external security, see Peter Katzenstein, *Cultural Norms and
National Security: Police and Military in Postwar Japan* (Ithaca, NY: Cornell University Press, 1996).

[20] Chung-in Moon, "Globalization: Challenges and Strategies," *Korea Focus* 3, no.
3 (May–June 1995), 64.

[21] TREVI was composed of ministers of the interior and justice of European Community (EC) member states whose purpose was to coordinate policy on terrorism (at Germany's initiative in 1975) and international crime. The Schengen
Accord also represented a convergence of internal and external security with

piracy, environmental pollution, or transnational crime as issues where international and domestic security converge.[22]

Multilateralism and Bureaucratic Innovation

If security is increasingly defined in postsovereign, globalized terms, then the modes of obtaining security should also change. As noted above, globalization means that both the agency and scope of threats have become more diverse and nonstate in form. This suggests that the payoffs for obtaining security through traditional means have lessened. Pollution, disease, and the transfer of technology and information cannot easily be controlled through national, unilateral means; they can be effectively dealt with only by applying national resources in multilateral fora or by encouraging transnational cooperation. Thus, one would expect globalized security processes to be reflected in a state's striving for regional coordination and cooperative security. In their relations, states should emphasize less exclusivity and bilateralism and more inclusivity and multilateralism as the best way to solve security problems. At the extreme end of the spectrum, globalization might downplay the importance of eternal ironclad alliances and encourage the growth of select transnational "policy coalitions" among national governments, nongovernmental organizations (NGOs), and individuals specific to each problem.[23]

Bureaucratic innovation should also be evident in response to the new challenges of globalization. For example, in the United States, the Clinton administration created the position of undersecretary for global affairs with a portfolio that includes environmental issues, promotion of democracy and human rights, population and migration issues, and law enforcement.[24] In a similar vein, the U.S. State Department's Foreign Service Institute now has a new core course for foreign service officers on narcotics trafficking, refugee flows, and environmental technologies.[25] One might also expect to see foreign-service bureaucracies placing greater emphasis on international organizations (IOs) and NGOs in terms of representation, placement, and leadership if these are recognized as the key vehicles of security and politics in a globalized world.

---

regard to common standards on border controls, pursuit of criminals across borders, asylum procedures, and refugees (Peter Katzenstein, "Regional Security Orders: Europe and Asia," manuscript, February 1998, 11–4).

[22] For example, see "Special Focus: China and Hong Kong," *Trends in Organized Crime* 2, no. 2 (Winter 1996), 1–55.

[23] Reinicke, "Global Public Policy," 134.

[24] Talbott, "Globalization and Diplomacy," 74.

[25] Ibid., 75.

Diffuse Reciprocity

Finally, globalized conceptions of security should be reflected in norms of diffuse reciprocity and international responsibility. These are admittedly more amorphous and harder to operationalize. Although some self-serving instrumental motives lie behind most diplomacy, there must be a strong sense of global responsibility and obligation that compels the state to act. Actions taken in the national interest must be balanced by the conviction that contributing to a universal, globalized value system will strengthen one's own values.

Korea's Globilization

If we compare the objectives of the *segyehwa* (globalization) program with the propositions laid out in the previous section, Korea appears to have developed globalized conceptions of security. In particular, the program exhibits three key traits one would associate with globalization: (1) greater multilateralism in diplomacy, (2) norms of international responsibility and obligation, and (3) bureaucratic innovation.

Inaugurated by the Kim Young Sam government in 1993–4, *segyehwa* has as its stated objectives raising South Korea's international competitiveness and preparing it to play a central role in the international arena. As then Foreign Minister Han Sung-joo, a key architect of *segyehwa* diplomacy, stated, "The internationalization of Korean society will be undertaken as Korea endeavors diplomatically to propel itself towards the world and the future. Domestic process and diplomatic enterprise will mutually influence and hopefully reinforce each other." According to this vision, Seoul would no longer allow the problem of North Korea to limit its foreign policy. Instead, South Korean diplomacy would be more supportive of universal values of freedom, justice, peace, and welfare. This would be exemplified by Korea's active participation in arms control and nonproliferation regimes, multilateral institutions, global economic integration, human-rights regimes, regional-security cooperation, and environmentally responsible production practices. In all cases, Korea would play a unique role as an intermediary between developed countries and lesser developed countries (LDCs).[26]

---

[26] Han Sung-joo, "Korea and World Order in the Next Century" (address to the Seoul Forum for International Affairs, 17 December 1993, reprinted in Han Sung-joo, *Korea in a Changing World Order: Democracy, Diplomacy, and Future Developments* [Seoul: OREUM, 1995], 56). In the same volume, see idem, "New Korea's Diplomacy toward the World and the Future" (address before the Korean Council on Foreign Affairs, 31 May 1993, 13–31), and "Emerging New World Order and Korea's New Diplomacy" (address before the Korean Association of International Studies, 26 August 1993, 38–46).

The vision sounded both ambitious and ambiguous, the latter most likely a strategic choice by the Kim Young Sam government, as almost every domestic- or foreign-policy initiative or reform was couched in the language of *segyehwa*. For example, in the political arena, globalization took the form of anticorruption drives and clean-government campaigns.[27] In the social arena, it meant greater attentiveness to quality-of-life and social-welfare issues.[28] In the arena of economics, *segyehwa* encompassed everything from rooting out corruption in business practices, deregulating financial institutions, and passing Foreign Direct Investment (FDI) reforms to more innocuous things such as holding language and classes in Western dining etiquette.

Segyehwa was also related to nationalism in that one of the purposes of "internationalizing" Korea was to promote it as a "rags to riches" success story. In other words, in order for Korea to be accepted globally as a country that went from the total destruction of 1953 to become a free-market democracy and a member of the elite OECD, Korea had to shed the aberrant traits that defined its Cold War identity. As Samuel Kim notes in Chapter 1 of this volume, *segyehwa* in this sense was a way of projecting a new national identity and role conception for Korea.[29] Therefore, reducing the strong interventionist role of the state, rooting out the last vestiges of military-authoritarian politics, and disavowing the neomercantilist tradition in trade practices were imperative parts of *segyehwa*'s "normalizing" of Korea.

Most significant, *segyehwa* translated to aspirations for a more active role in multilateral diplomacy. As one scholar noted, Korean foreign policy must cast off its traditional moorings. "It is no longer sufficient to anchor our Northeast Asian diplomacy on relations with Japan and the United States. It is necessary to conduct multilateral diplomacy to deal more independently with the four powers surrounding the Korean Peninsula."[30] In this spirit, *segyehwa* proponents argue, Seoul sought a larger role in various regional institutions and international organizations. For example, in the ASEAN Regional Forum (ARF), where the ROK is a dialogue partner, Seoul proposed extending the ARF to include

---

[27] Victor Cha, "Politics and Democracy under the Kim Young Sam Government: Something Old, Something New," *Asian Survey* 33, no. 9 (September 1993), 849–63.

[28] Sunhyuk Kim, "State and Civil Society in South Korea's Democratization," ibid. 37, no. 12 (December 1997), 1135–44.

[29] See Chapter 1 of this volume.

[30] Yoon Young-kwan, "Globalization: Towards a New Nationalism in Korea," *Sasang Quarterly*, Winter 1994, reprinted in *Korea Focus* (January–February 1995), 24–5. See also Kim Jin-Hyun, "Preparing for the Twenty-first Century: Korea's Globalization Policy and Its Implications for Future Korea-U.S. Relations," in *Korea's Turn to Globalization: and Korea-U.S. Economic Cooperation* (South Orange, NJ: Seton Hall, Stillman School of Business, 1996), 5.

the six-party Northeast Asia Security Dialogue.[31] It has also played prominent roles in Asian Pacific Economic Cooperation (APEC), CSCAP, and
the Northeast Asian Cooperation Dialogue, hosting meetings of these
groups in Seoul.[32] Upon admission to the United Nations in 1991, the
ROK immediately sought a nonpermanent seat on the Security Council,
and it is currently the fifteenth largest contributor to the U.N. regular
budget (0.95 percent of the total U.N. budget).[33] ROK membership and
participation in U.N. organs and/or committees have increased dramatically, from only two prior to 1991 to thirteen in 1998.[34]

The ROK has also sought more proactive roles in multilateral fora
more generally. Aside from the U.N. contributions, Seoul increased its
memberships in international governmental organizations from nineteen in 1960 to forty-eight by the mid-1990s and now spends as much as
$12.9 million annually in support of these activities ($8.8 million in
1998). Similarly, participation in NGOs increased from 102 in 1960 to
more than 1,000 in 1995.[35] South Korea also boosted its position as a
provider of international aid. Its total Official Development Assistance
(ODA) expenditures increased from $57.48 million in 1991 to $159
million in 1996, with grants to Africa, Vietnam, and other LDCs. During
the same period, outright grants-in-aid increased from $25 million to $53
million and contributions to international organizations from $5.8 mil-
lion to $30 million.[36] The Korea Overseas International Cooperation
Agency (KOICA) was established in April 1991 (before the Kim Young
Sam administration), and international fellowship programs were instituted to bring African, Southeast Asian, and Eastern European students

[31] Charles Morrison, ed., *Asia-Pacific Security Outlook* (Honolulu, HI: East-West
Center, 1997), 70–1; and Ministry of National Defense (hereafter MND),
Defense White Paper, 1997–1998 (Seoul, 1998), 82–3.
[32] MND, *Defense White Paper, 1997–1998*, 32–3.
[33] By comparison, China's contribution amounts to 0.9 percent of the total U.N.
regular budget, and North Korea's, 0.03 percent. The ROK ranking in this context has risen from twentieth in 1992. See Chapter 9 in this volume; also see
March 1999 figures located at the MOFA website http://www.mofat.go.kr/
en_default.html.
[34] These are the Security Council, the Economic and Social Council, the Children's Fund, the Commission on Narcotic Drugs, and the Crime Prevention
and Criminal Justice, Human Rights, Program and Coordination, Information, Outer Space, Development Program (UNDP), Social Development, Population and Development, and Status of Women committees (see Chapter 9
in this volume). Peacekeeping Operations (PKO) contributions are discussed
later in this section.
[35] Samuel Kim, "North Korea and the United Nations," *International Journal of
Korean Studies* (Spring 1997), 77–109, table on p. 86.
[36] See *http://www.mofat.go.kr/en_default.html*. Also see Chapter 8 in this volume for
more detailed data.

to Korea for language and engineering training. An embryonic version of the American Peace Corps sent 130 young Koreans to Asia, Africa, Latin American, and the Middle East.[37] As another analyst noted, a new sense of global concern appeared to infuse Korean behavior. "[Korea] must share and shoulder the responsibility of leading and guiding the crusades against such global problems as AIDS, poverty, boat people, family disintegration, urbanization, drugs, crime, nuclear disarmament, human rights violations and tyrant-dictatorships in many underdeveloped countries."[38]

Moreover, proponents contend that this *segyehwa* trend has been evident in the security arena. Since 1994 the ROK has sought to diversify its portfolio of military-related international activities. These efforts included exchanges of high-ranking officers, mutual port calls, new assignments of military attachés abroad, defense academy exchange programs, and exchanges of information about technology and the defense industry. The Ministry of National Defense also instituted a wide range of working-level policy talks with Japan, Germany, Australia, Great Britain, France, and Canada in addition to those with the United States.[39]

Support of U.N. peacekeeping operations (PKO) is another facet of Korea's security globalization. ROK armed forces have taken part in five peacekeeping operations in Africa, South Asia, and the former Soviet Union (see table 10.1). In addition, in 1995 the National Defense College instituted revisions to the curriculum allowing for study of U.N. peacekeeping operations and requirements as well as a program to send three to four officers yearly to PKO training courses in Europe and Canada.[40] Like other nations participating in peacekeeping operations, the ROK since 1995 has also designated national equipment and units for the U.N. Standby Agreement.[41]

Finally, the ROK has supported multilateral arms control and weapons conventions because these are considered critical to the *segyehwa* vision

---

[37] KOICA, interviews and site visit by author, Seoul, September 1991; also see http://www.koica.or.kr/english/index2.html.
[38] Kim, "Preparing for the Twenty-first Century," 9.
[39] MND, *Defense White Paper, 1997–1998*, 81–2.
[40] For details on South Korean PKO training abroad, see ibid., 93.
[41] The Standby Agreement is the peacetime designation of national forces to enable rapid U.N. responses to contingencies. The ROK commitment amounts to one infantry battalion (540 personnel); one heavy-construction engineering unit (130 personnel); one medical-support unit (80 personnel); two explosives-disposal units (11 personnel); a rescue unit (10-15 personnel); and military observers (36 personnel). Sixty-two nations have made similar commitments in principle, but only six have exchanged memoranda of understanding to substantiate these commitments (South Korea has not) (see ibid., 92–3; and Chapter 9 in this volume).

Table 10.1   South Korean U.N. PKO Participation, 1993–7

Place	Troop Size/Type	Period	Status
Somalia (UNOSOM)	252/engineers	July 1993– March 1994	Withdrawn
Angola (UNAVEM)	198/engineers	October 1995– December 1996	Withdrawn
Angola	6/administrative staff	February 1996– February 1997	Withdrawn
Western Sahara (MINURSO)	Medical staff (a)	September 1994	Active
IndiaPakistan (UNMOGIP)	9–10/military observers	November 1994	Active
Georgia (UNOMIG)	3–5/military observers	October 1994	Active (b)

Source: Adapted from MND, *Defense White Paper, 1998*, 149.
Note: a) Approximately 222 personnel have been rotated at six-month intervals since the start of the mission; b) South Korean personnel also took part in U.N. peacekeeping operations in Cambodia (UNTAC) in 1992–3 and in South Africa (UNOMSA) in 1994, but their numbers were extremely small (i.e., no more than six individuals for administrative tasks in each operation).

of postconflict peacebuilding, nonproliferation, and preventive diplomacy. Most recently, Seoul signed on to the Comprehensive Test Ban Treaty (CTBT); the Nuclear Suppliers Group and the Zangger Committee (to control the export and import of nuclear equipment, materials, and technology); and the U.N. Arms Register (to report the export or import of offensive conventional weapons, i.e., tanks, armored vehicles, field artillery) (see table 10.2).

Segyehwa proponents are correct in highlighting these activities as evidence that globalization's imperatives are permeating South Korean security policies. In spite of this, many aspects of Korean behavior still do not fit this vision. Although the rhetoric of globalization highlights Korea's new emphasis on IOs and transnational organizations, the numbers do not necessarily bear this out. For example, even though Korea is the sixth largest contributor of funds to some sixty trade-related international organizations, Korean nationals staff only twenty of these bodies.[42] Similarly, although the ROK ranks fifteenth among 184 U.N. member nations in terms of fiscal contribution, it ranks only fiftieth in terms of

[42] Yoon, "Globalization," 23.

Table 10.2 ROK Membership in Multilateral Arms Control Conventions, 1975–98

Treaty/Agreement	Membership	Membership Status
Nonproliferation (NPT)	Yes	Since 1975
Peaceful Use of Nuclear Energy	Yes	Since 1990
CTBT	Yes	Since 1996
Nuclear Suppliers Group/Zangger	Yes	Since 1995
Chemical Weapons Convention (CWC)	Yes	Since 1997
Biological Weapons Convention (BWC)	Yes	Since 1975
Missile Technology Control Regime	No	Seeks membership (currently under U.S.–ROK 1978 missile agreement)
U.N. Arms Register	Yes	Since 1993
CCW (antipersonnel land mines)	No	Declares exception based on national security needs

Source: Compiled from MND, *Defense White Paper, 1998*, 143–8.

the number of its U.N. employees in managerial positions.[43] While this certainly may be a function of the politics of IOs (indeed, a Korean national vied for the chairmanship of the World Trade Organization [WTO] and lost), it also reflects a bias in the foreign-service bureaucracy that still accords lesser status and training for positions in IOs and other nonnational organizations. An alternative explanation posited for the low Korean representation in such organizations is language barriers. The United Nations, for example, requires fluency in English and one additional language, a requirement that many South Koreans cannot meet. But this is more symptomatic of the general problem than a solution to it. It again reflects deficiencies in a foreign-service language-training curriculum and organizational culture that do not encourage Korean "internationalists" in this direction.

A closer look at Korean PKO and ODA activities generates similarly uninspiring findings. In the former case, although the ROK appears

[43] Lee, "Attitudinal Reform toward Globalization," 93.

quite active, gross contributions to the U.N. PKO budget have decreased annually since 1995 (from $5.26 million to $5 million in 1997). Moreover, the share of PKO support in both monetary and manpower terms is relatively less than that of South Korea's peer countries (e.g., Pakistan, Bangladesh, Jordan, Poland, Russia, and Canada each contribute more than one thousand personnel) and proportionally less than would be expected given Korea's comparative ranking in terms of contribution to the regular U.N. budget (i.e., in the top eighth or ninth percentile).[44] Regarding ODA, in spite of yearly aggregate increases from 1991 to 1995, the percentage of GNP accounted for by ODA remained constant at 0.02–0.03 percent, representing no real increases in commitments since 1991.[45] Moreover, this figure is below the average ratio of ODA to GNP for OECD countries (0.27 percent) as well as below that of the ROK's peer economies (e.g., Spain, at 0.23 percent; Austria, at 0.34 percent; and the Netherlands, at 0.80 percent).

Similarly, while norms of international responsibility are prominent in rhetoric, the predominant rationalization is still quid pro quo diplomacy. A good illustration of this is again Korean attitudes toward U.N. peacekeeping operations. Korea's participation and contributions help to project an image of a multilateralist and internationally responsible country. This image was not tarnished when Seoul opposed a larger Japanese role in peacekeeping operations in the early 1990s. Most observers simply attributed Korea's opposition to its deep-seated trepidations concerning renewed Japanese militarism. However, Seoul opposed Japanese peacekeeping for purely self-interested reasons: It wanted to preempt the heightened international pressures on Korea to increase its own peacekeeping role that would be attendant on a larger Japanese role. In addition, ROK government statements clearly reveal that the primary incentive structure by which PKO participation is justified is parochial rather than international (i.e., "to enable the ROK to justify its call for help from member states in the event of hostilities on the Korean peninsula").[46]

Self-interested, instrumentalist thinking is also apparent in some Korean arguments about arms control and APEC. While Korean commitments to these conventions are admirable, government statements clearly indicate that such internationalist cooperation is qualified by three conditions: (1) Korea's right to curtail participation and adherence as dictated by the domestic security situation; (2) consistency between these international conventions and the direction of domestic policies

---

[44] See Chapter 9 of this volume for elaboration on these figures.
[45] See table 8.5 in this volume.
[46] MND, *Defense White Paper, 1997–98,* 86. It is only after this statement that the white paper goes on to cite ROK military globalization as another incentive for PKO participation.

on economics, science, and technology; and (3) a guarantee that North
Korean missiles and weapons of mass destruction (WMD) can be controlled by international non-proliferation regimes.[47] These principles
make ROK arms control and nonproliferation commitments far from
close-ended.

Regarding APEC, participation is seen as desirable because Seoul's
membership and leadership in the body would provide even greater
leverage against the North (as some analysts put it, the North would be
forced into "defensive cooperation" with the South). In addition, participation is necessary because Korea does not benefit from any subre-
gional economic networks like the China-Taiwan-overseas Chinese,
Japan and Southeast Asia, or Association of Southeast Asian Nations
(ASEAN) networks.[48] Thus, although Korea's language in support of
APEC is in line with what one would expect from a country whose security attitudes increasingly are permeated by globalization processes, the
rationale behind the rhetoric – that is, competition with the North and
the necessity of avoiding exclusion from regional groupings – is less in
tune with norms of international obligation and collaboration.[49] As Lee
Hong-koo stated, diffuse reciprocity is an important principle that must
undergird any globalization-influenced country's rationale for cooperation, but Korea in many ways lacks this.[50]

The United States and Korea

The contradictions in Korea's globalization policies are most apparent
with regard to Korea's relationship with the United States. If Korean
security conceptions were truly globalist, one might expect developments along two axes: (1) the emergence of issues in the alliance that
operate at the nexus of internal and external security and nonphysical
security; and (2) compelling arguments for a somewhat reduced role for
the United States as Korea looked to its future. This would not necessarily mean an outright abrogation of alliance ties, but it would certainly
mean a much greater emphasis on multilateralism over bilateralism in
foreign affairs.

---

[47] Ibid., 103–4.
[48] Yong Chool Ha and Taehyun Kim, "Reflections on APEC: A Korean View," in
eds. Donald Emmerson and Kenneth Pyle, *From APEC to Xanadu: Creating a
Viable Community in the Post–Cold War Pacific* (Armonk, NY: M. E. Sharpe, 1997),
148–73.
[49] Indeed, the alternative to APEC participation is for Korea to create its own sub-
regional grouping involving the South, the Korean-Chinese overseas community, and the North (Ha and Kim, "Reflections on APEC," 168).
[50] Lee, "Attitudinal Reform toward Globalization," 93–4.

SOFA

To a certain extent, issues along the first axis have been present. The renegotiation of the status-of-forces agreement (SOFA) over the past two years is one example of globalization-induced convergence of internal and external security issues. Originally instituted in the mid-1960s, SOFA defines the rights and restrictions of U.S. military personnel in Korea. A primary issue in the renegotiations was the legal jurisdiction for off-base crimes committed by American servicemen. The results of these negotiations were extremely advantageous to the United States, protecting servicemen from Korean domestic law and detention. For this reason, of some forty-seven thousand crimes allegedly committed by U.S. servicemen from 1967 to 1992, only 2 percent were actually tried in Korean courts (compared to 31 percent in Japan and 21 percent in the Philippines).

When serious negotiations on SOFA revision started, the ROK wanted to strengthen domestic criminal jurisdiction over U.S. servicemen's actions as well as other issues (e.g., labor rights for Korean nationals employed on U.S. bases). Although the United States was sympathetic to Seoul's concerns, it had concerns of its own about how American servicemen would be treated under the Korean legal system.[51] This was a prickly issue in U.S.-ROK relations that gave rise to a groundswell of anti-American sentiment and popular antipathy to the civil-military externalities of the defense treaty.

The specific origin of this issue was political (i.e., the Okinawa rape and renegotiation of the U.S.-Japan SOFA), but the broader underlying cause was linked to globalization. Globalization and development changed the nature of civil-military relations regarding U.S. forces in Korea (USFK) in such a way that USFK were no longer seen as "saviors" who enjoyed special privileges within the host nation. The SOFA revision blurred distinctions between the host nation's internal security and its national security.

Missile Technology

Similarly, the debate on missile technology illustrates how nonphysical security has affected the contours of the alliance. Seoul has been interested

---

[51] For example, Seoul wanted custody at or before indictment (instead of after conviction), as well as the right of appeals to a higher court (where Korean prosecutors have a 90 percent success rate in cases of double-jeopardy appeals). The United States agreed to custody but disagreed regarding which crimes should be covered. The United States also wanted an official to be present during questioning to prevent coerced confessions and the right to cross-examine accusers (as in U.S. law).

in developing longer-range cruise missiles and terminating a 1979 agree-ment with the United States that restricts missile ranges to 112 miles.[52] In lieu of this, the ROK wants to join the missile technology control regime (MTCR), which would effectively allow missiles with a maximum range of 186 miles.[53] The United States opposes this on the grounds that Seoul does not need longer-range missiles for its primary security contingency (a ground war with North Korea) and that for that reason the devel-opment of such capabilities would only incite acute security-dilemma spirals with Japan and be generally destabilizing to the region.

This dispute is a function of globalization because the driving force behind it is the increasing accessibility of such missile technologies. The South Koreans have intimated that should the United States continue to oppose their plan, they would seek the technology through other parties (i.e., Russia). Indeed the added irony of this issue is that the desire for new technologies and greater power projection is couched in the global-ization language of commitments to arms control. As the Ministry of National Defense's white paper states, "The ROK is now affiliated with just about every international treaty and agreement devised to control proliferation of the weapons of mass destruction except the MTCR."[54]

Bilateralism Preferred over Multilateralism

Globalization therefore has fueled some of the recent issue-specific troubles in the U.S.-ROK alliance relationship. However, South Korea's overall outlooks and attitudes toward the alliance show little change in spite of the imperatives of globalization. Rather than frame the future in terms of multilateralism and regional-security communities, Seoul has emphasized with relatively greater enthusiasm the longevity and stead-fastness of the bilateral alliance as the key ROK security priority for the future. This has been the assumption across virtually the entire political

---

[52] For a concise overview of missile development on the peninsula and in the region more generally, see David Wiencek, "Missile Proliferation in Asia," in eds. William Carpenter and David Wiencek, *Asian Security Handbook* (Armonk, NY: M. E. Sharpe, 1996), 63–78.

[53] MTCR signatories (currently twenty-eight nations) are expected to enforce voluntary embargoes on the transfer of missile technology (i.e., "Category I" missiles with 500-kg warheads and a range of 330+ km). South Korea currently deploys the French Exocet (42 km) antiship missile and two versions (air- and ship-launch) of the American Harpoon missile (120 km). By comparison, North Korea deploys reverse-engineered Styx and Silkworm cruise missiles (41–95 km) and a modified Silkworm of longer range (160 km). North Korea also possesses an active ballistic-missile program, ranging from Scud B and Scud C (300–550 km) missiles to the longer-range No-Dong series (I and II) of 1,500+ km and the Taepo-Dong series (2,000+ km).

[54] MND, *Defense White Paper, 1997–98*, 106.

spectrum (with the possible exception of students). Critics of the alliance (including Kim Dae Jung in his opposition days) now speak of retaining the alliance unconditionally even after unification. Multilateralists also temper their advocacy for more varied external policies by embedding it in the solid foundation of the U.S.-ROK alliance.[55] This bilateralist obsession runs counter to globalization's predictions of behavior and preferences at the more multilateralist end of the continuum.

There is an additional contradiction in ROK behavior in this regard. Globalization's predictions are incorrect not only in that strict bilateralism dominates Korea's future security strategies but in that those who do not advocate bilateralism instead advocate unilateralism and self-help strategies. Nowhere is this more evident than in South Korean procurement patterns. Plans for force improvements that extend into the twenty-first century increasingly emphasize acquisition of power projection capabilities.[56] The ROK Navy (ROKN) is in the midst of completing the first stage of the KDX Destroyer Program, which entails developing 3,200-ton destroyers (KDX1) to replace old Gearing ships acquired from the U.S. Navy in the 1960s and 1970s. There are also plans for construction by the year 2006 of nine 4,300-ton destroyers (KDX2) with an operating range of four thousand miles and, eventually, acquisition of state-of-the-art Aegis destroyers (KDX3) starting in 2010. An active submarine program is also under way. The completion of twelve new 1,200-ton 209-class submarines is expected by 2001. Concurrently, there are plans to build six 1,500-ton submarines by 2002 (the SSU program), and there are some calls for development of 3,000-ton submarines. In 1995 a South Korean trading firm purchased two Kiev aircraft carriers (the *Minsk* and the *Novorossiyskk*) from Russia, ostensibly for scrap metal, but many believe that they were purchased so that their technology could be used in future domestic development (the navy has talked about developing a 12,000-ton transport ship that could serve as a small aircraft carrier by 2010). Other programs include the planned purchase of four AWACS early-warning aircraft from the United States by 2010 at a cost of $1.7 billion; CN-235 transport planes (from Spain and Indonesia); inflight refueling capabilities; and development of a longer-range fighter plane (KTX 2).[57]

[55] Yoon, "Globalization," 23–5.
[56] Details for procurement programs refer to the period prior to the IMF liquidity crisis.
[57] On these points, see MND, *Defense White Paper, 1997–1998*; "Defense Ministry Pushes Destroyer Plan," *Korea Herald*, 8 June 1998; Myung-ho Moon, "Debate on a Blue Water Navy," *Munhwa Ilbo*, 8 April 1997; "Military Concerned about Defense Budget Cuts," *Korea Herald*, 7 February 1998; Morrison, *Asia-Pacific Security Outlook*; "Major Military Procurement Projects to Be Delayed or

All of these programs give the ROK military a new force-projection-capability dimension. Moreover, these programs are being given a high priority in the ROK's overall security outlook for the next ten to fifteen years. At a time when most of the military budget has been subject to post-Cold War reductions, portions dedicated to force improvement increased between 1996 and 1997.[58] Moreover, although the economic crisis in late 1997 led to postponement or cancellation of a number of defense-related projects in early 1998 (including the scheduled AWACS purchases), two projects that were initially cut back but then reinstated in supplementary budgets were the acquisitions of SSU submarines and KDX destroyers, again highlighting the emphasis placed on projecting naval power in the region.[59]

The rationale for these programs is about as nonglobalist as one can imagine. Force projection and blue-water naval capabilities are desired less for the purpose of future maritime coordination or cooperative security than for self-help reasons:

> The ROK [can] not presently deal with regional contingencies. The ROK depends entirely on the United States to handle military crises off the Korean Peninsula and would find it difficult to manage a contingency involving China or Japan over the next 15 years if the United States were no longer present. Thus ... the ROK should begin now to build up its naval and air forces to deal with a range of regional contingencies.... the future purpose of the ROK Navy will be to deal with future adversaries invading Korean maritime territory. These adversaries ... will be equipped with platforms and weapons of high speed, long range, high precision, stealthiness, and destructive power.... Thus, the ROKN must develop a force capable of conducting effective sea-denial operations, which involve combined hit-and-run tactics, covert attacks, offensive and defensive mining, and submarine coastal defense operations.[60]

Canceled," *Korea Times*, 8 January 1998; "South Korea to Buy Eight CN-235 Indonesian Military Aircraft," *Korea Herald*, 20 November 1997; *Korea's Seapower and National Development in the Era of Globalization* (Seoul: Sejong Institute, 1995); Yong-sup Han, "Korea's Security Strategy for Twenty-first Century: Cooperation and Conflict," *Korea Focus* 5, no. 4 (July–August 1997); Joon-ho Do, "Security Strategy for Twenty-first Century," *Wolgan Choson*, 25 November 1993; Seo-hang Lee, "Naval Power as an Instrument of Foreign Policy," *Korea Focus* 5, no. 2 (March–April 1997).

[58] The actual increase was marginal (from 28 percent to 28.9 percent of the budget), but in its annual report, the ROK defense ministry highlighted this as a significant turnaround (MND, *Defense White Paper, 1997–1998*, 191–2).

[59] The revised budget, which includes funds for the KDX2 and SSU programs, is subject to approval by the National Assembly in September 1998 ("Defense Ministry Pushes Destroyer Plan"; and *Xinhua News Agency*, 7 June 1998).

[60] Korea Institute for Defense Analyses and Center for Naval Analyses, *Prospects for U.S.-Korean Naval Relations in the 21st Century* (Seoul, February 1995), 11–2; see also Moon, "Debate on a Blue Water Navy."

Granted these are military rationalizations for procurement; however, they resonate with a public sentiment that looks upon Korea's security future in nonintegrative terms. There is little sense that security is seen in cooperative or peace-building terms and a stronger affinity to understanding needs in pure self-help and competitive terms.

Korean Identity and Policies

To what are these contradictions attributable? Why does Korea vacillate between behavior and traits that do and do not reflect adjustments to the influences of globalization? How does one explain the gap between the rhetoric of multilateralism and the practice of bilateralism (or unilateralism)?

The primary causes may be identity and values. Although there is an external impetus for globalization, there are internal qualities that resist these imperatives. When the forces for globalization are refracted through this prism of Korean identity, the behavior that emerges reflects a tension between globalization pressures on the one hand and localization imperatives on the other.

Realist Mindsets

These localization impulses derive from a mixture of qualities. First, the ROK's strategic prism remains firmly entrenched in a classic realist mindset.[61] This mindset is the residue of history and certain immutable geopolitical traits. Because Korea is a border state for the major powers and a relatively weak power in relation to its immediate neighbors, its history has been characterized by the bitter experience of penetration from outside in the nineteenth century, the loss of sovereignty in the early twentieth century, and then division by war. Even in the post–Cold War era, its strategic situation is characterized by proximity to a hyperrealist state in North Korea and a neorealist state in China.[62] The combination of historically definitive experiences in a traditionally (and contemporarily) security-scarce region naturally makes balance of power politics the primary template for the Korean strategic mindset.

This is evident, for example, in views on Korean unification. As Patrick Morgan observes, South Koreans view the future as highly competitive and suspicious. "States surrounding Korea are potential threats, inherently

---

[61] Patrick Morgan, "The U.S.-ROK Strategic Relationship: A Liberalist Analysis," in Donald Clark et al., *U.S.-Korean Relations* (Claremont, CA: Keck Center, 1995); Cha, "Realism, Liberalism, and the Durability of the U.S.-South Korean Alliance."

[62] My thanks to Samuel Kim for raising this point.

uneasy about the emergence of a stronger Korea, bound to compete for influence on the peninsula as in the past. Thus Korea has to prepare to use its elbows in the regional jockeying for power and influence that will take place."[63] In planning their grand strategy with regard to Northeast Asia, therefore, Koreans place less credence in more globalized scenarios of a united Korea nested in a web of cooperative regional-security communities and much more credence in scenarios of a reunified Korea that must provide for itself in a region of powers with aggressive tendencies. The latter scenarios are externalizations of Korea's own strategic mindset, which again reflects well the fixation with security in narrow power-politics terms. For this reason, prescriptions about the future reflect assumptions of "time's cycle" (rather than "time's arrow"), in which security dynamics around the peninsula after watershed events such as the end of the Cold War or unification will resemble the struggles of the past rather than a more globalized cooperative security for the future.[64] While their rhetoric is laced with the language of globalization, Koreans remain firmly entrenched in balance-of-power thinking.

Relative-Gains Diplomacy

Another quality from which these localization impulses derive is the grounding of diplomacy in a relative-gains mindset. This mentality again grows out of the accumulated experience of Korea's tough neighborhood and in particular its experience as a divided country. Survival and development in a security-scarce environment and in constant competition with the proximate Northern threat has caused almost all diplomacy to be seen through the lens of relative-gains competition with North Korea.[65]

This may seem anachronistic today as the South has clearly won this competition. However, because South Korea's identity and legitimacy as a state since 1948 have been defined almost wholly in juxtaposition to the North, this mentality continues to inform policy, which naturally inhibits an internationalist policy and diffuse reciprocity more typical of globalization.

Analysts have pointed to developments such as the Roh Tae Woo regime's successful *nordpolitik* with Communist powers or the South's practice of sports diplomacy as watersheds in a foreign policy increasingly

---

[63] Morgan, "The U.S.-ROK Strategic Relationship," 98.

[64] On "time's arrow" see Robert Jervis, "The Future of World Politics," *International Security* (Winter 1991–2).

[65] For similar observations, see Han Sung-joo, "The Korean Peninsula: Today and Tomorrow" (address before the Asia Society, New York, 30 September 1994, reprinted in *Korea in a Changing World Order,* 84–95).

less mired in zero-sum relative-gains mindsets.[66] However, these too were motivated by relative-gains and zero-sum mindsets regarding North Korea. The two primary fruits of *nordpolitik* and sports diplomacy (i.e., Seoul's hosting of the 1986 Asiad and the 1988 Olympiad) were normalization with the Soviet Union in 1990 and with China in 1992. These events were of course welcomed in the language of economic interdependence, tension reduction, and security cooperation, yet the true benefit as seen by planners in Seoul was that they amounted to the ultimate diplomatic coup over the ROK's northern rival. *Nordpolitik* and sports diplomacy effectively won over the North's two primary Cold War patrons and closed the circle in terms of isolating and cutting the North off from any significant supporters in the international arena. This instrumentalist calculation of every policy in the context of the zero-sum competition with the North explains why the ROK may support regional-security endeavors, but not as a response to globalization pressures. It also helps to explain the general absence of diffuse-reciprocity norms and the focus on quid pro quo diplomacy.[67]

Reactive Nationalism

The third factor is reactive nationalism. Korean identity is strongly negative in strain. Nationalism has run the gamut from the antimodernization of the nineteenth century to the anti-Japanism of the colonial period to the anti-Communism of the Cold War to anti-Americanism of students in the 1980s, and, some observe, to the current anti-IMFism of the era of economic crisis and austerity. Today the two major national holidays in Korea – *samilchol* and *kwangbokchol* – celebrate Korean patriotism in anti-Japan terms. The central event in the vast celebrations of fifty years of Korean independence in 1995 was the razing of the National Museum (which formerly housed the Japanese colonial headquarters).[68] While negative nationalism has certainly been a reaction to the events of each era, this anti-internationalist identity has been rooted in three deeper factors.

[66] Chung-in Moon and Seok-soo Lee, "The Post–Cold War Security Agenda of Korea: Inertia, New Thinking, and Assessments," *Pacific Review* 8, no. 1 (1995).
[67] Again, the analytical distinction here is not that Korea is the only country that practices this type of diplomacy but that relative to others, it places a much greater emphasis on specific reciprocity as a condition of its external interaction.
[68] By contrast, the American celebration of patriotism on 4 July is not as negatively constructed. It is more a pro-American holiday than an anti-British one; this is reflected in its symbolism, which on the whole does not resurrect images of resistance and demonization of the enemy.

First is the Choson tradition of neo-Confucianism. The Korean value system is still grounded in nearly six centuries (1392–1910) of Confucian teachings, which emphasized rejection of things foreign, equating them with uncultured barbarianism.[69] This tradition fosters a mentality that chooses to ignore things foreign rather than learn from them. Furthermore, Korea's homogeneity and its insecurities as the historical victim in the region only serve to reinforce this antiforeign bias in a xenophobia anathema to globalization.[70]

The second is Korea's twentieth-century development experience. In addition to the strongly negative components of Korean identity, one very positive component was economic prosperity. This prosperity in turn was based on a development strategy that since the 1960s has emphasized a strong state with an interventionist role and neomercantilist protectionism, which cause Korean identity and conceptions of the state to go against the grain of globalization.[71] Nowhere is this more manifest than in the mode of implementation of the *segyehwa* program by the Kim Young Sam administration. As Chung-in Moon notes, this implementation had an oxymoronic quality, as globalization was implemented "top-down" as a government strategy, while globalization itself is a bottom-up phenomenon predicated on the dissolution of statism.[72]

The third factor is Korea's democratization experience. Globalization processes appear to have little effect on younger generations of Koreans, who tend to be more isolationist and nationalist than progressive and internationalist in their outlook. This in part is a function of the contradictions between Korea's democratization struggles and its Cold War security imperatives. Successive generations of students who stood up against past military-authoritarian regimes in the South perceived direct associations between the strength and intransigence of these regimes

---

[69] Lee, "Attitudinal Reform toward Globalization," 86.

[70] One manifestation of this is the "Seoul-hak" school, which sees Korea as the future metropolis at the center of the world because of its racial homogeneity and in the unique position of being at the center of four world spheres (see ibid., 86–7; Kim, "Preparing for the Twenty-first Century," 6; and Kim Sang-ki, "Traditionalism and Universalism," *Korea Focus* 2, no. 1 [January–February 1994], 26–7).

[71] Yoon, "Globalization," 14–5. As Hong-koo Lee states, this is evident in Korean and British attitudes toward FDI. Koreans are much more likely than the British to frame this as foreign penetration and subjugation (Lee, "Attitudinal Reform toward Globalization," 88–9).

[72] Moon, "Globalization," 62. It should be noted that the literature does not limit the process of globalization to a "bottom-up" phenomenon, nor does it assume that this process is normatively preferable to others. I am indebted to Samuel Kim for raising this point.

and the level of support they received from foreign powers, especially the United States and Japan. This only served to reinforce an antiforeign nationalism and an inherent distrust of outsiders.[73]

These three factors complicate the globalization challenge for Korea. On the one hand, Korea's economic capabilities and rising position in the status hierarchy require it to embrace globalization challenges. On the other hand, these policies sometimes run counter to certain deeply rooted aspects of Korean identity. The result is policy and behavior that is often inconsistent and incomplete.

Conclusion

This chapter examines globalization and Korean security from two perspectives. First, it highlights and addresses the relative absence of hypothesis-generating studies on the effect of globalization processes on security behavior. Second, viewing Korean security in this context, it describes three general ways by which security policy must meet the challenges of globalization: (1) adapting policy to intermestic issues, (2) increasing openness to bureaucratic innovation and multilateralism; and (3) increasing emphasis on diffuse reciprocity. Certain aspects of ROK strategic behavior have met the challenges of globalization processes; however, some policies and attitudes have deviated from this trend. In the U.S.-ROK alliance, globalization's effects were reflected in the emergence of specific issues that have caused problems in the relationship recently; at the same time, however, the Korean obsession with the longevity of this security alliance resists the impulses of globalization. These inconsistencies in the empirical realm further confirm that globalization is far from a homogenizing process in international relations. As James Rosenau states, "At one extreme are adaptations which accept the boundary-broadening processes and make the best of them by integrating them into local customs and practices. At the other extreme are responses intended to ward off the globalizing processes by resort to ideological purities, closed borders, and economic isolation, to mention only the main ways in which boundaries are heightened."[74] In the latter case, globalization highlights and articulates differences more than sameness among national and regional entities. This is evident in the Korean case. Inconsistencies in Korean behavior toward globalization are a function of national structures and values that interact with globalization

[73] John Oh, "Anti-Americanism and Anti-Authoritarian Politics in Korea," *In Depth* (Spring 1994).
[74] Rosenau, "Dynamics of Globalization," 252.

forces. For this reason, globalization's effects are always refracted through the prism of national identity.

What of the future? Can the Kim Dae Jung administration better meet the challenges of globalization? The initial assessment appears positive. Kim Dae Jung's "sunshine" or engagement policy for North Korea is a departure from decades of zero-sum, relative-gains thinking about inter-Korean competition. Moreover, his policy statements echo many of the wider visions for diplomacy set out by Han Sung-joo when globalization was first introduced, early in the Kim Young Sam administration. However, enthusiasm about such visions faded eventually under the previous administration, and experience teaches one to temper any optimism about the future. Regardless of the outcome, however, the performance of the current administration will provide interesting conceptual insights into the degree to which individual leadership factors influence adjusting to globalization pressures.

CHAPTER 11

Korea's *Segyehwa* Drive: Promise versus Performance

Samuel S. Kim

Segyehwa's Promise

Internationalization-cum-globalization had its antecedents in parlance and policy beginning in the early 1980s. Indeed, for the first time in the history of Korean politics, legitimacy disappeared as an issue in the 1992 presidential election. None of the three leading candidates – Kim Young Sam, Kim Dae Jung, and Chung Ju Young – had a military background; the paramount issue was economic revitalization. Kim Young Sam promised to create "a New Korea" (*sin Hankuk ch'angjo*) and cure the "Korean disease," under which he lumped together all that is wrong with the Korean society and the Korean state – endemic corruption at all levels of society, a decaying work ethic, regional factionalism and animosity, excessive and conspicuous consumption by the nouveux riches, and a faltering economy, to name but a few symptoms. The Kim Young Sam presidency thus got off to a stellar start, with his performance rating soaring as high as 90 percent in the first year (however, it had dropped to 13.9 percent by the end of 1997). Riding on the crest of such procedural legitimacy as the first civilian president in more than thirty years, President Kim Young Sam immediately launched a series of anticorruption and demilitarizing reform measures, including dismantling of the *Hanahoe* (One-mind society), a secret military clique. In addition, in early 1994 the Economic Planning Board, still responsible for the overall national economic strategy, outlined the "twelve tasks" necessary for the full "globalization" of the Korean economy.[1]

However, it was not until 17 November 1994 that President Kim Young

[1] See Barry K. Gills, "Economic Liberalisation and Reform in South Korea in the 1990s: A 'Coming of Age' or a Case of 'Graduation Blues'?" *Third World Quarterly* 17, no. 4 (1996), 677.

Sam formally outlined his own vision of globalization, in a visit to Sydney, Australia, following the APEC summit meeting. That the so-called Sydney Declaration was more than a flash in the pan was made evident in a major reorganization of the executive branch of the government, eliminating overnight the jobs of about one thousand civil servants, including two cabinet ministers, three vice-ministers, four assistant ministers, and twenty-three directors-general. Shortly thereafter, President Kim engineered a major cabinet reshuffle better suited for the all-out globalization drive.

Globalization was also granted an imprimatur in President Kim's 1995 New Year's address and his New Year's press conference at the Blue House. A Presidential *Segyehwa* Promotion Committee (PSPC) was established in January 1995 with a mandate to give shape and substance to his globalization visions and goals broadly delineated in the preceding weeks. Specifically, the PSPC was to work out policies and programs in six priority areas: (1) education, (2) legal and economic systems, (3) politics and the mass media, (4) national and local administrations, (5) the environment, and (6) culture and consciousness.[2] As noted in Chapter 1, *segyehwa* was Seoul's answer to Pyongyang's *juche* in the politics of competitive national-identity legitimation and delegitimation. Since early 1995, a "*segyehwa* fever" has swept the country, as no other buzzword has been more commonly used – and misused – among politicians, policymakers, business entrepreneurs, academicians, and journalists, most of whom stress the positive aspects of globalization.[3]

What's in, of, and by Segyehwa?

The stage was thus set for the word game to be played out in the politics of everyday life in South Korea during much of the Kim Young Sam administration. Not surprisingly, *segyehwa* meant something different to different groups – it was a strategic principle, a mobilizing slogan, a hegemonic ideology, or a new national-identity badge for a state aspiring to

---

[2] The PSPC was made up of three supervising members and ten advisory members; after six months of study, research, and debates, it issued a 207-page report in August 1995. See Presidential Segyehwa Promotion Committee (PSPC), *Segyehwa ui pichon kwa chonryak* [Globalization vision and strategy] (Seoul: Presidential Segyehwa Promotion Committee, August 1995).

[3] See Young Sae Lee, "Globalization in Korea: Prospects, Problems, and Policy," *Korea's Economy 1997* 13 (1997), 36–40; Chung-in Moon, "Globalization: Challenges and Strategies," *Korea Focus* 3, no. 3 (May–June 1995), 62–77; Gills, "Economic Liberalisation and Reform in South Korea in the 1990s"; Gerardo R. Ungson, Richard M. Steers, and Seung-Ho Park, *Korean Enterprise: The Quest for Globalization* (Boston: Harvard Business School Press, 1997); Lee Hong-koo, "Attitudinal Reform toward Globalization," *Korea Focus* 2, no. 2 (March–April 1994), 85–94; and PSPC, *Segyehwa ui pichon kwa chonryak*.

advanced world-class status. Of course, for some domestic critics, it was nothing but political sloganeering aimed at finding an escape route from a web of multiplying domestic political and economic difficulties. For the Korean conglomerates (*chaebol*), it meant having their cake and eating it too – to be free of state monitoring and supervision without giving up politically connected loans or state control of labor unions while at the same going global to escape rising wage and political demands from labor unions at home. For many economists it was a necessity, not a choice, a strategy for survival of the fittest in the neo-Darwinian global marketplace.

Still, *segyehwa* can be seen as Kim Young Sam's way of projecting and enacting a new Korean national identity and role conception, moving away from and beyond inter-Korean competition to the center of the action not only in the Asia-Pacific region but also in the world community. In a speech entitled, "The Vision for the Development of Korea in the 21st Century," delivered before the newly established PSPC on 25 January 1995, President Kim Young Sam proclaimed, "The national goal in the *segyehwa* era is to construct *a unified state* that will be the center of the world and [that] people all over the world will want to come [to], invest [in] and live in."[4] Writing in early 1995, Kang In Duk, unification minister in the Kim Dae Jung government, argued that *segyehwa* was both a means and an end of Korean reunification.[5]

All the same, *segyehwa* was seen by many as the necessary passport to the Organization for Economic Cooperation and Development (OECD) and the U.N. Security Council. "To Make Korea a Central Player on the World Stage" has become the standard justification for Kim Young Sam's *segyehwa* drive. Having inherited the accomplishments of President Roh's *Nordpolitik*, the Kim Young Sam administration was determined to chart a new course toward international status. In enunciating "five fundamentals" of the New Diplomacy" (i.e., globalism, diversification, multidimensionalism, regional cooperation, and future orientation) in May 1993, Foreign Minister Han Sung-Joo declared that "our diplomacy will no longer become hostage to [North Korea]."[6] A year later, all five fundamentals of the New Diplomacy were collapsed into an all-out campaign

---

[4] Cited in Kang In Duk, "South Korea's Strategy toward North Korea in Connection with Its 'Segyehwa' Drive," *East Asian Review* 7, no. 1 (Spring 1995), 55–70, quote on 56, emphasis added.

[5] Ibid.

[6] Sung-Joo Han, "New Korea's Diplomacy toward the World and the Future," in *Segyehwa sidae ui Hankuk oyekyo* [Korean diplomacy in an era of globalization: speeches of Foreign Minister Han Sung-Joo, March 1993–December 1994] (Seoul: Chisik samopsa, 1995), 77. In a spirit of globalization, this volume is published in both Korean and English, with some speeches in Korean and others in English.

for globalization. "The reason why Korea has been striving for globalization, trying to induce foreign investment, liberalizing its financial market, and preparing to join OECD is," Foreign Minister Han declared, "to successfully meet the challenge of the post–UR [Uruguay Round] international order. Korea has to face and overcome new challenges such as interdependence and globalization of issues, and the best means is to enhance competitiveness. This means [that] Korea's economy has a primary role to play. Yet as this endeavor has much to do with [the] changes in [the] international arena, foreign policy also has an important role to play. Precisely, here resides the task of foreign policy in this post-UR international order."[7]

According to the PSPC report released in August 1995, *segyehwa* means or refers to both objective and subjective – spontaneous and managerial – aspects of the same globalization dynamics: (1) the changing conditions in the global village, (2) a new paradigm (new cognitive framework) required by the changing global conditions, and (3) a new vision and strategy needed in order to become an advanced world-class country in the twenty-first century.[8] For the Kim Young Sam government, *segyehwa* reflected the growing recognition that with the birth of the new global trading system (the World Trade Organization, or WTO), a strategic offensive staged by advanced industrial countries, especially the United States, and an intensifying race for global competitiveness, South Korea could no longer rely on state-led market protection and strategic intervention. There is a sense in which *segyehwa* can be viewed as a more open and market-conforming strategy for enhancing Korea's global competitiveness. Tellingly, one of the many tasks deemed necessary for the full globalization of the Korean economy was effectively forestalling the movement toward regionalism.[9]

Faced with a likely financial meltdown in late 1997, President-Elect Kim Dae Jung quickly reversed his earlier stand against the International Monetary Fund (IMF), becoming perhaps the world's most outspoken champion of the controversial institution. No state leader in recent years has embraced the basic concept of globalization in an inaugural address as President Kim Dae Jung did. The information revolution is transforming the age of many national economies into an age of one world economy, turning the world into a global village." In an article written for the *Korea Times* in early November 1998, President Kim Dae Jung made a great leap from globalization to "universal globalism," which he described as resting on such universal values as "freedom, human rights,

---

[7] Ibid., 532.
[8] This theme runs throughout the report, especially in the preface. See PSPC, *Segyehwa ui pichon kwa chonryak.*
[9] Gills, "Economic Liberalisation and Reform in South Korea in the 1990s," 677.

justice, peace and efficiency." The most decisive change in the transition from the era of nationalism to an era of universal globalism is "informationization." It is no longer possible or desirable to run the national economy as a unit, nor is it necessarily patriotic for Koreans to buy only products made in Korea. In an era of informationization and a borderless global economy, the culture industry, which encompasses movies, databases, and computer games, has become one of the world's most fundamental industries.[10]

Thanks to the "greatest crisis since the Korean War," Kim Dae Jung started calling shots even before his formal inauguration in late February 1998. By any reckoning, the new administration had a stellar jumpstart with a series of high-profile promissory notes: (1) that a collusive link between the state and capital (crony capitalism) is the root cause of the economic crisis; (2) that the signature identity of his administration is the parallel pursuit of participatory democracy and a free market economy – liberal market democracy, not market Leninism – as "two sides of a coin and two wheels of a cart" pulling Korea out of its current crisis to full recovery; (3) that such participatory market democracy means "a grand compromise through dialogue" – "I will consult with you on all issues; you, in turn, must help me if only for one year when the nation is standing on the brink of disaster"; and (4) that political reform must precede everything else – to wit, "a small but effective government" will launch structural reforms in almost all sectors of the economy, including the public sector, financial and capital markets, the corporate sector, the labor market, and foreign trade, so as to speed up Korea's globalization train with a new conductor at the helm.

The new administration's diagnosis of what went wrong with the Korean economy is of some interest as it reveals the logic of the diagnosis and the prescription being formulated. According to Lee Kyu-Sung (Yi Kyu-song), finance and economy minister in the Kim Dae Jung government, the current economic crisis can be explained almost exclusively in terms of failures of the previous administration(s): the cumulative detrimental effect of a government-controlled economy; a wavering globalization policy; and the inability or unwillingness to restructure the economy in order to keep pace with the changing conditions of the world economy.[11] From this follows the pronouncement of the "five great reforms": (1) enhanced transparency of corporate management; (2) an end to the practice of guaranteeing loans among *chaebol* subsidiaries; (3) the building of a healthy financial structure; (4) concentration on core

---

[10] Kim Dae Jung, "Era of 'Universal Globalism' Dawning," *Korea Times*, 4 November 1998 (Internet version).
[11] See *Wolgan Chosun* [Monthly Korea], August 1998, 169–72.

business lines among the *chaebol* and support for small and medium-sized enterprises (SMEs); and (5) increased accountability on the part of majority shareholders and managers. In practice, the five great reforms have been translated into four separate but interconnected and interdependent sectors: banking, *chaebol*, the labor market, and public enterprise. Yet, diplomacy in the era of globalization is said to demand a change in thinking, embracing national *and* collective security.

Segyehwa's Performance

For any state in the post–Cold War world, which is becoming increasingly interdependent and fragmented, it is one thing to announce a policy of globalization and quite another to give it substance. As Gills and Gills argue in Chapter 2, globalization by any definition requires a "strategic choice" about the basic structure and goals of the economy and the society, that will determine the nature and direction of their developmental trajectory. A strategic choice is not only a matter of prioritizing one set of policy goals over another; it also involves the *speed* and *sequence* of the prioritized reforms. The challenge was and remains the same: how to make such a strategic choice in the face of the conflicting "intermestic" objectives and pressures. It is worth noting in this connection that South Korea is a quintessential trading state with one of the highest trade/GDP ratios among the major economies: Seoul's trade/GDP ratio increased from about 18 percent in 1960 to 58 percent in 1996 (75 percent in 1998), compared to 17 percent for Japan, 24 percent for the United States, and the world's average of 43 percent.[12] This means that there is no easy exit from globalization that would not entail a major economic disaster. The strategic choice for Korea is no longer, if it ever was, one between exit and embracement; it is one of constant adaptation to the logic of globalization dynamics and quickening economic, cultural, and social product cycles. In the Korean case, the chant "globalize or perish" has become, in effect, "trade or perish."

Tellingly, President Kim Young Sam's *segyehwa* drive started with a bang but ended with a whimper. During his five-year term in office, from February 1993 to February 1998, and extending to the first year of the Kim Dae Jung administration, Korea's performance declined noticeably according to all economic indicators. The greatest irony of all is that the single greatest gap between promise and performance lies in Korea's steadily declining globalization ranking. As tables 11.1 and 11.2 show, the so-called *segyehwa*-driven administration somehow managed to garner the lowest possible ranking in the "internationalization/globalization"

[12] World Bank, *World Development Indicators 1998 CD-ROM*, table 1.5.

Table 11.1 Korea's Select Globalization Performance Indicators, 1991–8

Category	1991[a]	1992	1993	1994	1995	1996	1997	1998
Globalization Rank /N=	4/15	6/15	11/15	44/48	40/48	43/46	45/46	46/46
Competitiveness Ranking N=	3/15	5/15	6/15	24/48	26/48	27/46	30/46	35/46
GDP (current $bn) [b] [MOFE]	294.1	307.9	332.8	380.7	456.5	484.4	442.6	304.3
(GDP Growth Rate)	(9.1)	(5.1)	(5.8)	(8.3)	(8.9)	(6.8)	(5.0)	(−5.8)
GNP per capita(U.S.$) [MOFE]	6,757	6,958	7,484	8,467	10,037	10,543	10,307	6,823
GNP per capita (ppp)	8,320	9,250	9,710	10,656	11,594		13,590	
Imports (U.S.$bn) [MOFE]	81.5	81.5	83.8	102.3	135.1	150.3	144.6	93.3
Exports (U.S.$bn) [MOFE]	71.9	76.5	82.2	96.0	125.1	129.7	136.2	132.3
Trade/GDP (%)			49.9	52.1	56.9	57.8	63.4	74.5
Total External Liabilities $bn	39.1	42.8	43.8	56.8	78.4	104.7	154.4	152.5
(Rate of Increase %)	(23.5)	(9.4)	(2.5)	(29.6)	(38.0)	(33.5)	(47.5)	(−1.2)
Current Account Balance ($bn)	−8.3	−3.9	1.0	−3.9	−8.5	−23.0	−8.2	40.0
U.S. Dollar/KW Exchange Rate	1:760	1:788	1:808	1:789	1:775	1:844	1:1415	1:1208
Foreign Exchange Reserves ($bn)			20.2	25.7	32.7	33.2	20.4	52.0
Unemployment Rate (%)	2.3	2.4	2.8	2.4	2.0	2.0	2.6	6.8
FDI in Korea ($bn)	1.39	0.89	1.04	1.32	1.94	3.20	7.0	8.9
% of Global FDI Flows	1.2	0.7	0.6	0.8	1.8	2.3	1.75	1.38
OFDI ($bn)	1.5	1.2	1.9	3.6	4.9	6.2	5.7	5.1
ODA ($mn) [c]	80.0	93.7	64.0	127.7	187.5	396.9	133.9	
HDI Rank/N=	35/160	34/160	31/174	29/174	32/175	30/174	30/174	
GEM Rank/N=			90/116	78/174	73/175	83/174	78/174	
GDI Rank/N=			37/130	31/174	35/175	37/174	30/174	
R&D As % of GDP	1.93	2.08	2.3	2.58	2.69	2.81		
# of Diplomatic Relations	148	169	174	175	182	182	183	183
IGO Membership			46	47	48	50	51	52
INGO Membership			999	1034	1072	1138	1200	1250

ROK's U.N. Budget (%)	0.69	0.69	0.69	0.69	0.8	0.817	0.82	0.955
Defense Budget (KW trillion)[b]	74.8	84.1	95.7	104.7	115.1	127.4	143.5	143.8
Growth Rate (%)	12.3	12.8	9.5	9.4	9.9	10.7	12.7	0.2
Defense/GNP (%)	4	3.6	3.6	3.4	3.3	3.2	3.3	3.2
Defense/Government Budget (%)		25.3	25.2	24.2	22.2	20.7	21.5	20.9
Defense Burden-sharing with U.S. ($mn)[c]	150	180	220	260	300	330	363	399

Note:

[a] As of the end of the year.

[b] In billions of current U.S. dollars.

[c] In millions of current U.S. dollars.

Sources: Adapted from International Institute for Management Development IMD (Lausanne, Switzerland), *World Competitiveness Yearbook 1998*; ROK Ministry of Finance and Economy (MOFE); United Nations Development Programme, *Human Development Reports 1991–99* (New York: Oxford University Press, 1991–9); World Bank, *World Development Report 1998/99* (New York: Oxford University Press, 1999); *Oekyo paekso 1998* [Diplomatic white paper 1998] (Seoul: Ministry of Foreign Affairs and Trade, 1998); *Yearbook of International Organizations 1994/1995-1998/99* (Muchen: K. G. Saur, 1995, 1996, 1997, 1998); *Defense White Paper 1997-1998* (Seoul: Ministry of National Defense, 1998); *Defense White Paper 1998* (Seoul: Ministry of National Defense, 1999).

Table 11.2 Korea's Ranking in World Competitiveness Input Factors, 1994–9

	Criteria	4/1994	4/1995	4/1996	4/1997	4/1998	4/1999
World Competitiveness	Based on 6 input factors below	32/46	26/46	27/46	30/46	35/46	38/47
Domestic Economy	28 criteria: Macroeconomic evaluation of the domestic economy	9/46	7/46	4/46	13/46	34/46	43/47
Internationalization (Globalization)	40 criteria: Extent to which the country participates in international trade and investment	44/46	40/46	43/46	45/46	46/46	40/47
Government	43 criteria: Extent to which government policies and practices are conducive to competitiveness	35/46	18/46	33/46	32/46	34/46	37/47
Finance	20 criteria: Performance of capital markets and quality of financial services	42/46	37/46	40/46	43/46	45/46	41/47
Infrastructure	30 criteria: Extent to which natural, technical, and communication resources are adequate to serve the basic needs of businesses	36/46	35/46	34/46	34/46	31/46	30/47
Management	34 criteria: Extent to which companies are managed in an innovative, profitable, and responsible manner	37/46	27/46	28/46	26/46	34/46	42/47

Science and Technology	20 criteria: Scientific and technological capacity	24/46	24/46	25/46	22/46	28/46	28/47
People	44 criteria: Availability and qualifications of human resources	23/46	21/46	21/46	22/46	22/46	31/47

Source: Adapted from International Institute for Management Development (Lausanne, Switzerland), *World Competitiveness Yearbook 1998* in http://www.imd.ch/wcy/factors/f2data.html and *World Competitiveness Yearbook 1999* in http://www.imd.ch/wcy/factors/overall.html.

input category, moving from eleventh place among the fifteen emerging market economies in 1993 to last place among the forty-six advanced and emerging market economies in the world in 1998, while its global competitiveness ranking dropped from sixth place in 1993 to thirty-fifth place in 1998. During the first year of the Kim Dae Jung government, Korea's globalization rank improved slightly from forty-sixth place in 1998 to fortieth place in 1999 (as of 21 April 1999), while Korea's global competitiveness ranking continued to decline (from thirty-fifth place in 1998 to thirty-eighth place in 1999) (see table 11.2). Korea's total external liabilities ballooned from $43.8 billion in 1993 to $154.4 billion at the end of 1997, while its foreign-exchange reserves dropped from $20.2 billion in 1993 to a dangerously low level of $3.9 billion in early December 1997, triggering the single largest IMF rescue operation in IMF history. Korea's per capita GNP dropped from $10,543 in 1996 to $9,511 in 1997 and then plunged to $6,750 in 1998, lower even than the $6,745 registered in 1991, and national unemployment has already more than tripled, from 2.0 percent in 1997 to 7.6 by the end of 1998, leaving 1.65 million people out of work in an economy that until recently had to import foreign workers for the "dirty, dangerous, and difficult" jobs (the 3Ds); and the unemployment rate reached 8.7 percent by February 1999, surpassing the previous all-time record of 8.4 percent set back in the 1960s. As detailed in Chapter 3, the 1997 economic crisis has brought about devastating social consequences for most sectors of Korean society, especially workers, with the most striking impact being the substantial shrinkage of the middle class from the Korean political-economy map (see tables 3.3 and 3.4).

The starting point for explaining such a steady decline in Korean performance in the 1990s is to recognize that since 1987 profound changes have occurred in relations between the state and society in general and among the state, capital, and labor in particular. The chronic discrepancy between policy pronouncements (promise) and performance in Korea's *segyehwa* drive during the Kim Young Sam administration and all the grand rhetoric without significant progress in structural reform during the first year of the Kim Dae Jung administration reflect the ineluctable fact that the *belle époque* of the much-touted developmental state has long since disappeared and a new democratic state has been trying hard to cope with the twin challenges of democratic consolidation within and globalization from without. As pointed out by Barry K. Gills and Dongsook S. Gills in Chapter 2 and Yong Cheol Kim and Chung-in Moon in Chapter 3, if democratization enhanced the power of civil society in general and workers in particular – the number of labor unions tripled from 2,534 in 1985 to 7,527 in 1992 and real wages rose by almost 50 percent between 1987 and 1990 – globalization favored both the opening of the domestic market and the *chaebol*'s going global. In the process, the requirements of democratic consolidation at home and competitiveness in the global marketplace have become mutually competitive and even conflictive, even as the labor unions and the *chaebol* have become more powerful and independent at the expense of the state.

Faced with competing pressures on both the domestic and the external front, President Kim Young Sam showed himself to be an inept patriarchal ruler, incapable of coming to grips with the complicated issues of a country experiencing political, economic, and social turbulence. He proved to be a weak executive, waffling on one issue after another, reigning through a revolving-door cabinet but not actually leading or governing. During his five years in office, he replaced the chief economic planner (the deputy prime minister) seven times, the senior economic secretary to the president six times, the prime minister four times, and the foreign affairs minister three times. In mid-1995, only one member of his original twenty-five cabinet ministers remained.

Nonetheless, it would be wrong to paint President Kim Young Sam as the sole culprit, ignoring the underlying social norms, values, and structures that defined the possible and the permissible in the Korean state and society. At the end of 1998, more than a full year after the IMF stewardship, just about everyone – including Korea's militant trade unions, the Kim Dae Jung government, and even the IMF – viewed curbing the power and profligacy of the *chaebol* as the heart of structural reform. And yet the top five *chaebol*, the Big Five – already the Frankensteinian *deus ex machina* of the Korean political economy, accounting for a whopping 40 percent of GNP and 44 percent of total exports – are growing bigger and bigger by crowding out SMEs, by gobbling up the available credit (more than three-quarters of all new corporate bonds and commercial paper issued in 1998), and by doubling their expansion plans.[13] Although more than ten of the twenty-five *chaebol* just below the Big Five (Hanbo, Kia, Jinro, Daenong, Newcore, and Halla) went belly up in 1997–8, the "too big to fail" thinking remains in the saddle. For a more synthetic analysis, it is useful to look at *segyehwa*'s performance in all the specified domains – economic, sociocultural, diplomatic, and security.

Economic Segyehwa

As Chapters 2–5 show, the increasing scale and sophistication of Korea's economy and the rapidly changing context of globalization dynamics

---

[13] See "The *Chaebol* That Ate Korea," *The Economist*, 14 November 1998, 67–8; and "Showdown in Seoul," *Business Week*, 14 December 1998, 56–7.

exerted ever-increasing pressures on South Korea at a time when the authoritarian developmental state of the past had been replaced by a new democratic one experiencing growing tension with the *chaebol* and labor. What emerged was not "social concertation" – a trilateral state-capital-labor collaboration – but an uneasy and fragile balance of power often leading to a social and political stalemate and a policymaking gridlock. Against this backdrop, as Gills and Gills argue in Chapter 2, President Kim Young Sam made an "external opening first" strategic decision, as against a "deconcentration first" one, with the aim of promoting Korea's global competitiveness. Far from achieving or improving its putative objectives, this strategic decision led to progressive decline in practically all performance categories, especially in globalization and global competitiveness (table 11.2).

What accounts for such a dismal gap between promise and performance? Despite the rhetorical support of the globalization policy as a shortcut to advanced world-class status – who could oppose such a national ego trip? – there has in effect occurred a kind of state-capital-labor collaboration in the pursuit of an overly leveraged expansion based on a synergy of the so-called too-big-to-fail theory – *taema pulsa ron* ("a big horse can't die) – and a "can-do mentality." As C. S. Eliot Kang explains in Chapter 4, the sharp increase in wage levels in South Korea and the growing challenge of low-wage competition from China and Southeast Asian countries worked against each other, chipping away the competitiveness of Korea's labor-intensive industries. During the 1986–95 period, the average annual wage increase was 15.3 percent in South Korea, compared to 9.85 percent in Taiwan and 2.7 percent in Japan, whereas the annual productivity increases were 9.2 percent, 6.4 percent, and 3.1 percent, respectively.

Faced with this situation, the Big Five, especially Daewoo, Hyundai, and Samsung, have gone global in the 1990s, spearheading Korea's outward foreign direct investment (OFDI) but without "globalizing" much of their corporate thinking, culture, and behavior. It may not be an exaggeration to say that the "globalization" of the Big Five was a quick way to escape from multiple and multiplying problems at home, such as skyrocketing wages, labor-union militancy and never-ending labor-management disputes, high interest rates, and even state supervision. As a consequence, the deeply rooted features and problems of the *chaebol* – mindless expansion and diversification aimed at size rather than profitability, reckless borrowing and dangerously high debt/equity ratios rather than a solid equity base, an archaic, Confucian governing style and structure with no transparency and accountability to speak of, and monopolistic rent-seeking (moral hazard) behavior – have increased rather than ameliorated. Worse, *chaebol* globalization was indebted globalization, as the *chaebol* relied on foreign loans for global expansion via OFDI. As Kim points out in Chapter 5, among Korea's large overseas investments in 1995, the ratio of debt to equity was more than 927 percent, and the profit ratios, based on total assets, equity capital, and total sales, were all in the red. The extremely high debt/equity ratio was inevitable because the Big Five preferred the relatively low-interest loans offered in the host country to the high-interest loans offered at home. In going global via indebted OFDI, then, the Big Five increased Korea's foreign indebtedness to U.S. $93 billion by mid-1996, and climbed even further as the country headed for financial meltdown in late 1997. As of the end of 1998, more than a year after the financial crisis, the debt-to-equity ratio of the Big Five stood at 526.5 percent for Daewoo, followed by Hyundai at 449.3 percent, SK at 354.9 percent, LG at 341.0 percent, and Samsung at 275.7 percent. The case of Daewoo, Korea's second-largest *chaebol*, is a textbook case of mindless globalization. As its chairman, Kim Woo-Choong, pushed his overseas empire-building drive under the slogan of "global vision," buying dilapidated auto and home appliance plants in Eastern Europe and Third World countries, Daewoo's debts skyrocketed from $19 billion in 1995 to $50 billion in 1998, more than five times its equity.

Such *chaebol* behavior was aided and abetted by the globalization-cum-deregulation drive of the Kim Young Sam administration. As shown in Chapters 4–5, the government adopted various measures – outlined in the Five-Year New Economic Plan for 1993–7 and the Long-Term Economic Design for the Twenty-First Century – to encourage the *chaebol*'s OFDI as a part of the effort to deregulate domestic capital and financial markets. As a result, Korea's annual OFDI more than tripled, from $1.9 billion in 1993 to $6.2 billion in 1996 (see tables 5.1 and 11.1). The government failed to establish a system of state monitoring, supervision, and accountability due in part to the mistaken belief that deregulation means an end of state monitoring and supervision and in part to the embedded state-capital collusion (*chungkyung yuchaek*). In the end, the Kim Young Sam government made *the right strategic decision* of financial liberalization in *the wrong sequence*. To accelerate financial globalization as an entry ticket price for OECD membership in 1995 but without modern banking and legal systems in place, while at the same time keeping restrictions on long-term foreign investments, proved to be a sure recipe for disaster.

The absence of state monitoring or a warning system of any kind was made evident, tragically, in the government's inaction from July to early December 1997 in the face of the unfolding Asian crisis. In November 1997, when IMF Managing Director Michel Camdessus paid a secret visit to Seoul and informed South Korean economic officials that South Korea's crumbling finances required the IMF's intervention, government officials flatly responded, "You're crazy; our system works" (Chapter 8). As Chae-Jin Lee suggests, such a response "betrayed either misplaced overconfidence or blind nationalistic pride," to be sure, but it also high-lights with particular clarity a total absence of state monitoring, supervision, and accountability. In short, there was no early warning system of any kind to rely upon. Only a few days later, a newly appointed deputy prime minister appealed to the IMF for an immediate rescue program.

Deregulation without state monitoring and supervision led to a dramatic but indebted increase in OFDI as well as a massive domestic lending spree that encouraged further investment in risky and speculative ventures. In the end, the reform measures that the Kim Young Sam government managed to enact only made the country more vulnerable to rapid transfers of "hot money," the ugly side of economic globalization. Another example of Seoul's wrongly sequenced strategic decisions during the Kim Young Sam administration was the continuing restrictions on FDI because of an abiding fear of foreign domination, a fear rooted in the unhappy history of Japanese colonialism. "Ironically," as Peter Beck writes, "over-reliance on loans rather than FDI would ultimately prove to be the undoing of Korea's developmental state, with the ultimate loss of state autonomy coming with the acceptance of the conditions attached to the IMF Stand-by Agreement last November."[14] In short, Korea's financial crisis in late 1997 is a textbook example, an almost unavoidable outcome of the moral hazard of the *chaebol*.[15]

Table 11.3 compares Korea's economic performance during the first year of the economic crisis – from November 1997 to November 1998 – to the performance of other Asian countries. It is worth noting that of the ten countries, South Korea has the lowest scores in consumer confidence (suggesting the extent of depression in the domestic economy) and foreign direct investment (suggesting the extent to which Korea is closed or lacks globalization in a critical dimension). In a recent survey and rating of the business environments of sixty countries by the Economist Intelligence Unit (EIU) based on such indicators as market potential, tax and labor-market policies, infrastructure skills, and the political environment, Korea was ranked twenty-ninth in 1994–8 – and twenty-seventh for 1999–2003 – lower than all the other East Asian countries in the sample.[16]

---

[14] Peter M. Beck, "Creating a Favorable Environment for Foreign Direct Investment in Korea" (paper presented at the conference "The Republic of Korea after 50 Years: Continuity and Convergence," Georgetown University, 2–3 October 1998), 3.

[15] See D. M. Leipziger, "Public and Private Interests in Korea: Views on Moral Hazard and Crisis Resolution," EDI discussion paper (Washington, DC: World Bank, May 1998).

[16] See *The Economist* (London), 21 November 1998, 108.

Table 11.3 Korea's Economic Performance Evaluation in Comparative Asian Perspective, 1997–8

Country	Financial Reform	Political Reform	Consumer Confidence	Corporate Sector	Foreign Investment
Thailand	B+	A–	C–	C	C
Japan	C	C	D	B–	B+
Malaysia	D	F	C+	F	C
Indonesia	D	C–	D	D	C–
Singapore	B+	C–	B–	A	C–
Taiwan	B	A–	B	A	B
Hong Kong	B+	B–	C+	A–	A–
China	C+	D	B–	C–	B+
Philippines	B+	A	C–	C	B–
South Korea	B	B	D	C	C–

Source: Adapted from *Business Week* (23 November 1998), 70–2.

Despite the government's efforts to reduce the *chaebol*'s indebted expansion, the Big Five's debt-to-equity ratios, which ranged from 370 percent to 570 percent, have actually increased rather than decreased during the first year of the Kim Dae Jung government.

Social and Cultural Segyehwa

Culture has always remained part of international politics and commerce. Because of the advances in communications and information technology and growing global interconnectedness in economics, politics, society, culture, and security, the links among economic, social, and cultural globalizations have intensified and blurred in a two-way process of global interconnectedness and interdependence. Korea has remained more of a decision *taker* than a decision *maker* in the area of sociocultural globalization. For example, if America's cultural and knowledge products have already become America's largest or second-largest export (depending on one's definition), one would search in vain to find in Korea's exports any made-in-Korea cultural products, whether computer software, music, movies, TV programs, or books.

Part of the problem has to do with the fact that English has become the *lingua franca* of globalization, – the language of 85 percent of home pages on the World Wide Web and 80 percent of the information on the world's computers. Fueled by the cyberspace revolution and the dominance of American pop culture, the United States acts as globalization's principal agent and advocate. But part of the problem also has to do with the rooted Hermit Kingdom complex. Writing in late 1993, Lee Hong-Koo –

who served as prime minister in the Kim Young Sam government in 1994–6 – argued with remarkable clairvoyance that several major attitudinal and normative obstacles (e.g., rigid neo-Confucian ethical concepts, the myth of national homogeneity, limited experience with cultural diversity, fear of foreign powers, and anti-internationalization) stood in the way of Korea's globalization drive and that such cultural exclusivism must be overcome if Korea was to meet the challenges of globalization.[17] In a similar vein, in February 1994 President Kim Young Sam inveighed against the lack of "a solid public consensus" on the importance of internationalization and the persistence of the Hermit Kingdom mentality. All of this is to say that the greater the chasm between Korea's cultural orientation and the norms and rules of the globalization game, the more wrenching will be Korea's globalization learning and adaptation.

President Kim Dae Jung, as he stated in his inaugural address, envisioned the new millennium, less than two years away, as an era of informationization, in which "intangible knowledge and information will be the driving power for economic development"; hence the globalization of the Korean culture and Korean diplomacy "will center around the economy and culture."[18] Measured in terms of various science and technology development indexes, such as the ratio of research and development (R&D) investment to GNP, the number of researchers, the number of patent rights obtained, and the number of research papers published in international journals, Korea is no match for advanced countries such as the United States and Japan.

Nonetheless, there can be no doubt that globalization as a multidimensional process is coming to Korea, with new social and cultural products, practices, norms, and actors challenging Korea's traditional values and Korea's national identity as a homogeneous people. Is Korea still the world's most Confucian – status-conscious – place in an era of globalization? That workers and women are the most oppressed and exploited groups in the Confucian social order and that foreign migrant workers are present in the putatively homogeneous nation-state provide an empirical basis for assessing the normative and practical consequences of sociocultural globalization.

The interplay of globalization and Korean workers and women has produced variegated and somewhat paradoxical consequences. Without question, the transition to democracy in 1987 has greatly enhanced the power and status of Korean workers. To a certain extent, Korea's successful transition to democracy was made possible by what was happening in the world at large – democratic globalization, the so-called third wave of

[17] Lee, "Attitudinal Reform toward Globalization."
[18] *Korea Herald*, 26 February 1998.

global democratization. In the democratic consolidation process beginning in 1988, Korea joined with greater confidence and exposure various international intergovernmental and nongovernmental organizations – including the United Nations, the International Labor Organization (ILO), and the Organization for Economic Cooperation and Development (OECD) – and signed a multitude of international human-rights treaties. Of course, joining as many international organizations as possible became an integral part of its intensive drive to improve its international status and its projection of a new national identity not only as a newly industrialized country (NIC) but also, and more importantly, as a newly democratizing country (NDC) on the global stage.

All in all, the image factor that inevitably accompanied Korea's greater participation in a world of international institutions and treaties has engendered nontrivial socialization effects. In the highly status-conscious Korean society, where ranking is often used as a way to locate any group in the pecking order, as Seungsook Moon argues in Chapter 6, Korean women seized the wide chasm between the nation's economic standing as the world's eleventh largest economy and its social standing measured in terms of women's status in various international categories, such as the Gender-Related Development Index (GDI) and the Gender Empowerment Measure (GEM) of the United Nations Development Programme (UNDP) (see table 11.1). The point is not that Korean women were socialized by universal human rights norms from without but that they have seized upon the opportunities of sociocultural globalization engendered by the United Nations and U.N.-sponsored global conferences or conventions. Korean women have been developing critical social movements of various sorts, but the U.N. politics of human rights have also provided a legitimating platform for setting in motion within Korea the politics of continuing legislative adaptation to better prepare the country's positions on a great variety of global issues and problems while at the same time facilitating the formation of transnational nongovernment organization (NGO) coalitions. When South Korea applied for membership in the OECD in 1995, for example, the OECD's Trade Union Advisory Committee made South Korea's admission conditional on its compliance with ILO requirements (Chapter 3). The international legitimation of the women's movement in Korea, which is facilitated by the growing awareness of the universality of human rights in general and the increasing acceptance of gender equality as a measure of social progress in particular, underscores the positive normative spillovers of sociocultural globalization.

As Kim and Moon argue in Chapter 3, globalization has not only fostered democratization of industrial labor relations through the amendment of the existing labor laws but also strengthened workers' political and organizational power by lifting bans on multiple unionism, labor unions' political activities, and third-party intervention in labor-management disputes. Similarly, as Seungsook Moon points out in Chapter 6, South Korea's women's policy has emerged in the space created by economic, political, and sociocultural globalization, but the major site of struggle, bargaining, and negotiation between the state and the women's movement has been the enactment of laws and their revision for the elimination of discrimination against women in employment and in their family or kinship group, as well as in society in general. Despite the constraints and limitations resulting from traditional values and organizational resources, Korean women's movements have served as the chief catalyst for enacting a series of women's rights laws on equal employment, infant and child care, sexual violence, and domestic violence.

And yet the most recent Asian-cum-Korean economic crisis has had a devastating impact on all social groups, especially workers, women, and children. That Korea's social-welfare spending remained the lowest in the OECD did not have much sociopolitical impact as long as Korea enjoyed a seemingly virtuous circle of high economic growth rates and full employment with job security. But as the Asian economic crisis got under way in 1997, causing a panic among international hedge-fund managers and the massive exodus of hot money, the virtual nonexistence of the social safety net left Korean workers badly exposed when the IMF bailout program brought skyrocketing unemployment (Chapter 3). During the first half of 1998, South Korea experienced a sharper drop in consumption (28 percent) than any other country in the twentieth century, while the unemployment rate rose from an average of slightly higher than 2 percent in 1991–7 to nearly 8 percent by the end of 1998. If the underemployed are included, the total number of unemployed is estimated to have reached 3–4 million (as against about 1.8 million) as of mid-1998. Not surprisingly, then, Korean workers see more evil than good in globalization (Chapter 3). For Korean women, however, the gap between promise and performance was evident even before the outset of the economic crisis in late 1997. As table 11.1 shows, Korea's ranking in the UNDP's human development index (HDI) rose from thirty-fifth place in 1991 to thirtieth place in 1997, but Korea's ranking in GEM remained far behind in the seventy-eighth to eighty-third range in 1996–7. In the wake of the recent economic crisis, women are the first to be sacked and the last to be hired, even as the population of Korea's "economic orphans" seems to be growing exponentially.

In short, globalization has produced the paradoxical consequence of strengthening workers and women by creating more democratic space for grassroots labor and women's movements and by introducing global human-rights norms, while at the same time reducing the welfare system as a drag on the state's global competitiveness in the global marketplace and thus weakening the state's capacity and willingness to provide a welfare safety net for the worst-off in society. As Seungsook Moon puts it in Chapter 6, in the long run, the economic crisis can dismantle women's policy by accelerating privatization, which tends to undermine the state's capacity to provide welfare services. If economic globalization has exerted variegated but mostly detrimental effects on the development of women's policy in Korea, the normative effects of political and socio-cultural globalization have been largely positive for the advancement of women's rights and welfare in Korea.

One of the most remarkable effects of globalization in the 1990s, according to Katharine H. S. Moon (Chapter 7), is the presence of some 370,000 migrant workers from China and South and Southeast Asia challenging Korea's self-identity as a homogeneous people and what it means to be "Korean" in a rapidly changing and globalizing world. In striking contrast to Tokyo's ethnically oriented attitudes and policies toward foreign migrant workers, Seoul shied away from any policy of ethnic preference toward Korean-Chinese migrant workers even though they make up the largest single group of foreign migrant workers. The reason has less to do with South Koreans being less nationalistic than Japanese – they are not – and more to do with the divided politics of Korean nationalism. In addition, Seoul's attitudes toward ethnic Chinese-Koreans in China's northeastern provinces, inhabited by the world's largest Korean diaspora (more than 2 million of a total overseas Korean population of 5.7 million), loom as a kind of Sword of Damocles over Sino-ROK relations. Organizations such as Damui (Reclaim) in South Korea, with more than 50,000 members, are advancing the irredentist claim, "Manchuria was ours but was taken away [and] ... maybe, one day, it'll be ours again." Damui's irredentist activities have already provoked Beijing's strong protests, and Seoul has acknowledged that such activities need to be curbed.[19]

With a growing, floating population of foreign migrant workers in their midst, South Koreans as a people and a government are for the first time being accused of being racist and exploitative abusers of human rights intent on using foreign workers only for economic gain and 3D work. How could Korea sustain its globalization-cum-status drive as a world-class advanced nation in the face of such a challenge? A national identity is not a property or object frozen in time or some immutable attribute transmitted from generation to generation but subject to recurrent reinterpretation and renegotiation. It may be reconceptualized as an ongoing negotiating process in the course of which the self attempts,

---

[19] Paul H. Kreisberg, "Threat Environment for a United Korea: 2010," *Korean Journal of Defense Analysis* 8, no. 1 (Summer 1996), 84–5.

especially in those problematic moments of ambiguity and challenge, to secure an identity that others do not bestow, while others attempt to bestow an identity that the self does not appropriate.[20] The impact of such negotiating processes is most obvious in some quick-fix revisions of the citizenship law by the Ministry of Justice, establishing gender equality in citizenship requirements for foreign-born spouses of South Koreans. Whether the changes are "epoch-making" or merely a function of "changing times and globalization" is a matter of opinion. As Katharine Moon argues, "Korean nationalism still seems to be more about resisting the power of the already powerful rather than about beating up on the poor and powerless." And she concurs with Seungsook Moon (Chapter 6) on the positive effects of political and sociocultural globalization that "the civic movements' adoption of the normative aspects of globalization – human rights and democratization – as a form of resistance to the elite-directed forms of economic globalization may also help thwart national-istic abuses toward migrant workers."

The tension between nationalism and globalism, another example of the glaring discrepancy between policy pronouncement and policy performance of the Kim Dae Jung government, was made manifest when the Ministry of Justice announced in August 1998 a legislation plan for a special law that would accord 5.2 million ethnic Koreans abroad legal status virtually equal to that of Korean citizens at home. The main objec-tive of this proposed legislative plan, according to the ministry, is to give those overseas Koreans a stronger sense of belonging as members of the Korean ethnonational community and provide them with more oppor-tunities to contribute to the economic development of their motherland. Not only would this hypernationalistic legislative sleight of hand directly contradict the spirit and letter of President Kim Dae Jung's professed globalism but it would create legal and diplomatic disputes with the host countries of overseas Koreans, most of whom (about 60 percent, or 3.1 million) are by birth or naturalization bona fide citizens of their respec-tive host states. China, Uzbekistan, and Kazakhstan lost no time in mak-ing known through diplomatic channels their strong displeasure and the likelihood of trouble ahead. Against this backdrop, the Ministry of Foreign Affairs and Trade (MOFAT) has already expressed opposition to the proposed legislation for fear that it might create serious diplomatic and legal disputes with China and some other foreign countries, only to rankle some hypernationalistic overseas Koreans. Nonetheless, the Kim

[20] For such a synthetic formulation of national identity theory, see Lowell Ditt-mer and Samuel Kim, "In Search of a Theory of National Identity," and Samuel Kim and Lowell Dittmer, "Whither China's Quest for National Identity?" in *China's Quest for National Identity*, ed. Lowell Dittmer and Samuel Kim (Ithaca, NY: Cornell University Press, 1993), 1–31 and 237–90.

Dae Jung government was forced to revise the dual-citizenship bill dras-tically to accommodate Beijing's demand. The revised bill, if enacted by the National Assembly, would effectively exclude ethnic Koreans in China by extending the benefits of the new law to only those overseas Koreans who emigrated *after* the establishment of the ROK in 1948.

The controversy over the dual-citizenship bill underscores the ineluctable fact that despite the rising globalization and globalism cho-rus, deep down Korea remains mired in the cocoon of exclusive cultural nationalism. What is peculiar and troublesome in the South Korean case is that globalization seems to have engendered little, if any, positive effect on younger generations of Koreans, who tend to be more isolationist, nationalist, and leftist than older generations, with their more interna-tionalist outlook.[21]

The exclusiveness of Korean culture is also evident in the higher edu-cational system, a virtual carryover from the Japanese imperial period. The Korean higher educational system with its sterile emphasis on rote memorization of facts for "test-aholic" students and "tutor-aholic" par-ents is designed for status-obsessed Confucian society, but not suited at all for surviving or even prospering in a neo-Darwinian world of global-ization. As earlier noted, education was first among the six priority reform areas proposed by the PSPC. And yet virtually nothing further was said or done. The nation's preeminent institution of higher learning, Seoul National University (SNU), is not even ranked among the top one hundred universities in the world. SNU, the South Korean clone of Tokyo Imperial University (now simply Tokyo University), is perhaps without peer in at least one respect: Its faculty inbreeding ratio is at about 96 percent. Other top-tier universities (Korea University, Yonsei Univer-sity) are slightly better in this respect, with only 80–89 percent of their faculty coming from alumni. Not surprisingly, recent survey data show that South Korean professors published the least number of research papers in international academic journals among the twenty-nine mem-ber states of the OECD. The number of academic articles was only 1.3 per 10,000 people, compared to 12 in Britain, 10.6 in the United States, and 7.3 in France, despite the fact that Korea has one of the world's highest Ph.D./population ratios. The number of patent applications was 6.3 per 10,000 people, compared to 33 to 39 per 10,000 in advanced countries.[22] The level of industrial technology is only 45–60 percent of those in advanced OECD member countries. It remains to be seen whether the flurry of university reform measures proposed in September 1998 by

---

[21] Lee, "Attitudinal Reform toward Globalization," 90; see also Chapter 10, of this volume.

[22] *Korea Herald*, 9 September, 7 November, 24 November 1998 (Internet version).

the largely self-educated reformist president with no connection of any kind with the old-boy alumni network with any of Korea's top universities will make any headway.

Although "politics and the mass media" were singled out as the third globalization priority reform area, there has been little change in the structures and practices of Korean politics and mass media, especially local newspapers. If Korean journalists defied newspaper owners in the 1980s to fight for democracy and establish one of the freest presses in Asia, at the risk of losing their jobs or ending up in prison, the same cannot be said about the globalization drive. Instead, Korean journalists became part of the problem – Korea Inc. – with abiding "suspicion of globalization as a hidden agenda of foreign investors bent on taking over Korean companies at a low price."[23]

The inability of local newspapers to foretell the outbreak of the financial crisis in late 1997, even in the wake of the Thai economic crisis of July 1997, which rapidly besieged other East Asian countries, speaks volumes about the low quality and poor credibility of Korean journalism. Since most of South Korea's big names in mass media are owned and controlled by family or *chaebol* groups – *Chosun Ilbo* (Bang Woo Young and family), *Dong-A Ilbo* (Kim Byung Kwan and family), *JoongAng Ilbo* (Samsung), *Hankuk Ilbo* (Chang Jae Kook and family) – they parrot *chaebol*-style managerial practices: excessive dependence on deficit-financing, mindless expansion and cutthroat competition, and uniformity in style, favoring color printing and lowbrow tabloids at the expense of quality reporting and in-depth critical analysis.[24] Faced with a credibility problem when the country's bubble economy burst, the media launched hypernationalistic scapegoating and large-scale campaigns urging the people to stop spending, exactly the opposite of what was needed to prevent the country from sliding into a major depression.

Diplomatic Segyehwa

At the level of policy pronouncements and global interconnectedness, Korean foreign policy has gone a long way toward globalization. The triumph of *nordpolitik* entailed Seoul's growing diplomatic expansion and diversification in the 1990s. The number of countries having formal diplomatic relations with the ROK steadily increased from 126 in 1985 (before the inauguration of *nordpolitik*) to 146 in 1990 to 183 by the end

[23] Shim Jae Hoon, "Same Old Story," *Far Eastern Economic Review*, 5 November 1998, 23.

[24] Nam Si-uk, "How to Surmount Journalism Crisis," *Korea Focus* 6, no. 4 (July–August 1998).

of 1998. Seoul's membership in intergovernmental organizations (IGOs) increased from thirty-six in 1985 to fifty-two in 1998, and its membership in international intergovernmental organizations (INGOs) increased from 686 to 1,250 in the same period (see table 11.1). Beyond the numbers, however, practically all of globalization accomplishments of Korean foreign policy came about in the 1990s: ROK-Soviet normalization (1990), U.N. membership (1991), ROK-PRC normalization (1992), OECD membership (1996), and U.N. Security Council membership (1996-97). As earlier noted, *segyehwa* diplomacy was initiated by Foreign Minister Han Sung-Joo in May 1993 as a key component of, and a point of departure for, the "new diplomacy" (*sin oekyo*). Indeed, central to the new diplomacy were "five fundamentals" (globalism, diversification, multidimensionalism, regional cooperation, and future orientation), all of which were intended in principle to expand and diversify the number and scope of diplomatic relations via regionalization and globalization so as to break away from the U.S.-ROK bilateral straightjacket, to play the role of peacemaking intermediary between developed and developing countries in multilateral fora, to overcome Seoul's one-dimensional preoccupation with national-security issues, and to transcend the tragic legacies of the past (the Korean War) in its accelerated, future-oriented march toward globalization. A strong, healthy, competitive economy is both a means and an ends of the new *segyehwa* diplomacy. On the one hand, it is an indispensable means for realizing the five fundamentals of *segyehwa* diplomacy; on the other, *segyehwa* diplomacy itself was designed to enhance Korea's global competitiveness in what Han called the "post-UR international order."

More than anything else, *segyehwa* diplomacy may be seen as President Kim Young Sam's way of projecting a new national identity and role as a "world-class advanced nation" and of moving beyond inter-Korean competition toward the center of action, not only in the Asia-Pacific region but also within the world community. This is what Han meant when he declared that "our diplomacy will no longer become hostage to it [North Korea]." That the Sydney Declaration came about in the midst of President Kim Young Sam's summit diplomacy is hardly surprising. On the eve of Korea's financial crisis in November 1997, Seoul dropped out of the Group of Seventy-Seven (the United Nations' 134-member Third World caucus) in order to join the Vinci Group (the advanced developed countries' economic caucus).[25] Even before becoming an OECD member in 1996, Seoul started its foreign-aid program – overseas development assistance (ODA) – albeit rather modestly in both scale and scope

[25] Ministry of Foreign Affairs and Trade, *1998 Oyekyo Paekso* [1998 diplomatic white paper], chapter 2 (Internet version).

(see tables 8.2 and 11.1). In the wake of the economic crisis, Seoul initially indicated that it might have to freeze its financial contributions to the United Nations at the 1997 level for the next three years. But the Kim Dae Jung government decided not only to pay its U.N. dues in full but also to increase its contributions to the United Nations and related programs (Chapter 9). In fact, Seoul's U.N. assessment is not only sixteen times that of Pyongyang but also higher than that of China. Despite the recent economic crisis, the U.N. assessment highlighted the dramatic contrast between the rise of South Korea and the decline of North Korea in the U.N. politics of collective legitimation and delegitimation.[26]

Perhaps the most striking feature of Seoul's diplomatic globalization during the Kim Young Sam administration is the extent to which it was driven by a desire for status via summit diplomacy. Unlike the Clinton administration, the Korean government created no new cabinet position to cope with "intermestic" challenges. Nor was there any evidence that Korea's ambassadors served as supersalespeople for economic diplomacy. If indeed globalization demands a fundamental reconceptualization of the state's roles – its possibilities and limitations – in a shrinking world, there is no evidence that such a transformation took place in Korean foreign-policy thinking during the Kim Young Sam government. If Korean diplomacy is defined in traditional terms or even in terms of global diplomatic interconnectedness, there is no doubt about its success, especially in the United Nations (Chapter 9). Defined in substantive terms – that is, in terms of meeting the multiple intermestic challenges or in terms of enhancing Korea's competitiveness in the global marketplace – *segyehwa* diplomacy was a failure.

As Chae-Jin Lee and Victor Cha point out in Chapters 8 and 10, globalization is Janus-faced, providing both a challenge and an opportunity in the conduct of Korean foreign relations – a challenge to the realist paradigm and nationalistic conception of "security" narrowly defined and an opportunity to advance through the shortening product cycles and global competitiveness ranking by constantly adapting to the pressures and requirements of globalization dynamics. Viewed in this light, President Kim Young Sam's *segyehwa* diplomacy was at best "only a limited success" (Chapter 9). But B. C. Koh concludes Chapter 9 with a more positive assessment of Seoul's *segyehwa* diplomacy as made manifest in the United Nations: It is in this quintessentially globalist organization, he says, that Seoul has managed to make globalization a reality. With the end of the Cold War and the progressive triumph of Seoul's *nordpolitik*,

---

[26] For further analysis along this line, see Samuel S. Kim, "North Korea and the United Nations," *International Journal of Korean Studies* 1, no. 1 (Spring 1997), 77–110.

the nature of Seoul's conflict with former socialist adversaries was transformed, making it possible for Seoul to enter into a wide range of non-zero-sum relationships with new diplomatic and trading partners and a host of international organizations, including the United Nations.

The impact of the economic crisis on Korean foreign policy is palpable, especially the prominence of economic diplomacy. The Ministry of Foreign Affairs (MOFA) became the Ministry of Foreign Affairs and Trade (MOFAT), with Korea's ambassadors – and even President Kim Dae Jung himself – more actively engaged in an international investment road show, even as some fourteen overseas diplomatic missions had to be closed by the end of 1998 as a cost-saving measure (about $10 million a year). In mid-July 1998, the MOFAT decided to form a task force to help Korean firms cope with antidumping tariffs and other trade barriers by Korea's major trade partners. The task force, composed of ministry officials, trade experts, businessmen, and officials from related organizations, will focus on scrapping antidumping tariffs already imposed on Korean products and provide legal and administrative supports for Korean firms engaging in legal procedures against foreign companies presently trying to levy antidumping tariffs. The task force will also concentrate its efforts on collecting information on the sentiments against Korean products in foreign countries so that some preventive measures can be taken.[27]

Time and again, President Kim Dae Jung has stressed in his proactive summit diplomacy the importance of culture, knowledge, and information. In his address to the Japanese parliament in early October 1998, he declared that culture develops through contacts and exchanges with other cultures, and promised to gradually lift a fifty-three-year ban on the importation of Japanese cultural products. Indeed, Seoul decided on 20 October 1998 to gradually allow the importation of Japanese pop culture, starting with select movies and cartoons but for now excluding the more popular performance arts, music, animations, video games, videos, and television broadcasts. Apparently, this was President Kim's "gift" to Tokyo, needed in order to achieve gains in other areas of the bilateral deal.[28] Despite, or perhaps because of, the ongoing economic crisis, the government is also actively promoting knowledge-based industries (culture, tourism, information-telecommunications and design industries, and Internet-based business-to-business electronic-commerce systems) as the chief catalyst for a second economic takeoff in the coming years. When the annual number of foreign tourists arriving passed the 4-million mark, for the first time, on 10 December 1998, with the single largest

[27] *Seoul Yonhap* in English, 16 July 1998, in FBIS-EAS-98-197 (16 July 1998).
[28] *Korea Herald*, 10 October 1998 (Internet edition).

increase coming from Japan (a 15.6 percent increase over 1997) – generating a surplus of $3.5 billion, thus reversing 1997's deficit of $1.1 billion – the president of the Korea National Tourism Organization (KNTO) quickly responded, "We believe that the TV commercial in which President Kim Dae-jung promoted Korean tourism was very effective in spreading the image of Korea as a safe country to visit."[29]

Security Segyehwa

What does it mean to be or feel "secure" in an era of globalization? As Cha suggests in Chapter 10, in recent years both the agency and the scope of "threat" as well as the sources and effects of security globalization have become more complex, diverse, multidimensional, nonstate, and nonmilitary than ever before. The extent of South Korea's security globalization can be assessed in terms of the shifting balance between national security narrowly defined and human security broadly defined, and between unilateral-cum-bilateral and multilateral cooperative security. To what extent and in what specific way is the meaning of security redefined and acted out in multilateral cooperative-security terms? How much diplomatic capital is mobilized in South Korea's participation in the development of such synergistic conception of human security as against the traditional Realpolitik conception of national interest and security narrowed construed? Or is South Korea too caught up in the post–Cold War efforts in various parts of the world to develop "information warfare techniques"? Whatever the extent of implementation, the PSPC breaks new conceptual and normative ground in espousing the concept of "human security" (*inkan anpo*) as an integral part of a new *segyehwa* paradigm.[30]

The antinomies of Korea's security globalization are made manifest in the interplay of multilateral cooperative security engagement and unilateral-cum-bilateral security behavior.[31] On the multilateral cooperative security side, South Korea participated as of early 1999 in eight U.N. Peacekeeping Operations (UNPKOs), albeit on an extremely modest scale (see table 9.3). South Korea has become a signatory of most of the relevant multilateral arms control and disarmament conventions, including the Non-Proliferation Treaty (NPT), the Comprehensive Test Ban Treaty (CTBT), the Chemical Weapons Convention (CWC), and the Biological Weapons Convention (BWC) (see table 10.2). Seoul has also

[29] Ibid.
[30] *Segyehwa ui pichon kwa chonryak*, 151, 204.
[31] See Chung-in Moon and Seok-soo Lee, "The Post–Cold War Security Agenda of Korea: Inertia, New Thinking, and Assessments," *Pacific Review* 8, no. 1 (1995), 99–115.

utilized its position as a member of the ASEAN Regional Forum (ARF) to seek support for its efforts to maintain peace and stability on the Korean Peninsula via the Korean Armistice Agreement, to implement the 1994 U.S.-DPRK Agreed Framework via the multilateral consortium known as the Korean Peninsula Energy Development Organization (KEDO) in New York and the Four-Party Peace Talks, designed to replace the existing armistice accord with a new peace mechanism. Seoul has also proposed a six-party Northeast Asia Security Dialogue (NEASED), involving the two Koreas, the United States, China, Japan, and Russia, to explore measures for building confidence on the Korean Peninsula.

Despite the situation-specific changes and shifts in Seoul's definition of the regional and global situations, there remains at the core a deeply rooted Realpolitik world view that military power buys both soft security (international status) and hard security (deterrence). The United States, the United Nations, and other multilateral security regimes or fora are supplements to, not substitutes for, Seoul's independent security. To promote security globalization, according to the Ministry of National Defense, is to foster powerful, first-rate armed forces, to develop international military relations, and to improve international competitiveness (Chapter 8). Defying the post–Cold War global trends, Seoul's defense budget increased by an average of 11 percent annually in the 1990s (see tables 8.3 and 11.1). Even the economic crisis has hardly made a dent, as the defense budget for 1999 declined by only a trifling 0.2 percent. Seoul has also attempted to expand and diversify its security *segyehwa* by gradually de-Americanizing its international military relations and gradually increasing its military exchanges with Japan, Russia, and China. Much to the United States' chagrin, Seoul has also begun diversifying the sources of its military procurement by increasing its imports of military hardware from France, Britain, and other Western countries and by acquiring Russian weapons systems in repayment of outstanding loans. All the same, Seoul has joined the ugly, subversive side of military and security globalization as a supplier to the international arms trade. In the period 1992–6, fifty-two countries, in a six-tier pecking order, supplied the international arms: the United States, as the first-tier supplier, preempting a whopping 40–50 percent of the market, while South Korea, as a member of the fifth tier, supplied only 1–2 percent of the market. It is worth noting in this connection that Seoul is behind Pyongyang (a third-tier supplier, with 5–10 percent of the market) but ahead of Tokyo (a sixth-tier supplier with 0–1 percent of the market).[32]

With the Kim Dae Jung government came a shift from nationalist to

---

[32] International Institute for Strategic Studies, *The Military Balance, 1997/98* (London: Oxford University Press, 1997), 264.

multilateral cooperative security in the form of "independent collective security." Central to the "independent collective security" thinking is the proposition that "collective security" is not more important than "independent security" but that it is important to "independent security" as the source of state security. The president wants to strengthen "independent security capabilities" without neglecting "collective security" (i.e., the ROK-U.S. security arrangement) while at the same time making the "utmost efforts to bring the four-party meeting to success." Such "independent collective security" thinking – having one's security cake and eating it too – is also made manifest in President Kim Dae Jung's Northern policy, known as the "sunshine policy": Seoul would not tolerate military provocation of any kind; at the same time, it pledges not to undermine or absorb the North and to accelerate functional cooperation starting first in those areas of mutual interest or on which they can most readily reach agreement. President Kim pledged that the ROK would no longer stand in the way of allied powers' improving their bilateral relations with the DPRK.[33]

And yet President Kim Dae Jung's "independent collective security" thinking and "sunshine policy" are not so much evidence of a paradigm shift as they are the result of cost-effective adaptation to changing situations in the North and South. On 12 January 1998, President-Elect Kim told IMF Managing Director Michel Camdessus that "for now, because of such matters as economic recovery, administrative reform, and improving international trust, we have little [few] resources to spare for large-scale North-South programs. We will make no haste with [on] North-South issues."[34] Despite the imperatives of globalization, which have fueled some of the recent issue-specific troubles in the U.S.-ROK alliance relationship, as Cha argues in Chapter 10, Seoul's overall attitudes toward the alliance show little if any change. Despite the deepening economic problems and continuing trade-related disputes with the United States, Seoul's share of the costs for the United States Force in Korea (USFK) has more than doubled in the 1990s, from U.S. $150 million in 1991 to $399 million in 1998 (see table 11.1).[35] The recent economic crisis has sharpened an ongoing ROK-U.S. dispute over the sharing of costs for the USFK, with Washington demanding that Seoul contribute $440 million for 1999, while Seoul wants to scale back to the 1994 level of $260 million because of the current economic crisis. Even the *Korea Times*, an English-language daily not noted for radical or anti-American views, joined the

---

[33] For the text of the inaugural speech where these ideas and principles are enunciated, see *Korea Herald*, 26 February 1998 (Internet version).

[34] FBIS-EAS-98-082 (23 March 1998) (Internet version).

[35] See also Ministry of National Defense, *Defense White Paper 1997–1998* (Seoul: Ministry of National Defense, Republic of Korea, 1998), 228.

fray attacking the U.S. demand as unreasonable, unfair, and downright self-serving. Washington keeps its thirty-seven thousand troops in Korea for its own strategic interests, not because Korea wants them there. Besides, instead of demanding more rent-seeking (burden sharing), Washington should be grateful to Seoul for the use of land rent-free since the rent for the land the USFK occupies amounted to no less than $1.57 billion in 1997.[36] Nonetheless, the presence of American troops is so crucial to ROK security that even the liberal globalist President Kim Dae Jung wants to keep American troops in a reunified Korea.

At least in theory, globalization undermines the traditional realist paradigm and geostrategic determinism. And yet the zero-sum mentality and the realist Realpolitik perspective still dominate South Korean leaders' perception of their security environment. Not only is there a gap between the rhetoric of multilateralism and the practice of unilateralism-cum-bilateralism but there is a gap between the elite's and people's perceptions of security issues, as the overwhelming majority of South Koreans were not overly concerned about national-security issues. In response to a question about what was most important for South Korea's national security, the respondents in a national opinion survey conducted on 10 June 1995 mentioned the need for political stability (38.6 percent), economic prosperity (23.2 percent), citizens' security consciousness (25.1 percent), increased military capabilities (7.9 percent), and expanded diplomatic relations (4.1 percent) (Chapter 8). Of course, the survey results would have been different if it had been conducted a year earlier, in the heat of the nuclear crisis. Still, there is no denying the perception gaps regarding security issues between the elite and the people in many countries, including South Korea.

To what are these antinomies of security *segyehwa* attributable? Both Lee and Cha explain Seoul's abiding security thinking and behavior in terms of the zero-sum mentality and the traditional realist mindset. In Lee's view, the liberal assumption that "economic interdependence would discourage states from using force against each other because warfare would threaten each side's prosperity" has not been embraced by South Korean national-security managers. Likewise, the theoretical claim of liberal institutionalists that international organizations can alter state preferences, change state behavior, and cause states to turn from conflict to cooperation does not hold up too well in Seoul's security *segyehwa*,[37] although Koh may well take issue with this argument. For Cha,

---

[36] Editorial, *Korea Times*, 18 October 1998 (Internet version).

[37] For the debate between structural realists and liberal institutionalists, see John J. Mearsheimer, "The False Promise of International Institutions," *International Security* 19, no. 3 (Winter 1994–5), 5–49; Robert O. Keohane and Lisa L. Martin, "The Promise of Institutional Theory," ibid. 20, no. 1 (Summer 1995),

however, the primary cause of Seoul's security thinking and behavior lies in the "realist mindset," which in turn is a function of rooted national identity and values: "Although there is an external impetus for globalization, there are internal qualities that resist these imperatives. When the forces for globalization are refracted through this prism of Korean identity, the behavior that emerges reflects a tension between globalization pressures on the one hand and localization imperatives on the other."

To a significant extent, Pyongyang's hypernationalistic security thinking and behavior has the paradoxical consequences of simultaneously strengthening Seoul's unilateral *and* multilateral security impulses. Indeed, what complicates Seoul's security *segyehwa* is its *sui generis* divided polity. Even under the best of circumstances, incomplete nation-states such as the two Koreas are said to be primed for a zero-sum, often violent politics of competitive legitimation and delegitimation to maximize their exclusive security and legitimacy. By any reckoning, however, Pyongyang's hypernationalistic security or insecurity behavior is just the thing to fuel Seoul's zero-sum mentality and realist mindset. There is little doubt about the North Korean leadership's determination to use all the available instruments of national military power to avert absorption by the South. Even without going nuclear, North Korea commands massive, forward-based forces deployed along the northern side of the so-called demilitarized zone (DMZ) on the Korean Peninsula. Moreover, North Korea is believed to have the world's third-largest inventory of chemical weapons, as well as an impressive array of delivery systems. Consider the grim consequences of another Korean war as depicted by the top U.S. military brass in a 1994 report: "If war broke out in Korea, it would cost 52,000 US military casualties, killed or wounded, and 490,000 South Korean casualties in the first ninety days.... North Korea could pound Seoul with five thousand rounds of artillery within the first twelve hours."[38] Whether the Cold War has ended or not, whether the era of globalization has arrived or not, there is no easy escape for South Korean leaders from viewing their goals and means of security *segyehwa* in local rather than global terms.

Whither *Segyehwa?*

Given the above, Korea's *segyehwa* drive leads to one obvious and somewhat paradoxical conclusion: Perhaps more than any other state in the

39–51; Charles A. Kupchan and Clifford A. Kupchan, "The Promise of Collective Security," ibid., 52–61; John Gerald Ruggie, "The False Premise of Realism," ibid., 62–70; and Alexander Wendt, "Constructing International Politics," ibid., 71–81.

[38] *Korea Times* 18 September 1998 (Internet version).

1990s, South Korea under Kim Young Sam extolled globalization un-abashedly, only to achieve so little. As virtually all the chapters in this volume suggest or imply, the jury is still out on the future of *segyehwa* under the Kim Dae Jung government. Despite the seemingly principled pronouncements about the parallel pursuit of participatory democracy and a liberal market economy, the transition from an era of nation-alism to an era of "universal globalism" and the corresponding major structural reforms in all sectors of the state, society, and economy, how-ever, the gaps between *segyehwa* promise and *segyehwa* performance remain wide and deep at the end of the first year of the new government. In many respects, the Republic of Korea remains far from being or becoming an attractive, advanced, and globalized world-class country that people all over the world would want to come to, invest in, and live in.

A pessimistic answer to the question – whither *segyehwa?* – is that the country still seems like a strange and depressing political environment where many formal motions are made but there is no actual movement. With no progress of any kind in political reform, the rival parties have spent most of their legislative time in the partisan power politics of mutual recrimination and bloodletting. Indeed, the democratic state is now caught between a recalcitrant *chaebol* and militant labor. The state-capital collusion – Korea Inc. – has been replaced by a tug of war between the government and the *chaebol* and more recently between the govern-ment and labor. As a result, the corporate (*chaebol*) restructuring – the heart of structural reform, needed to avert a second economic crisis – occurs at a snail's pace. Of course, corporate restructuring is not possible without some labor market flexibility or mass "IMFiring." Given the inability of the state to formulate and implement a consistent and coher-ent globalization policy at a pace commensurate with the requirements of globalization dynamics, doing more and more seems to be achieving less and less.

An optimistic answer to the question – whither *segyehwa?* – is that Korea's economy in early 1999 began to show signs of bottoming out. This is suggested by some rebound in the external credit rating, interest rates, tourism, and exports, especially favorable exports in semiconduc-tors and automobiles, all riding on such favorable seasonal but volatile variables as a low U.S. dollar, low interest rates, and low petroleum prices on international markets – the "new three lows." Yielding to presidential and public pressure, in early December 1998, the Big Five agreed in prin-ciple on a set of sweeping reform programs and once again pledged full observance of the five principles of *chaebol* reform they had agreed upon earlier in the year: (1) the elimination of cross-subsidiary credit guaran-tees, (2) the introduction of consolidated financial statements, (3) the improvement of the capital structure by putting the owners' personal assets to company finances and lowering the debt-equity ratios, (4) the achievement of transparency in corporate governance and business transactions, and (5) the streamlining of octopus-like businesses to three to five core industries. The government-business agreement on corporate restructuring is no more than a joint statement of reciprocal quid pro quos: The Big Five will reduce the number of their subsidiaries by up to 70 percent by the year 2000, for which they will receive comprehensive tax breaks and other benefits, including debt-for-equity swaps by creditors, thus bringing back the moral hazard (socialization of risks). The agreement could turn into just another piece of paper if either party fails to live up to its end of the bargain. By and large, this latest agreement is no different from the agreement reached between President Kim and the Big Five earlier in the year.

The nature and consequences of globalization for both developed and developing countries are for the first time being hotly debated, with various competing prescriptive measures being suggested, thanks to the East Asian economic crisis of 1997–8. There is general agreement among the analysts of the Korean state, society, and economy that the main causes of the greatest crisis ever to hit Korea since the Korean War are largely endogenous, the external factors (e.g., the contagious effects of changes in the foreign-exchange rate and interest rates, the panic behavior of international short-term hedge fund managers) serving only as the trigger. But there is no agreement on which among the many domestic factors played the most determinative role.

For analytical convenience and simplicity, the contending explanations can be reduced to three different, if not mutually exclusive, broad explanations, representing three levels of analysis. One explanation has to do with policy and leadership. Essentially, this explanation contends that the Korean crisis is an inevitable outcome of the Kim Young Sam government's poor performance in the areas of policy and leadership. The Kim Young Sam government, in cahoots with the *chaebol* – state-capital collusion (*chungkyong yuchaek*) – has brought about the crisis. Not surprisingly, this is the most popular explanation in Korea. It has led to a politics of finger-pointing and scapegoating, which too often has degenerated into the zero-sum politics of mutual assured destruction (MAD) South Korean style, with two of President Kim Young Sam's top economic advisors (Kang Kyong-Shik and Kim In-Ho) initially going to prison, then tried and acquitted, for "policy mistakes and complacency," not for criminal wrongdoing. To cite another example, during the first six months of 1998, under the liberal, human-rights administration of Kim Dae Jung, the prosecutor's office, the police, and the Agency for National Security Planning (ANSP) made use of the dubious practice of wiretapping on 3,580 occasions, a considerable jump from about 2,400 occasions in 1996 under the Kim Young Sam administration. The prosecutor's office in fact seems more politicized now than during the Kim Young Sam administration.[39]

The problem with this first explanation is that it does not fully demonstrate why such a policy and leadership failure occurred in spite of the numerous attempts by both the Roh and Kim governments over at least ten years to reform the very features of the system that caused the economic crisis, such as rigid labor markets, highly leveraged and indebted expansion of the *chaebol*, and the archaic banking and financial systems, or why human-rights abuses and politically motivated prosecution of opposition politicians have continued under the new administration.

A second explanation for the failure of the *segyehwa* drive and the onset of the economic crisis is a systemic failure: Since 1987, there have been profound changes in state-capital-labor relations, with the consequence that the *chaebol* and labor have become more powerful and independent at the expense of the state. Caught between the powerful *chaebol* and militant labor as well as between the requirements of democratic consolidation at home and the requirements of enhancing Korea's competitiveness in the global marketplace, the state muddled through by redefining its globalization drive in symbolically popular terms of a grand national ego trip. The problem has less to do with democracy per se than with the way in which it was practiced – "immature democracy" – with the greatest damage to the Korean economy coming from ten years of systemic incongruence and gridlock.[40]

The third explanation locates the root cause of the Korean crisis in the deeply embedded cultural and ideational variables; according to this explanation, Korea's cultural nationalism and Realpolitik mindset act as a powerful and persistent constraint on the *segyehwa* drive. Put succinctly, no fundamental learning – no paradigm shift – has occurred in the course of Korea's *segyehwa* drive, only situation-specific tactical adaptation.[41]

---

[39] *Korea Herald,* 19 October 1998 (Internet version).

[40] See Chung-in Moon and Jongryn Mo, "Democracy and the Origins of the 1997 Korean Economic Crisis," in eds. Jongryun Mo and Chung-in Moon, *Democracy and the Korean Economy* (Stanford, CA: Hoover Institution Press, 1999), 171–98.

[41] Learning theory suddenly became hot in the wake of the Gorbachev revolution in the Soviet Union, the end of the Cold War, and the collapse of the Soviet Union. The sudden prominence of learning theory suggests as well that mainstream international-relations theory, especially realism and neorealism, is in a state of unprecedented disarray. For a sample of the burgeoning literature on learning theory, see George Breslauer and Philip Tetlock, eds., *Learning in U.S. and Soviet Foreign Policy* (Boulder, CO: Westview Press, 1991); Ernst Haas, *When Knowledge Is Power: Three Models of Change in International Organizations* (Berkeley, CA: University of California Press, 1990); Alastair Johnston, "Learning versus Adaptation: Explaining Change in Chinese Arms Control Policy in the 1980s and 1990s," *China Journal* 35 (January 1996), 27–61; Jack Levy,

There is ample evidence that Seoul has developed a more sophisticated and constructive U.N. diplomacy (Chapter 9). However, there is less evidence that Seoul's diplomatic *segyehwa*, with its extensive linkages and participation in the world of international organizations in the 1990s, has led to a paradigm shift from unilateral self-help to cooperative common security. All the policy shifts and changes in the 1990s can be better seen as adaptive or instrumental learning rather than cognitive or normative learning at the basic level of world view and national identity. And yet, this very ROK-U.N. interaction, intentionally or unintentionally, widened and deepened the ambit of Korea's involvement in the U.N. system, eroding and blurring the boundary between externally conditioned and internally determined policies. As Koh concludes in Chapter 9, globalization as a two-way process "will ineluctably lead to the globalization of South Korea itself – in the sense of transforming South Korean thinking and behavior, both at the individual and collective level, in the direction of meeting global standards. Slowly but surely, then, the gap between *segyehwa* and globalization will be bridged." Viewed in this light, the apparent absence of cognitive or normative learning at this point in time does not necessarily mean that Seoul's Realpolitik views are immutably predetermined or that changes conducive to cooperative common security are totally lacking or cannot occur in the future. The adaptive-cognitive learning distinction, therefore, may be better seen as a continuum rather than a dichotomy.

The Kim Dae Jung government now faces a number of critical challenges with regard to the three broad explanations provided for the failure of the *segyehwa* drive and the economic crisis, each of which involves strategic decisions about how to survive and prosper in an increasingly interconnected and interdependent Darwinian world with high payoffs for the fittest and high penalties for the least adaptable.

At the most basic level, that of world view and national identity, there remains the challenge of replacing antiglobalization beliefs and behaviors with a system of beliefs and behaviors that extends beyond the diplomatic domain and into social relations more generally. Just as nondemocratic beliefs and practices complicate the task of democratic consolidation far more than they do democratic transition, nationalistic beliefs and practices at the societal level would make the task of globalization performance far more difficult than they do globalization pronouncements.

"Learning and Foreign Policy: Sweeping a Conceptual Minefield," *International Organization* 48, no. 2 (Spring 1994), 279–312; Dan Reiter, "Learning, Realism, and Alliances: The Weight of the Shadow of the Past," *World Politics* 46 (July 1994), 490–526; and Janice Gross Stein, "Political Learning by Doing: Gorbachev as Uncommitted Thinker and Motivated Learner," *International Organization* 48, no. 2 (Spring 1994), 155–83.

One of the major consequences of the division of the peninsula and the ensuing politics of competitive legitimation and delegitimation that South Korea would have to overcome if its *segyehwa* drive were successful is the bias toward bigness – a "bigger is better and biggest is best" edifice complex – as a defensive mechanism for coping with its national identity angst as a small *and* divided nation surrounded by big and powerful neighbors (China, Russia, and Japan). The incomplete, 105-story Yuk-yong Hotel in Pyongyang, rising to a height of more than three hundred meters, seventy meters taller than any other hotel in the world, and the omnipresence of monuments (more than thirty-five thousand), are symptomatic of North Korea's *Juche*-style edifice complex. The South Korean equivalent is the *chaebol,* which are too dangerous if left uncontrolled yet nearly impossible to control without causing serious dislocations in the labor market, banking, and export sectors and without the state's deviating too far from its market-economy principles.[42]

That size had traditionally been the most important measure of status inevitably propelled the *chaebol's* reckless expansion, sending false signals to Korean resource allocators and fair business competition at home and abroad. In the end, it was the *chaebol's* reckless expansion and diversification aimed at increasing their size rather than their profitability and specialization that caused Korea's financial crisis. D. M. Leipziger put it in the form of the following proposition: "excessively risky investments – regulation + corruption + high interest rates = corporate sector meltdown."[43]

Missing from the rational-choice analysis of the *chaebol's* size-driven behavior is the emotional national-identity factor: the *chaebol's* reckless expansion and diversification in order to increase their size reflects and effects a generalized aggressive impulse to cope with or at least compensate for the national-identity angst Korea feels as a small and divided nation in a region long dominated by big and powerful states. The eco-developmental "small is beautiful" principle[44] and the idea that creativity and innovation can thrive in small, flexible, and ever-adapting systems still remain largely alien to Korean political-economy thinking and behavior. That the United States (a lone superpower), Singapore (a ministate), and Russia (a failed state) ranked respectively first, second, and last among the forty-six developed and emerging market economy

---

[42] For an argument along this line, see Samuel S. Kim, "The Impact of the Division of Korea on South Korean Politics: The Challenge of Competitive Legitimation," in *Korean Democracy toward a New Horizon* (Seoul: Korean Political Science Association, 1995), 57–90.

[43] Leipziger, "Public and Private Interests in Korea," 11.

[44] E. F. Schumacher, *Small Is Beautiful: A Study of Economics as If People Mattered* (New York: Harper & Row, 1973).

countries on the world competitiveness scoreboard in the last five years (1995–9) speaks volumes about the relative importance of *size* versus *speed* (in information technology, innovations, and state action).[45]

At the systemic level, what the role of the state is or should be and how to rethink the nature, form, and content of participatory democratic politics in the face of the complex intermeshing of local, national, and globalization processes are questions that the *segyehwa* pronouncements cannot simply skate over. Just as President Kim Young Sam's *segyehwa* drive was initiated by the government as a state-enhancing, top-down strategic plan, President Kim Dae Jung's espousal of participatory democracy and a liberal market economy as "two wheels of a cart" and the "Second Nation-Building Movement," in practice, seemed like top-down, command-and-control reform plans. Instead of using market principles, the government resorted to command-and-control-style arm-twisting to get the Big Five to follow the state guidelines for corporate restructuring and reform. The launching of the Second Nation-Building Movement in mid-August 1998 is another example of a top-down reform movement – "a guided democracy" Korean style. As a vast network is taking shape at the central and local levels and as its political structure and substance become more visible, the state-initiated nationwide campaign is facing formidable resistance in both political and civil-society circles. Even many who stress the importance of noble objectives (e.g., two-way political communication between the people and the government, realization of a market democracy, adoption of a new value system based on universalism and globalism, rebuilding a knowledge- and information-based economy, promoting a constructive relationship between labor and management) are increasingly concerned about the efficacy and appropriateness of a reform movement that relies on government funds, manpower, and agency. Some critics point to the legal absurdity of a body created by presidential decree to work on reorganization of state agencies and structures established under the Constitution and related laws.

A more serious challenge for the state is how to carry out "social concertation" successfully since so many European social democracies abandoned it in the face of globalization challenges. In the Korean context, such social concertation (a labor-management-government trilateral commission) and the relationship between the state and women are all the more desirable, all the more necessary, and yet all the more problematic. As pointed out in Chapter 3, such social partnership is difficult to establish due to the lack of social trust, the lack of strong top-level

---

[45] See International Institute for Management Development, *World Competitiveness Yearbook 1999* in http://www.imd.ch/wcy/factors/overall.html.

labor associations, and the lack of institutional links between political parties and labor interests.

Despite, or perhaps because of, the remarkable transition to democracy in 1987, the ascendancy of a civilian government in 1992, and the first-ever victory of an opposition candidate in 1997, the politics of fragmentation prevail. In a sense, South Korea, chronically plagued by fratricidal regional factionalism and searing labor-management conflict, remains to be geographically, socially, and politically unified within its own borders. In what South Koreans call the "IMF era," Korea seems to have acquired a new national identity as a "People's Republic of Endless Strikes" – the government striking against the opposition party, the opposition striking back at the government, Big Labor striking against Big Business (the *chaebol*), Big Business striking against Big Labor and the government, the Yongnam region striking against the Honam region (whose per capita income has been one-quarter that of Yongnam) and now the Honam region striking against the Yongnam region with a vengeance, one faction of Korean Buddhism striking violently against another faction, and so on. The politics of fragmentation and confrontation does not stop at the water's edge. Tellingly, the opposition Grand National Party debuted at the 1999 annual session of the United Nations Human Rights Commission in Geneva as a Korean human rights NGO to accuse the Kim Dae Jung government of alleged torture, political surveillance, illegal wiretapping, and other political skullduggery and civil liberty abuses.

Finally, at the level of policy formulation and implementation, the Kim Dae Jung government is now faced with a series of challenges, as was the Kim Young Sam government, each of which will involve, in a larger sense, a strategic decision regarding how to meet and minimize the clear and continuing dangers of systemic vulnerability, relational sensitivity, and structural dependency that globalization poses and how to redefine the role of the state as a knowledge-intensive and information-intensive partner, catalyst, and facilitator, not as a direct commander or provider of economic growth and prosperity. Specifically, policymaking and policy-implementing challenges include but are not limited to the following:

- Making *segyehwa* compatible with domestic social and political stability without regressing into backlash hypernationalist politics.
- Developing a social-welfare and safety-net system in the face of the relentless competitiveness in world marketplaces.
- Formulating and implementing a liberal trade policy, removing capital controls, opening financial markets to foreign investors, and downsizing the role of the state in the economy without giving up the state's monitoring and supervisory role.

- Formulating and implementing a policy shift away from foreign borrowing to foreign direct investment in Korea in order to undo thirty years of a bureaucratic Great Wall designed to keep FDI out and to minimize the moral hazard and rent-seeking behaviors of domestic *chaebol* and international hedge-fund managers, especially in view of the fact that the government itself has been the greatest obstacle to foreign investment.
- Encouraging and stimulating the technological innovation and development necessary for maximizing productivity, quality, and specialization, and surviving and even prospering in the world of fierce knowledge-intensive and information-intensive competition.

Predicting the future of *segyehwa* or the future of Korea, always hazardous, has never been more so than today, when the country is experiencing the greatest crisis since the Korean War even as the global economic system to which it is now widely connected and in which it is deeply enmeshed undergoes a profound turbulence as well. The old developmental state has already been discredited beyond redemption and an alternative state – a competent, efficient, knowledge-intensive, and adaptable state – is not yet in the offing.

Still, it is possible to speak of three plausible future scenarios: breakdown, breakthrough, and muddling through. The breakdown scenario is the most pessimistic, but its possibility should not be prematurely dismissed. How or whether the Kim Dae Jung government can carry out the parallel pursuit of participatory democracy and a market economy, meeting the twin challenges of enhancing Korea's competitiveness in the global marketplace and enhancing social and economic well-being and stability at home, remains to be seen. As it is, if the rate of economic recovery is insufficient to meet the rising expectations of the people, the penalty for this failure may put more strains on legitimacy, risking democratic breakdown and/or a hypernationalistic backlash.

The most optimistic scenario – breakthrough – proceeds from the premise that the current crisis is really a blessing in disguise, providing President Kim Dae Jung with a once-in-a-generation opportunity for a paradigmatic change. That is, the crisis is and becomes a great teacher of the reality principle and a great generator of national consensus, helping the reformist and liberal president to break through all the cultural, institutional, and political barriers standing in the way.

The third scenario – muddling through – sees continuing systemic incongruence and policymaking gridlock, some marginal sector-specific, time-specific changes, but no fundamental paradigmatic change. This scenario is likely to come about if the Korean economy makes a quick rebound, if not full recovery, helped by external seasonable variables undermining the crisis-induced sense of national urgency and consensus for major structural reform, especially *chaebol* and labor market reform and restructuring.

At the dawn of the new millennium, the Republic of Korea stands at a crossroads. Although written more than a century ago, the opening statement of Charles Dickens's *A Tale of Two Cities* (1859) seems even more appropriate now as a characterization of the Korean situation today: "It was the best of times, it was the worst of times, it was the age of wisdom, it was the age of foolishness, it was the epoch of belief, it was the epoch of incredulity, it was the season of Light, it was the season of Darkness, it was the spring of hope, it was the winter of despair."

Bibliography

Books

Agarwal, Bina, ed. *Structures of Patriarchy: State, Community and Household in Modernizing Asia.* London: Zed Press, 1988.

Alvarez, Sonia. "The (Trans)formation of Feminism(s) and Gender Politics in Democratizing Brazil,"in ed. Jane S. Jaquette., *The Women's Movement in Latin America: Participation and Democracy* 2nd ed. Boulder, CO: Westview Press, 1994.

Amsden, Alice H. *Asia's Next Giant: South Korea and Late Industrialization.* New York: Oxford University Press, 1989.

Appiah, Kwame Anthony. "Cosmopolitan Patriots," in *Cosmopolitics: Thinking and Feeling beyond the Nation,* eds. Pheng Cheah and Bruce Robbins. Minneapolis, MN: University of Minnesota Press, 1998.

Arato, Andrew and Jean Cohen, *Civil Society and Political Theory.* Cambridge, MA: MIT Press, 1992.

Bedeski, Robert, *The Transformation of South Korea: Reform and Reconstruction in the Sixth Republic under Roh Tae Woo 1987–1992.* London: Routledge, 1994.

Beneria, Lourdes, ed. *Women and Development: The Sexual Division of Labor in Rural Societies.* New York: Praeger, 1982.

Boserup, Esther. *Women's Role in Economic Development.* New York: St. Martin's Press, 1970.

Brecher, Jeremy and Tim Costello. *Global Village or Global Pillage: Economic Reconstruction from the Bottom Up.* Boston: South End Press, 1994.

Breslauer, George, and Philip Tetlock, eds. *Learning in U.S. and Soviet Foreign Policy.* Boulder, CO: Westview Press, 1991.

Brunhes, Bernard. "Labor Flexibility in Enterprise: A Comparison of Firms in Four European Countries," in OECD, *Labour Market Flexibility: Trends in Enterprises.* Paris: OECD, 1989.

Brydon, Lynne and Sylvia Chant, eds. *Women in the Third World: Gender Issues in Rural and Urban Areas.* New Brunswick, NJ: Rutgers University Press, 1989.

Chatterji, Partha. "The Nation and Its Women," in *The Nation and Its Fragmentations: Colonial and Postcolonial Histories.* Princeton, NJ: Princeton University Press, 1993.

Chi, Tong Uk, *Kankoku no Zokubatsu, Gunbatsu, Zaibatsu* [South Korea's kin groups, military groups, and business groups]. Tokyo: Chuo Koron, 1997.

Cho, Dong Seok. *The South Korean Chaebol*. Seoul: Maeil Kyungje Shinmunsa, 1997.

Cho, Eun. *Cholbanui kyonghom cholbanui mosori: yosong choch'aikui hyonjang* [Experience of the half voice of the half: a scene from the women's policy]. Seoul: Miraemidiô, 1996.

Cho, Hwa-Soon. *Let the Weak Be Strong: A Women's Struggle for Justice*. Bloomington: Meyerstone Books, 1988.

Choi, Jang-Jip. *Hankookui nodong undongkwa kooga* [Labor movement and the state in South Korea]. Seoul: Yeolumsa, 1988.

Choi, Jang Jip. "Political Cleavages in South Korea," in *State and Society in Contemporary Korea*. ed. Hagen Koo. Ithaca, NY: Cornell University Press, 1993.

Choi, Seoung-No. *The Analysis of the 30 Korean Big Business Groups for 1996*. Seoul: Korea Economic Research Institute, 1996.

Chu, Hun-han. "Social Protests and Political Democratization in Taiwan," in ed. Murray A. Rubinstein, *The Other Taiwan: 1945 to the Present*, Armonk, NY, and London: M. E. Sharpe, 1994.

Chu, Yun-han. "The Realignment of Business-Government Relations and Regime Transition in Taiwan," in ed. Andrew MacIntyre, *Business and Government in Industrializing Asia*, Ithaca, NY: Cornell University Press, 1994.

Cox, Robert. "Democracy in Hard Times: Economic Globalization and the Limits to Liberal Democracy," in McGrew, Anthony. ed. *The Transormation of Democracy? Globalization and Territorial Democracy*. Cambridge, UK: Polity Press, 1997.

Dickenson, Donna. "Counting Women In: Globalization, Democratization and the Women's Movement," in ed. Anthony McGrew, *The Transformation of Democracy? Globalization and Territorial Democracy*, London: Polity Press, 1997.

Dittmer, Lowell and Samuel S. Kim. "In Search of a Theory of National Identity," in eds. Lowell Dittmer and Samuel S. Kim, *China's Quest for National Identity*, Ithaca, NY: Cornell University Press, 1993.

Doremus, Paul N, William W. Keller, Louis W. Pauly, and Simon Reich. *The Myth of the Global Corporation*. Princeton, NJ: Princeton University Press, 1998.

Escobar, Arturo and Sonia Alvarez, eds. *The Making of Social Movements in Latin America*. Boulder, CO: Westview Press, 1992.

Evans, Peter B., Harold K. Jacobson, Robert Putnam, eds. *Double-Edged Diplomacy: International Bargaining and Domestic Politics* (Berkeley, CA: University of California Press, 1993).

Falk, Richard. *Law in an Emerging Global Village: A Post-Westphalian Perspective*. Ardsley, NY: Transnational Publishers, 1998.

Frankel, Jeffrey F. "Liberalization of Korea's Foreign-Exchange Markets and the Role of Trade Relations with the United States," in eds. Jongryn Mo and Ramon H. Myers, *Shaping A New Economic Relationship: The Republic of Korea and the United States*, Stanford, CA: Hoover Institution Press, 1993.

Freeman, Gary and Jongryn Mo. "Japan and the Asian NICs as New Countries of Destination," eds. P. J. Lloyd and Lynne S. Williams, *International Trade and Migration in the APEC Region*, New York: Oxford University Press, 1996

Friedman, Thomas L. The Lexus and the Olive Tree. New York: Farrar, Straus and Giroux, 1999.

Gereffi, Gary and Miguel Korzeniewicz, eds. *Commodity Chains and Global Capitalism*. Westport, CN: Greenwood Press, 1994.

Gills, Barry K., ed. *Globalization and the Politics of Resistance*. London: Macmillan, forthcoming.

Gills, Barry K. "Korean Capitalism and Democracy," in eds. Barry K. Gills, J. Rocamora, and R. Wilson, *Low Intensity Democracy: Political Power in the New World Order*, London: Pluto Press, 1993.

Ginsberg, Faye D. and Rayna Rapp, eds. *Conceiving the New World Order: The Global Politics of Reproduction*. Berkeley, CA: University of California Press, 1995.

Goetschy, Janine and Jacques Rojot. "French Industrial Relations," in eds. Greg J. Bamber and Russell D. Lansbury, *International and Comparative Industrial Relations: A Study of Developed Market Economics*. London: Allen & Unwin, 1987.

Ha, Yong Chool and Taehyun Kim. "Reflections on APEC: A Korean View," in *From APEC to Xanadu: Creating a Viable Community in the Post–Cold War Pacific*. Armonk, NY: M.E. Sharpe, 1997.

Haas, Ernst. *When Knowledge Is Power: Three Models of Change in International Organizations*. Berkeley, CA: University of California Press, 1990.

Haggard, Stephan. *The Pathways from Periphery: The Politics of Growth in the Newly Industrializing Countries*. Ithaca, NY: Cornell University Press, 1990.

Haggard, Stephan and Chung-in Moon "The State, Politics, and Economic Development in Postwar South Korea," in ed. Hagen Koo, *State and Society in Contemporary Korea*. Ithaca, NY: Cornell University Press, 1993.

Hall, John A, ed. *Civil Society: Theory, History and Comparison*. Cambridge, UK: Polity Press, 1995.

Han, Sung-Joo. *Korea in a Changing World: Democracy, Diplomacy, and Future Developments*. Seoul: OREUM, 1995.

Han, Sung-Joo. *Segyehwa sidae ui Hankuk oyekyo* [Korean diplomacy in an era of globalization: speeches of Foreign Minister Han Sung-Joo, March 1993–December 1994]. Seoul: Chisik samopsa, 1995.

Hartmann, Betsy. *Reproductive Rights and Wrongs: The Global Politics of Population Control and Contraceptive Choice*, rev. ed. Boston: South End Press, 1995.

Hasegawa, Keitaro. *Ajia daitenkan to Nippon* [The shift of the Asian MEGA trend]. Tokyo: Kobunsha, 1997.

Held, David. *Democracy and the Global Order*. Stanford, CA: Stanford University Press, 1995.

Held, David; Anthony McGrew; David Goldblatt; and Jonathan Perraton. *Global Transformations*. Stanford, CA: Stanford University Press, 1999.

Hirst, Paul and Grahame Thompson. *Globalization in Question?* Cambridge, UK: Polity Press, 1996.

Hoogvelt, Ankie. *Globalisation and the Postcolonial World*. London: Macmillan, 1997.

Hsiung, Ping-Chun. *Living Rooms as Factories: Class, Gender, and the Satellite Factory System in Taiwan*. Philadelphia, PA: Temple University Press, 1996.

Huntington, Samuel. *The Clash of Civilizations and the Remaking of World Order*. New York: Simon & Schuster, 1996.

International Institute for Management Development (IMD). *World Competitiveness Yearbook 1991-99*, Lausanne, Switzerland, 1991–99.

International Institute for Strategic Studies. *The Military Balance, 1997/98*. London: Oxford University Press, 1997.

International Monetary Fund. *Direction of Trade Statistics Yearbook, 1997*. Washington, DC, 1997.

International Monetary Fund. *Korea: Memorandum on the Economic Program*. Seoul, 1997, mimeographed.

Jaquette, Jane, ed. *The Women's Movement in Latin America: Feminism and the Transition to Democracy.* London: Unwin Hyman, 1989.

Johnson, Chalmers. "Political Institutions and Economic Performance: The Government-Business Relationship in Japan, South Korea, and Taiwan," in ed. Frederic C. Deyo, *The Political Economy of the New Asian Industrialism,* Ithaca, NY: Cornell University Press, 1987.

Jones, Leroy P. and Il Sakong. *Government, Business, and Entrepreneurship in Economic Development: The Korean Case.* Cambridge, MA: Harvard University Press, 1980.

Kang, Jun-man. *Kim Young-sam ideologi* [Kim Young Sam's ideology]. Seoul: Kaimagowon, 1995.

Katzenstein, Peter J. *Culture, Norms, and National Security: Police and Military in Postwar Japan.* New York: Columbia University Press, 1996.

Katzenstein, Peter J. *Small States in World Markets: Industrial Policy in Europe.* Ithaca, NY: Cornell University Press, 1985.

Keane, John, ed. *Civil Society and the State: New European Perspectives.* London: Verso, 1988.

Kim, Dae Jung. *Daejung Kyungjaeron* [Mass-Participatory Economics]. Seoul: Cheongsa, 1986.

Kim, Eun Mee. *Big Business, Strong State: Collusion and Conflict in South Korean Development. 1960–1990.* Albany, NY: State University of New York Press, 1997.

Kim, Jin-hyun. "Preparing for the 21st Century: Korea's Globalization Policy and its Implications for Future Korea-U.S. Relations," in *Korea's Turn to Globalization: and Korea-U.S. Economic Cooperation.* South Orange, NJ: Stillman School of Business, Seton Hall, 1996.

Kim, Kihwan. "The Political Economy of U.S.-Korea Trade Friction in the 1980s: A Korean Perspective," in eds. Jongryn Mo and Ramon H. Myers, *Shaping A New Economic Relationship: The Republic of Korea and the United States,* Stanford, CA: Hoover Institution Press, 1993.

Kim, Samuel S., "The Impact of the Division of Korea on South Korean Politics: The Challenge of Competitive Legitimation," in *Korean Democracy toward a New Horizon.* Seoul: Korean Political Science Association, 1995.

Kim, Samuel S. and Lowell Dittmer, "Whither China's Quest for National Identity?" in eds. Lowell Dittmer and Samuel S. Kim, *China's Quest for National Identity.* Ithaca, NY: Cornell University Press, 1993.

Kim, Seung Kyong. *Class Struggle or Family Struggle? The Lives of Women Factory Workers in South Korea.* Cambridge, UK: Cambridge University Press, 1997.

Kim, Wan-Soo and Bokyeun Han. "Trade Pressures in Koreas Foreign Economic Frictions," in *Korea's Economic Diplomacy: Survival as a Trading Nation,* IPE Program of the Sejong Institute. Seoul: Sejong Institute, 1995.

Kim, Yong Cheol. "The State and Labor in South Korea," in ed. Martin Landsberg, *The Rush to Development: Economic Change and Political Struggle in South Korea.* New York: Monthly Review Press, 1993.

Kim, Yong Cheol. *The State and Labor in South Korea: A Coalition Analysis.* Ph. D. dissertation, Ohio State University, 1994.

King, Ambrose. "State Confucianism and Its Transformation: The Restructuring of the State-Society Relation in Taiwan," in ed. Tu Wei-Ming, *Confucian Traditions in East Asian Modernity.* Cambridge, MA: Harvard University Press, 1996.

Kitamura, Kayoko and Tsuneo Tanaka, eds. *Examining Asia's Tigers: Nine Economies Challenging Common Structural Problems.* Tokyo: Institute of Developing Economies, 1997.

Klare, Michael, and Yogesh Chandrani, eds. *World Security: Challenges for a New Century.* New York: St. Martin's Press, 1998.

Koo, Hagen. "Strong State and Contentious Society," in ed. Hagen Koo, *State and Society in Contemporary Korea.* Ithaca, NY: Cornell University Press, 1993.

Korea International Labor Foundation. *Handbook of the Social Agreement and New Labor Laws of Korea.* Seoul: Korean International Labor Foundation, 1998.

Korea International Labor Foundation. *Labor Reform in Korea Toward the 21st Century.* Seoul: Korean International Labor Foundation, 1998.

Korean Women's Development Institute. *Yosong Baikso* [White paper on women]. Seoul, 1991.

Korea's Seapower and National Development in the Era of Globalization. Seoul: Sejong Institute, 1995.

Kung, Lydia. *Factory Women in Taiwan.* Ann Arbor, MI: UMI Research Press, 1983.

Kuwahara, Yasuo. "Japanese Industrial Relations," in eds. Greg J. Bamber and Russell D. Lansbury *International and Comparative Industrial Relations: A Study of Developed Market Economics.* London: Allen & Unwin, 1987.

Leacock, Eleanor, Helen Safa, and contributors, eds. *Women's Work: Development and the Division of Labor by Gender.* South Hadley, MA: Bergin & Garvey Publishers, Inc., 1986.

Lee, Kyu Uck and Jae Hyung Lee. *Business Group* (Chaebol) *in Korea: Characteristics and Government Policy.* Seoul: Korea Industrial Economics and Trade, 1996.

Lee, Won-Duck. *Nosa Gaehyeck: Miraelul Weehan Seontaek* [Reform of Labor-Business: The Choice for the Future]. Seoul: Korea Labor Institute, 1997.

Lett, Denise Potrzeba. *In Pursuit of Status: The Making of South Korea's "New" Urban Middle Class.* Cambridge, MA: Harvard University Press, 1998.

Lloyd, P. J. "Globalisation, Foreign Investment, and Migration," in eds. P. J. Lloyd and Lynne S. Williams, *International Trade and Migration in the APEC Region,* New York: Oxford University Press, 1996.

Lu Yi et al., eds. *Qiuji: Yige shijiexing de xuanze* [Global citizenship: a worldwide choice]. Shanghai: Baijia chubanshe, 1989.

Management Efficiency Research Institute. *Analysis of Financial Statements–Thirty Major Business Groups in Korea.* Seoul: Management Efficiency Research Institute, 1985–96.

Matear, Ann. "'Desde la protesta a la propuesta': The Institutionalization of the Women's Movement in Chile," in ed. Elizabeth Dore, *Gender Politics in Latin America: Debates in Theory and Practice.* New York: Monthly Review Press, 1997.

McGrew, Anthony, ed. *The Transformation of Democracy? Globalization and Territorial Democracy.* Cambridge, UK: Polity Press, 1997.

McMichael, Philip. *Development and Social Change: A Global Perspective.* Thousand Oaks, CA: Pine Forge Press, 1996.

Millburn, Thomas W. "Successful and Unsuccessful Forecasting in International Relations," in *Forecasting in International Relations: Theory, Methods, Problems, Prospects,* eds. Nazli Choucri and Thomas W. Robinson. San Francisco: W. H. Freeman and Co., 1978.

Ministry of Finance and Economy (MOFE). *1997 International Investment Trends.* Seoul: MOFE, 1998.

Ministry of Finance and Economy (MOFE). *Challenge and Chance: Korea's Response to the New Economic Reality.* Seoul: MOFE, 1998.

Ministry of Finance and Economy (MOFE). *Economy's Trends in Foreign Investment and Technology.* Seoul: MOFE, 1997.

Ministry of Finance and Economy (MOFE). *International Investment Trends*. Seoul: MOFE, 1998.

Ministry of Finance and Economy (MOFE). *Statistical Data on Foreign Direct Investment*. Seoul: MOFE, 1997.

Ministry of Finance and Economy (MOFE). *Statistical Data on Foreign Direct Investment* (unpublished data). Seoul: MOFE, 1998.

Ministry of Finance and Economy (MOFE). *Trends in International Investment Technology Inducement*. Seoul: MOFE, 1998.

Ministry of Finance and Economy and Korea Development Institute. *DJnomics: Kookmikwa Hamkkae Naeilul Yeonda* [Djnomics; Open Tomorrow with the People]. Seoul: Daehan Minkook Jungpu, 1998.

Ministry of Foreign Affairs (MOFA). *Chuyo oegyo munje haesol: Yu-en anbori isaguk hwaltong p'yongka* [Major foreign policy issues: an assessment of the activities as a member of the Security Council]. Seoul: MOFA, 1998.

Ministry of Foreign Affairs (MOFA). *Che 50 ch'a Yu-en ch'onghoe kyolgwa 1996* [The results of the Fiftieth U.N. General Assembly]. Seoul: MOFA, 1996.

Ministry of Foreign Affairs (MOFA). *Che 51 ch'a Yu-en ch'onghoe kyolgwa 1996* [The results of the Fifty-First U.N. General Assembly]. Seoul: MOFA, 1997.

Ministry of Foreign Affairs and Trade (MOFAT). *1998 Oyekyo paekso* [1998 diplomatic white paper]. Seoul: MOFAT, 1998.

Ministry of Foreign Affairs and Trade (MOFAT). *Yu-en kaeyo mit urinara waui kwangye* [An overview of the United Nations and our country's relations with the U.N.]. Seoul: MOFAT, 2 March 1999.

Ministry of National Defense (MOND). *Defense White Paper 1997–1998*. Seoul: MOND, 1998.

Ministry of National Defense (MOND). *Defense White Paper 1998*. Seoul: MOND, 1999.

Mittelman, James H., ed. *Globalization: Critical Reflections*. Boulder, CO: Lynne Rienner, 1997.

Mo, Jongryn and Chung-in Moon. "Democracy and the Origins of the 1997 Korean Economic Crisis," in eds. Jongryn Mo and Chung-in Moon, *Democracy and the Korean Economy*. Stanford, CA: Hoover Institution Press, 1999.

Moon, Chung-in. "Changing Patterns of Business-Government Relations in South Korea," in ed. Andrew MacIntyre, *Business and Government in Industrializing Asia*. Ithaca, NY: Cornell University Press, 1994.

Moon, Chung-in. "In the Shadow of Broken Cheers: The Dynamics of Globalization in South Korea," in eds. Jeffrey Hart and Aseem Prakash, *Globalization and Governance*. (forthcoming).

Moon, Chung-in and Jongryn Mo. "Democracy and the Origins of the 1997 Korean Economic Crisis," in eds. Jongryun Mo and Chung-in Moon *Democracy the Korean Economy*. (Stanford, CA: Hoover Institution Press, 1999).

Moon, Chung-in and Jongryn Mo. eds. *Democratization and Globalization in Korea*. Seoul: Yonsei University Press, 1999.

Moon, Chung-in and Kim Yong Cheol. "A Circle of Paradox: Development, Politics, and Democracy in South Korea," in ed. Adrian Leftwich, *Democracy and Development: Theory and Practice*. London: Polity Press, 1996.

Moon, Seungsook. "Economic Development and Gender Politics in South Korea, 1963–1992." Ph.D. dissertation. Brandeis University, 1994.

Morgan, Patrick. "The U.S.-ROK Strategic Relationship: A Liberalist Analysis," In Donald Clark et al., *U.S.-Korean Relations*. Claremont: Keck Center, 1995.

Morrison, Charles, ed. *Asia-Pacific Security Outlook*. Honolulu, HI: East-West Center, 1997.

Nash, June and Maria P. Fernandez-Kelly, eds. *Women, Men, and the International Division of Labor*. Albany, NY: State University of New York Press, 1983.

New Industry Management Academy. *Financial Analysis of the South Korean 30 Chaebol*. Seoul: New Industry Management Academy, 1998.

Ogle, George E. *South Korea: Dissent Within the Economic Miracle*. Atlantic Highlands, NJ: Zed Books, 1990.

Ohmae, Kenichi. *The Borderless World*. London: Collins, 1990.

Oka, Takashi. *Prying Open the Door: Foreign Workers in Japan*. Washington, DC: Carnegie Endowment for Peace, 1994.

Oman, Charles. *Globalisation and Regionalisation: The Challenge for Developing Countries*. Paris: OECD, 1994.

Ong, Aihwa. *Spirits of Resistance and Capitalist Discipline: Factory Women in Malaysia*. Albany, NY: State University of New York, 1987.

Organization for Economic Cooperation and Development (OECD). *Trade, Employment, and Labour Standard: A Study of Core Workers Rights and International Trade*. Paris, 1996.

Park, Heh-Rahn. "Narratives of Migration: From the Formation of Korean Chinese Nationality in the PRC to the Emergence of Korean Chinese Migrants in South Korea." Ph.D. dissertation, University of Washington, 1996.

Pempel, T. J. and Keiichi Tsunekawa, "Corporatism without Labor? The Japanese Anomaly," in eds. Philippe C. Schmitter and Gerhard Lehmbruch, *Trends Toward Corporatist Intermediation*. London: Sage Publications, 1979.

Presidential *Segyehwa* Promotion Committee (PSPC), *Segyehwa ui pichon kwa chonryak* [Globalization vision and strategy]. Seoul: Presidential *Segyehwa* Promotion Committee, August 1995.

Prospects for U.S.-Korean Naval Relations in the 21st Century. Seoul: Korea Institute for Defense Analyses and Center for Naval Analyses, February 1994.

Przeworski, Adam. *Capitalism and Social Democracy*. Cambridge, UK: Cambridge University Press, 1985.

Reich, Robert. *The Work of Nations*. New York: Vintage Books, 1992.

Rhee, Jong-Chan. *The State and Industry in South Korea: the Limists of the Authoritarian State*. New York: Routledge, 1994.

Robertson, Roland. *Globalization: Social Theory and Global Culture*. London: Sage, 1992.

Robison, Richard and David S. G. Goodman, eds. *The New Rich in Asia: Mobile Phones, McDonalds' and Middle-class Revolution*. New York: Routledge, 1996.

Rodrik, Dani. *Has Globalization Gone Too Far?* Washington, DC: Institute for International Economics, 1997.

Rosenau, James. *Along the Domestic-Foreign Frontier: Exploring Governance in a Turbulent World*. New York: Cambridge University Press, 1997.

Sachs, Jeffrey D. "Ten Trends in Global Competitiveness in 1998," in *Global Competitiveness Report 1998*, http://www.weforum.org/publications/GCR/sachs.asp.

Samsung Group. "Samsung's Global Strategy and Operation," in *Samsung Strategic Report*. Seoul: Samsung Group, 1997.

Sarangbang (Center for Human Rights in South Korea). *Human Rights in South Korea–A Perspective from Within*. Seoul: Korea Human Rights Network, 1996.

Sassen, Saskia. "Toward a Feminist Analytics of the Global Economy," in *Globalization and Its Discontents*. New York: Columbia University Press, 1998.

Schain, Martin A. "Corporatism and Industrial Relations in France," in eds. Philip G. Cerny and Martin A. Schain, *French Politics and Public Policy*. London: Frances Printer, 1980.

Schumacher, E. F. *Small Is Beautiful: A Study of Economics as If People Mattered*. New York: Harper & Row, 1973.

Seager, Joni. *The State of Women in the World Atlas*, second ed. New York: Penguin Reference, 1997.

Sen, Gita and Carol. *Grown Development, Crises, and Alternative Visions: Third World Women's Perspective*. New York: Monthly Review Press, 1987.

Shinn, James, ed. *Weaving the Net: Conditional Engagement with China*. New York: Council on Foreign Relations Press, 1996.

Silliman, G. Sidney and Lela Garner Noble. *Organizing for Democracy: NGOs, Civil Society, and the Philippine State*. Honolulu: University of Hawaii Press, 1998.

Simon, Denis Fred, ed. *Techno-Security in an Age of Globalization*. Armonk, NY: M. E. Sharpe, 1997.

Steven, Rob. *Classes in Contemporary Japan*. Cambridge, UK: Cambridge University Press, 1983.

Strange, Susan. *The Retreat of the State: The Diffusion of Power in the World Economy*. New York: Cambridge University Press, 1996.

UNCTAD. *World Investment Report 1997*. New York and Geneva: United Nations, 1997.

UNCTAD. *World Investment Report 1998*. New York and Geneva: United Nations, 1998.

UNDP, *Human Development Report 1991–99* New York: Oxford University Press, 1991–9.

Ungson, Gerardo, Richard M. Steers, and Seoung-Ho Park. *Korean Enterprise: The Quest for Globalization*. Cambridge, MA: Harvard Business School Press, 1997.

United Nations, Department of Public Information. "Assembly to Consider Scale of Assessment for 1998–2000, Budget for 1998–1999, at Conclusion of Current Segment Tonight," U.N. Press Release G/A 9389, 22 December 1997. New York, 22 December 1997.

Wade, Robert. *Governing the Market: Economic Theory and the Role of Government in Asian Industrialization*. Princeton, NJ: Princeton University Press, 1990.

Wallerstein, Immanuel. *The Modern World System*. New York: Academic Press, 1974.

Wang, Yen-Kyun. "Exchange Rates, Current Account Balance of Korea, and U.S.-Korea Negotiations on Exchange-Rate Policy," in eds. Jongryn Mo and Ramon H. Myers, *Shaping A New Economic Relationship: The Republic of Korea and the United States*, Stanford, CA: Hoover Institution Press, 1993.

Wang, Yizhou. *Dangdai guoji zhengzhi xilun* [Analysis of contemporary international politics]. Shanghai: Renmin chubanshe, 1995.

Wang, Yoon-Jong. *Mooyekkwa Nodong Gijoonui Yeongae* [Links between International Trade and Labor Standards]. Seoul: Research Institute for International Economic Policy, 1996.

Watson, Justin. *The Christian Coalition: Dreams of Restoration, Demand for Recognition*. New York: St. Martin's Press, 1997.

White, Gordon. *In Search of Civil Society: Market Reform and Social Change in Contemporary China*. Oxford: Clarendon Press, 1996.

Wickramasekara, Piyasiri. "Recent Trends in Temporary Labour Migration in Asia," in *OECD, Migration and the Labour Market in Asia*. Paris, 1996.

Wiencek, David. "Missile Proliferation in Asia," in eds. William Carpenter and David Wiencek, *Asian Security Handbook*. Armonk, NY: M.E. Sharpe, 1996.

Wolf, Diane. *Factory Daughters: Gender, Household Dynamics, and Rural Industrialization in Java.* Berkeley, CA: University of California Press, 1994.

Woo, Jung-En. *Race to the Shift: State and Finance in Korean Industrialization.* New York: Columbia University Press, 1991.

World Bank. *The East Asian Miracle: Economic Growth and Public Policy.* New York: Oxford University Press, 1993.

World Bank. *World Development Indicators 1998 CD-ROM.* Washington, DC: World Bank 1998.

World Bank. *World Development Report 1991.* New York: Oxford University Press, 1991.

World Bank. *World Development Report 1997: The State in a Changing World.* New York, 1997,

World Bank. *World Development Report 1998/99: Knowledge for Development.* New York: Oxford University Press, 1998.

Yohsino, Michael Y. and Srinivasa U. Rangan. *Strategic Alliances: An Entrepreneurial Approach to Globalization.* Boston, MA: Harvard Business School Press, 1995.

Young, Kate, Carol Wolkowitz, and Roslyn McCullagh. eds. *Of Marriage and the Market: Women's Subordination Internationally and Its Lessons.* London: CES Books, 1981.

Articles

Anderson, Benedict. "The New World Disorder," *New Left Review* 193 (May–June 1992).

Bae, Yong Ho. "Nodong Gijoonkwa Mooyeok Goyong Ganui Kwangae" [The relationship between the labor standard, international trade, and employment], *Journal of Legislative Research* 242 (December 1996).

Bank of Korea. "Introduction of Laws Related to Liquid Assets and Mutual Funds," *Monthly Economics Indicators* (January 1999).

Beck, Peter M. "Creating a Favorable Environment for Foreign Direct Investment in Korea" (paper presented at the conference "The Republic of Korea after 50 Years: Continuity and Convergence," Georgetown University, 2–3 October 1998).

Beinart, Peter. "An Illusion for Our Time: The False Promise of Globalization," *New Republic* (20 October 1997).

Bello, Walden. "The Answer: De-Globalize," *Far Eastern Economic Review* (29 April 1999).

Blaney, David L. and Mustapha Kamal Pasha. "Civil Society and Democracy in the Third World: Ambiguities and Historical Possibilities," *Studies in Comparative International Development* 28 (1993).

Blumenthal, W. Michael. "The World Economy and Technological Change," *Foreign Affairs* 66, no. 3 (1987–8).

Bobrow, Davis D. and James J. Na. "Korea's Affair with Globalization: Deconstructing Segyehwa" (paper presented to the conference "Democratization and Globalization in Korea: Assessments and Prospects" in conjunction with the Seventeenth World Congress of the International Political Science Association, Seoul, Korea, 18–19 August 1997).

Cha, Victor. "Politics and Democracy under the Kim Young Sam Government: Something Old, Something New," *Asian Survey* 33, no. 9 (September 1993).

Cha, Victor. "Realism, Liberalism and the Durability of the U.S.-South Korean Alliance," *Asian Survey* 37 (July 1997).

"The *Chaebol* That Ate Korea," *The Economist* 14 (November 1998).

Choi, Jang Jip. "A Korea's Political Economy: Search for a Solution," *Korea Focus* 6 (March–April 1998).

Cohen, Benjamin. "Phoenix Risen: The Resurrection of Global Finance," *World Politics* 48, no. 2 (1996).

Cohen, Eliot. "A Revolution in Warfare," *Foreign Affairs* 75, no. 2 (1996).

Cohen, Roger. "Redrawing the Free Market: Amid a Global Financial Crisis, Calls for Regulation Spread," *New York Times* (14 November 1998).

Cumings, Bruce. "The Northeast Political Economy," *International Organization* 38 (1984).

Do, Joon-ho. "Security Strategy for 21st Century," *Wolgan Choson* 25 (November 1993).

Dong, Wonmo. "University Students in South Korean Politics: Patterns of Radicalization in the 1980s," *Journal of International Affairs* 40, no. 2 (1987).

Falk, Richard A. "Resisting 'Globalization-from-above' through 'Globalization-from-below'," *New Political Economy* 2 (1997).

Falk, Richard A. "State of Siege: Will Globalization Win Out?" *International Affairs* 73, no. 1 (1997).

Farhi, Paul and Megan Rosenfeld. "American Pop Penetrates Worldwide," *Washington Post*, 25 October 1998.

Fine, Robert. "Civil Society Theory, Enlightenment and Critique," *Democratization* 4 (1997).

Freedman, Lawrence. "International Security: Changing Targets," *Foreign Policy* 110 (Spring 1998).

Friedman, Milton. "Internationalization of the U.S. Economy," *Fraser Forum* (February 1989).

Gills, Barry K. "Economic Liberalisation and Reform in South Korea in the 1990s: A 'Coming of Age' or a Case of 'Graduation Blues'?" *Third World Quarterly* 17, no. 4 (1996).

Gills, Barry K. "Editorial: 'Globalization' and the 'Politics of Resistance'," *New Political Economy* 2 (1997).

Godson, Roy. "Criminal Threats to U.S. Interests in Hong Kong and China" (testimony before the Senate Foreign Relations Committee, East Asian and Pacific Affairs Subcommittee, 10 April 1997).

Gold, Thomas. "The Resurgence of Civil Society in China," *Journal of Democracy* 1 (1990).

Goldblatt, David et al. "Economic Globalization and the Nation-State: Shifting Balances of Power," *Alternatives* 22, no. 3 (1997).

Gromyko, Anatolly. "The Present Is Not a Shrine for Contemplation," *Pravda*, 14 April 1998, in FBIS-SOV-98-119 (Internet version).

Haas, Richard, "Paradigm Lost," *Foreign Affairs* 74, no. 1 (1995).

Hamre, John. "How Do Free Trade and Globalization Impinge on U.S. Security and How Does Defense Policy Affect U.S. Economic Welfare?" The Council on Foreign Relations, 5 June 1998, in hppt://www.foreignrelations.org/studies/transcripts/hamre.html.

Han, Bae-Sun. "The South Korea's Overseas Investment in Peril," *Maeil Kyungje Shinmun* (20 November 1997).

Han, Yong-sup. "Korea's Security Strategy for 21st Century: Cooperation and Conflict," *Korea Focus* 5 no. 4 (July–August, 1997).

Hankuk Ilbo, "The Train Named the Big Beal Is Arriving at a Terminus," *Hankuk Ilbo* (24 March 1999).

Held, David. "Democracy and Globalization," *Global Governance* 3 (1997).

Hyundai Group. "Overseas Investment," Hyundai Group website at http://www.hyundai.net.

Hyundai Group. "21st Century Vision," Hyundai Group website at http://www.hyundai.net.

Ikenberry, G. John. "Patterns and Theories of the Globalization Paradigm," (paper presented to the conference on "Democratization and Globalization in Korea: Assessments and Prospects," in conjunction with the Seventeenth World Congress of the International Political Science Association, Seoul, Korea, 18–19 August 1997).

Im, Young-Il. "Nodong Undongui Jaedowhawa Siminkwon" [Institutionalization of labor movements and citizenship], *Economy and Society* 34 (Summer 1997).

Iversen, Torben. "Power, Flexibility, and the Breakdown of Centralized Wage Bargaining: Denmark and Sweden in Comparative Perspective," *Comparative Politics* 28, no. 4 (July 1996).

Jervis, Robert. "The Future of World Politics," *International Security* 16, no. 3 (Winter 1991–2).

Johnston, Alastair. "Learning versus Adaptation: Explaining Change in Chinese Arms Control Policy in the 1980s and 1990s," *China Journal* 35 (January 1996).

Kang, In Duk. "South Korea's Strategy toward North Korea in Connection with Its '*Segyehwa*' Drive," *East Asian Review* 7, no. 1 (Spring 1995).

Katz, Harry C. "The Decentralization of Collective Bargaining: A Literature Review and Comparative Analysis," *Industrial and Labor Relations Review* 47 (October 1993).

Keizai Kikaku-cho Chosa-kyoku. "Ajia Keizai 1997" [*The Asian Economy, 1997*]. Tokyo: Okura-sho Insatsu-kyoku, 1997.

Keller, William W. and Janne E. Nolan. "The Arms Trade: Business as Usual?" *Foreign Policy*, 109 (Winter 1997–8).

Keohane, Robert O. and Lisa L. Martin. "The Promise of Institutional Theory," *International Security* 20, no. 1 (Summer 1995).

Keohane, Robert O. and Joseph S. Nye, Jr. "Power and Interdependence in the Information Age," *Foreign Affairs* 77 (September–October 1998).

Kim, Dae Jung. "Era of 'Universal Globalism' Dawning," *Korea Times* 4 (November 1998).

Kim, June. "Nodong Beop Gaejung Nonuiui Baekyungkwa Pilryoseong" [Background and necessity of the revision of labor laws], *Journal of Legislative Research* 238 (April 1996).

Kim, Nak-Hoon. "1997 Economic Forecast," *Maeil Kyungje Shinmun* (3 February 1997).

Kim, Samuel S. "North Korea and the United Nations," *International Journal of Korean Studies* 1 no. 1 (Spring 1997).

Kim, Sang-ki. "Traditionalism and Universalism," *Korea Focus* 2, no. 1 (January–February 1994).

Kim, Su-Jin. "Hankook Nodong Chohapui Hyunhwangkwa Jeonmang" [The present condition and prospect of Korean labor unions], *Economy and Society* 25 (Spring 1995).

Kim, Sunhyuk. "State and Civil Society in South Korea's Democratization," *Asian Survey* 37 no. 12 (1997).

Kim, Yong Cheol. "Industrial Reform and Labor Backlash in South Korea: Genesis, Process, and Termination of the January Strike" (paper presented at the Seventeenth World Congress of the International Political Science Association, Seoul, Korea, 1997).

Klare, Michael. "The Next Great Arms Race," *Foreign Affairs* 72, no. 3 (1993).

Korean Embassy in Washington, D.C. "Reform and Globalization Policy of President Kim Young-Sam," Korean Overseas Information Service at *http://korea.emb.washington.dc.us/*1995–7.

Korean Embassy in Washington, D.C. "President Kim Young Sam's Three Year Pursuit of Change and Reform," Korea Overseas Information Service at http://korea.emb.washington.dc.us, 1995–7.

Korea Labor Institute. "Nosa Kwangae" [Labor-business relations]. *Quartery Labor Review* 11, no. 2 (1998).

Krasner, Stephen. "Compromising Westphalia," *International Security* 20, no. 3 (1995).

Kreisberg, Paul H. "Threat Environment for a United Korea: 2010," *Korean Journal of Defense Analysis* 8, no. 1 (Summer 1996).

Kristof, Nicholas D. and David E. Sanger. "How U.S. Wooed Asia to Let Cash Flow In," *New York Times*, 16 February 1999.

Kristof, Nicholas D. and Sheryl WuDunn. "World Markets, None of Them an Island," *New York Times*, 17 February 1999.

Kristof, Nicholas D. and Sheryl WuDunn. "The World's Ills May Be Obvious, But Their Cure Is Not," *New York Times*, 18 February 1999.

Kristof, Nicholas D. and Edward Wyatt. "Who Sank, or Swam, in Choppy Currents of a World Cash Ocean," *New York Times*, 15 February 1999.

Kupchan, Charles A. and Clifford A. Kupchan. "The Promise of Collective Security," *International Security* 20, no. 1 (Summer 1995).

Lancaster, John. "Barbie, 'Titanic' Show Good Side of U.S.," in *Washington Post*, 27 October 1998.

Lee, Byungtae. "Kunro Gijoon Beop Gaejungaeseoui Nodongja Sangkwa Jaengjum" [The image of workers and issues in revising labor standard laws], *Journal of Legislative Research* 238 (April 1996).

Lee, Eui Chul. "The Big Business Group's Overseas Investment Boom," *Monthly Chosun* (1996).

Lee, Hong-koo. "Attitudinal Reform toward Globalization," *Korea Focus* 2, no. 2 (March–April 1994).

Lee, Hye-kyung. "The Employment of Foreign Workers in Korea: Issues and Policy Suggestions," *International Sociology* 12, no. 3 (1997).

Lee, Kyu Min. "Overview of the South Korean Overseas Investment," *Donga Ilbo* (25 January 1997).

Lee, Mi-Kyoung. "Kukgaui chulsan chongchaek" [A feminist analysis of the state policy on birth], *Yosonghaknonjip* 6 (1989).

Lee, Seo-hang. "Naval Power as an Instrument of Foreign Policy," *Korea Focus* 5, no. 2 (March–April 1997).

Lee, Seung Hun. "Do Not Unleash *Chaebol* Again," *Shindonga* (1994).

Lee, Won-Duck. "Hankook Nodong Undongui Miraenun Mooeok Inga?" [What is the future of the Korean Labor Movement?], *Quarterly Labor Review* 9, no. 1 (1996).

Lee, Young Sae. "Globalization in Korea: Prospects, Problems, and Policy," *Korea's Economy 1997* 13 (1997).

Leipziger, D. M. "Public and Private Interests in Korea: Views on Moral Hazard and Crisis Resolution," *EDI Discussion Paper* (Washington, DC: World Bank, May 1998).

Levy, Jack. "Learning and Foreign Policy: Sweeping a Conceptual Minefield," *International Organization* 48, no. 2 (spring 1994).

Long, Yongtu. "On Economic Globalization," *Guangming ribao*, 30 October 1998, in FBIS-CHI-98-313 (Internet version).

Mansbach, Richard W. and Dong Won Suh. "A Tumultuous Season: Globalization and the Korean Case," *Asian Perspective* 22, no. 2 (1998).

Matthew, Richard and George Shambaugh, "Sex, Drugs, and Heavy Metal: Transnational Threats and National Vulnerabilities," *Security Dialogue* 29, no. 2 (1998).

Mearsheimer, John J. "The False Promise of International Institutions," *International Security* 19, no. 3 (Winter 1994–5).

Milner, Helen. "International Political Economy: Beyond Hegemonic Stability," *Foreign Policy* 110 (1998).

Mittelman, James. "The Globalisation Challenge: Surviving at the Margins," *Third World Quarterly* 15, no. 3 (1994).

Moon, Chung-in. "Globalization: Challenges and Strategies," *Korea Focus* 3, no. 3 (May–June 1995).

Moon, Chung-in and Seok-soo Lee. "The Post–Cold War Security Agenda of Korea: Inertia, New Thinking, and Assessments," *Pacific Review* 8, no. 1 (1995).

Nam, Si-uk. "How to Surmount Journalism Crisis," *Korea Focus* 6, no. 4 (July–August 1998).

Nye, Joseph, and William Owens. "America's Information Edge," *Foreign Affairs* 75, no. 2 (1998).

OECD Economics Outlook 62 (December 1997).

Oh, John. "Anti-Americanism and Anti-Authoritarian Politics in Korea," *In Depth* 4, no. 2 (1994).

Ohmae, Kenichi. "The Rise of the Region State," *Foreign Affairs* (Spring 1993).

Park, Hyun Ok. "*Segyehwa*: Globalization and Nationalism in Korea," *Journal of the International Institute* (Internet version), 4, no. 1 (1996).

Park, Sang Young. "Booming of the Overseas Subsidiaries by the South Korean Big Business," *Weekly Magazine Newspaper* (August 1997).

Parsley, Ed and Terrence Clernan. "Reforms Boost Capital Flows," *Far Eastern Economic Review* (26 May 1994).

Perraton, Jonathan et al. "The Globalization of Economic Activity," *New Political Economy* 2, no. 2 (1997).

Peterson, V. Spike. "The Politics of Identification in the Context of Globalization," *Women's Studies International Forum* 19 (1996).

"President Kim Addresses Inaugural Ceremony," *Current Topics* (25 February 1998).

Putnam, Robert. "Diplomacy and Domestic Politics: The Logic of Two-Level Games," *International Organization* 42 (Summer 1988).

Reinicke, Wolfgang. "Global Public Policy," *Foreign Affairs* 76, no. 6 (1997).

Reiter, Dan. "Learning, Realism, and Alliances: The Weight of the Shadow of the Past," *World Politics* 46 (July 1994).

Rodrik, Dani. "Sense and Nonsense in the Globalization Debate," *Foreign Policy* 107 (Summer 1997).

Rosenau, James N. "The Dynamics of Globalization: Toward an Operational Formulation," *Security Dialogues* 27, no. 3 (1996).

Ruggie, John Gerald. "At Home Abroad, Abroad at Home: International Liberalisation and Domestic Stability in the New World Economy," *Millennium: Journal of International Studies* 24, no. 3 (1994).

Ruggie, John Gerald. "The False Premise of Realism," *International Security* 20, no. 1 (Summer 1995).

Sachs, Jeffrey. "International Economics: Unlocking the Mysteries of Globalization," *Foreign Policy* 110 (Spring 1998).

Seoul Kyungje Shinmun. "Large Overseas Investment Increases," *Seoul Kyungje Shinmun,* (7 September 1996).

Shim, Jae Hoon. "Same Old Story," *Far Eastern Economic Review,* 5 November 1998.

Shin, Wha-Soo. "Take a Jakarta Drift by the South Korean Corporations," *Seoul Kyungje Shinmun,* 17 October 1997.

"Special Focus: China and Hong Kong." *Trends in Organized Crime* 2, no. 2 (Winter 1996).

Stein, Janice Gross. "Political Learning by Doing: Gorbachev as Uncommitted Thinker and Motivated Learner," *International Organization* 48, no. 2 (Spring 1994).

Strange, Susan. "The Defective State," *Daedalus* 124, no. 2 (1995).

Talbott, Strobe. "Globalization and Diplomacy: A Practitioner's Perspective," *Foreign Policy* (Fall 1997).

Thelen, Kathleen. "Beyond Corporatism: Toward a New Framework for the Study of Labor in Advanced Capitalism," *Comparative Politics* 27, no. 1 (October 1994).

"Thinking about Globalisation: Popular Myths and Economic Facts," *The Economist* (London), http://www.economist.com/editorial/freeforall/18-1-98/sb0225.html.

Uchitelle, Louis. "Globalization Has Not Severed Corporations' National Links," *New York Times* (30 April 1998).

Wang, Yizhou. "New Security Concept in Globalization," *Beijing Review* 42, no. 7 (February 15–21, 1997).

Waxman, Sharon. "Holly Attuned to World Markets," *Washington Post,* 26 October 1998.

Wendt, Alexander. "Constructing International Politics," *International Security* 20, no. 1 (Summer 1995).

Windolf, Paul. "Productivity Coalitions and the Future of Corporatism," *Industrial Relations* 28 (Winter 1989).

Yoon, Sanghyun. "South Korea's Kim Young Sam Government: Political Agendas," *Asian Survey* 36 (May 1996).

Yoon, Young-kwan. "Globalization: Towards a New Nationalism in Korea," *Sasang* (Winter 1994).

Yu, Hyun-Seok. "Moohan kyungjaeng sidaeui nosakwangae" [Korean labor-business relations in the era of unlimited competitiveness], in *Asia wa segyewa: Dong asia kookgaui daeung* [Asia and Globalization: Reactions of East Asian States]. Seoul: Sejong Institute, 1998.

Yun, Kun-ha. "Samsung Seeks Capital Injection from Intel," *Korea Herald,* 21 February 1998.

Index